AT RISK

Latino Children's Health

EDITED BY
RAFAEL PÉREZ-ESCAMILLA
HUGO MELGAR-QUIÑONEZ

Arte Público Press
Houston, Texas

At Risk: Latino Children's Health is funded by grants from the Californi Endowment, the Marguerite Casey Foundation, the Houston Arts Alliance throug the City of Houston, the W.K. Kellogg Foundation, the Simmons Foundation an the Texas Commission on the Arts. We are grateful for their support.

Recovering the past, creating the future

Arte Público Press
University of Houston
452 Cullen Performance Hall
Houston, Texas 77204-2004

Cover design and cover photo by Pilar Espino

At Risk: Latino Children's Health / edited by Rafael Pérez-Escamilla and
Hugo Melgar-Quiñonez.
   p. cm.
   Includes bibliographical references.
   ISBN: 978-1-55885-708-7 (alk. paper)
  1. Children—Health and hygiene—United States. 2. Hispanic Americans—Social
conditions. 3. Hispanic Americans—Economic conditions. I. Pérez-
Escamilla, Rafael. II. Melgar-Quiñonez, Hugo.
[DNLM: 1. Child Welfare—United States. 2. Health Policy—United States.
3. Hispanic Americans—United States. 4. Socioeconomic Factors—United
States. WA 320]
RJ102.A87 2011
362.198'920089968—dc23   2011025 36
                                                    CP

11 12 13 14 15 16 17 18   10 9 8 7 6 5 4 3 2 1

CONTENTS

iii

To Sofia, Alejandro and Rafaelito.
In memory of my father, Ricardo Pérez Escamilla.
—RPE

To the ones who preceded us in the search
for a better and more dignified life.
—HMQ

INTRODUCTION

LATINO CHILDREN SOCIOECONOMIC, DEMOGRAPHIC AND HEALTH PROFILE

Rafael Pérez-Escamilla[1] and Hugo Melgar-Quiñonez[2]

Introduction[3]

Latinos will continue to account for over half of the population growth in the USA in the decades to come. Thus, the future of the country is very much tied to the health and wellbeing of Latino children. Overall Latinos in the United States confront higher rates of poverty, as well as lower levels of school education and English proficiency, and less access to the nation's health care services, which is highly determined by the financial resources available to the families, and policies affecting millions of Latino immigrants and migrant farm workers. Thus, social and environmental factors strongly influence the health status of Latino children in the United States. These factors also help explain the fact that millions of Latinos in the United States lack access to enough

[1]Yale School of Public Health. Dr. Peréz-Escamilla was partly supported by the Connecticut NIH EXPORT Center of Excellence for Eliminating Health Disparities among Latinos (CEHDL), NIH-NCMHD grant P20MD001765.
[2]Department of Human Nutrition, OSU Extension, The Ohio State University.
[3]The views expressed in this book are those of the authors and do not necessarily reflect the views of the NIH or NCMHD.

nutritionally adequate foods for a healthy and active life. Almost 27% of Latino households faced food insecurity in 2009, compared to a national rate of 14.7%. About 75% of Mexican-American adults are overweight or obese and over 20% of the children have a Body Mass Index above the 95-percentile for age and gender. Disparities in risk factors for subsequent obesity among Latinos can be detected since infancy. While Latinos have a higher rate of breastfeeding than the general population, supplementation with infant formula starting very early on after birth is also higher when compared to other ethnic groups. Suboptimal dietary and lifestyle behaviors increase the risk of obesity and the development of chronic diseases among Latino children and youth. The rate of diabetes in Latino adults is 50% higher than among the general population. If the current trends in obesity persist half of the Latino children in the United States will develop type 2 diabetes during their lifetime. In addition to obesity and chronic diseases, Latino children are more likely than their white counterparts to grow up in environments strongly affected by violence and opportunities for abusing addictive substances, both of which have negative consequences on their psychosocial and emotional development, as well as their mental health.

At Risk: Latino Children's Health examines key maternal, child and youth issues that affect the wellbeing of our very diverse Latino communities. In Chapter One, Flores et al. analyze key Latino childhood health issues, including childhood obesity, within the context of a socio-ecological framework perspective. A framework that strongly acknowledges the major influence that the physical and psychosocial environments where Latino children are born and grow have on their lifestyles including dietary and physical activity habits. Segura-Pérez et al. in Chapter Two review the evidence behind the effectiveness of community health workers (CHW) or *promotores de salud* at improving the health of Latino children. Their chapter first covers prenatal care, a key issue for addressing the childhood obesity epidemic as there is strong evidence suggesting that the intrauterine environment the fetus is exposed to influences the risk of childhood obesity and the development of chronic diseases later on in life. They also address CHW-led programs for dealing with childhood asthma, immunizations and youth sex education. Infant feeding practices are important determinants of maternal and child health and also influence childhood obesity risk. In Chapter Three, Chapman and Zubieta address the factors that influence breastfeeding and complementary feeding choices among Latino infants. They also review optimal infant feeding promotion approaches, including breast-feeding peer counseling models that are likely to help improve infant feeding behaviors. Olvera, George and Kaiser in Chapter Four present a critical review of the evidence on the influence of parental feeding styles on eating behaviors of children. Because food preferences get established very early on in life, this area of inquiry is crucial for understanding how to protect young Latino children against the risk of obesity and how to maximize their health through fostering optimal caregiver-child feeding interactions. Nutrition is essential not only for physical health but also for attaining adequate academic achievement. Children receive a substantial amount of their nutrition at school, ideal setting for also exposing children to sound nutrition education. Thus, the review by Woodward Lopez and Gosliner in Chapter Five on school feeding programs and how they affect the health and wellbeing of Latino children is very timely. Food insecurity is prevalent in Latino households. This is unfortunate as household food insecurity has consistently been identified as a major nutritional and psycho-emotional stressor. Television viewing has consistently been identified as a risk factor for childhood obesity. In Chapter Six, Mendoza and Barroso examine the evidence for an association between television viewing and physical inactivity, and provide best practice examples of community-based approaches that can be used to both reduce television viewing time and increase physical activity levels of Latino children. Melgar-Quiñonez and Pérez-Escamilla in Chapter Seven review the evidence of an association between food insecurity and the physical and psycho-emotional development of Latino children. They discuss the impact of food insecurity as multifold since this phenomenon not only affects the quantity of the food available but also the quality of the foods families consume.

Accidents and violence are the major cause of premature death among young Latinos. Thus, in Chapter Eight, Vaca and Anderson review recent epidemiological trends regarding violence-related injuries and motor vehicle accidents among Latino youth and propose ways to address them, including ways to curve alcohol consumption. Castro et al.

in Chapter Nine also address the major concern on substance abuse among Latino youth. They present results from a recent innovative study that conducted an in-depth examination of the relationship between parental acculturation trajectories and substance abuse (alcohol, tobacco, marijuana) among Latino adolescents. *At Risk* concludes in Chapter Ten with a health economics analysis by Treviño of type 2 diabetes and ways to prevent or address this major public health epidemic that disproportionately affects Latinos through lifestyle modification approaches including diet and physical activity. As illustrated in this chapter, the risk for type 2 diabetes starts to develop very early on in life and obesity is a major risk factor for this condition. Thus, cost-effective approaches to curve this epidemic need to start since gestation and need to be based on the socio-ecological framework emphasized throughout this book.

Our intention in this book is not only to discuss the existence of major challenge and problems but also to provide examples and suggestions with each chapter as to which policies and programmatic approaches may be relevant for improving the health and wellness of Latino children. Although *At Risk* does not include a specific chapter on health care access we fully acknowledge the relevance of this and other topics (e.g. immigration reform) for the health of Latino children and their families. Thus the reader is advised to read recent reviews in these rapidly evolving areas of concern.

References

Melgar-Quiñonez, H. (2008). "The growing Latino community: New challenges for nutrition and health professionals in the United States." *Clinical Nutrition Insight*, *34*(7):1-4

Pérez-Escamilla R., Garcia J., & Song D. (2010). "Health care access among Hispanic immigrants: Alguien está escuchando? [is anybody listening?]." *NAPA Bull*, *34*:47-67.

Pérez-Escamilla R. (2010) "Health care access among latinos: Implications for social and health care reforms." *Journal of Hispanic Higher Education*, *9*: 43-60.

CHAPTER ONE

LATINO CHILDREN'S HEALTH AND THE ENVIRONMENT

George R. Flores, Emma V. Sanchez-Vaznaugh, Lisa G.-Rosas,
Liz U. Schwarte, Robert Garcia, Sandra R. Viera, Mariah S. Lafleur,
Manal J. Aboelata, Seth H. Strongin and Amanda M. Navarro

. . . If you grow up in a neighborhood with a good school, where it's safe, where you can walk and play outside, where you have a regular doctor and where you have access to good food, you are more likely to live a long and healthy life. On the other hand, if you grow up in a neighborhood where you're not safe, where your school is failing you and where you do not have a place to go when you are sick or need a basic grocery store, then you are far more likely to live a shorter life, to earn less money, to be party to or victim of violence and to be far less healthy emotionally and physically. If you are . . . Latino, you are likely to face not just one of those challenges, but many or all of them at once.

(Policy Link, *2010*)

Introduction

Generally speaking, health and wellness is influenced to a greater degree by environments where children are born, grow, play and go to school than by genetics or the medical care that children receive (McGinnis, Williams-Russo et al., 2002). The social, political, economic and physical conditions in the environment shape children's physical, emotional and social wellbeing through each developmental stage (WHO Commission on Social Determinants of Health, 2008; Braveman & Barclay, 2009). These conditions are commonly referred to as *social and environmental determinants of health* (Marmot, 2000; Subramanian, Belli et al., 2002; WHO Commission on Social Determinants of Health, 2008).

Relative to non-Hispanic whites, Latino children that experience less favorable environments are at risk for poorer health outcomes (Carter-Pokras, Zambrana et al., 2007). In Spanish, the term *bienestar* conveys a sense of health and wellbeing that extends beyond physical wellness and that reflects favorable social and environmental conditions. It stands to reason that efforts to improve the health and wellbeing of Latino children ought to address their environments as well.

This chapter reviews scientific literature to identify environmental conditions commonly experienced by Latino children that have bearing on their health during childhood and throughout life. We provide promising models from Latino communities working toward healthier environments. Finally, we list policy goals for policymakers and the public to improve environments for healthier, safer, more productive Latino children, families and communities.

The determinants of health are illustrated in Figure 1 as a sphere of environments that interact with behavior and biology, and that are shaped by policies and interventions. Scientists examining the factors that lead to health and wellbeing use a broad systems view, based on the understanding that health outcomes are the result of multiple determinants—social, behavioral, environmental and genetic—that work in concert through complex interactions (Hernandez & Blazer, 2006). Environments may have direct (i.e., exposure causes illness) or indirect (i.e., exposure influences behavior to cause illness) impacts on health. Community-level health advocates recognize that many environmental conditions can be shaped through policy change to bring about favorable health outcomes (Center for Health Improvement, 2009). The general understanding is that distinct environments operate in unique ways to influence children's health and wellness, and that policies largely determine the extent to which environments can optimize health and support healthy behaviors.

Figure 1.

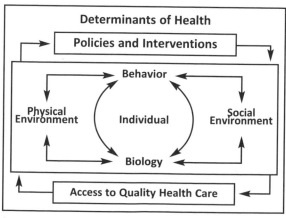

Source: HHS, 2000.

In Figure 2, Diez-Roux and Mair describe processes through which neighborhood environments contribute to health and health inequalities (Diez-Roux and Mair, 2010). For example, characteristics of the physical environment such as lack of safety in public spaces can affect the nature of social interactions within the neighborhood, which in turn has consequences for the ability of neighbors to advocate for improved public safety. Additionally, environments can induce stress. While some environmentally mediated behaviors (e.g., physical activity in school) may buffer the adverse effects of stress, exposure to stress-inducing environments may be a factor in leading children to adopt unhealthy behaviors (e.g., diet, smoking) as mechanisms to cope. Environmental conditions illustrated in Figure 2 are amenable to policy interventions, ranging from policies that minimize resource inequalities to those that target neighborhood-level features such as increasing access to healthy food.

Besides operating across the life course, the impact of environments can be modified by personal characteristics. For example, some children may possess certain characteristics that could increase their vulnerability to adverse neighborhood conditions, while others with similar characteristics may have families with resources to permit overcoming deficiencies or hazards in their neighborhoods (Diez-Roux et al., 2010). Additionally, a single environmental agent may influence multiple personal, social and structural characteristics and health outcomes for many children, and over a lifetime. For example, a policy that improves neighborhood walk-ability can simultaneously benefit children's physical fitness, reduce stress, increase safety, strengthen social connections and improve neighborhood aesthetics. In effect, that single policy may have multi-

Figure 2.

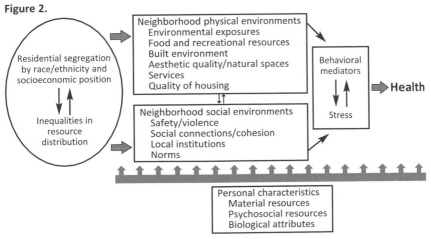

Diez-Roux AV, C Mair. Neighborhoods and health Ann. N.Y. Acad. Sci. 1186 (2010) 125–145.

ple benefits by preventing obesity, and reducing the risk of diabetes, cancer and heart disease later in life.

Environmental conditions may have profound and long-term effects on health at all stages of life, from pregnancy through childhood and adulthood (Braveman et al., 2009). Sensitive and critical periods of development, such as the prenatal period, early childhood and the school years present windows of opportunity to promote lifelong health and wellbeing through policies that can shape environments. Health care services are important, but alone are insufficient to produce health and wellness for children (Wizemann & Anderson, 2009). The holistic notion of *bienestar* requires health-supportive environments (i.e., in places where children are born, grow, play and go to school) for optimal health and wellbeing throughout the lifespan.

Environments and Health—The Evidence

To investigate how the physical and social features of environments impact the health and wellbeing of Latino children, we selected from studies identified by key terms in the scientific literature. We also examined selected "best available" unpublished sources of community-based research and program evaluations. We found in the literature that some types of environments overlap with others (e.g., food and physical activity environments in neighborhoods and in schools), just as the actual environments do in our surroundings. Thus, our discussion of food and physical activity environments, for example, is presented in multiple sections of the chapter. Further, many of the references and examples are drawn from work to prevent childhood obesity. Since obesity is a precursor of multiple chronic diseases (Visscher & Seidell, 2001) and is influenced by behavioral factors such as diet (Bray & Popkin, 1998; Peters, 2003) and physical activity (Jimenez-Pavón, Kelly j., 2010), this field offers the most salient and accessible evidence to demonstrate the links between the environment and children's health.

There is a growing, but still insufficient, evidence base in the published scientific literature specific to Latino children that illuminates the nexus of environments and health. Consequently, to develop this chapter, we also applied our considerable collective practical experience with environments and Latino children's health.

HOME AND NEIGHBORHOOD

The home environment is most closely associated with early childhood development and reflects family structure, socioeconomic status, culture and other factors. Many Latino children experience home environments different than non-Hispanic children with regard to Spanish-language use, food availability and types, male parent involvement in rearing and introduction to reading; but the effect of poverty on how children experience environments is greater than that of ethnicity (Bradley, Corwyn et al., 2001). In many places across the United States, Latinos overall, but particularly recent Latino immigrants (Ramirez & de la Cruz, 2002) are the poorest population group. Latino children living in poor urban neighborhoods may have inadequate housing, experience crowded and unsafe living conditions and be exposed to toxins, traffic and other hazards. Latino children in remote rural areas, especially those supported by seasonal labor at risk of economic and food insecurity and lack of health insurance, may have limited access to transportation and be far from essential services like medical care and healthy food sources.

Neighborhoods play a critical role with regard to health (Kawachi & Berkman, 2003) because residents share common exposure to environmental risks and health-supporting opportunities. Physical and social features of neighborhood environments are linked with a wide range of health outcomes, especially among adults (O'Campo, Xue, Wang et al. 1997; Winkleby & Cubbin 2003; Robert & Reither 2004; Mujahid, Roux, Shen et al. 2008; Diez-Roux & Mair 2010) but also among children (Carter & Dubois, 2010; Singh, Siahpush et al., 2010).

Because Latino children are more likely to live in socioeconomically disadvantaged neighborhoods than even poorer non-Hispanic white children (Acevedo-Garcia, Osypuk et al., 2008) and evidence indicates that these neighborhoods offer fewer health promoting opportunities (Larson, Story & Nelson 2009; Lovasi, Hutson, Guerra et al. 2009; Singh, Siahpush & Kogan 2010), Latino children are especially at risk of multiple health damaging exposures and deprivation.

Neighborhood environments that recent immigrants from Mexico and Central America encounter in the United States may contrast sharply with the environments that they experienced in their home countries. Latino immigrants are primarily concentrated in six states (California, New York, Florida, Texas, New Jersey and Illinois), however over the past 15 years, greater dispersal of Latinos throughout the United States has occurred (Capps, Passel, Perez-Lopez et al., 2003). Neighborhoods more recently settled by Latino immigrants tend to have limited capacity to assist Spanish-speaking, low income and less well-educated populations, whereas neighborhoods populated by Latinos for generations tend to have fewer language barriers and greater Latino political representation. Thus, programs and services developed by and for populations in well-established Latino neighborhoods may not be directly transferable to newer Latino neighborhoods. Still, most low-income Latinos, both immigrants and U.S.-born, live in segregated neighborhoods that offer inexpensive housing, comfortable language, trusted relationships and familiar goods. These neighborhoods often have fewer structural resources to support healthy behavior such as grocery stores and parks, school yards that are open for recreation after-hours, sidewalks and streets that are safe for walking and biking, clean air and water (Schulz, Williams, Israel et al., 2002).

FOOD ENVIRONMENTS

The food environment refers to the availability of food retailers, including convenience stores, supermarkets and fast food restaurants (Morland, Wing & Diez Roux 2002; Morland, Wing, Diez Roux et al. 2002; Morland, Diez Roux & Wing 2006) within cities, neighborhoods or near schools.

Several descriptive studies have shown that access to healthy food environments is unequally distributed by race/ethnicity and class, where minority and poor neighborhoods typically have the least access to supermarkets and the highest concentration of convenience stores and fast food restaurants (Papas, Alberg, Ewing et al. 2007; Black & Macinko 2008; Larson, Story & Nelson 2009; Lovasi, Hutson, Guerra et al. 2009).

A limited but growing number of investigations have characterized food environments in Latino neighborhoods. For example, a study in Los Angeles found fewer supermarkets in Latino neighborhoods than non-Hispanic white neighborhoods (Shaffer, 2002). Another recent study that used U.S. Census and commercial food store data reported that neighborhoods in a Texas locality with a high percentage of Hispanic residents had almost four times the number of convenience stores compared to neighborhoods with a low percentage of Hispanic residents (Lisabeth, Sanchez et al., 2010). Although local convenience stores are potential sources of culturally favored fruits and vegetables, research in Latino neighborhoods in Chicago found this not to be the case (Grigsby-Toussaint, Zenk et al., 2010). In addition to convenience store availability, studies have shown that a greater number of fast food outlets are found in minority compared with non-Hispanic white neighborhoods (Larson, Story et al., 2009; Lovasi, Hutson et al., 2009).

A recent review of the food environment-obesity literature reported that access to supermarkets was inversely related to body weight and concluded that this was the strongest and most consistent association across the studies reviewed (Lovasi et al., 2009). Similarly, a study using national data documented that supermarket availability was inversely associated with the adolescent body mass index (BMI) (Powell, Auld et al., 2007). The same study reported a positive association between the number of convenience stores and BMI.

Although availability and density of fast food restaurants in disadvantaged neighborhoods is widely considered a contributor to obesity, the limited evidence of these linkages is equivocal: some studies showed an association while others did not (Lovasi et al., 2009). Despite increasing interest in this area, there is still insufficient research to fully understand the associations between neighborhood supermarkets, fast food and convenience stores, diet and obesity among Latino children (Larson, Story and Nelson 2009; Lovasi, Hutson, Guerra et al. 2009). Nevertheless, previously mentioned studies documenting a preponderance of smaller grocery and convenience stores in Latino neighborhoods may translate into fewer healthy food options for Latino children.

Prices constitute an important component of the food environment. Recent economic studies document the influence of food prices on children's body weight. One study found that higher prices for fruits and vegetables were associated with higher BMI, while higher fast food prices were related to lower BMI (Powell, 2009). Although Latinos represent a small proportion of the population under investigation (Powell & Bao, 2009; Powell, Zhao et al., 2009), findings from these studies may have important implications for Latino children. Despite living under the same roof of those who grow our nation's food, children of agricultural workers may not have ready and affordable access to fresh nutritious food at home or at school (Weigel, Armijos et al., 2007). Further, compared with whites, Latino children are more likely to live in poverty (Suro, Kocchar et al., 2007) and poverty is associated with greater consumption of energy-dense foods and lower quality diets (Drewnowski & Specter, 2004).

Farmers' markets and community gardens are growing in popularity and have been highlighted as a potential tool in addressing poor food environments. Although more research is needed to understand accessibility of farmers' markets and their influence on consumption of fruits and vegetables and obesity, preliminary research of the Supplemntal Nutrition Program for Women Infants and Children (WIC) Farmers' Market Nutrition Program suggests that providing coupons for purchase of allowed foods at these markets increases fruit and vegetable consumption (McCormack, Laska et al., 2010). However, farmers' markets and community gardens may not always be accessible for Latino populations; and the quality and prices of produce may differ between farmers' market venues, depending on the neighborhood demographics.

Traditional food outlets sometimes carry a unique connotation in Latino neighborhoods where a variety of ready-to-eat foods are commonly offered by street vendors. Despite their popularity, little research has been conducted to understand the impact of street vendors on Latino children's health. Observational studies have noted a consistent customer base for street vending of ice cream and candy on property adjacent to elementary and middle schools that have implemented policies prohibiting on-campus sales of such products (Healthy Eating and Active Communities, 2010). While policies to restrict street vending have been implemented (with varying degrees of enforcement) in a number of places, assessment of street vending in Latino communities needs to consider the range of food offerings as well as the impact on jobs and economics, cultural traditions and access to healthy alternatives (Woodward-Lopez & Flores, 2006).

Sugar-sweetened beverages have unique implications for Latino children. In 2009, Mexico and the United States were respectively the first and fourth largest per capita consumers of Coca-Cola products worldwide (Coca-Cola Co, 2010). Recent studies suggest that sugar-sweetened beverages are one of single largest contributors to the obesity epidemic (Vartanian, Shwarts et al., 2007; Brownell & Freiden, 2009). Forty-one percent of children (ages 2-11), 62% of adolescents (ages 12-17) and 24% of adults in California drink at least one soda or other sugar-sweetened beverage every day (Babey, Jones et al., 2009). Rising consumption of sugary drinks is likely due to a variety of factors, including larger portion sizes, pervasive marketing and increasing accessibility of these products. Marketers spend close to $500 million dollars a year to reach children and adolescents, including targeting Latino youth, with messages about sugar-sweetened drinks, more than they spend on any other category of food or beverage (Berkeley Media Studies Group, 2009).

Compounding the influence of food and beverage marketing on Latino children, prominent Latino civic and health organizations may accept support from and have longstanding loyalties to the food and beverage industries, including major purveyors of beer, soda, snack foods and fast foods (National Council of La Raza, 2009). The food and beverage industry plays a vital role in many Latino neighborhoods, fueling commerce, jobs and donations for programs and celebrations. Consequently, policy measures to improve health that involve regulating the food and beverage industry are not always met with support from prominent organizations that speak for Latino children (Geiger & Hamburger, 2010).

PHYSICAL ACTIVITY ENVIRONMENTS

There is strong evidence that consistent and vigorous physical activity in combination with healthy nutrition is instrumental to prevent obesity and its complications, such as type 2 diabetes, coronary heart disease, hypertension, sleep apnea and some cancers (U.S. Department of Health and Human Services 2001; U.S. Department of Health and Human Services and U.S. Department of Education 2001; U.S. Department of Health and Human Services 2002; White House Task Force on Childhood Obesity 2010). Neighborhood environments also matter when it comes to physical activity (Sallis & Glanz, 2009). Access to safe recreational facilities, such as parks, playgrounds, open spaces and trails, has been demonstrated to increase physical activity among youth and adolescents (Babey, Brown et al., 2005). However, compared with white and high socioeconomic status populations, minority and low-income communities have less access to public and private facilities for recreation (Sallis et al., 2009). Lack of access to safe parks in particular is a significant barrier to physical activity for Latino children and youth. In California, more than 29% of Latino adolescents do not have access to a safe park as compared with 22% of non-Hispanic white teens (Babey et al., 2005).

Compared to 8.5% of non-Hispanic white parents, more than 41% of Latino parents reported lack of neighborhood safety as a problem in relation to their children's physical activity (Babey et al., 2005). Furthermore, Latino parents of nine- to thirteen-year-old children report more obstacles to their children's physical activity than non-Hispanic white parents, including a lack of local opportunities, transportation problems, cost of participation in organized sports and safety concerns (Duke, Huhman et al., 2003). As a result, a far lower percentage of Latino youth participate in organized physical activity outside of a school setting than non-Hispanic children (Duke, Huhman et al., 2003). Neighborhood environments that support and promote physical activity among youth are measured not only by access to parks and recreational facilities, but also by safety, walkability and bikeability, access to organized sports and joint-use of school facilities for after-school recreation in the neighborhood as well as school and community design (Sallis et al., 2009).

Television and Advertising

Television viewing and exposure to advertisements is associated with multiple adverse health consequences such as obesity (Saelens, Sallis et al., 2002), alcohol consumption (Smith & Foxcroft, 2009) and smoking (Charlesworth & Glantz, 2005). TV viewing replaces activities like playing with friends, being physically active, playing outside, reading, doing homework and doing chores (Bickham & Rich, 2006).

Children see tens of thousands of TV commercials each year (American Academy of Child and Adolescent Psychiatry, 2001), two-thirds of which are for unhealthy food and drinks (McGinnis, Appleton et al., 2005). During the after-school time period, ads targeting children tend to focus on promotion of fast food and sugary drinks (Jago, Baranowski et al., 2005; Viner & Cole, 2005).

On average, two- to five-year-old children spend 32 hours a week, and their six- to eleven-year-old counterparts spend about 28 hours a week watching television, DVDs, DVR and videos or using a game console (McDonough, 2009). One study found that young children of Hispanic mothers whose dominant language was Spanish spent less time in front of the TV than children whose mothers spoke mostly English (Thompson, Sibinga et al., 2010).

Older Hispanic youth average about 1½ times as much of media exposure daily, compared to white youth (Rideout, Foehr et al., 2010). Children's programming on Spanish-language TV is scant, so children in Spanish-speaking households may be more likely than children in English-speaking households to be exposed to adult content and advertising that is predominantly for unhealthy foods like sugary drinks and fast food (Thompson, Flores et al., 2008).

Despite industry self-regulation in response to pressure from the public and from Congress, 73% of the foods advertised on television to children are for products in the poorest nutritional category, and cartoon characters continue to be used to get children to influence parental food purchasing decisions (Kunkel, McKinley et al., 2009).

Advertising also influences and encourages smoking and alcohol consumption. Children see on average, about 2,000 beer and wine ads on TV each year (Strasburger, 2002) and although tobacco ads are banned on TV, young people still see characters smoking in movies and on TV, which has been associated with smoking initiation (Charlesworth et al., 2005). Some television and magazine ads for alcohol, such as "alcopop," which combine the sweet taste of soda pop in a liquor-branded malt beverage, target youth, especially girls and Latinos (Jernigan & Ostorff, 2005).

TOBACCO AND OTHER ENVIRONMENTAL TOXINS

Tobacco use and exposure to second-hand smoke are toxins that can cause health problems for children and later in life. Children and teens are at greater health risk from tobacco use and exposure to second-hand smoke than adults because their respiratory, immune and nervous systems are still developing. Due to lower rates of tobacco use among Latino adults, Latino children may have a lower risk of exposure to second-hand smoke than African-American or non-Hispanic white children (U.S. Department of Health and Human Services, 2007), although a study by Acevedo-Garcia and colleagues found that the tobacco industry aggressively targeted immigrant groups, including Latinos (Acevedo-Garcia, Barbeau et al., 2004).

Tobacco users almost always begin during adolescence while 16.7% of Latino high school students report using tobacco (Center for Disease Control and Prevention, 2008), 6.8% of Latino middle school students report tobacco use (Center for Disease Control and Prevention, 2006). Tobacco use among Latino high school students is slightly below the national average, but Latino middle school students were more likely than any other subgroup to report tobacco use (Center for Disease Control and Prevention, 2006).

Latino children living in substandard housing or poor neighborhoods have a higher risk of exposure to toxins that may adversely affect their health than children not living in such places (Morello-Frosch & Jesdale, 2006; Carter-Pokras et al., 2007). Latino children may be more vulnerable to the effects of toxic exposures than other children due to co-existing factors such as poor nutrition, stress and lack of access to health care (Carter-Pokras et al., 2007). Exposure to household mold, a common problem in sub-standard housing, is a frequent finding in Latino children with asthma (Natalie, Freeman et al., 2003).

Exposure to toxins such as lead, hazardous air pollutants and pesticides is a relatively common risk for Latino children. Because Latinos account for 90% of the farm worker population in the United States, their children can be chronically exposed to the widespread use of agricultural pesticides. Although children may not work directly in the fields, they are exposed to pesticides through drift from applications to nearby fields and as a result of residues on farm workers' shoes and clothing that are brought into the home. Inadvertently, Latino children living in substandard housing may be exposed to indoor pesticides used to treat infestations as well.

The National Institute of Environmental Health Sciences joined with the Environmental Protection Agency to fund the CHAMACOS (Center for the Health Assessment of Mothers and Children of Salinas) study in 1999 which found that children of Mexican immigrants residing in the agricultural community of Salinas, California, have higher pesticide exposure levels than the general U.S. population and than Mexican-American children in general (Bradman, Whitaker et al., 2007). Exposures were found to be associated with developmental deficits and behavioral problems (Eskenazi, Rosas et al., 2008; Rosas & Eskenazi, 2008).

The presence of lead in the blood of children is abnormal and almost always due to lead exposure in the child's environment. Health effects of lead include damage to the brain and nervous system, behavior and learning problems such as hyperactivity, slowed growth and hearing problems (Agency for Toxic Substances and Disease Registry, 2007). Latino children are more likely than non-Hispanic white children to have high blood lead levels on screening tests (Meyer, Pivetz et al., 2003). Children residing in older dwellings with lead paint, exposed to industrial sources of lead or consuming food contaminated with lead are at risk of lead intoxication (Handley, Hall et al., 2007).

Some Latino children have been found to have high blood lead levels from ingesting *greta*, a traditional laxative made in Mexico, and from Mexican tamarind and other flavored candies and their wrappers. Latino children have also been exposed to the lead dust-laden clothing of household members that are employed in places where contact with lead commonly occurs (radiator repair, furniture refinishing, etc.) (Flattery, Gambatese, Shlag et al. 1993; Gourtney, Kilpatrick, Buchannan et al. 2002).

Latino children have higher levels of exposure to hazardous air pollutants compared to non-Hispanic whites (Morello-Frosch et al., 2006). Hazardous air pollutants have been linked to a range of health conditions including cardiovascular disease (Brook, Rajagopalan et al., 2010), respiratory disease, poorer performance on neurodevelopmental tests and cancer. Air pollutants may exacerbate symptoms in children with asthma (Leikauf, 2002). Latino children living in low-income neighborhoods are more likely than children not similarly located to be exposed to air pollutants from adjacent industry such as metal finishing, manufacturing, farming and train and truck transportation corridors (Carter-Pokras, Zambrana et al., 2007).

COMMUNITY DESIGN AND TRANSPORTATION

Community design and transportation is increasingly reported to have indirect and direct impacts on children's health. Community design that supports safety, walking and biking promotes healthy behaviors, whereas community design that favors cars and urban sprawl can be detrimental to health. For example, mounting evidence suggests that living near safe walkable green spaces, having access to public transit and the presence of sidewalks and bike lanes increases the likelihood of physical activity, including active transportation (e.g., bicycling, walking) (Frank, Andresen et al., 2004; Galea, Freudenberg et al., 2005; Frank, Saelens et al., 2007). In contrast, community and transportation design that fails to accommodate mixed-use, infill and inter-connectedness has been associated with poor nutrition and decreased physical activity, which may lead to obesity and chronic diseases (Morland, Wing et al., 2002).

Residential segregation and inequity lie at the center of the "place, space and race" basis for unequal geography of opportunity (Acevedo-Garcia et al., 2008). For Latino communities, "smart growth" has largely failed to address issues of social equity and environmental justice. The social and environmental effects of sprawl, the relationship between sprawl and concentrated poverty and community-based regionalism linking cities and suburbs need to be considered in relation to Latino children's health (Pastor, 2007).

Latino children and others living in low-income urban communities are challenged by an over-abundance of unhealthy businesses such as liquor stores and fast food outlets, poor street lighting, vacant buildings and limited access to adequate and affordable transportation, despite sometimes being saturated with railroads, highways and diesel truck traffic (Acevedo-Garcia et al., 2008). In comparison, residents of rural areas are challenged by insufficiency of community resources, long distances to services and lack of multi-modal transportation options including sidewalks, bike lanes and public transit.

Walking to and from school is a healthy and convenient means for children to gain beneficial minutes of physical activity each day (Safe Routes to School), however walking to school may be unsafe in some Latino communities. Schools with high proportion of students of color are less likely to be served by well-maintained, continuous pedestrian facilities (Ross & Marcus, 2009). In 1999, Latinos made up almost a third of the California's population but accounted for 40% of all pedestrian injuries and 43% of pedestrian deaths (Ohland & Corless, 2000). Latino children are disproportionately at risk for motor vehicle injury due to failed immigration policy that does not allow undocumented immigrants to obtain driver's licenses—if these were allowed, immigrants could obtain training and be able to drive safely (Cooper, Wilder et al., 2005).

Bicycling has been found to be an important mode of transportation for recent Latino immigrants in California (Handy, 2009). While this type of physical activity can enhance health, it can increase risk for injury and death in places lacking bike paths, safe crossings and adequate lighting. Improving walking and biking conditions in low-income communities and communities of color would not only improve safety and lower the risk of injuries and fatalities, but would also generate economic development within those neighborhoods, bringing businesses and essential services within walking distance of residential areas (Handy, 2009).

SAFETY AND VIOLENCE

Safety is a top environmental priority in Latino communities—that is, preventing both unintentional and intentional injury. Violence exacts a disproportionate burden on young people, families, neighborhoods and cities. Disproportionately high rates of community and street violence, as well as a common perception of higher crime are commonly attributed to low-income communities and communities of color. Whether the fear is perceived or real, concerns about neighborhood safety and violence discourage outdoor physical activity including play, walking, biking, going to the store and social interaction with neighbors, and are linked to the onset of chronic diseases (Cecil-Karb & Grogan-Kaylor, 2009; Duncan, Johnson et al., 2009).

Violence along with food and activity-related chronic diseases are most pervasive in disenfranchised communities, where they occur together and with severity, making them fundamental equity issues. Violence influences where people live, work and shop, whether parents let children play outside and walk to school, and whether there is a grocery store or places for employment in the community.

Further, violence and the resulting trauma is linked long-term to the onset of chronic diseases, the most costly and quickly rising portion of unsustainable health care costs for individuals, businesses and government. One study found that over 75% of urban elementary school children living in high-violence neighborhoods had been exposed to community violence (Duncan et al., 2009). Among Latinos between the ages of 10 and 24, homicide is the second leading cause of death (Cecil-Karb et al., 2009). Many urban youth experience trauma and may have post traumatic stress disorder from exposure to violence (Prevention Institute, 2010).

SCHOOL ENVIRONMENTS

Schools offer unique opportunities to teach children critical lifelong habits, including healthy eating and regular vigorous physical activity through didactic as well as normative approaches. Because schools reach most children during critical developmental periods, these settings are increasingly becoming a central focus for policy and environmental strategies to prevent childhood obesity at the population level (Sallis & Glanz, 2009; Story, Nanney et al., 2009). The food environment inside schools is shaped by multiple factors, including federal policies and programs such as the National School Breakfast and Lunch programs, as well as district and individual school nutritional policies and resources.

Although there is growing interest in and research on the multilevel associations between the school food environment, diet and obesity (Kann, Grunbaum et al., 2005; Delva, O'Malley et al., 2007; Story, Kaphingst et al., 2007), relatively little research documents the nature and magnitude of the effect of the school food environment on Latino children's health above and beyond individual and school-level characteristics. A recently published study of Latino children in K-2nd grades in three San Diego school districts did not find significant associations between school and community measures with BMI, although they identified a significant relationship between parental characteristics and child's BMI (Elder, Arredondo et al.). Longitudinal, multilevel research on the influences of the school food environment on diet, physical activity and obesity among Latino children is nearly absent from the published research.

In addition to the food environment in schools, concern is growing over the food environment *outside* schools (Gittelsohn & Kumar, 2007; Simon, Kwan et al., 2008; Zenk & Powell, 2008). Descriptive studies using national data have shown that fast food restaurant proximity to schools was greater for high schools compared to middle and elementary schools (Simon et al., 2008; Sturm, 2008). Similarly, studies have found that the availability of convenience stores was particularly greater in high schools and schools with higher concentration of Hispanic students (Sturm & Datar, 2005).

A study using a large sample of children 12-17 years old in California found that fast food restaurant proximity to schools was associated with fewer consumption of fruits and vegetables, higher consumption of sodas and greater likelihood of overweight relative to students whose schools were not near a fast food restaurant (Davis & Carpenter, 2008). This study reported that the influence of proximity of fast food venues to schools on obesity was not different for Hispanic children.

At the local level, a study found that of all food outlets within walking distance of a school, 63% were those that offered unhealthy food (Kipke, Iverson et al., 2007) in a predominantly Hispanic California community. Additional research is needed to improve our understanding of how proximity of unhealthy food outlets close to schools with high concentrations of Latinos may impact Latino children's health.

Schools are also an important venue for children to be physically active. For many Latino children, particularly those that lack access to safe parks and other places to play, physical education in school can offer the opportunity to get the recommended daily amount of physical activity. Physical activity during school has been shown to reduce obesity, improve physical health (UCLA Center to Eliminate Health Disparities and Samuels and Associates, 2007) as well as academic performance and to promote youth development (Field, Diego et al., 2001; Coe, Pivarnik et al., 2006).

In California, where more than 49% of all public school students are Latinos, state law requires physical education (Garcia & Fenwick, 2009). Over half the school districts audited from 2004 to 2009 did not enforce physical education laws that require an average of 20 minutes per day of physical education in elementary school and 40 minutes in middle and high school (The City Project, 2010). Failure to enforce physical education requirements disproportionately harms children of color and low-income children including Latinos.

The percentage of Latino fifth-, seventh- and ninth-grade students that passed six of six fitness criteria on the California statewide physical fitness test was the lowest of any race or ethnicity for each grade tested (California Department of Education, 2010). Because Latino children are more likely to live in poor neighborhoods with limited resources for physical activities, schools may be the only public facilities where children can play safely. However, school grounds are locked after hours in many Latino neighborhoods. As a result, some Latino children experience real barriers to regular physical activity outside of school, which could partly explain why they are less physically fit than their peers.

Promising Strategies for Healthier Environments

Scientific research alone does not yet provide a sufficiently robust base of evidence to drive a policy agenda to improve environments for healthier Latino children. Certainly, more and high quality research is needed that targets Latinos and the places where Latino children live. But, we cannot wait for results from research that targets Latino children to materialize, because the problems owing to adverse environments are too great and the cost of inaction is intolerable.

Community experience and engagement in promising strategies, coupled with the best available evidence, provides the necessary catalyst for policy action to create healthier environments. Across the nation, environmental conditions are being improved in places where Latino children live, play, and go to school through a variety of policy and systems change strategies.

It is crucial to document promising models and lessons to benefit replication and sustainability. Improved nutrition and physical activity environments, tobacco-free communities and the development and implementation of policies ensuring safe, sustainable and equitable environments are measures of progress toward the ultimate goal of improved health outcomes for Latino children.

Aiming at building healthy environments through policy change, community members are developing their skills as advocates, building collaborations, influencing decision-makers and strengthening the fabric of their communities. These actions are leading to health-supportive environments and social norms that will result in healthier Latino children.

In this section, we present a selection of promising, policy-driven, practice-based models that are changing environments in Latino communities to increase opportunities for healthy eating and physical activity, prevent tobacco use and asthma triggers, engage community residents and youth in productive environmental change efforts, and improve safety and crime prevention. The models provide empirical evidence that community-driven efforts to improve environments can succeed in reducing factors associated with unhealthy behaviors and poor health outcomes, and increase factors associated with healthy behaviors and favorable health outcomes. In addition, the models provide valuable lessons that other communities can learn from and adapt to their unique circumstances. Formative and/or summative evaluations of many of these models are helping to build the base of knowledge needed to improve programs and policies aimed at creating healthier environments for Latino children.

Healthy Food and Beverage Access in Communities

Latino communities are using a variety of novel strategies to increase access to healthy foods and beverages in neighborhoods, including working with local restaurants to create healthier options and provide nutrition information, implementing farmers' markets in areas with limited access to fresh produce, and partnering with corner stores to offer fresh fruits and vegetables along with other healthier foods and beverages. Below are some examples of interventions that demonstrate what it takes to transform resource-poor environments into environments that make it easier for families to choose healthy foods and beverages.

Mercado la Paloma: Improving the restaurant nutrition environment

Restaurant owners at Mercado La Paloma have come together to improve the nutrition environment in a South Los Angeles neighborhood that is predominantly Latino and has one of the highest rates of obese children (37%) in the state (Madsen, Weedn et al., 2010). *La Salud Tiene Sabor* is a Mercado la Paloma program led by independently owned restaurants, Esperanza Community Housing Corporation and the Los Angeles County Public Health Department, to empower community residents and families to make healthy food choices via access to healthy selections and nutrition information on menus and menu boards. All restaurants have had their recipes professionally analyzed for nutritional content, received input on how to modify menu items that could be prepared in a healthier manner and display calorie information on their menu boards. *Promotoras* have played an important role in the Mercado to promote the needed changes. An evaluation of the *La Salud Tiene Sabor* program is currently underway with support from the Robert Wood Johnson Foundation Salud America! research program to document and disseminate lessons learned at the Mercado.

Holyoke Food and Fitness Initiative

Nuestras Raíces, a grassroots, community-based organization in Holyoke, Massachusetts, addresses environmental, economic development, substance abuse and food security issues in Latino neighborhoods (Nuestras Raíces). Established in 1992 by the predominantly Puerto Rican members of La Finquita community garden, *Nuestras Raíces* is currently collaborating with the Holyoke Health Center, community-based agencies, governmental institutions, community residents and youth leaders on the Holyoke Food and Fitness Policy Council (HFFPC) with funding from the W.K. Kellogg Foundation's Food and Fitness Initiative. HFFPC is pursuing a policy-driven systems change agenda to create access to healthy foods and fitness opportunities for families and children through strategies such as land use, transportation and healthy food retailing while addressing underlying conditions of poverty, blight and social injustice.

HEALTHY BODEGAS: HEALTHIER OPTIONS IN NEW YORK CITY CORNER STORES

In New York City, the public health department is working to increase the availability of healthier food choices in small stores/bodegas through the Healthy Bodegas Initiative (New York City Department of Health and Mental Hygiene, 2009). Since 2005, the Healthy Bodegas Initiative has worked with more than 1,000 bodegas in primarily Latino neighborhoods in East and Central Harlem, the South Bronx and Central Brooklyn to increase access to and promote healthy foods, such as fresh fruits and vegetables, whole grain bread, low-fat milk and dairy products and low-salt and no-sugar-added canned goods. The Initiative also aims to reduce advertising of unhealthy foods and beverages.

CCROPP FARMERS' MARKETS: MAKING PRODUCE AVAILABLE IN FOOD DESERTS

Many of the predominately Latino and low-income residents of California's Central Valley, one of our nation's richest agricultural regions, lack easy access to the fruits and vegetables grown and harvested in the area (Samuels & Associates, 2010). Even those that work in the agricultural fields may not have markets available in their neighborhoods to access fresh fruits and vegetables nor the economic resources to afford produce of relative high quality. The Central California Regional Obesity Prevention Program (CCROPP) sites, established with the support of The California Endowment, are working to improve the nutrition and physical activity environments in these communities. In seven counties, CCROPP partners have expanded existing farmers' markets to offer more fruits and vegetables, established produce sales at flea markets and produce stands on school campuses, offered electronic benefit transactions (EBT), WIC and/or senior nutrition vouchers for use at markets and stands and engaged community support for markets. Through their work, CCROPP partners have increased local and regional access to healthy foods in the Central Valley, attracted diverse customers, increased collaboration between communities, schools, public health departments, farmers, vendors and food assistance programs, and supported production and consumption of local produce.

BUEN PROVECHO: PROMOTING PRODUCE IN PUERTO RICAN NEIGHBORHOODS IN CHICAGO

In addition to a farmers' market, a produce mobile and a physical activity program, The Puerto Rican Cultural Center in Humboldt Park, Chicago, is implementing *Buen Provecho* (Consortium to Lower Obesity in Chicago's Children, 2010). The restaurants offer healthier menu item choices that include fresh produce, smaller portion sizes and/or cooking with healthier oils, an intervention involving promotion of healthier menus and produce-focused items in local restaurants. In return for point of purchase in-store promotion of these healthier items, businesses get a window decal identifying them as a *Buen Provecho* participant and are listed in year-round local newspaper advertisements. This intervention is creating an environment for Latino residents in this area of Chicago that allows healthy foods to be the norm.

IMPROVING PHYSICAL ACTIVITY ENVIRONMENTS

Improving access to safe places to play and opportunities for physical activity is critical when addressing environmental strategies to improve community health. In Latino communities around the country, work is being done to improve existing parks and recreation spaces or to create new ones, make communities more walkable and bikeable, and to increase physical activity levels during physical education classes in schools. Noteworthy examples include the following:

THE ALBUQUERQUE ALLIANCE FOR ACTIVE LIVING

The Alliance advocates changing city and school district planning and development policies to support walking, bicycling and transit use. The focus is on increasing funding for pedestrian improvements at the city and regional level, and raising standards for street design to allow for safe and comfortable pedestrian movement.

Founded in 2001 as an Active Living by Design Program (Philip, Mark et al., 2009), the Alliance works with the predominantly Hispanic Atrisco neighborhood on targeted promotions, programs and physical projects. The *Vecinos* Bike Recycle Program has fixed and given approximately 100 used bicycles to neighborhood children and adults. The city has donated space at a vacant library for the bike repair shop, where used bikes and an office are housed. The Alliance also is helping to create a network of walking paths through the Ditches with Trails program. *Vecinos del Bosque*, a neighborhood within Atrisco is one of two pilot project areas that will improve neglected irrigation ditch right-of-ways to support pedestrian trails. Publicizing access to and improving the trails along the ditches, as well as on the streets, will greatly enhance walking routes to schools.

LATINO ADVOCACY FOR PARKS AND RECREATION

The urban park movement in Los Angeles and beyond has drawn on Latino community leadership to create safe places for play and physical activity in park-poor, income-poor communities. The recently established Los Angeles State Historic Park, a park in downtown Los Angeles; the Rio de Los Angeles State Park at Taylor Yard along the Los Angeles River; and the Ascot Hills Park in northeast

Los Angeles, for example, resulted in part from Latino grassroots activists and advocates fighting city hall and wealthy developers in and out of court—and winning. Successful strategies included community empowerment, multidisciplinary research and analysis, new and traditional media campaigns, policy and legal advocacy outside the courts and access to justice through the courts (Garcia & White, 2006; The City Project, 2010).

The struggles to create the Los Angeles State Historic Park and Rio de Los Angeles State Park led to the formation of the Alianza de los Pueblos del Río. The Alianza is working to ensure that the Los Angeles River Revitalization Master Plan promotes democratic participation and equitable results in greening 52 miles along the River with healthy parks, schools and communities. The Alianza formed when its leaders decided that the greening of the River was a symbolic and literal convergence of a myriad of issues confronting the Latino population and other communities of color and low-income communities. The agenda of the Alianza has grown into a comprehensive new platform of urban and Latino environmentalism, or the "browning of the green movement." Part legal strategy, part organizing principle, this "urban greening *con salsa* movement" has put immigrants and low-income families at the center of an issue that has traditionally focused on flora and fauna (George, 2006; Garcia, Rawson et al., 2009).

LOS ANGELES UNIFIED SCHOOL DISTRICT–PHYSICAL EDUCATION AND CIVIL RIGHTS

Los Angeles Unified School District (LAUSD) is the second largest school district in the United States and serves over 600,000 students, 73% of whom are Latino (California Department of Education, 2010). Multiple audits by the California Department of Education found that LAUSD was not enforcing state physical education requirements requiring an average of 20 minutes of physical education in elementary schools every day and 40 minutes in middle and high schools.

In response to a community campaign, LAUSD adopted a plan to enforce physical education requirements (Los Angeles Unified School District, 2009). The school district is enforcing education and civil rights laws to help promote academic performance and youth development and reduce obesity and diabetes. The plan seeks to ensure that schools provide properly credentialed physical education teachers, meet the physical education minute requirements, maintain reasonable class size averages, and provide quality facilities for physical education (Garcia et al., 2009; Los Angeles Unified School District, 2009).

Diverse allies are advocating for the U.S. Department of Education to recognize Los Angeles as a bellwether for action to ensure that public schools across the country provide physical education (California Center for Public Health Advocacy, California LULAC et al., 2010).

ACTIVE LIVING LOGAN SQUARE

The primarily Latino population in the Logan Square neighborhood of Chicago is served by a neighborhood association with 48 years of experience in building partnerships (Gomez-Feliciano, McCreary et al., 2009). Their efforts enhance school environments and practices to support physical activity before, during and after the school day; and create safe, inviting places for activity that connect to surrounding communities. The partnership's participatory approach involved a variety of community stakeholders in developing and implementing affordable, accessible, culturally acceptable and sustainable physical activities for children and their families. The partnership successfully piloted Open Streets (temporary street closures) and advocated for development of an elevated rails-to-trails project. The partnership changed the culture at a local elementary school to support healthy behaviors through new policies and programs.

PREVENTING TOBACCO USE AND ASTHMA TRIGGERS

Community-driven efforts for healthier social norms about tobacco use provide some of the greatest public health success stories of our times. We are on the cusp of implementing landmark federal and state policies that will improve air quality, reduce environmental degradation, improve asthma management and reduce asthma triggers. In recent years, many community-level efforts have surfaced to reduce tobacco use and to reduce asthma triggers. Two noteworthy efforts are featured here:

INDIANA LATINO HEALTH INSTITUTE

The Indiana Latino Institute (ILI) works to address the multitude of health issues caused by the use and promotion of tobacco products among Latinos nationwide (Indiana Latino Institute, 2010). ILI has brought together local businesses and partner organizations to support clean, comprehensive air ordinances as well as establish smoke-free businesses. Their focus has been on Latino-owned businesses and businesses that employ Latinos or that are frequented by Latinos as patrons. As a result of the ILI efforts, over 200 businesses in Indiana have gone "smoke-free."

COMMUNITY ACTION TO FIGHT ASTHMA (CAFA): UNITING ADVOCATES

Initially focused on treating and managing the disease, CAFA has taken up policy advocacy and prevention. Affiliates throughout California are working to shape local, regional and state policies to reduce the environmental triggers of asthma for school-aged children. CAFA's statewide network serves many predominantly Latino communities, and in Southern California CAFA is supported by the National Latino Research Center (CAFA, 2009). In the Merced Mariposa Coalition, Spanish-speaking community members are critical in the coalition's strategic planning process and assist in shaping its agenda and future projects.

COMMUNITY RESIDENT AND YOUTH ENGAGEMENT

Community resident and youth engagement are at the core of Latino communities' advocacy efforts to create healthy environments. Community residents and youth are leading change in their communities in the face of competing priorities. In many cases, they are focused on the survival of their families. Many parents work more than one job to feed and house their children. Language barriers and anti-immigrant sentiment present additional challenges. The following are but a few examples of residents and youth mobilizing to improve environments in Latino communities.

DENVER URBAN GARDENS

Working with school officials, teachers, parents and supportive community members, The LiveWell Colorado Denver Urban Gardens (DUG) Initiative is working to promote healthy eating and active living (HEAL) in three low-income, mostly Latino neighborhoods in Denver County, CO (Leeman-Castillo, 2010). DUG provides opportunities for participants to supplement their diet with produce grown in nearby public gardens integrated with other environmental approaches to promote changes in their community food systems. For example, the Fairview school garden and youth market is a learning laboratory for students, as well as a place to address neighborhood needs for access to fresh produce, job skills and to connect with neighbors.

More than 50% of community gardeners meet national guidelines for fruit and vegetable intake, compared to 25% of non-gardeners. As well as eating better and being more active, gardeners are more involved in social activities, view their neighborhoods as more beautiful and have stronger ties to their neighborhoods. Ninety-five percent of community gardeners give away some of the produce they grow to friends, family and people in need; 60% specifically donate to food assistance programs (University of Colorado Denver School of Public Health, 2008). Organizations like Denver Urban Gardens, are increasingly needed to inform local government institutions, private developers and policy-makers about the complex web of sustainable practices and policies needed to support urban agriculture ranging from water conservation, land tenure, waste management, recycling and community building—all essential ingredients for a sustainable food production system.

PIÑEROS Y CAMPESINOS UNIDOS DEL NOROESTE

In the rural town of Woodburn, Oregon, where the population is more than 50% Latino, the farm workers union has a history of organizing and advocacy for labor and housing issues. The 5,700+ members of the union, as well as farm workers' spouses and children, are now using community engagement to address healthy food access and physical activity right along with voter registration and immigration reform, as shared priorities (Ashley, Aboelata, Sims et al., 2008) through the "capaces" coalition. As a result, children in Woodburn have greater opportunities for healthy nutrition and physical activity.

GREENFIELD WALKING GROUP: BAKERSFIELD, CALIFORNIA

A parent-led walking group serves as the local resident task force to the Central California Regional Obesity Prevention Program and is reversing barriers to healthy eating and safe walking in their rural, predominantly Latino neighborhood in Kern County, California (Samuels, Schwarte et al., 2009). Walking group members have increased access to safe physical activity, improved neighborhood safety, cleaned the park of trash and drug paraphernalia, decreased gang activity, gained support from local government leadership, increased social support among Greenfield walking group members and built overall community cohesion. Along the way, their energy, success and fun have attracted many new participants. Now famous, they are also showing communities throughout the region how to mobilize for a healthier, safer environment.

JUNTAS PODEMOS: POLICY RECOMMENDATIONS FOR LATINO CHILDREN

Juntas Podemos brings together public health researchers, Latino community leaders and families to develop effective policy recommendations for physical activity in a growing settlement of recent immigrants from West Columbia, South Carolina (Torres, 2009). Photovoice is being used to collect data from mothers and community stakeholders, and document and analyze the issues. Based on the findings from the data collection, involved residents are developing recommendations targeting physical activity among Latino children, and are disseminating them to local and state-level policy-makers.

VIOLENCE PREVENTION AND SAFETY

Recognizing the link between violence prevention and health-supportive environments, those working to improve health in Latino communities have focused on reducing violence and creating safer places for community residents and families to live, work and play through strategies such as crime prevention through environmental design (CPTED) (see for example, Center for Crime Prevention Through Environmental Design).

The following strategies have not only created access to places to play and learn, but also helped to deter criminal activity and the perception of crime. A unified approach to addressing safety and violence issues that assembles people from multiple fields (including healthy eating and active living advocates) and combines their strengths can forge a path that simultaneously promotes safety, health and health equity. Such collaboratives have the capacity to solve complex root problems, benefiting society overall and, in particular communities of color and low-income communities (Prevention Institute, 2010).

RECLAIMING LAUDERBACH PARK

Friends of Lauderbach Park, in Chula Vista California, is a group of students, *promotoras*, community organizations, city staff and elected officials, that collaborated to revitalize a favorite community park that had deteriorated over the years (Samuels & Associates, 2010). Improvements to Lauderbach Park included reducing the height of bushes and lowering the chain-link fence to make a once-hidden area more visible and thereby less inviting to criminal activity. Other changes included new landscaping and lighting, a children's play area and restrooms, drinking fountain, more picnic tables and trash cans and enhanced pedestrian pathways. As a result of these changes and a stronger partnership with city officials including law enforcement, residents have gained a greater sense of hope and pride which has helped to sustain the health promoting changes at Lauderbach Park.

CULTIVATING PEACE IN SALINAS

Libraries are not often considered when thinking about violence prevention. However, a simple, yet innovative, change in practice has resulted in more young people reading, engaging in meaningful opportunities, having a safe place to gather and connecting with their community (Prevention Institute, 2008). A partnership between the library and schools in Salinas, California, was established to provide all students with library cards, free of charge and application-free. The library has seen a significant increase in library usage by young people and their families since this change in city policy. In order to continue to build momentum and draw more young people to its safe and imaginative space, the library has eliminated fines and fees for the first year to enable students to learn about using the library. Through cross-sector collaboration and implementation of one element of a broader plan for violence prevention for the entire city, community residents and local public officials have created safe spaces for youth.

Conclusions

This chapter presents both scientific evidence and real-life examples of environmental conditions that shape the health and wellness of Latino children. Descriptive and cross-sectional studies provide evidence that Latino children confront multiple inequitable conditions within the social and physical environments that surround them where they live, go to school and play. Critical examination of the impact that adverse environments can have on health outcomes suggests that the health and wellness of millions of Latino children is being compromised.

It is evident that community-driven measures to create equitable and health-supportive environments in Latino neighborhoods constitute a growing body of promising practices ripe for broad replication. The most successful approaches are those that use community organizing to strengthen the democratic process by creating space for voices that are not in positions of power to push for change. Community and organizational leaders in many places have stepped forward to promote the health of Latino children by championing environmental policy and systems changes that have the potential to benefit many children for generations to come.

In recent years, Latino-elected officials in California and elsewhere have authored some of the nation's most significant legislation for healthy school and community nutrition environments including environmental justice. Appointments of Latino community residents to influential civic decision-making and advisory bodies are striking evidence of achievement and sustainability of the movement for healthy environments. Still, too many Latinos are deterred from civic engagement, and there is a relative dearth of Latinos prominent in the smart growth and regional equity movements (Pastor, 2007).

To drive policy improvements, both rigorously scientific as well as empirical evidence is needed from various disciplines to elucidate how environments influence health outcomes of Latinos along the lifecourse. Carefully constructed longitudinal studies are also needed because it could take many years for the impact of environmental exposures on Latino children's health to manifest. However, even good science sometimes is not sufficient to create the political will for change, especially if there are countervailing forces that stand to benefit from the widespread socioeconomic, racial/ethnic and environmental disparities that mirror health inequalities.

While the initiative of Latino communities and the leadership of key elected officials are laudable, the nation's economic downturn presents a formidable but not impossible challenge to communities needing resources for environmental improvement. There is unprecedented opportunity to advance healthy and equitable environments through well-resourced policy efforts such as the national priorities for childhood obesity prevention, health care reform, environmental protection including green economy and equitable transportation system reform.

Furthermore, given the size, growth and youth of the Latino population, efforts to improve environments in Latino communities must be considered a smart and necessary investment for the health and wellbeing of the nation.

Bienestar underlines the need for policy and systems change to create equitable and health-supportive social and physical environments. To generate sustainable improvements in the health and wellness of Latino children, we propose several policy goals as follows:

Policy Goals for Latino Children's Health and the Environment

Social and physical environmental policies promote health and equity for all Latino children. The public, policy makers and business are aware and support high quality health care and schools, along with efforts to change environments to improve health.

Decision-makers enact federal, state and local policies only after thoroughly considering the impact on health and equity (i.e. "health in all policies") to ensure a standard of living adequate for the health and wellbeing of all people.

Latino families, community leaders and systems serving Latino communities have the tools and resources to work together to ensure healthy and safe environments for children. Grassroots leaders, *promotoras*, community and health organizations, public agencies, schools and businesses contribute expertise and energy to catalyze and monitor healthy and safe environments where Latino children live, go to school, develop and play.

Latino communities are full partners in the development of a green economy and sustainable environment. Green jobs, smart growth, environmental planning, sustainable agriculture, community development and transportation system reform aim for equitable involvement of and benefit to Latinos as the nation's largest minority and stewards of the environment for generations to come.

A robust research agenda elucidates the nexus of Latino children's health and the environment. Government and private foundations support multidisciplinary research from a systems science approach, and culturally competent community-engaged research that involves indigenous investigators to inform policy and environmental improvements and purposeful community engagement.

References

Acevedo-Garcia, D., Barbeau, E., Bishop, J. A., Pan, J., & Emmons, K. M. (2004). "Undoing an epidemiological paradox: the tobacco industry's targeting of U.S. Immigrants." *Am J Public Health, 94*(12): 2188-93.

Acevedo-Garcia, D., Osypuk, T. L., McArdle, N., & Williams, D. R. (2008). "Toward a policy-relevant analysis of geographic and racial/ethnic disparities in child health." *Health Aff, 27*(2): 321-333.

Agency for Toxic Substances and Disease Registry (2007). Toxicological profile for lead, U.S. Department of Health and Human Services, Public Health Service.

American Academy of Child and Adolescent Psychiatry. (2001). Facts for families: Children and watching TV. Accessed September, 13, 2010, from http://www.aacap.org/galleries/FactsForFamilies/54_children_and_watching_tv.pdf

Ashley, L., Aboelata, M., Sims, J., & Adler-McDonald, S. (2008). Mapping the movement for healthy food and activity environments in the United States. Accessed August, 13, 2010, from http://www.preventioninstitute.org/component/jlibrary/article/id-61/127.html

Babey, S., Brown, E., & Hastert, T. (2005). Access to safe parks helps increase physical activity among teenagers. Accessed September, 1, 2010, from http://www.healthpolicy.ucla.edu/pubs/files/TeenActivity_PB_120605.pdf

Babey, S. H., Jones, M., Yu, H., & Goldstein, H. (2009). Bubbling over: Soda consumption and its link to obesity in California. Accessed September 9, 2010, from http://healthpolicy.ucla.edu/pubs/Publication.aspx?pubID=375.

Berkeley Media Studies Group. (2009). Sugar water gets a facelift: what marketing does for soda. Accessed September, 1, 2010, from http://www.preventioninstitute.org/component/jlibrary/article/id-171/127.html

Bickham, D. S., & Rich, M. (2006). "Is television viewing associated with social isolation? Roles of exposure time, viewing context and violent content." *Archives of Pediatric Adolescent Medicine, 160*(4): 387-92.

Bradley, R., Corwyn, R., McAdoo, H., & Coll, C. (2001) The home environments of children in the United States Part 1: Variations by Age, Ethnicity, and Poverty Status. *Child Developent, 72*(6):1844-67.

Bradman, A., Whitaker, D., Quiros, L., Castorina, R., Henn, B. C., Nishioka, M., Morgan, J., Barr, D. B., Harnly, M., Brisbin, J. A., Sheldon, L. S., McKone, T. E., & Eskenazi, B. (2007). "Pesticides and their metabolites in the homes and urine of farm worker children living in the Salinas Valley, CA." *J Expo Sci Environ Epidemiol, 17*(4): 331-49.

Braveman, P., & Barclay, C. (2009). "Health disparities beginning in childhood: a life-course perspective." *Pediatrics, 124*(Supplement_3): S163-175.

Bray, G. A., & Popkin, B. M. (1998). "Dietary fat intake does affect obesity!" *Am J Clin Nutr, 68*(6): 1157-73.

Brook, R., Rajagopalan, S., Pope, C., III., Brook, J., Bhatnagar, A., Diez-Roux, A., Holguin, F., Hong, Y., Luepker, R., Mittleman, M., Peters, A., Siscovick, D., Smith, S., Jr., Whitsel, L., & Kaufman, J. (2010). "Particulate matter air pollution and cardiovascular disease: An update to the scientific statement from the American Heart Association." *Circulation, 121*(21): 2331-2378.

Brownell, K., & Freiden, T. (2009). "Ounces of prevention—The public policy case for taxes on sugared beverages." *New England Journal of Medicine, 360*(18): 1805-8.

CAFA. (2009). Resident and community involvement in policy advocacy. Accessed September, 2010, from http://www.calendow.org/uploadedFiles/Publications/By_Topic/Disparities/Asthma/90109_CAE_CAFAResComm_5.pdf

California Center for Public Health Advocacy, California LULAC, The City Project, California Pan Ethnic Health Work, Prevention Institute and Public Health Law and Policy (2010). Letter to Secretary Arne Duncan.

California Department of Education. (2010). 2008-09 California Physical Fitness Report: Hispanic or Latino. Accessed September, 1, 2010, from http://data1.cde.ca.gov/dataquest/PhysFitness/PFTestSt2007.asp?RptNumber=20&cYear=2008-09&cChoice=PFTest1

California Department of Education. (2010). Student enrollment in the LAUSD: 2008-2009. Accessed September 27, 2010, from http://dq.cde.ca.gov/dataquest/DistEnr2.asp?TheName=&cSelect=1964733—LOS+ANGELES+UNIFIED&cChoice=DistEnrEth&cYear=2008-09&cLevel=District&cTopic=Enrollment&myTimeFrame=S&submit1=Submit

California Department of Education (2010). Spreadsheets of pubic schools audited for physical education compliance from 2005-2009, obtained by The City Project from the California Department of Education under the California Public Records Act. Los Angeles. http://www.cityprojectca.org

Capps, R., Passel, J., Perez-Lopez, D., & Fiz, M. (2003). The New Neighbors: A User's Guide to Data on Immigrants in the U.S. Accessed September, 9, 2010, from http://www.urban.org/uploadedPDF/310844_the_new_neighbors.pdf

Carter-Pokras, O., Zambrana, R., Poppell, Logie, L., & Guerrero-Preston, L. (2007). The environmental health of Latino children. *Journal of Pediatric Health Care, 21*(5): 307-14.

Carter, M., & Dubois, L. (2010). Neighbourhoods and child adiposity: A critical appraisal of the literature. *Health & Place, 16*(3): 616-628.

Cecil-Karb, R., & Grogan-Kaylor, A. (2009). Childhood body mass index in community context: Neighborhood safety, television viewing, and growth trajectories of BMI. *Health Soc Work, 34*(3): 169-77.

Center for Crime Prevention Through Environmental Design. Accessed August, 28, 2010, from www.designcentreforcpted.org

Center for Disease Control and Prevention. (2006). National youth tobacco survey and key prevalence indicators. Accessed September, 1, 2010, from http://www.cdc.gov/tobacco/data_statistics/surveys/nyts/pdfs/indicators.pdf

Center for Disease Control and Prevention (2008). Cigarette use among high school students United States, 1991-2007. Accessed September 1, 2010, from http://www.cdc.gov/mmwr/preview/mmwrhtml/mm5725a3.htm

Center for Health Improvement. (2009). Tackling obesity by building healthy communities: Changing policies through innovative collaborations. Accessed September 1, 2010, from http://www.chipolicy.org/pdf/Issue_Briefs/CHIObesityBriefFinal.pdf

Charlesworth, A., & Glantz, S. (2005). Smoking in the movies increases adolescent smoking: A review. *Pediatrics, 116*(6): 1516-1528.

Coca-Cola Co. (2010). Per capita consumption of company beverage products. Accessed September, 1, 2010, from http://www.thecoca-colacompany.com/ourcompany/ar/pdf/2009-per-capita-consumption.pdf

Coe, D., Pivarnik, C., Womack, C., Reeves, M., & Malina, R. (2006). Effect of physical education and activity levels on academic achievement in children. *Med Schi Sprt Exrc, 38*: 1215-1219.

Consortium to Lower Obesity in Chicago's Children. (2010). Accessed September 27, 2010, from http://www.clocc.net

Cooper, J., Wilder, T., Lankina, E., Geyer, J., Ragland, D., Macias, E., & Wainer, A. (2005). Traffic safety among latino populations in California: Current status and policy recommendations. Accessed September, 17, 2010, from http://ideas.repec.org/p/cdl/itsrrp/87309.html

Davis, B., & Carpenter, C. (2008). Proximity of fast-food restaurants to schools and adolescent obesity. *Am J Public Health, 99*(3): 505-10.

Delva, J., O'Malley, P., & Johnston, L. (2007). Availability of more-healthy and less-healthy food choices in american schools: A national study of grade, racial/ethnic, and socioeconomic differences. *American Journal of Preventive Medicine, 33*(4, Supplement 1): S226-S239.

Diez-Roux, A., & Mair, C. (2010). Neighborhoods and health. *Ann. N.Y. Acad. Sci, 1186*: 125-145.

Drewnowski, A, & Specter, S. (2004). Poverty and obesity: The role of energy density and energy costs. *Am J Clin Nutr, 79*(1): 6-16.

Duke, J., Huhman, M., & Heitzer, C. (2003). Physical activity levels among children aged 9-13 years old. *Morbidity and Mortality Weekley Report, 52*: 785-788.

Duncan, D., Johnson, R., Molinar, B., & Azrael, D. (2009). Association between neighborhood safety and overweight status among urban adolescents. *BMC Public Health, 34*(3): 169-77.

Elder, J. P., Arredondo, E. M., Campbell, N., Baquero, B., Duerksen, S., Ayala, G., Crespo, N. C., Slymen, D., & McKenzie, T. "Individual, family, and community environmental correlates of obesity in Latino elementary school children. *Journal of School Health, 80*(1): 20-30.

Eskenazi, B., Rosas, L. G., Marks, A. R., Bradman, A., Harley, K., Holland, N., Johnson, C., Fenster, L., & Barr, D. B. (2008). Pesticide toxicity and the developing brain. *Basic Clin Pharmacol Toxicol, 102*(2): 228-36.

Field, T., Diego, M., & Sanders, C. (2001). Exercise is positively related to adolescent's relationships and academics. *Adolescence, 36*: 105-110.

Frank, L., Andresen, M., & Schmid, T. (2004). Obesity relationships with community design, physical activity and time spent in cars. *American Journal of Preventive Medicine, 27*: 87-96.

Frank, L., Saelens, B., Powell, K., & Chapman, J. (2007). Stepping toward causation: Do built environments or neighborhood and travel preferences explain physical activity, driving, and obesity? *Social Science & Medicine, 65*(9): 1898-1914.

Galea, S., Freudenberg, N., & Vlahov, D. (2005). Cities and population health. *Soc Sci Med, 60*(5): 1017-33.

Garcia, R., & Fenwick, C. (2009). Social science, equal justice, and public health policy: Lessons from Los Angeles. *Journal of Public Health Policy, 30*: S26-S32.

Garcia, R., Rawson, Z., Yellot, M., & Zaldana, C. (2009). Economic stimulus, green space, and equal justice 3-5, 8-9. Accessed September, 9, 2010, from http://www.cityprojectca.org/blog/archives/1450

Garcia, R., & White, A. (2006). Healthy parks, schools and communities: Mapping green access and equity for the Los Angeles region., The City Project. 2010.

Geiger, K., & Hamburger, T. (2010). Soda drink tax battle shifts to states. *Los Angeles Times*, News, February, 21.

George, E. (2006). Browning the Green Movement. Accessed August, 30, 2006, from http://www.wcvi.org/press_room/press_clippings/2006/LAalt_091 706.html

Gittelsohn, J., & Kumar, M. (2007). Preventing childhood obesity and diabetes: Is it time to move out of the school? *Pediatric Diabetes, 8*(s9): 55-69.

Gomez-Feliciano, L., McCreary, L., Sadowsky, R., Peterson, S., Hernandez, B., McElmurry, B., & Park, C. (2009). Active living logan square: Joining together to create opportunities for physical activity. *American Journal of Preventive Medicine, 37*(6S2): 361-367.

Grigsby-Toussaint, D. S., Zenk, S. N., Odoms-Young, A., Ruggiero, L., & Moise, I. (2010). Availability of commonly consumed and culturally specific fruits and vegetables in african-american and Latino neighborhoods. *Journal of the American Dietetic Association, 110*(5): 746-752.

Handley, M. A., Hall, C., Sanford, E., Diaz, E., Gonzalez-Mendez, E., Drace, K., Wilson, R., Villalobos, M., & Croughan, M. (2007). Globalization, binational communities, and imported food risks: Results of an outbreak investigation of lead poisoning in Monterey County, California. *Am J Public Health, 97*(5): 900-6.

Handy, S. (2009). Walking, bycicling, and health. Accessed September, 18, 2010, from http://www.policylink.org/atf/cf/%7B97c6d565-bb43-406d-a6d5-eca3bbf35af0%7D/HEALTHTRANS_FULLBOOK_FINAL.PDF

Healthy Eating and Active Communities (2010). Phase 1 Evaluation Findings (2005-2008). Samuels & Associates, Center for Weight and Health, UC Berkeley; Center to Eliminate Health Disparities, UC Los Angeles; Abundantia Consulting; and Field Research Corporation. Accessed September 1, 2010, from http://www.calendow.org/uploadedFiles/Publications/By_Topic/Disparities/Obesity_and_Diabetes/HEACEvalFINAL.pdf?n=4174

Hernandez, L., & Blazer, D., Eds. (2006). Genes, behavior and the social environment: Moving beyond the nature/nurture debate. Institute of Medicine. Washington, D.C., National Academy Press.

Indiana Latino Institute. (2010). Preventing Secondhand Smoke Exposure. Accessed September, 16, 2010, from http://www.indianalatino.com/english/tobacco.asp

Jago, R., Baranowski, T., Baranowski, J., Thompson, D., & Greaves, K. (2005). BMI from 3-6 y of age is predicted by TV viewing and physical activity, not diet. *International Journal of Obesity, 29*(6).

Jernigan, D., & Ostorff, C. (2005). Alcohol advertising and youth: A measured approach. *Journal of Public Health Policy, 26*: 312-325.

Jimenez-Pavón, D., Kelly, J., & Reilly, J. J. (2010). Associations between objectively measured habitual physical activity and adiposity in children and adolescents: Systematic review. *International Journal of Pediatric Obesity,* 5(1): 3-18.

Kann, L., Grunbaum, J., McKenna, M. L., Wechsler, H., & Galuska, D. A. (2005). Competitive foods and beverages available for purchase in secondary schools—Selected sites, United States, 2004. *Journal of School Health,* 75(10): 370-374.

Kawachi, I., & Berkman, L. F. (2003). Ch. 1: Introduction. Neighborhoods and Health. I. Kawachi, Berkman, L.F., Oxford University Press: 1-17.

Kipke, M. D., Iverson, E., Moore, D., Booker, C., Ruelas, V., Peters, A. L., & Kaufman, F. (2007). Food and park environments: Neighborhood-level risks for childhood obesity in east Los Angeles. *Journal of Adolescent Health,* 40(4): 325-333.

Kunkel, D., McKinley, C., & Wright, P. (2009). The impact of industry self-regulation on the nutritional quality of foods advertised on television to children. Accessed September, 2010, from http://www.childrennow.org/uploads/documents/adstudy_2009.pdf

Larson, N. I., Story, M. T., & Nelson, M. C. (2009). Neighborhood environments: Disparities in access to healthy foods in the U.S. *Am J Prev Med,* 36(1): 74-81.

Leeman-Castillo, B. (2010). Denver Urban Gardens. Accessed September, 10, 2010, from http://dug.org/gardens

Leikauf, G. D. (2002). Hazardous air pollutants and asthma. *Environ Health Perspect, 110* Suppl 4: 505-26.

Lisabeth, L. D., Sanchez, B. N., Escobar, J., Hughes, R., Meurer, W. J., Zuniga, B., Garcia, N., Brown, D. L., & Morgenstern, L. B. (2010). The food environment in an urban Mexican-American community. *Health Place, 16*(3): 598-605.

Los Angeles Unified School District (2009) Physical Education Programs— Grades K-12. Accessed from http://www.cityprojectca.org/blog/wp-content/uploads/2010/02/lausd-phys-ed-civil-rights-plan.pdf

Lovasi, G. S., Hutson, M. A., Guerra, M., & Neckerman, K. M. (2009). Built environments and obesity in disadvantaged populations. *Epidemiol Rev, 31*: 7-20.

Madsen, K. A., Weedn, A. E., & Crawford, P. B. (2010). Disparities in peaks, plateaus, and declines in prevalence of high BMI among adolescents. *Pediatrics, 126*(3): 434-42.

Marmot, M. (2000). Multilevel approaches to understanding social determinants. Social Epidemiology. L. Berkman & I. Kawachi, Oxford University Press: 349-367.

McCormack, L. A., Laska, M. N., Larson, N. I., & Story, M. (2010). Review of the nutritional implications of farmers' markets and community gardens: A call for evaluation and research efforts. *J Am Diet Assoc, 110*(3): 399-408.

McDonough, P. (2009). TV viewing among kids at an eight year high. Accessed November 11, 2009, 2009, from http://blog.nielsen.com/nielsenwire/media_entertainment/tv-viewing-among-kids-at-an-eight-year-high

McGinnis, J., Appleton, J., & Kraak, V., Eds. (2005). Food marketing to children and youth: Threat or opportunity. Washington, National Academy Press.

McGinnis, J., Williams-Russo, P., & Knickman, J. (2002). The case for more active policy attention to health promotion. *Health Affairs, 21*(2): 78-93.

Meyer, P., Pivetz, T., Dignam, T., Homa, D., Schoonover, J., & Brody, D. (2003). Surveillance for elevated blood lead levels among children—United States, 1997-2001. *Korbidity and Mortality Weekly Report, 52*(SS10): 1-21.

Morello-Frosch, R., & Jesdale, B. M. (2006). Separate and unequal: residential segregation and estimated cancer risks associated with ambient air toxics in U.S. metropolitan areas. *Environ Health Perspect, 114*(3): 386-93.

Morland, K., Wing, S., Diez Roux, A., & Poole, C. (2002). Neighborhood characteristics associated with the location of food stores and food service places. *Am J Prev Med, 22*(1): 23-9.

Natalie, C., Freeman, D., Schneider, D., & McGarvey, P. (2003). Household exposure factors, asthma, and school absenteeism in a predominantly Hispanic community. *Journal of Exposure Analysis and Enviromental Epidemiology, 13*: 169-176.

National Council of La Raza. (2009). Annual Report. Accessed August, 30, 2010, from http://www.nclr.org/images/uploads/publications/file__NCLR _Annual_Report_2009.pdf

New York City Department of Health and Mental Hygiene. (2009). Healthy Bodegas Initiative. Accessed September, 1, 2010, from http://www.nyc.gov /html/doh/html/cdp/cdp_pan_hbi.shtml

Nuestras Raíces. Accessed September, 1, 2010, from http://www.nuestras-raices.org/en

Ohland, G., & Corless, J. (2000). Dangerous by design: Pedestrian safety in California. Accessed September, 10, 2010, from http://www.transact.org/ca/design/Dangerous%20by%20Design.pdf

Pastor, M. (2007). ¿Quién es más urbanista? Latinos and smart growth. Growing smarter achieving livable communities, environmental justice, and regional equity. R. Bullard. Cambridge, MIT Press.

Peters, J. C. (2003). Dietary fat and body weight control. *Lipids, 38*(2): 123-7.

Philip, B., Mark, D., Rich, B., Risa, W., Joanne, L., & Sarah, L. S. (2009). The active living by design national program: Community initiatives and lessons learned." *American Journal of Preventive Medicine, 37*(6): S313-S321.

Policy Link. (2010). Healthy communities matter: The importance of place to the health of boys of color. Accessed August, 28, 2010, from http://www.policylink.org/site/apps/nlnet/content2.aspx?c=lkIXLbMN-JrE&b=5136581&ct=8501273

Powell, L. M. (2009). Fast food costs and adolescent body mass index: Evidence from panel data. *Journal of Health Economics, 28*(5): 963-970.

Powell, L. M., Auld, M. C., Chaloupka, F. J., O'Malley, P. M., & Johnston, L. D. (2007). Associations between access to food stores and adolescent body mass index. *American Journal of Preventive Medicine Bridging the Gap—Research Informing Practice and Policy for Healthy Youth Behavior 33*(4, Supplement 1): S301-S307.

Powell, L. M., & Bao, Y. (2009). Food prices, access to food outlets and child weight. *Econ Hum Biol, 7*(1): 64-72.

Powell, L. M., Zhao, Z., & Wang, Y. (2009). Food prices and fruit and vegetable consumption among young American adults. *Health Place, 15*(4): 1064-70.

Prevention Institute. (2010). Addressing the intersection: Preventing violence and promoting healthy eating and physical activity. Accessed September, 10, 2010, from http://www.preventioninstitute.org/component/jlibrary/article/id-267/288.html

Prevention Institute. (2008). Cultivating peace in Salinas: A framework for violence prevention. Accessed August, 28, 2010, from http://www.eatbettermovemore.org/pdf/Cultivating_Peace.pdf

Ramirez, R., & de la Cruz, G. (2002). The Hispanic population in the United States: 2002 current population reports. Accessed September, 9, 2010, from http://www.census.gov/prod/2003pubs/p20-545.pdf

Rideout, V., Foehr, U., & Roberts, D. (2010). Generation M2: Media in the lives of 8-18-year-olds. A Kaiser Family Foundation Study. Accessed June, 30, 2010, from http:www.kff.org/entmedia/upload/8010.pdf

Rosas, L. G., & Eskenazi, B. (2008). Pesticides and child neurodevelopment. *Curr Opin Pediatr, 20*(2): 191-7.

Ross, C., & Marcus, M. (2009). Roadways and health: Making the case for collaboration. Accessed September, 18, 2010, from http://www.policylink.org/

atf/cf/%7B97c6d565-bb43-406d-a6d5-eca3bbf35af0%7D/HEALTH.
TRANS_FULLBOOK_FINAL.PDF

Saelens, B. E., Sallis, J. F., Nader, P. R., Broyles, S. L., Berry, C. C., & Taras, H. L. (2002). Home environmental influences on children's television watching from early to middle childhood. *J Dev Behav Pediatr, 23*(3): 127-32.

Safe Routes to School. Accessed August, 30, 2010, from www.saferoutesto school.org

Sallis, J. F., & Glanz, K. (2009). Physical activity and food environments: solutions to the obesity epidemic. *Milbank Q, 87*(1): 123-54.

Samuels & Associates (2011). Healthy eating active communities and Central California Regional Obesity Prevention Program Final Evaluation Synthesis Report. Accesed July 12, 2011, from http://www.samuelsandssociates.com/ samuels/upload/ourlatest/HEAC_CCROPP_Final_Report_2010.pdf

Samuels & Associates. (2010). Increasing access to health food in the Central Valley through farmers' markets and produce stands. Accessed August, 2010, from http://www.calendow.org/uploadedFiles/Publications/By_ Topic/Disparities/Obesity_and_Diabetes/CCROPP%20Increasing%20AC CESS%20FINAL.pdf

Samuels, S., Schwarte, L., Clayson, Z., & Casey, M. (2009). Engaging communities in changing nutrition and physical activity environments. Accessed September, 15, 2010, from http://www.calendow.org/uploadedFiles/Publications/By_Topic/Disparities/Obesity_and_Diabetes/HEAC_CCROPP_En gagingCommunities.Updated.FINAL.5.pdf

Schulz, A., Williams, D., Israel, B., & Lempert, L. (2002). Racial and spatial relations as fundamental determinants of health in detroit. *Milbank Quarterly, 80*(4).

Shaffer, A. (2002). The persistence if LA's grocery gap: the need for a new food policy and approach for market development. http://departments.oxy.edu/ uepi/cfj/publications/Supermarket%20Report%20November%202002.pdf

Simon, P. A., Kwan, D., Angelescu, A., Shih, M., & Fielding, J. E. (2008). Proximity of fast food restaurants to schools: do neighborhood income and type of school matter? *Prev Med, 47*(3): 284-8.

Singh, G. K., Siahpush, M., & Kogan, M. D. (2010). Neighborhood socioeconomic conditions, built environments, and childhood obesity. *Health Aff, 29*(3): 503-512.

Smith, L. A., & Foxcroft, D. R. (2009). The effect of alcohol advertising, marketing and portrayal on drinking behaviour in young people: Systematic review of prospective cohort studies. *BMC Public Health, 9*: 51.

Story, M., Kaphingst, K. M., Robinson-O'Brien, R., & Glanz, K. (2007). Creating healthy food and eating environments: Policy and environmental approaches. *Annu Rev Public Health, 29*: 253-272.

Story, M., Nanney, M. S., & Schwartz, M. B. (2009). Schools and obesity prevention: creating school environments and policies to promote healthy eating and physical activity. *Milbank Q, 87*(1): 71-100.

Strasburger, V. (2002). Alcohol adversiting and adolescents. *Pediatr Clin North Am, 49*(2): 353-76.

Sturm, R. (2008). Disparities in the food environment surrounding U.S. middle and high schools. *Public Health, 122*(7): 681-90.

Sturm, R., & Datar, A. (2005). Body mass index in elementary school children, metropolitan area food prices and food outlet density. *Public Health (Elsevier) Public Health (Elsevier) J1—Public Health (Elsevier), 119*(12): 1059-1068.

Subramanian, S. V., Belli, P., & Kawachi, I. (2002). The macroeconomic determinants of health. *Annu Rev Public Health, 23*: 287-302.

Suro, R., Kocchar, R., Passel, J., Escobar, G., Tafoya, S., Fry, R., Benevides, D., & Wunsch, M. (2007). The American Community—Hispanics: 2004. Accessed August 23, 2010, from http://www.census.gov/prod/2007pubs/acs-03.pdf

The City Project. (2010). Ascot Hills Park Watch and Countdown. Accessed September, 8, 2010, from http://www.flickr.com/photos/cityprojectca/sets/72157624175148551

Thompson, D., Flores, G., Ebel, B., & Christakis, D. (2008). *Comida en venta*: After-school advertising on Spanish-language television in the United States. *Journal of Pediatrics, 152*(4): 576-81.

Thompson, D., Sibinga, E., Jennings, J., Bair-Merritt, M., & Christakis, D. (2010). Television viewing by young hispanic children: Evidence of heterogeneity. *Archives of Pedriatric Adolescence, 164*(2): 174-179.

Torres, M. (2009). Juntas podemos (Together we can): Empowering Latinas to shape policy to prevent childhood obesity. Accessed September, 1, 2010, from http://www.salud-america.org/Files/Grantees/torresm.pdf

UCLA Center to Eliminate Health Disparities and Samuels and Associates. (2007). Failing fitness: Physical activity and physical education in schools. Accessed September 1, 2010, from http://www.healthyeatingactivecommunities.org/downloads/Schools/Failing_Fitness_01_2007.pdf

University of Colorado Denver School of Public Health (2008). Localizing health and wellness in West Denver: An evalation of the 2007 Live Well Denver Urban Garden Program.

U.S. Department of Health and Human Services. (2007). Children and second-hand smoke exposure: Excerpts from the health consequences of involuntary exposure to tobacco smoke. Accessed September, 1, 2010, from http://www.surgeongeneral.gov/library/smokeexposure/report/fullreport.pdf

Vartanian, L., Shwarts, M., & Brownell, K. (2007). Effects of soft drink consumption on nutrition and health: a systematic review and meta analysis." *American Journal of Public Health, 97*: 667-75.

Viner, R., & Cole, T. (2005). Television viewing predicts adult body mass index. *Journal of Pediatrics, 147*(4): 429-35.

Visscher, T. L., & Seidell, J. C. (2001). The public health impact of obesity. *Annu Rev Public Health, 22*: 355-75.

Weigel, M., Armijos, R., Hall, Y., Ramirez, Y., & Orozco, R. (2007). The household food insecurity and health outcomes of U.S.-Mexico border migrant and seasonal farm workers. *Immigrant and Minority Health, 9*(3): 157-69.

WHO Commission on Social Determinants of Health. (2008). Closing the gap in a generation: Health equity through action on the social determinants of health. Accessed September 27, 2010, from http://whqlibdoc.who.int/publications/2008/9789241563703_eng.pdf

Wizemann, T., & Anderson, K. (2009). Focusing on children's health: Community approaches to addressing health disparities. Workshop Summary. Institute of Medicine, National Academy Press.

Woodward-Lopez, G., & Flores, G. (2006). Obesity in Latino communities: Prevention, principles and action. Accessed September 9th, 2010, from http://www.lchc.org/research/documents/Obesity_in_Latino_Communities.pdf

Zenk, S., & Powell, L. (2008). U. S. secondary schools and food outlets. *Health & Place, 14*(2): 336-346.

CHAPTER TWO

IMPACT OF *PROMOTORES DE SALUD* ON PREGNANCY AND CHILD HEALTH OUTCOMES

Sofia Segura-Pérez,[1,2] Hector Balcazar[3,4] and Katherine Morel[1,2]

Introduction

The foundation of a healthy nation is the health and wellbeing of its children. Almost a quarter of the children (22%) in the United States are Latino, and it is estimated that for the year 2050 over a third (35%) of them will be of Latino origin (Pew Hispanic Center, 2008). Efforts for achieving children's optimal health need to begin even before they are born. For example facilitating mothers' access to adequate prenatal care can make a difference. Once children are born, access to appropriate preventive pediatric health care services becomes paramount. These services include timely physical examinations, immunizations and adequate health care access for diverse medical needs.

In the United States lack of health insurance coverage and poverty is strongly associated with lack of access to health care (Scott & Hi, 2004). Recent data show that 9.9% of U.S. children do not have health insurance with this percentage being higher among those living in poverty (15.7%) and among Latino children (Figure 1). The latter have the highest prevalence of unmet medical needs, and are more likely to delay care due to cost and to lack a usual place for health care (Figure 2) (Bloom et al., 2009).

[1]Hispanic Heath Council.
[2]Connecticut NIH EXPORT Center for Eliminating Health Disparities among Latinos.
[3]University of Texas, School of Public Health, Health Science Center Houston, El Paso Regional Campus.
[4]Hispanic Health Disparities Research Center, El Paso, Texas.

Figure 1. Percentage of U.S. Children without Health Insurance by Race and Hispanic/Latino Origin.

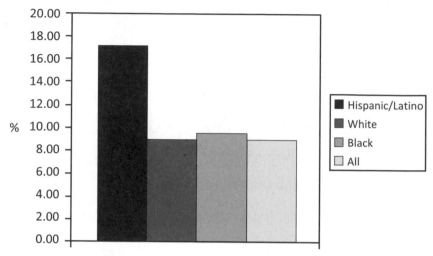

Source: Bloom B., Cohen R. A., Freeman G. Summary health statistics for U.S. Children: National Health Interview Survey, 2008. *National Center for Health Statistics. Vital Health Stat, 10*(244).2009.

Figure 2. Percentage of U.S. Children with Unmet Medical Needs and Delayed Care Due to Cost by Race and Hispanic/Latino Origin.

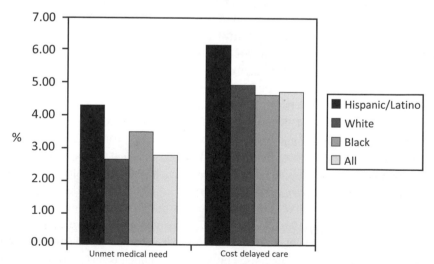

Source: Bloom B., Cohen R. A., Freeman G. Summary health statistics for U.S. Children: National Health Interview Survey, 2008. *National Center for Health Statistics. Vital Health Stat, 10*(244).2009.

Compared with their white counterparts, pregnant Latinas are less likely to report receiving prenatal care during their first trimester of pregnancy (70.2% vs. 57.6%, respectively), and more likely to start receiving it during their last trimester or to not receive prenatal care at all (7.5% vs. 12.2%) (National Center for Health Statistics, 2009).

While poverty and lack of health insurance are important determinants of access to health care services for Latino children, there are also other factors affecting this negative outcome. In a cross-sectional study in Boston, language problems and lack of transportation were identified by Latino parents as important barriers for accessing medical care for their children (Flores et al., 1998). Consistent with these findings, a comprehensive review identified the following key health insurance barriers among Latino children: a) financial, b) non-financial such as lack of awareness of availability of state medical services benefits along with complexity of application process, fear and mistrust of government funded services, logistics (lack of transportation and childcare, and inconvenient office hours) and limited English proficiency and c) social policies. In addition to conducting a formal literature review, the authors gathered evidence from interviews with front-line service personnel, reviewed outreach waiver requests approved by U.S. Department of Health and Human Services, in eight states, and examined socio-demographic and health care access indicators at the national level and from the nine states with the largest Latino population (Zambrana & Carter-Pokras, 2004). Another study that used a national U.S. database of children with special health care needs found that 14% of them were living in households where English was not the primary language. Furthermore, these children were more likely to be of Latino origin, to be poor, to have parents with low level of education and to reside in urban areas (Yu & Singh, 2009).

Thus, improving and maintaining the health of Latino children requires a multilevel culturally appropriate comprehensive approach that takes into account the socioeconomic context of the communities where children from this ethnic group live and grow. One of the strategies that has been recommended to reduce health care access disparities among Latinos is through the use of *Promotores de Salud* or Community Health Workers (CHWs) (Yu & Singh, 2009; Chin et al., 2009). CHWs are also known by an array of other names including lay health educators, peer educators or counselors, outreach worker educators, or health advisors.[5] CHWs are recognized by the World Health Organization [WHO] (World Health Organization, 2007) as playing a relevant role in improving child health worldwide and describes them as an important health resource to reach underserved populations. The WHO recommends that "CHWs should

---

[5]The term CHWs and *promotores de salud* will be used interchangeably in this chapter.

be members of the community where they work, should be selected by the communities, should be answerable to the communities for their activities, should be supported by the health system but not necessarily as part of its organization, and have shorter training than professional workers." Thus, CHWs should be trusted members with a strong commitment to their communities with the skills needed to become effective liaisons between their clients and the health care system through a process of community empowerment. A recent U.S. report from the Community Health Worker National Workforce Study (U.S. Department of Health and Human Services, 2007) estimates that there are approximately 86,000 CHWs in the country, 67% of whom are paid and the rest are volunteers. According to this report, CHWs are ethnically/racially diverse, 35% are Latino/Hispanic, 39% white, and 15.5% African American. Most CHWs are women (82%), and have completed high school or more (92.6%). A high percentage of them are working in the areas of women's health, nutrition, child health, prenatal care, immunizations and sex education.

The main objective of this chapter is to review the literature on the impact of the CHWs on the health of Latino children living in the United States. The review focuses on areas that address the needs of Latino children from conception through adolescence. The specific themes covered fall within the areas of prenatal and postpartum care (including health education, family nutrition, smoking cessation and mental health, stress management, mother-child interaction and preventive health services and screenings), and children health (immunizations, asthma and sex education). The chapter concludes with policy implications and priorities for future research.

Methods

This systematic review began with an initial exploratory search in Pubmed to identify the main areas where *promotores de salud*/CHWs had been used to impact children's health. This search used the following initial key words: *promotora*, peer counselor, community health worker, outreach worker or patient navigator in combination with child health, maternal and child health, Hispanics or Latinos. Breastfeeding studies were excluded as another chapter in this book concentrates on that topic. Of the abstracts originally obtained through this first search only five met the inclusion criteria (Malchodi, 2003; Warrick, 1992; Taylor, 2000; Meister et al., 1992; Krieger, 2009).

A second search was then conducted using a combination of the following CHW-related terms (*promotora*, peer counselor, outreach worker, patient educator, patient navigator, outreach worker) paired with each possible health outcome, ethnicity (Hispanic vs. Latino), farm workers, developmental stages of children/youth (children, adolescent, youth, teenager) and using the United States as a unique location. This second search was limited to articles published within the last 10 years for all topic categories except for adolescent health or when authors considered the article relevant enough to include it as part of the review. The evidence available for youth was limited, thus for this topic articles published within the last 20 years were considered. Utilizing this search approach a Pubmed and Web of Science investigation was completed utilizing all selected terms. The resulting 171 unique articles were compiled and divided into the following categories: prenatal care, breastfeeding, asthma, vaccinations, nutrition, HIV, sex education, smoking cessation, drug use and mental health. All the abstracts of these articles were then reviewed by a panel of three experts and were selected for inclusion if they met the following criteria: (i) conducted in the United States, (ii) Latinos/Hispanics were at least 10% of the study's population, and (iii) CHWs were used to improve the health of children. In the case of asthma only randomized controlled trials (RCTs) were considered as for this topic there was a critical body of evidence based on the strongest epidemiological research design. The two searches combined resulted in a total of 27 papers that met the expected criteria broken down into the following categories: Maternal and child care (n=8 studies), asthma and immunizations (n=15) and adolescent health focusing on HIV/Sex Education (n=4). Among the asthma papers there were 7 asthma studies excluded because they were not RCTs. No studies met the inclusion criteria for CHWs and adolescent drug use, mental health and medication adherence. Thus Latino youth health is represented in this chapter by the HIV and sex education domains.

Results

I) Maternal and Child Health

Addressing the needs of women during pregnancy and at birth has major implications for improving infant birth outcomes as well as the child's wellbeing later on in life. This section reviews the studies that have examined the influence of *promotores de salud*/CHWs on prenatal and postnatal maternal-child health outcomes. These studies can be grouped into two broad categories: 1) prenatal care and postpartum periods including health and nutrition education and 2) clinical settings/teams in the areas of smoking cessation and reduction, mental health and stress during pregnancy.

1) Maternal Nutrition Counseling and Education.

a) Health education. One of the key studies that provided an initial account of the use of *promotores de salud* for pregnant women was the program *Un*

Comienzo Sano (A Healthy Beginning) developed in Arizona for Latino farm communities (Meister et al., 1992). This study described how prenatal care service delivery can be incorporated in an informal rather than a formal medical model of service delivery. Three components of the intervention were evaluated: 1) the use of a Spanish-language prenatal education guide, *Un Comienzo Sano*; 2) the utilization of a delivery system of indigenous health educators or *promotores de salud*; and 3) the use of a support network of local health professionals. The evaluation conducted yielded positive results for all the three components of the intervention. A total of 147 women living in three migrant and seasonal farm worker border communities participated. This non-randomized community participatory study suggested that: 1) the prenatal curriculum was culturally sensitive, 2) peer workers were accepted by the target community and 3) the model did not threaten the established professional medical staff. These findings called for more in-depth studies of *promotores de salud* as indigenous health educators (Warrick et al., 1992).

b) NUTRITION AND COMMUNITY OUTREACH. *Promotores de salud* studies have consistently shown that the peer educator model can easily be adapted in the context of key programs that serve mothers and infants such as the Special Supplemental Nutrition Program for Women, Infants and Children (WIC). A qualitative study that provides a description of the use of *promotores de salud* (peer educators) was done through the Maryland WIC 5 A Day Promotion Program (Anliker, 1999). In this study that included pregnant, lactating and postpartum women the peer educators played a critical role in the delivery of a series of three bimonthly 45-minute nutrition education sessions and in data collection activities. The peer educators reinforced goal-related behaviors associated with the nutrition session via phone calls. A pre-post non-randomized study design included 1443 women in the intervention group and 1679 women in the control group attending 15 WIC sites. Peer educators were successful at improving fruit and vegetables intake. These results need to be interpreted with caution given the pilot nature of the study. An interesting aspect of this study is that it documented the potential participation of *promotores de salud* not only as interventionists but also as data collectors. The study also described a very crucial role that *promotores de salud* play in many interventions, that is, as recruiters of program participants. This is a key function that cannot be underestimated given the challenges in recruiting hard-to-reach and vulnerable minority populations. One of the important lessons described by researchers in this study is the need for intensive training and support for peer educators and the provision of an environment that supports their efforts. This challenge was confirmed by a study in Arizona that identified the need to "empower" *promotores de salud,* so that a supportive environment is created within the non-medical delivery system (Meister, 1992).

*La Cocina Saludable (*The Healthy Kitchen), a project developed in Colorado, is a good example of "empowerment" of *promotores de salud* (Taylor et al., 2000). This nutrition education program utilized 36 trained Latino grandmothers and grandmother figures or *abuelas* as nutrition educators, to deliver five lessons-units to teach nutrition messages for improving nutrition knowledge, skills and behaviors among mothers and their preschool children. Culturally appropriate bilingual materials were developed including flip charts and *La Cocina Saludable* Resource Guide, and kitchen utensils were used as incentives. The study used a pre-post design to test the impact of the program in the *abuela* educators, and in 337 program participants. This non-randomized study found positive outcomes in nutrition knowledge, skills and self-reported nutrition-related behaviors for both the peer educators or *abuelas*, and program participants. One additional component of this unique *promotora de salud* model was that it was guided by the Stages of Change Model for tailoring the nutrition education delivery.

c) HEALTH CARE OUTREACH. A comprehensive study conducted by researchers in Denver, Colorado, tested a 3-arm RCT to examine the impacts of prenatal and infancy home visiting by paraprofessionals, as compared to nurses, among two- to four-year-old children (Olds et al., 2004). The home visiting program sought to improve: 1) fetal and maternal health during pregnancy, 2) parental care to improve children's health and 3) maternal use of family planning methods. Of the 735 women who were randomized, 47% were Mexican American.

Results showed that both paraprofessionals and nurses had positive effects on different outcomes as compared to the control group. Two years after the program ended, women who were visited by the paraprofessional had fewer subsequent miscarriages and low birth weight newborns as compared to the control group. Mothers and children visited by the paraprofessional displayed greater sensitivity and responsiveness toward one another and had home environments that were more supportive as compared to the control group. The authors however, caution that these findings need to be replicated before warranting public investment. Nevertheless, this study provides an important examination of how extending the medical model to the community model using *promotores de salud* may prove to be a worthwhile investment in the community for addressing the health needs of low-income pregnant women and their children.

2) MATERNAL SMOKING CESSATION AND MENTAL HEALTH SERVICES

a) SMOKING CESSATION. The positive impact of peer counseling has also been reported for pregnant women in the context of smoking cessation and reduction in clinic settings. This illustrates the flexibility of the *promotora de salud* approach for improving a variety of health outcomes for mothers and their children (Malchodi et al., 2003). Using a prospective randomized control design, 142 pregnant women who were smokers at the time of the study were selected to participate in either a peer-led smoking cessation program plus usual care or as part of a control group who received usual care only. Trained peer counselors who came from the same socio-environmental and cultural milieu of study participants were trained using research guidelines for smoking cessation in addition to basic strategies for motivational counseling. Peer counselors delivered the intervention based on eight sessions or client contacts to support and reinforce "stop smoking" messages. A major finding of this study was that peer counselors were significantly more likely to reduce the reported number of cigarettes smoked per day during pregnancy (confirmed by biomarkers of cigarette use) when compared to the women in the usual care group. As expected, a statistically significant negative association was observed between infant birth weight and maternal cigarettes smoked per day during pregnancy. Of great significance for this type of intervention using peer educators is that the impact on smoking cessation reduction was greatest among women who were heavier smokers. This finding speaks to the opportunities to tailor specific *promotores de salud* interventions to the needs of high-risk populations.

b) MENTAL HEALTH AND STRESS. The utilization of *promotores de salud* in combination with nurses is an approach to clinic services that enhances the capacity of extending support beyond the usual medical setting. This is illustrated by a program based on applying a conceptual framework to a nurse-community health worker approach for addressing mental health and stress outcomes in Medicaid-insured pregnant women (Roman et al., 2007). The main thrust of the combined nurse-community health worker model is centered on an ecological stress conceptual framework for addressing stress and mental health among pregnant women. The framework is particularly relevant as it takes into account the contextual environments where women live, the different stressors present in different environments and the psychosocial factors influencing the response to these stressors. The use of conceptual frameworks for providing context to the work of *promotores de salud* has indeed become a key methodological strategy in the public health prevention field (Balcazar et al., 2006; Anders et al., 2006). It is in this contextual development framework, that Roman et al. (2009) delineated in their RCT the primary roles of nurses and community health workers to address mental health and stress during pregnancy. In this trial they specifically compared a nurse-community health worker team intervention (experimental group) with a standard community care approach. A total of 613 women were randomly assigned to the experimental or control groups. The objectives of the intervention were to: 1) decrease depressive symptoms, 2) decreased perceived stress and 3) improved psychosocial resources. Using a variety of statistical techniques appropriate to the modeling of variables included in their conceptual framework, the results showed that the first two objectives were met. Of great significance was the observation that the reductions in depressive symptoms were more pronounced among women with low psychosocial resources and high stress. Thus, the authors provided a good argument for combining a clinical nurse with a community-based approach utilizing CHWs. More specifically, the dual focus consisted of CHWs assisting women through a supportive relationship to cope with stressors in their lives in addition to nurses who focused more on addressing complex health issues. This unique and well-designed study provides crucial empirical evidence that the clinic-based model targeting the pregnancy and postpartum periods can extend its reach through a community model and capture hard-to-reach women (through well-defined screening and intervention processes) who may suffer from depression and high stress levels and/or low psychosocial resources. The authors recommended that CHWs be included as paid providers of care within the context of Medicaid programs serving underserved communities. Financial and funding models for CHWs have been described in the literature and serve as templates for advancing the practice and utilization of this needed workforce (Dower et al., 2006).

From the analyses of the different studies utilizing *promotores de salud* in the context of maternal and child health, there is a clear pattern of successful results observed from their work. *Promotores de salud* have played a key role in recruiting women in both, the prenatal and postnatal periods, and thus have facilitated the access of a variety of maternal and child health services. Outreach to hard-to-reach women and their children have been accomplished by having *promotores de salud* working closely with communities to bring programs and services within and outside the medical system. They have also served a primary role as health educators, counselors and as "social supporters" for delivering a variety of programs and services including nutrition education, smoking cessation and mental health. Salient to the role of *promotores de salud*, is their capacity to be integrated with the medical model of services and health professionals at the clinical level and beyond, to serve Latino women and their children taking into consideration the integration of the clinic-community environment which is consistent with a true "prevention" model of health and wellbeing.

II) Children Health

This section reviews the impact of CHWs on two key child health indicators, immunizations and management of childhood asthma.

1) CHILDREN IMMUNIZATIONS

According to the 2007 National Immunization Survey (NIS) 77.4% of U.S. children between the ages of 19-35 months had been immunized as recommended by the Advisory Committee on Immunization Practices (ACIP). However, a wide range in coverage within states and local areas was noted. This survey also found lower coverage rates for some vaccination series among children living in poverty (National Center for Immunization and Respiratory Diseases, CDC 2008). Through the years, studies have reported immunization disparities among children living in poverty (Chin et al., 2009; Anderson et al., 1997; Brenner et al., 2001). In the United States, children are required to meet a full immunization schedule before entering school. As a result, immunizations levels among five- to six-year-olds are almost 100%. However, for infant and younger children there is not a single strategy in place for assuring timely immunizations among them. Those living in poverty and belonging to ethnic minorities seem to be the most affected (Hinman, 1991; Dominguez et al., 2004). A study conducted with 688 Latino mothers of children aged 12 to 36 months from two low-income Los Angeles neighborhoods found poor prenatal care, lack of close family members, not being the first born, and relocation during the child's lifetime as factors associated with inadequate immunization (Anderson et al.,1997). Another study looking into immunization patterns among a cohort of inner-city Latino and African-American infants found that while 75% of them were up to date with their vaccines at 3 months, only 41% of them were at 7 months. Participation in the WIC program, breastfeeding intention and infant's grandmother living at home were baseline determinants for proper immunization at 3 months while maternal employment and low-perceived barriers were factors identified for continuation of vaccinations at 7 months (Brenner et al., 2001).

The use of reminder cards sent to parents by medical offices is one strategy that has been used to improve timely vaccinations among children. This approach has been shown to be successful when cards are tailored to the target population. A non-randomized study was conducted at a community clinic in Colorado using reminder vaccinations cards provided to families of children that were not up to date on their immunization schedule (Hicks et al, 2007). This intervention resulted in a significant increase in the number of up-to-date vaccines, from 61.3% at baseline to 73.4% at study termination (p=.004). This clinic served a high number of low-income Latino, Spanish-speaking families, therefore, these reminder cards were sent in the primary language of the client (Spanish or English). Each card had specific information regarding vaccines that seemed to be missing and invited families to present the card to the staff at the clinic for nurses to provide the vaccines. This study was also looking to decrease missed opportunities for vaccinations for eligible children attending clinical appointments due to other reasons. Therefore, posters were placed at examination rooms to remind health providers and clients to offer or ask for the vaccines during the clinical visit. However, this last strategy did not a have a significant impact on immunization levels. Even though CHWs were not used in this study, it is important to review those that have, as findings from this study suggest that it is likely that CHWs may play a positive role for expanding vaccination coverage through community outreach efforts.

A community wide randomized intervention that used a reminder, recall and outreach system (RRO) using CHWs was effective in raising childhood immunization rates in inner city Rochester, New York (Szilagyi et al., 2002). The target county was divided into three regions with different levels of poverty; inner-city Rochester, the rest of the city and the suburbs around the city. The target population was children between 0-2 years of age. The intervention was initially implemented in 8 medical office practices within the city and expanded to 10 later on the study. The RRO system used lay outreach workers from the community that were assigned to one or more practices within their area. Outreach workers were trained on how to follow strict RRO protocols for children that were behind their immunization schedule and on how to keep track of these children. This system consisted of multiple reminders such as phone calls, letters or a postcard as needed. When necessary, home visits were also used. In this study, 55% of the children were non-Hispanic white, 28% African American, 10% Hispanic and 7% belonged to other ethnic/racial groups. Increases in immunization rates were significant in all three geographical areas. The biggest impact was found among the 12-month-old inner-city children, immunization rates increased from 67% pre-intervention to 82% at three years and to 87% six years after the implementation of the RRO system. Likewise, immunization rates improved among 24-month-old children from 55% at baseline to 76% at three years and 84% at post-intervention.

An example of a citywide initiative using CHWs to improve the immunizations rates and health care access in the community is the Northern Manhattan Community Voices Collaborative. A partnership among academic institutions, community-based organizations and health providers. This collaborative serves a culturally diverse community, of which half are Latino/Hispanics living in Harlem, Washington Heights and Inwood neighborhoods in New York City. This initiative began in 2000, at a time when the study children immunizations rates were very low (57%) and maternal and child health indicators were very poor. As part of this initiative, CHWs worked with the community to have better access to health care, including immunization programs and asthma management. Since its inception CHWs facilitated the health care enrollment of 30,000 individuals, helped 8,000 children to be fully immunized and assisted 4,000 families with asthma management (Perez et al., 2006). These findings are in agreement with a review (Wasserman et al., 2007) that documented how community-level interventions that include CHWs can raise immunizations using free walk-in clinics. The lack of a formal national system to ensure timely immunizations among young children disproportionably affects children from poor families and those that belong to ethnic minorities. Therefore, the combination of a tracking system using reminders from medical offices and outreach at home through the use of CHWs is likely to have a positive effect in improving vaccination rates among underserved populations. Thus, CHWs initiatives such as the Northern Manhattan Community Voices Collaborative need to be supported and expanded.

2) CHILDHOOD ASTHMA

Asthma is a chronic respiratory disease characterized by symptoms such as coughing, wheezing, shortness of breath, rapid breathing and chest tightness related to airflow obstruction. The etiology of asthma is not well understood but it is clear that it is multifactorial involving interactions between genetic and environmental factors. Asthma is one of the main reasons given by parents for explaining daytime activity limitations among preschoolers (National Center for Health Statistics, 2009).

During the period of 1980-1999 asthma prevalence in the United States increased a remarkable 74% (Mannino et al., 1998). According to the 2008 National Health Interview Survey, in the United States there are millions of individuals with a lifetime diagnosis of asthma of whom 14% are children. Asthma is in fact the leading chronic disease among children with 9.4% of them having a current diagnosis of asthma.

Children living in poverty have a higher prevalence of both a lifetime diagnosis of asthma (18% vs. 13%) and current asthma (12% vs. 9%) compared to their better off counterparts. Likewise, asthma morbidity and mortality is higher in inner-city urban areas (Crain et al., 2002; Gern, 2010).

When compared with non-Hispanic whites, Latino children are more likely to live in poverty (7.2% vs 24%), to be in fair/poor health (1.2% vs 2.4%) and to lack health insurance (25.7% vs 7.8%) (Bloom et al., 2009). Asthma prevalence among Latino children is 11% for lifetime diagnosis and 6.8% for current asthma (Figure 3).

However, studies using data from national surveys comparing prevalence throughout the years among Latino subgroups had found lifetime prevalence for

Figure 3. Percentage of U.S. Children with a Lifetime Diagnosis of Asthma and Current Asthma by Race and Hispanic/Latino Origin.

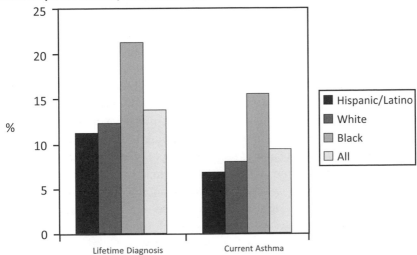

Source: Bloom B., Cohen R. A., Freeman G.. Summary health statistics for U.S. Children: National Health Interview Survey, 2008. *National Center for Health Statistics. Vital Health Stat, 10*(244).2009.

Puerto Ricans as high as 26% and for current asthma as high as 12% (Lara et al., 1999; Lara et al., 2006).

Evidence-based medical guidelines for asthma diagnosis and treatment in children have been developed by the National Heart, Lung and Blood Association (NHLBI). Besides, proper assessment, monitoring of symptoms and medication use; these guidelines also advise on how best to control for environmental factors. They also call for the identification of asthma triggers, and provision of asthma education for patients and their families to improve the self-management of the disease.

CHWs have been used to extend asthma education beyond the clinical setting and to improve asthma health outcomes among low-income children. A recent systematic review assessed the effectiveness of CHWs in the delivery of asthma environmental education to families with affected children (Postma et al., 2009). This review, based on seven RCTs concluded that CHWs can be very effective at reducing specific asthma triggers, asthma symptoms, daytime activity limitations and use of unscheduled clinical care including emergency room use. These studies included two- to sixteen-year-old low-income children with current asthma. Four of these studies included Latinos, ranging from 10% to 92% of their total sample. In most studies, CHWs were from the target community, shared a similar ethnic background and spoke the same language as their clients, and all had experienced asthma themselves or had a close family member with asthma. The CHW training background was not described in detail in several studies. In those that described it the timing, length and place of the training differed substantially. In most studies, CHWs worked with clients in identifying asthma triggers in their homes and used this information to develop an action plan to reduce exposure at home and to improve asthma self-management. However, not all studies reported provided information on other aspects of asthma care, including medications. In all the studies the CHWs provided pillow and mattress encasements for dust mite avoidance, and additional resources as needed to fit individual needs (e.g., mouse traps, pest infestation treatments). In several instances the specific actions taken were based on an allergic sensitivity test. The asthma affected families received three to nine home visits, each lasting between 60 and 150 minutes, during a timeframe lasting between six weeks to one year. The authors concluded that although CHWs seem to be very effective at improving asthma health outcomes there were mixed results for trigger/allergen reduction behaviors. Further research is needed to better link theory with practice, and to better understand the pathways through which CHWs improve asthma outcomes.

One of the studies included in the systematic review by Postma et al. was the Seattle-King County Healthy Homes Project (Krieger et al., 2005), an initiative seeking to reduce asthma triggers and exposures at home based on home environmental assessments. Low-income households receiving multiple visits from a CHW and resources to reduce asthma environmental exposure (High Intensity Group, HIG) had a significant improvement in caretaker's actions to reduce home asthma triggers. As a result there was a lower use of urgent medical services, less child's asthma symptoms and improvement of caregiver quality of life when compared to those families receiving a single visit from a CHW and only pillow or mattress encasements as resources to reduce environmental exposure (Low Intensity Group, LIG). The authors attributed the intervention effectiveness to: (i) the comprehensive asthma trigger education provided by the CHW, (ii) their ability to establish a quick rapport with their clients, (iii) the provision of multiple resources to reduce allergen exposure and (iv) the strategy to simultaneously reduce multiple indoor allergens.

In this study the CHW from the HIG conducted an environmental assessment of the home, developed an action plan with the client and provided resources during the first visit. In addition, 4-8 home visits were conducted by the CHW to support the implementation of the action plan, provide education, social support and various other resources to decrease asthma triggers at home. The low-intensity group received only one CHW visit consisting of an environmental assessment, an action plan, education and provision of pillow and mattress encasements to reduce exposure. The improvements in health outcomes remained at 6 months post interventions in the HIG. However, there was no data collected 6 month post intervention for the LIG, since most of them received the multiple visits format at the end of the one-year study. A cost-effectiveness analysis based on utilization of urgent health care during the last two months of the study estimated that the range of saving per child in the HIG was between $201 and $334 compared with savings between $185 and $315 per child in the LIG.

Another study that was part of the Postma et al. review and which deserves to be highlighted was The Community Action against Asthma Intervention (Parker et al., 2008). This CHW intervention was adapted from the Seattle-King County Healthy Homes Project. It showed a significant positive impact on the health of the children with asthma and their caregivers and mixed results in measures aimed to reduce asthma triggers in the group receiving CHW services. This study was conducted in two Detroit low-income neighborhoods with families of children with persistent asthma. Participants were assigned to a group receiving at least nine home visits from a CHW during a one-year period, or to a control group receiving an asthma booklet. The CHWs were trained as asthma environmental specialists through a four-week intensive course followed by periodic refreshers. In addition to asthma, topics such as tenant's rights, access to medical care and referrals to social programs were also part of the training. CHWs were trained and certified as integrated pest management specialists for the eradication of rodents or other pests without using chemical products. Among participants receiving the intervention, there was a significant improvement in health lung function outcomes including persistent coughs with and without exercise. The intervention group also experienced a significant reduction of asthma related unscheduled health care use, an improvement in proper treatment of asthma symptoms, and there was a significant reduction in caregiver depressive symptoms. It is important to note that in this study most of the caregiver behaviors to reduce exposure were also linked to resources provided by the study, and no change was noted in exposure to second-hand smoking, or smoking cessation among family members.

Most CHW home interventions have heavily focused in reducing exposure to indoor home triggers. Krieger et al. (2009) conducted a study involving CHWs, that in addition to asthma trigger reduction education, provided information about asthma medical self-management. In this study they compared the benefits of using a team of medical nurses in the clinic plus a CHW conducting home visitations versus a model of using only a nurse at the clinical setting. Low-income clients receiving asthma education and support by both nurses at clinics and the CHW at home had better caretaker quality of life and the child more asthma symptom-free days when compared with those only receiving education and care from nurses at clinics. Furthermore, all the secondary outcomes measured significantly improved in the intervention group including day activity limitation, asthma attacks within the last 3 months and child school or adult work absenteeism. In this one-year intervention nurses at the clinic completed an initial intake form, conducted an allergy test and developed an individualized self-management medical plan. A well-coordinated health care team action plan was indeed developed for each client based on these initial findings. In the "only nurse" group, clients received education at the first visit and were offered three follow-up visits, referral to social services, school nurses and help accessing medical services. In the intervention group, CHWs reviewed with their clients their asthma self-management plan, access to medical care, results from the allergy test and the home environmental list findings, based on which an action plan was developed with the client to reduce exposure to home triggers. All the participants in this study were provided with allergen-bedding encasements for the child. The asthma affected households were followed up an average of 4.5 times by the CHW who maintained regular communication with nurses and medical providers. The intervention group (i.e., nurse and CHW) experienced more benefits for asthma control. However there were positive improvements in important areas of asthma self-management in both groups. Thus, the authors recommend having nurses at medical settings for those clients that refuse home visitations. It is important to underscore that the nurses in this study were trained to assess the patient's social and medical barriers and to take a proactive approach addressing them.

Most of the CHW-led asthma studies have targeted the child's caretaker doing home visits and have not worked directly with the affected children. Thus, it is important to review a study done in rural Texas (Horner and Fouladi, 2008) where CHWs worked directly with school-age children in the school setting. This study concluded that school based CHW-led asthma education aimed at improving children's understanding and practical skills for asthma control was an effective way to improve asthma self-management. The sample included was formed by 183 school-age children, 46% of whom were Hispanic. Children in the 10 intervention schools received a 7-step asthma self management plan that addressed symptoms, management and skill practice in the use of a metered dose inhaler (MDI) and problem-solving exercises. Children in the 8 control schools received general information about important age-appropriate non-asthma related health topics. CHWs were trustworthy former schools volunteers who were part of the community, and that were already familiar with the school environment. They received a 16-hour training that included both review of the educational material combination as well as the practice sessions in both group and individual settings. Results showed that this school-based CWH intervention led to significant improvements in children's asthma knowledge, asthma self-efficacy and self-management, and metered-dose inhaler technique.

Across the asthma studies the areas where the CHW intervention had consistent significant beneficial impacts were: a) urgent asthma-related medical care visits; b) asthma morbidity and daytime activity limitations among children; and c) on caretaker's quality of life by either reducing depression and/or improving self-reported quality of life. On the other hand, findings regarding reductions in indoor asthma trigger and caretaker's actions to reduce it were mixed. In some instances improvements were mostly tied to use of trigger reduction resources provided by the study such as pillow and bedding encasements. Overall, areas that seem especially challenging to improve are decreasing child household exposure to second-hand smoking, increasing the frequency of washing or changing sheets and pest/pet management.

Future research studies need to recognize the importance of working very closely with smoking cessation initiatives for the better management of asthma. At the same time studies must take into account that most low-income housing does not provide separate laundry facilities within each household. In addition, pest infestation and poor pest control may be common among low-income housing. Thus, future studies should emphasize addressing asthma control through multiple channels appropriate for the reality of low-income households. The use of CHWs working directly with asthma-affected children in school settings seems to be a promising approach and deserves further consideration. All the intervention studies included in this review included Hispanic/Latino families. Due to the relatively high rate of asthma among Puerto Rican children and their families research is needed specific to this community.

III) YOUTH SEX EDUCATION

Peer educators have been used to increase adolescent awareness of the Human Immune Deficiency Virus Infection (HIV), Sexually Transmitted Diseases (STDs) and pregnancy in a variety of school- and health care-based facilities. Siegel and colleagues tested the effect of an intervention delivered by an adult health educator and a peer educator as compared to the usual health education curriculum (Siegel et al., 2001). In addition, within a year after the completion of the intervention, middle school teachers were trained to deliver the intervention to test the ability for regular school personnel to teach the curriculum. Thus at the end of the study period there were a total of three intervention groups and one control group. The following five outcomes were assessed: 1) HIV/AIDS and sexuality knowledge, 2) sex self-efficacy, 3) safe sex behavior intention, 4) sexual intercourse history and 5) sexual risk behaviors. Results were presented based on school level (middle vs. high school) and gender. Knowledge scores increased in all intervention groups in both middle and high school, but only reached significance among middle school males and females. Self-efficacy scores increased among intervention participants, but the difference only reached significance among middle and high school females. Improvements in safe sex behavior intention scores were significant among male and female middle school students but not among high school students. Intention to follow safe sex practices was lower for those who reported a sexual history. Intervention participants in each of the schools and of both genders, with the exception of high school females, reported less involvement in sexual exploration. However, this between-group difference was only statistically significant among female middle school students. In addition, while not reaching significance, intervention participants tended to engage less in sexual risk behaviors. There was also a significant interaction between gender and study group on sex activity status indicating that middle school-aged sexually active females were significantly more positively influenced by the intervention. It is important to note that Latino students reported lower knowledge, self-efficacy and safe behavior intention scores post-intervention as compared to other ethnic/racial groups. This may indicate that this population is more at risk and may benefit from additional interventions.

A clinic-based study compared the effectiveness of peer vs. provider delivered messages on Acquired Immunodeficiency Syndrome (AIDS) knowledge, attitudes and behaviors (Quirk et al., 1993). Both interventions combined showed a significantly positive effect on preventing sexual transmission of HIV through condom use, condom use with a spermicidal and preventing IV drug transmission by cleaning implements with bleach. However, further analyses showed that the peer intervention was more effective at delivering the message to clean implements with bleach as compared to the provider intervention, while the provider intervention was more effective at improving knowledge about unprotected sex as a carrier of HIV as compared to the peer intervention.

A sample of high school students in an alternative drop out prevention program were studied to test the effectiveness of peer educators in changing social norms associated with STD/AIDS risk behaviors. The intervention included two schoolwide presentations on STD/HIV facts including segments with an STD disease intervention specialist and a young person with AIDS, as well as two small group breakouts which included activities around decision-making and prevention strategies against STDs/HIV. Results from a pre/post intervention surveys suggest that peer educators do help change established AIDS risk behaviors social norms (O'Hara et al., 1996). For example, pre-intervention, when asked "would your good friends think it's okay if they knew you used condoms?" 55 answered yes while this number increased to 65% post-intervention. In addition, condom use at last intercourse increased significantly post-intervention (44.8% to 55.2%). The authors also reported a decrease in students who never used condoms and an increase in those who intended to use condoms, although these differences did not reach statistical significance. Finally, there was a significant increase in the percentage of student who reported discussing HIV/AIDS with other students (23.3% to 67.7%). Thus, this intervention achieved its goal of utilizing peer educators to alter social norms around safe sex behaviors.

A recent study tested the effectiveness of the "peer providers of reproductive health services to teen model" with a goal to determine how clinic visit patterns, birth control and condom use were modified (Brindis et al., 2005). Female teens were divided into 4 sub-categories while male teens were divided into 2 sub-categories based on which services they received. Groups included a clinic services only group, a clinic-outreach group, a clinic-phone follow-up group and a full model group that included all three components. Female clients were retrospectively assigned to one of the four groups based on their level of intervention exposure, while males could receive clinic only or clinic-outreach services. Overall, females were significantly more likely to report consistent birth control use, birth control use at last intercourse and use of effective birth control methods from first to last visit. However, females were significantly less likely to report consistent condom use between first and last visits. The authors sought to determine if the level of exposure of services affected the previously mentioned outcomes and reported that females exposed to multiple components had no greater benefits as compared to clinic-only patients. However, some subgroups of clients benefited from some components of the model more than others. For example, Hispanics assigned to the full model, who received clinic and outreach services, as well as follow-up phone calls were more likely than those in the clinic-only group to report consistent birth control use (Odds ratio: 1.7; 95% Confidence Interval: 1.33-2.08) and less likely to report a pregnancy (0.2; 0.01-0.66). Other sub-groups who benefited from the intervention were those born to teenage mothers and those who reported having at most one sexual partner in the previous six months. The only significant between-group difference for males was that clinic-outreach clients were less likely than clinic-only clients to report using birth control or condoms at their last visits as compared to their first.

In summary, our literature review linking adolescent health with community health workers identified two main topics, STD prevention and safer sexual activity practices. Studies were conducted in two contexts, clinic- and school-based interventions. All interventions led to improvements confirming the value of peer-based counseling around sensitive adolescent health topics.

Conclusions

Without exception, all the RCTs identified in this review showed positive outcomes associated with the use of *promotores de salud* /CHWs on maternal, child and youth health promotion and disease management interventions. The implications of these findings cannot be overstated. For example, a CHW smoking cessation interventions resulted in a significant reduction of the number of cigarettes smoked per day by pregnant women. This in turn was associated with a reduction in low birth weight (LBW) rates.

Our review calls for the development of health care delivery programs that integrate CHWs as part of health care management teams that include nurses. As an example, the combination of nurses at clinical settings with CHWs led to improved mental health outcomes among low-income pregnant women, including a reduction of depressive symptoms and stress during pregnancy. CHWs have also been effective at improving parenting skills at home, indicating that they can also help improve the wellbeing of the Latino child through culturally appropriate non-biomedical approaches.

In the area of child health CHWs were able to improve the timely immunization of young children. Furthermore, the asthma management studies showed a positive impact of CHWs in reduction of urgent/unscheduled medical care due to asthma, reduced asthma morbidity and on the quality of caretaker's life including less depressive symptoms. The latter is a very important finding as it was not a target of the intervention but shows that CHWs cannot only improve the physical health of the child affected by asthma but also the wellbeing of the child caretakers.

There were no RCTs examining the impact of CHWs working on Latino youth sex education. However the evidence from qualitative and intervention studies showed positive outcomes in the area of safe sex behaviors.

To conclude, the evidence strongly supports the effectiveness of CHWs at improving the health and wellbeing of low-income Latino children in the United States. Thus, it is encouraging that there are several citywide initiatives, some of which were reviewed in this chapter, that have incorporated CHWs in their health care delivery services. These scaled-up programs are likely to improve the health of low-income communities by providing better access to culturally competent health care services, including vaccinations and childhood asthma management. However, these programs do not appear to have been evaluated through rigorous process and outcome evaluation designs.

There is a need for studies that examine the impact of CHWs among Latino subgroups with different levels of acculturation. In most interventions Latinos/Hispanics were part of the samples included but in general the interventions were not specifically designed to assess the needs that different Latino subgroups have. There is also a need for assessing the cost effectiveness of different CHW models targeting different behaviors and health outcomes in clinical and community settings but most importantly as part of chronic care systems that include both clinic- and community-based care.

Policy Implications

Findings from this chapter have important policy implications for the incorporations of CHWs as part of health care management teams and community agencies. In particular they suggest the following:

Legislative action is needed for the reimbursement of services provided by CHWs.

The development of a comprehensive workforce for CHWs needs to include a systematic investment in training, capacity building and evaluation of credentialing processes for CHWs to serve as functional members of the health care system and beyond, including the educational system (i.e. schools), community-based organization and housing, among others.

Funding is needed for properly evaluating and understanding the cost-effectiveness of programs that include CHWs.

References

Anders, R., Balcazar, H., & Paez, L. (2006). Hispanic community-based participatory research using a promotores de salud model. *Hispanic Health Care International, 4* (2), 71-78.

Anderson, L. M., Wood, D. L., & Sherbourne, C. D. (1997). Maternal acculturation and childhood immunization levels among children in Latino families in Los Angeles. *American Journal of Public Health, 87*:2018-2021.

Anliker, J. (1999). Using peer educators in nutrition intervention research: Lessons learned from the Maryland WIC 5 a day promotion program. *Journal of Nutrition Education, 31*:347-354.

Balcazar, H., Alvarado, M., Hollen, M. L., Gonzalez-Cruz, Y., Hughes, O., Vazquez, E., & Lykens, K. (2006). Salud para su corazon-NCLR: A comprehensive Promotora outreach program to promote heart-healthy behaviors among hispanics. *Health Promotion Practice, 7*:68-77.

Bloom, B., Cohen, R. A., & Freeman, G. (2009). Summary health statistics for U.S. children: National Health Interview Survey, 2008. Vital and Health Statistics. Series 10, Data from the National Health Survey 1-81.

Brenner, R. A., Simons-Morton, B. G., Bhaskar, B., Das, A., & Clemens, J. D.; NIH-D.C. InitiativeImmunization Working Group. (2001). Prevalence and predictors of immunization among inner-city infants: a birth cohort study. *Pediatrics, 108*:661-670.

Brindis, C. D., Geierstanger, S. P., Wilcox, N., McCarter, V., & Hubbard, A. (2005). Evaluation of a peer provider reproductive health service model for adolescents. *Perspectives on Sexual and Reproductive Health, 37*:85-91.

Chin, M. H., Alexander-Young, M., & Burnet, D. L. (2009). Health care quality-improvement approaches to reducing child health disparities. *Pediatrics, 124 Suppl 3*:S224-236.

Crain, E. F., Walter, M., O'Connor, G. T., Mitchell, H., Gruchalla, R. S., Kattan, M., Malindzak, G. S., Enright, P., Evans, R. 3rd, Morgan, W., & Stout, J. W. (2002). Home and allergic characteristics of children with asthma in seven U.S. urban communities and design of an environmental intervention: the Inner-City Asthma Study. *Environmental Health Perspectives, 110*(9):939-45

Dominguez S. R., Parrott J. S., Lauderdale D. S., & Daum R. S. (2004). On-time immunization rates among children who enter Chicago public schools. *Pediatrics, 114*(6):e741-7.

Dower C., Knox M., Lindler V., & O'Neil E. (2006). Advancing Community Health Worker Practice and Utilization: The Focus on Financing. San Francisco, CA: National Fund for Medical Education.

Flores G., Abreu M., Olivar M. A., & Kastner B. (1998). Access barriers to health care for Latino children. *Archives of Pediatrics & Adolescent Medicine, 152*:1119-1125.

Gern J. E. (2010). The Urban Environment and Childhood Asthma study. *The Journal of Allergy and Clinical Immunology, 125*(3):545-9.

Hicks P., Tarr G. A. M., & Hicks X. P. (2007). Reminder cards and immunization rates among Latinos and the rural poor in Northeast Colorado. *Journal of the American Board of Family Medicine: JABFM, 20*:581-586.

Hinman A. R. (1991). What will it take to fully protect all American children with vaccines? *American Journal of Diseases of Children, 145*:559-562.

Horner S. D., & Fouladi R. T. (2008). Improvement of rural children's asthma self-management by lay health educators. *J Sch Health, 78*(9):506-13.

Krieger J., Takaro T. K., Song L., Beaudet N., & Edwards K. (2009). A randomized controlled trial of asthma self-management support comparing clinic-based nurses and in-home community health workers: The Seattle-King County Healthy Homes II Project. *Archives of Pediatrics & Adolescent Medicine, 163*:141-149.

Krieger J. W., Takaro T. K., Song L., & Weaver M. (2005). The Seattle-King County Healthy Homes Project: A randomized, controlled trial of a community health worker intervention to decrease exposure to indoor asthma triggers. *American Journal of Public Health, 95*(4):652-9

Lara M., Morgenstern H., Duan N., & Brook R. H. (1999). Elevated asthma morbidity in Puerto Rican children: A review of possible risk and prognostic factors. *The Western Journal of Medicine, 170* (2):75-84.

Lara M., Akinbami L., Flores G., & Morgenstern H. (2006). Heterogeneity of childhood asthma among Hispanic children: Puerto Rican children bear a disproportionate burden. *Pediatrics, 117*(1):43-53.

Malchodi C. S., Oncken C., Dornelas E. A., Caramanica L., Gregonis E., & Curry S. L. (2003). The effects of peer counseling on smoking cessation and reduction. *Obstetrics and Gynecology, 101*(3):504-10.

Mannino D. M., Homa, D. M., Pertowski, C. A., Ashizawa, A. Nixon, L. L., Johnson C. A., Ball L. B., Jack E., & Kang D. S. (1998). Surveillance for Asthma—United States, 1960-1995. April 24, 1998 / 47(SS-1);1-28 http://www.cdc.gov/mmwr/preview/mmwrhtml/00052262.htm (Accessed June 10, 2010)

Meister J. S., Warrick L. H., de Zapién J. G., & Wood A. H. (1992). Using lay health workers: case study of a community-based prenatal intervention. *Journal of Community Health, 17*:37-51.

National Center for Health Statistics (2009). Health, United States, 2008. Health, United States, 2008. http://www.ncbi.nlm.nih.gov.ezproxy.lib.uconn. edu/bookshelf/br.fcgi?book=healthus08 (Accessed June 12, 2010).

National Center for Immunization and Respiratory Diseases, CDC (2008). National, state, and local area vaccination coverage among children aged 19-35 months—United States, 2007. MMWR. *Morbidity and Mortality Weekly Report, 57*:961-966.

O'Hara P., Messick B. J., Fichtner R. R., & Parris D. (1996). A peer-led AIDS prevention program for students in an alternative school. *The Journal of School Health, 66*:176-182.

Olds D. L. et al. (2004). Effects of home visits by paraprofessionals and by nurses: age 4 follow-up results of a randomized trial. *Pediatrics, 114*:1560-1568.

Parker E. A., Israel B. A., Robins T. G., Mentz G., Xihong Lin, Brakefield-Caldwell W., Ramirez E., Edgren K. K., Salinas M., & Lewis L. (2008). Evaluation of Community Action Against Asthma: a community health worker intervention to improve children's asthma-related health by reducing household environmental triggers for asthma. *Health Education & Behavior: The Official Publication of the Society for Public Health Education, 35*(3):376-95.

Perez M., Findley S. E., Mejia M., & Martinez J. (2006). The impact of community health worker training and programs in NYC. *Journal of Health Care for the Poor and Underserved, 17*:26-43.

Pew Hispanic Center (2008). U.S. Population Projections: 2005-2050—Pew Hispanic Center. http://pewhispanic.org/reports/report.php?ReportID=85 (Accessed June 5, 2010)

Postma J., Karr C., & Kieckhefer G. (2009). Community health workers and environmental interventions for children with asthma: a systematic review. *The Journal of Asthma: Official Journal of the Association for the Care of Asthma, 46*(6):564-76.

Quirk M. E., Godkin M. A., & Schwenzfeier E. (1993). Evaluation of two AIDS prevention interventions for inner-city adolescent and young adult women. *American Journal of Preventive Medicine, 9*:21-26.

Roman L. A., Gardiner J. C., Lindsay J. K., Moore J. S., Luo Z., Baer L. J., Goddeeris J. H., Shoemaker A. L., Barton L. R., Fitzgerald H. E., & Paneth N. (2009). Alleviating perinatal depressive symptoms and stress: a nurse-community health worker randomized trial. *Archives of Women's Mental Health, 12:*379-391.

Roman L. A., Lindsay J. K., Moore J. S., Duthie P. A., Peck C., Barton L. R., Gebben M. R., & Baer L. J. (2007). Addressing mental health and stress in Medicaid-insured pregnant women using a nurse-community health worker home visiting team. *Public Health Nursing (Boston, Mass.) 24:*239-248.

Scott G., & Ni, H. (2004). Access to health care among Hispanic/Latino children. Adv Data. 2004. June 24;(344):1-20. http://www.ncbi.nlm.nih.gov. ezproxy.lib.uconn.edu/pubmed/15227813 (Accessed June 5, 2010)

Siegel D. M., Aten M. J., & Enaharo M. (2001). Long-term effects of a middle school- and high school-based human immunodeficiency virus sexual risk prevention intervention. *Archives of Pediatrics & Adolescent Medicine, 155:*1117-1126.

Szilagyi P. G., Schaffer S., Shone L., Barth R., Humiston S. G., Sandler M., & Rodewald L. E. (2002). Reducing geographic, racial, and ethnic disparities in childhood immunization rates by using reminder/recall interventions in urban primary care practices. *Pediatrics, 110*(5):e58

Taylor T., Serrano E., Anderson J., & Kendall P. (2000). Knowledge, skills, and behavior improvements on peer educators and low-income Hispanic participants after a stage of change-based bilingual nutrition education program. *Journal of Community Health, 25:*241-262.

U.S. Department of Health and Human Services (2007). Community Health Worker National Workforce Study.

Warrick L. H., Wood A. H., Meister J. S., & de Zapien J. G. (1992). Evaluation of a peer health worker prenatal outreach and education program for Hispanic farm worker families. *Journal of Community Health, 17:*13-26.

Wasserman M., Bender D., & Lee S. Y. D. (2007). Use of preventive maternal and child health services by Latina women: A review of published intervention studies. *Medical Care Research and Review, 64:*4-45.

Yu S. M., & Singh G. K. (2009). Household language use and health care access, unmet need, and family impact among CSHCN. *Pediatrics, 124 Suppl 4:*S414-419.

Zambrana R. E., & Carter-Pokras O. (2004). Improving health insurance coverage for Latino children: a review of barriers, challenges and State strategies. *Journal of the National Medical Association, 96:*508-523.

CHAPTER THREE

EARLY FEEDING PRACTICES: BREASTFEEDING AND COMPLEMENTARY FEEDING AMONG U.S. LATINOS

Donna J. Chapman[1] and Ana Claudia Zubieta[2]

Introduction

The period from birth to two years of age is a critical window for the development of the best possible growth, health and behavior (World Health Organization, 2002b). Breastfeeding has been recognized by U.S. (Gartner et al., 2005) and international health authorities (World Health Organization, 2002b) as the optimal method for feeding infants. Breastfeeding provides, not only the ideal blend of nutrients for a growing infant, but it also provides infants with immunological protection and developmental advantages not available through infant formula. The current recommendation from the American Academy of Pediatrics (AAP) is for U.S. infants to be exclusively breastfed (ie: receive no other foods or liquids, with the exception of medicine or vitamin drops) for the first 6 months of life (Gartner et al., 2005). At around 6 months, infant's iron stores start to become depleted and breast milk alone is insufficient to meet the growing nutritional requirements of the infant (Dewey, Cohen, Brown & Rivera, 2001). At that time, appropriate complementary foods should be introduced

---

[1]Connecticut Center for Eliminating Health Disparities Among Latinos, Yale School of Public Health, New Haven, CT.
[2]The Ohio State University, Department of Human Nutrition, Columbus, OH.

with continued breastfeeding at least through the first 12 months of life, and continuing as long as mutually desired (Gartner et al., 2005). Complementary foods are typically defined as nutrient containing solid and liquid foods given to infants in addition to breast milk (or formula) to meet the nutritional require-ments of the infant when milk alone no longer suffices. The process of intro-ducing infants to complementary foods is often called weaning and in some instances complementary foods are also referred to as weaning foods.

This chapter focuses on Latino practices related to breastfeeding and com-plementary feeding, by reviewing the scientific literature in the areas of infant feeding practices, barriers to meeting the current recommendations and inter-ventions which have been designed to promote optimal infant nutrition among Latinos in the U.S. National data describing infant feeding methods of Latinos can mask differences in the practices of Latino subgroups (Chapman, Mere-wood, Ackatia-Armah & Pérez-Escamilla, 2008). Since the U.S. Latino popula-tion is composed of multiple ethnic subgroups (ie. Mexican, Puerto Rican, other Central/South American origins), which may differ in their infant feeding tradi-tions, we have differentiated between the practices of these subgroups, whenev-er possible.

Methods

Manuscripts contained in this systematic literature review were identified from PubMed searches, by back-searching reference lists of selected articles and from the authors' personal libraries. We conducted two separate Medline searches (breastfeeding and complementary feeding) of the research published in English in the past 20 years (1990–May 2010).

The "breastfeeding" search used the following terms: breastfeeding, lacta-tion, Latinas, Hispanics, Puerto Rican, Mexican, immigrants. This section was organized into three parts (breastfeeding rates, breastfeeding barriers and breastfeeding interventions). Inclusion criteria for the "breastfeeding rates" sec-tion specified that publications must report breastfeeding initiation, duration or exclusivity rates of a predominantly Latina, U.S. sample or must separately report breastfeeding rates for Latinos. The "breastfeeding barriers" section included qualitative studies evaluating breastfeeding attitudes and barriers of predominantly Latina, U.S. samples, or attributing specific comments to Lati-nas, while the "interventions" section included randomized trials of breastfeed-ing interventions targeting U.S. Latinas.

For the "complementary feeding" search, the following terms were used: complementary foods, weaning foods, Latino/a, Hispanics, baby foods, cereals, finger foods, juice and WIC. To be included, articles must describe complementary feeding practices or attitudes in U.S. samples that were Latina or included a Latina subsample. For both sections, full text articles were obtained for abstracts appearing to meet the inclusion criteria. Relevant articles were reviewed and summarized.

BREASTFEEDING RATES: NATIONAL DATA

The 2004–2008 National Immunization Survey (NIS) data indicate that 73.4% of U.S. mothers initiate breastfeeding, with breastfeeding rates gradually declining such that by 6 and 12 months postpartum, only 41.7% and 21.0% of infants are breastfed, respectively (Scanlon, Grummer-Strawn, Li & Chen, 2010). U.S. rates of exclusive breastfeeding are significantly lower. Of the infants born in 2006, the exclusive breastfeeding rates at 3 and 6 months were 33.1 and 13.6%, respectively (Centers for Disease Control and Prevention, 2010a). It should be noted that no data from Puerto Rico are included in the NIS (Chapman & Pérez-Escamilla, 2009).

Overall, breastfeeding rates among the Latino population exceed the national average. U.S. data on Latinos from the 2004–2008 NIS reflect a high rate of breastfeeding initiation (80.4%), and breastfeeding rates at 6 and 12 months postpartum (pp) are 45.1% and 24%, respectively (Scanlon et al., 2010). Similarly, among infants born in 2006, the NIS exclusive breastfeeding rates among Latinos are slightly better than national rates, with 35.7 and 14.9% of Latinos exclusively breastfeeding at 3 and 6 months pp, respectively (Centers for Disease Control and Prevention, 2010a).

However, when the analyses are limited to infants who were ever breastfed, the results for Latinos are not so positive. Among breastfed infants born in 2006, the rates of supplementation with infant formula are highest among Latinos, compared to all U.S. ethnic groups. Nationally, 25.6% of breastfed infants are supplemented with formula within the first 2 days of life, compared to 34.9% of Latino breastfed infants (Centers for Disease Control and Prevention, 2010b).

BREASTFEEDING INITIATION

We identified 15 studies that reported breastfeeding initiation rates of U.S. Latinos (Table 1). In general, Latinos of Mexican or Central/South American origin have higher breastfeeding initiation rates than Puerto Ricans (Table 1). However, in one study conducted in a hospital working toward Baby Friendly certification in Puerto Rico, 96% of women initiated breastfeeding. Predictors of breastfeeding initiation identified among Mexicans and other non-Puerto Rican Latinos included immigrant status (Gibson-Davis & Brooks-Gunn, 2006) and shorter time living in the United States (Harley, Stamm & Eskenazi, 2007).

Table 1. Descriptive studies documenting breastfeeding outcomes among U.S. Latinos

Study	Location and Sample Size (#Latinos/ # enrolled)	Study Design	Latino Subgroup	Breastfeeding Initiation	Early EBF[a] Practices	Breastfeeding Duration
Anderson, 2004	Hartford, CT 161/161	Cross-sectional	Mostly Puerto Rican	50.3%	N/A[b]	N/A
Gibson-Davis, 2006	20 U.S. cities, 1142/4207	Longitudinal birth cohort from Fragile Families and Child Wellbeing Study	Mexicans, Puerto Ricans, Other	Covariate Adjusted proportions: Mexican Immigrant, 91% Mexican U.S. born, 53% Other Hispanic immigrants, 89% Other Hispanic U.S. born, 47% Puerto Rican, born in Puerto Rico, 59% Puerto Rican, born in U.S., 54%	N/A	Covariate adjusted proportions: BF[c] for ≥ 6 months Mexican immigrant: 59% Mexican U.S. born: 24% Non-Mexican Hispanic immigrant: 59% Non-Mexican U.S. born: 21%
Gorman, 1995	U.S.-Mexico border 197/197	Cross-sectional	Mexican	45.7%	42.4% EBF > 7 days[d]	15.9% BF ≥ 6 mo
Gorman, 2007	San Francisco, CA 1359/1635	Medical record review	Mostly Mexican, grouped as Spanish- vs. English-speakers	N/A	% EBF in hospital: 76.1% Spanish, 68.6% English	N/A
Gross, 2010	New York, NY 368/368	Longitudinal birth cohort of WIC[e] participants	25% Mexico, 25% Ecuador, 7% Dominican Republic, 43% other	81%	5% at 6 weeks pp.	N/A
Harley, 2007	Salinas, CA 490/490	Longitudinal birth cohort	100% Mexican	96%	Median EBF Duration, 1 mo.[d]	Median BF duration, 5 months

Hurley, 2008	Maryland, 117/767	Cross-sectional	Not specified	91%	N/A	N/A
Kersey, 2005	Chicago, IL 364/364	Cross-sectional	Mostly Mexican	87%	N/A	N/A
Kugyelka, 2004	Up-state New York 1032/2527	Medical record review	Mostly Puerto Rican	58.5% attempted to BF	Mean EBF[f] duration, 17 days	Mean duration of any BF, 48 days
Lee, 2009	Philadelphia, PA 200/1140	Longitudinal birth cohort	Puerto Rican and "Other Hispanic"	Adjusted odds ratio for BF initiation[g] Non-Hispanic white:1.0 Puerto Rican: OR[h]: 0.73 Other Hispanic: OR: 7.16 (p<0.001)	N/A	Adjusted OR for BF termination Non-Hispanic white:1.0 Puerto Rican: 1.44 Other Hispanic: 0.83 p<0.01
Newton, 2009	Boston, Massachusetts 349/349	Retrospective chart review	Mostly foreign-born from El Salvador and Dominican Republic	93.1%	27.5% EBF in hospital	N/A
Pachon, 1999	New York state 136/136	Cross-sectional	Puerto Rican South American Central American Dominican Republic	51.9%	EBF "at birth" 28% Puerto Ricans, 49% other Hispanic	N/A
Pérez-Escamilla, 1998	Hartford, Connecticut 144/144	Cross-sectional	Mostly Puerto Rican	50%	N/A	N/A
Pérez-Rios, 2008	Puerto Rico 1695/1695	Cross-sectional data from the Puerto Rico Reproductive Health Survey	Puerto Rican	61.5%	N/A	N/A

Table 1 continued.

Study	Location and Sample Size (#Latinos/ # enrolled)	Study Design	Latino Subgroup	Breastfeeding Initiation	Early EBF[a] Practices	Breastfeeding Duration
Petrova, 2007	New Jersey 47/307	Secondary analysis of prospective data	Not specified	N/A	44.7% EBF in hospital	N/A
Rivera-Lugo, 2007	San Juan, Puerto Rico 200/200	Semi-structured questionnaire	Puerto Rican	96.5%	N/A	N/A
Sussner, 2007	Northeastern U.S. 505/679	Secondary analysis of prospective data	Central/South America, Dominican Republic, Puerto Rico	76.7%	N/A	44.9% BF at 6 months pp

[a]EBF: Exclusive breastfeeding; [b]N/A: Not applicable; [c]BF: Breastfeeding; [d] EBF definition allowed water; [e]WIC: Special Supplemental Nutrition Program for Women, Infants and Children; [f] EBF data not specific regarding fluids other than breastmilk or formula; [g]BF initiation defined as having BF for at least 7 days; [h]OR: Odds ratio.

Among Puerto Ricans living in the U.S. mainland, predictors of breastfeeding initiation included higher levels of social capital and not being the head of the household (Anderson et al., 2004). Pérez-Escamilla and colleagues (1998) identified other factors predictive of breastfeeding initiation among Puerto Rican Latinas including fewer years living in the United States, not receiving prenatal advice to formula feed, primiparity, multiparity with previous breastfeeding experience, delivery of an infant that was not low-birth weight and younger age of the index child. In a diverse predominantly Latina sample (Sussner, Lindsay & Peterson, 2008), exclusive use of a woman's native language was predictive of breastfeeding initiation. Given the frequency with which proxy markers for increased levels of acculturation (ie. increased years in United States, born in United States, non-exclusive use of native language) are cited as predictors of the failure to initiate breastfeeding, future research should identify those aspects of U.S. culture which are strong disincentives of this practice.

EXCLUSIVE BREASTFEEDING (EBF) PRACTICES

Eight studies described the EBF practices of Hispanics in the United States (Table 1). Of the four studies (Gorman, Madlensky, Jackson, Ganiats & Boies, 2007; Newton, Chaudhuri, Grossman & Merewood, 2009; Pachon & Olson, 1999; Petrova, Hegyi & Mehta, 2007) that evaluated in-hospital EBF rates, all but one (Gorman et al., 2007) found that less than half of Latino infants were EBF at hospital discharge. Two studies reported EBF duration among U.S. Latinos (Harley et al., 2007; Kugyelka, Rasmussen & Frongillo, 2004). Although the mean EBF duration among Mexicans (1 month) was higher than those for Puerto Ricans (median 17 days), both rates are far below national recommendations. Factors associated with EBF included: foreign-born (Pachon & Olson, 1999), shorter time living in the United States (Harley et al., 2007), Spanish language-use and term delivery (Gorman et al., 2007), and BMI < or = 29.0 (Kugyelka et al., 2004). Newton and colleagues (Newton et al., 2009) identified other determinants of EBF among their Dominican and El Salvadorian immigrants including maternal age < 25 years, U.S.-born mother and doula support. Extensive research is necessary to better understand the factors surrounding the decision to introduce formula during the hospital stay, in order to better promote EBF during this critical period.

BREASTFEEDING CONTINUATION RATES

We identified six studies that reported data on postpartum breastfeeding rates among U.S. Latinas who initiated breastfeeding (Table 1). As was observed for breastfeeding initiation and exclusivity, postpartum breastfeeding rates were higher for Mexican Americans or other Latino groups, as compared to Puerto Ricans (Gorman, Byrd & VanDerslice, 1995; Harley et al., 2007; Kugyelka et al., 2004; Lee, Elo, McCollum & Culhane, 2009; Sussner et al., 2008). Immigrants were more likely to be breastfeeding at 6 months postpartum, compared to Latinas born in the United States (Gibson-Davis & Brooks-Gunn, 2006). Other determinants of longer breastfeeding duration included shorter time in the United States (Harley et al., 2007) and body mass index <29 kg/m² (Kugyelka et al., 2004). Sussner and colleagues also identified exclusive use of one's native language, maternal age > 30, non-smoking status, absence of depression and foreign-born maternal grandparents as predictors of longer breastfeeding duration (Sussner et al., 2008).

BREASTFEEDING BARRIERS AMONG U.S. LATINAS

We identified eight qualitative studies examining barriers to breastfeeding among Latinas. Two perceived disadvantages of breastfeeding described in nearly every study, by women from multiple Latino subgroups, were pain (Bunik et al., 2006; Gill, Reifsnider, Mann, Villarreal & Tinkle, 2004; Hannon, Willis, Bishop-Townsend, Martinez & Scrimshaw, 2000; Higgins, 2000; Kaufman, Deenadayalan & Karpati, 2010; Wood, Sasonoff & Beal, 1998) and uneasiness with breastfeeding in public (Bunik et al., 2006; Gill et al., 2004; Gorman et al., 1995; Hannon et al., 2000; Kaufman et al., 2010). Other concerns raised in these studies included perceived insufficient milk (Bunik et al., 2006; Gorman et al., 1995; Heinig et al., 2006; Wood et al., 1998), inconvenience (Bunik et al., 2006; Gill et al., 2004; Gorman et al., 1995; Higgins, 2000; Wood et al., 1998), poor diet quality or dietary restriction (Gill et al., 2004; Kaufman et al., 2010) and inadequate support from healthcare professionals (Gill et al., 2004; Heinig et al., 2006; Kaufman et al., 2010).

Some beliefs engrained in the Latino culture may contribute to suboptimal breastfeeding practices. In both the Mexican and Puerto Rican cultures, a chubby baby is perceived to be healthy and beautiful (Bunik et al., 2006; Higgins, 2000). Some mothers thought it would be too time-consuming to have a big, exclusively breastfed infant (Higgins, 2000). Instead, they supplemented with formula, or used formula exclusively. In pursuit of having a *"gordito"* infant, these mothers often overfed, causing the infant to spit up. In addition, the Latino culture holds grandmothers in high respect; however, not all Latino grandmothers breastfed exclusively, and many Puerto Rican grandmothers did not breastfeed at all (Higgins, 2000). Thus, many Latino grandmothers encourage formula use, based on their experiences (Bunik et al., 2006).

Some women reported Latino cultural factors, as reasons why they were not successful with breastfeeding. La Cuarentena is a traditional 40-day period of rest and recovery after delivery. Some Mexican-American women, who did not adhere to La Cuarentena, cited violation of this practice as a reason for poor breastfeeding outcomes (Bunik et al., 2006). Others endorsed the cultural belief that mothers experiencing negative emotions would damage their milk's flavor or quality (Bunik et al., 2006; Hannon et al., 2000).

The practice of providing infants with both breastmilk and formula is very common among U.S. Latinos (Centers for Disease Control and Prevention, 2010b), and is sometimes referred to as *"los dos"* (i.e. both breast milk and formula) (Bunik et al., 2006). Latinas reported that this combination allowed the health benefits of breastfeeding, but also provided the "vitamins" in formula. Formula was perceived as thicker than breast milk, and therefore richer. This practice was seen as acceptable, since Latinas received mixed messages from hospitals and WIC clinics, where they were encouraged to breastfeed, but simultaneously provided with free formula (Bunik et al., 2006).

BREASTFEEDING INTERVENTIONS TARGETING LATINAS

We identified seven randomized trials targeting Latinas and evaluating breastfeeding interventions delivered by either peer counselors (PC)/community health workers or by lactation consultants (Table 2). Breastfeeding peer counseling refers to the provision of breastfeeding education and support by local women who successfully breastfed their own children, and have received specialized training, enabling them to effectively promote breastfeeding in their communities (Chapman, Damio, Young & Pérez-Escamilla, 2004). Breastfeeding PC has been used in the United States and internationally, with the overwhelming majority of studies documenting a positive impact on breastfeeding outcomes (Chapman, Morel, Anderson, Damio & Pérez-Escamilla, 2010).

Chapman and colleagues (2004) evaluated the effectiveness of a PC program among a predominantly Puerto Rican population in Hartford, CT, and reported a significant increase in the breastfeeding initiation rate and marginally higher breastfeeding rates at 1 and 3 months pp in the intervention (vs. control) group. Anderson et al (2005) evaluated the efficacy of a more intensive PC intervention promoting EBF in the same community and demonstrated significant improvements in breastfeeding initiation and EBF rates (at hospital discharge and 3 months pp), along with lower incidence of infant diarrhea and a higher rate of maternal amenorrhea in the intervention (vs. control) group. In a unique study, Hopkinson et al. (2009) evaluated the impact of routine postpartum clinic appointments in which breastfeeding Mexican-born Latinas met with

Table 2. Randomized trials evaluating breastfeeding interventions among U.S. Latinos

Study	Location; # Latinos/ # enrolled	Latino Subgroup	Study Groups	Outcomes
Anderson, 2005	Hartford, CT 97/135	Mostly Puerto Rican	Intervention (n=90): Peer counseling (3 prenatal, daily perinatal, and 9 pp[e] home visits) Control (n=92): Standard care	Initiation [a]: I[b]: 91%, C[c]: 76% Any BF[d] at 3 months: I:49%, C:36% EBF[d] at 3 months[a]: I:27%, C: 3% Infant diarrhea by 3 months[a]: I: 18%, C: 38%
Bonuck, 2005 and 2006	Bronx, NY 191/338	Not specified	Intervention (n=163): Lactation consultant attempted 2 prenatal visits, 1 pp visit, telephone calls Control (n=175): Standard care	BF at week 20 pp[a]: I: 53%, C:39% EBF: No significant difference Infant Health: No significant differences in rates of otitis media, respiratory illness, gastrointestinal illness by group
Bunik, 2010	Denver, Colorado 300/341	Mexican	Intervention (n=161): Daily phone call from bilingual nurse through day 14 pp. Control (n=180): Standard care	No significant differences in any BF or predominant BF at 1,3 and 6 months pp.
Chapman 2004	Hartford, CT	Mostly Puerto Rican	Intervention (n=113): Peer counseling (1 prenatal, daily perinatal, 3 pp visits) Control (n=106): Standard care	Initiation[a]: I: 91%, C: 77% Any BF at 1 mo: RR[f], 95% CI[g]: 0.78 (0.50, 1.05) Any BF at 3 mo: RR, 95% CI: 0.78 (0.61, 1.0)
Hopkinson, 2009	Houston, TX	Mostly Mexican	Intervention (n=255): Scheduled to attend BF clinic Control (n=267): Received phone number of clinic	Week 4 outcomes EBF[a]: I, 17%, C: 10% Consumed water[h]:I: 20%,C:41 Consumed tea[h]:I:16%, C:28% Ounces of formula/day[h]: I:12, C: 14
Petrova, 2009	New Brunswick, NJ 91/104	Mostly Mexican	Intervention (n=52): 2 prenatal + 3 pp visits from lactation consultant Control (n=52): Standard care	EBF at 7 days: I: 46%, C: 29% EBF at 1 month: I: 30%, C: 24% EBF at 2 months: I: 25%, C: 18%
Sandy, 2009	New York City, NY 235/238	Mostly Dominican	I: FSW visits: prenatal (weekly), perinatal (1), postpartum (weekly). C: 1-2 prenatal FSW home visits	BF Initiation: No significant difference between those exposed vs. unexposed to intervention. Statistical analyses based on exposure to intervention, not by intention to treat

[a]p<0.05; [b]I: Intervention; [c]C: Control group; [d]EBF: Exclusive breastfeeding;[e]pp: postpartum;[f] RR: Relative risk;[g]95% Confidence interval; [h] p<0.01; [i]FSW: family support worker.

a PC. At 4 weeks postpartum, the intervention group was significantly more likely to be EBF during the past 24 hours than controls. Thus, among Mexican immigrants, a less intensive PC effort may be sufficient to improve breastfeeding outcomes.

Sandy et al. (2009) evaluated the impact of a family support worker (FSW) intervention which included a breastfeeding promotion component. This study, which was not analyzed on an intention to treat basis, showed no impact of the intervention on breastfeeding rates. The authors reported significant improvements in the EBF rates of participants *exposed* to the intervention; however, the results should be interpreted with caution as EBF was not clearly defined and outcome data were collected by the FSW.

Other types of breastfeeding support services have been evaluated among U.S. Latinas. In a series of publications, Bonuck and colleagues (2005, 2006) evaluated the impact of a 3-visit lactation consultant intervention to a study population that was 57% Latina. This intervention yielded significant improvements in breastfeeding rates at 5 months postpartum, but there were no significant differences in EBF rates or infant health outcomes by study group. In a more intensive intervention delivered by a lactation consultant, Petrova et al. reported increased rates of EBF in their intervention group (vs. control) at 1 week pp; however, this difference was not statistically significant and became negligible by 3 months. Bunik et al. (2010) evaluated the impact of a telephone-based, postpartum intervention delivered by bilingual nurses and observed no significant impact on breastfeeding rates between 1 and 6 months pp, suggesting that in-person contact may be essential in this population.

COMPLEMENTARY FEEDING GUIDELINES

The World Health Organization and the American Academy of Pediatrics recommend that complementary foods be introduced to infant's diets at 6 months of age (Gartner et al., 2005; World Health Organization, 2002a). WHO has published a set of guidelines on *quantity, consistency, meal frequency, energy density* and *nutrient content of foods* (World Health Organization, 2005). As with breastfeeding, the *quantity* of food offered needs to be based on the principles of responsive feeding. In regards to *consistency*, infants can eat pureed, mashed and semi-solid foods beginning at six months. Finger foods or infant snack foods, which required the ability of "munching" (up and down mandibular movements), can typically be eaten starting at eight months. By 12 months infants are able to chew (using their teeth) and are able to eat most "family foods" keeping in mind the need for nutrient dense foods. Regarding *meal frequency,* healthy infants should be provided meals (defined as milk only feeds, other foods, and combinations of milk feeds and other foods) four to five times a day, with one to two additional healthy snacks (e.g. fruit or vegetables, typically self-fed foods between meals). *Meal density* is linked to meal frequency, the more nutrient dense the meals, the less frequently the infant will require a meal. Due to the existing infant to infant variation, caregivers need to pay attention to infant hunger cues when deciding how frequently to feed. Finally, with respect to *nutrient content of foods* the general guideline is to feed a variety of foods to guarantee that nutrient needs are being met. Animal source foods (meat, fish, poultry, egg and milk) need to be eaten daily as they are rich in crucial nutrients such as iron, zinc, vitamin B12, calcium, fat and protein (World Health Organization, 2005). Fruits and vegetables need to be included early in an infant's diet as they are nutrient dense foods. It has also been shown that infants are more accepting of foods after they have been repeatedly exposed to them (Gerrish & Mennella, 2001). Regular cow's milk should not be introduced until twelve months of age and when introduced, it needs to be whole milk until the infant turns two years old.

Just as important as starting complementary foods at around six month of age, avoiding early weaning is crucial. Premature weaning can have harmful effects, such as infections, malnutrition and increased risk of chronic diseases later in life (World Health Organization, 2002a).

COMPLEMENTARY FEEDING PRACTICES OF LATINO SUBGROUPS

The initiation, the composition and the quantity of complementary foods vary widely among different ethnic, racial and social groups. Latinos in the United States are composed of many cultural, racial as well as social backgrounds. The larger proportions of Latinos in the United States are of Mexican, Puerto Rican, Cuban and Central American descent (Ramirez, 2004). We identified five studies describing complementary feeding practices of U.S. Latinos (Table 3).

Gross et al. (2009) studied urban Latinas participating in WIC and evaluated maternal perceptions of infant hunger, satiety and pressuring feeding styles. Many mothers associated crying with hunger and reported using pressuring feeding styles. These mothers seemed to be less likely to consider alternative causes for crying and thus fed their babies in the absence of hunger.

A qualitative study of healthcare providers, working primarily with Mexican Americans in Denver, CO, (Johnson, Clark, Goree, O'Connor & Zimmer, 2008), found that providers perceived that these mothers preferred bigger babies and were concerned when their babies had normal body weight, as the latter was perceived as being too thin. Providers also reported that Mexican-American

Table 3. Studies documenting complementary feeding practices of U.S. Latinos

Study	Location	Sample Size (#Latinos/ #enrolled)	Study Design	Latino Subgroup	Main Findings
Crocetti, 2004	Baltimore, MD	18/1C2	Cross-sectional	N/A[a]	Hispanic caregivers and those who breastfed (partial or exclusively) were less likely to introduce cereals early.
Gonzalez-Reyes, 2003	Hartford, CT	119/148	Longitudinal	Mostly Puerto Rican	99% of infants received solids and liquids (other than breastmilk or formula) before 6 months. Most infants received water (86.3%), juice (67.5%), cereals (84.5%) and baby foods other than cereals (60.5%) ≤ 4 months.
Gross, 2009	New York, NY	368/368	Longitudinal birth cohort of WIC[b] participants	N/A	70% of mothers believed that crying represented hunger and reported using pressuring feeding styles.
Heinig, 2006	Yolo, Solano and Sacramento, CA	39/65	Focus Groups	N/A	Planning for complementary feeding was rare. Mothers were not aware of links between health and complementary foods.
Menella, 2006 & Ziegler, 2006	Subset of the national Feeding Infants and Toddlers Study (FITS)	371/3022	Cross-sectional, telephone survey of children ages 4-24 months	N/A	Hispanic infants (4-5 months old) were more likely to be eating baby foods and less likely to be eating non-infant cereals, compared to non-Hispanic infants. Nearly all nutrients were not significantly different for Hispanics and non-Hispanics for meals and snacks.

[a]N/A: Not applicable; [b]WIC: Special Supplemental Nutrition Program for Women, Infants and Children

mothers introduced complementary foods before the recommended six months of age, often during the first month of life. This practice generated from maternal perception that their children need more calories, will sleep longer when given cereals, and will grow faster. Early introduction of solids conforms to cultural traditions and family pressures emphasizing the social dimension of eating with the family. In addition, providers suggest that Mexican mothers often offer their infants high-calorie, low nutrient-dense foods (e.g., chips or candy) to promote good behavior, to provide comfort following painful procedures and to convey love and attention. These foods were selected due to their low cost and high satisfaction reached (Johnson et al., 2008).

The work of Higgins (Higgins, 2000) supports the early introduction of cereal among Latinos, with mothers reporting the common practice of feeding rice cereal in a bottle, often as early as two months of age. This practice is contrary to current AAP recommendations, but was reported as promoting an early introduction to rice, a staple in the Latino diet (Higgins, 2000).

Focus groups examining the relationship among maternal beliefs, feeding intentions and infant-feeding behaviors among 65 (60% Latinas) mothers participating in WIC concluded these women rarely had a plan for introducing complementary foods (Heinig et al., 2006). Although health messages related to breastfeeding were well received and understood, few mothers recognized the link of complementary feeding with infant health. These mothers introduced solids, not to satisfy nutritional needs necessarily, but rather to respond to perceptions that their infants wanted foods or that their infants were developmentally ready to eat solid foods.

Crocetti et al. (2004), in a cross-sectional study during the 4-month well-baby check-up, concluded that the three most frequent reasons for early introduction of cereals were the perception that infants were not satisfied with breast milk or formula alone (80%), infants slept better at night (53%) and recommendation of family/friends (42%). This study also suggested that Latino (18% of sample) caregivers, in comparison to blacks (34% of sample), were less likely to introduce cereals earlier than 4 months of age [OR=0.2 (0.03-0.9)]. Moreover, caregivers who breastfed exclusively or partially with formula were less likely to introduce cereals early [OR= 0.4 (0.2-0.9)].

The Feeding Infants and Toddlers Study (FITS) is a national random sample of children aged 4-24 months, which assessed food and beverage intake for a 24-hour period (Mennella, Ziegler, Briefel & Novak, 2006). Cross-sectional data were collected via telephone surveys from mothers or primary caregivers of Latino (14%) and non-Latino (86%) infants and toddlers. Overall, Latino infants differentiated from non-Latino infants in numerous ways. Latino infants under 12 months of age were more likely to have ever been breastfed and fed pureed baby foods between the ages of 4 to 5 months when compared to non-Latino infants. Latino infants at ages 6 to 11 months were also more likely to be eating fresh fruits, fruit-flavored drinks, baby cookies and foods such as soups, rice and beans. A similar pattern of foods and drinks in addition to tortillas was observed among the 12- to 24-month-old Latino toddlers. Additionally, the FITS Study reported that at 6-11 months of age, Latino children had a significantly lower intake of carbohydrates at dinner and lower intake of saturated fat at afternoon snacks compared with non-Latino children (P<0.05).

In the FITS study, the main difference between Latino and non-Latino children's intakes occurred at 12-24 months of age (Ziegler, Hanson, Ponza, Novak & Hendricks, 2006). Latino toddlers aged 12-24 months had significantly (P<0.05) lower percentages of energy from fat and saturated fat at lunch and dinner, as well as a significantly (P<0.05) higher percentage of carbohydrates at lunch, when compared with non-Latino children. Whole grains, vegetables and fruits were the food groups typically lacking at meals and snacks for both Latinos and non-Latinos. Nutrient intake levels for nearly all nutrients were not significantly different between Latinos and non-Latinos for meals and snacks.

Gonzalez-Reyes (2003) evaluated infant feeding practices among a predominantly Puerto Rican population (N=148) in Hartford, CT. These prospectively collected data revealed unfavorable complementary feeding practices, with 99% of participants introducing solids and liquids other than breast milk or formula before 6 months of life. The majority of infants were introduced to water (86%), juice (68%), cereals (85%) and baby foods other than cereals (61%) at or before 4 months of age.

Determinants of very early (≤ 4 months) introduction of complementary foods were assessed. Maternal overweight/obesity and being a single mother were risk factors for early water consumption. Younger women and those enrolled in WIC were more likely to introduce baby foods early (vs. older women and those not enrolled in WIC), while women receiving Food Stamps were more likely to introduce juice and baby foods including cereals by 4 months (vs. those not receiving Foods Stamps). English-speaking women tended to be more likely to introduce baby cereals ≤ 4 months when compared to bilingual and Spanish-speakers (93.9%, 82.9%, 76.1% respectively, p=0.052). Women with a higher level of education were less likely to introduce juice ≤ 4 months (90% of those with 1-8 years of schooling, 71.9% if 9-11 years of schooling, 70.6% of high school graduates and 46.4% of those with more than a high school education, p<0.05).

The findings of this study imply that weaning is likely to be influenced by social (being single, young), cultural (ethnicity) and socioeconomic (WIC and food stamp participation) factors. To improve complementary feeding practices, interventions should consider all of those aspects.

COMPLEMENTARY FEEDING INTERVENTIONS

Our literature search did not identify a single intervention promoting optimal complementary feeding practices among Latinos. Based on the inappropriate complementary feeding practices that have been reported in the scientific literature, interventions targeting Latina mothers during pregnancy or shortly after delivery are in need. These interventions should include: a) effective parenting practices that address recognition of infants' hunger and satiety cues; b) the importance of appropriate timing of the introduction of quality complementary foods; c) clearly communicating the relationship between complementary feeding and long- and short-term health outcomes. An example of a relevant intervention is The Infant Feeding Series (TIFS), a six-lesson curriculum that addresses the transition to feeding solids, through parenting education and behavior change (Brophy-Herb, Silk, Horodynski, Mercer and Olson, 2009). This curriculum was pilot tested in black and Caucasian mothers. Results indicated that after receiving the intervention, mothers could more accurately identify infants' readiness for solids and reported increased feelings of self-efficacy about starting and maintaining healthful eating patterns. This, or a similar curriculum, needs to be adapted and pilot-tested with Latina mothers.

Implications

Although breastfeeding rates of Latinas are better than those of other U.S. ethnic groups, wide variation exists in the breastfeeding practices of Latinas. In general, women from Mexico or other Central/South American countries, where breastfeeding has been the cultural norm, have higher rates of breastfeeding initiation and duration, compared to Puerto Ricans. However, acculturation has been negatively associated with optimal breastfeeding outcomes. Several of the studies included in this review demonstrate that U.S. born Latinas are much less likely to initiate breastfeeding (Gibson-Davis & Brooks-Gunn, 2006; Harley et al., 2007; Rassin et al., 1993) or continue breastfeeding for extended periods (Gibson-Davis & Brooks-Gunn, 2006), compared to immigrants. Additionally, the prevalence of supplemental formula use among Latinas initiating breastfeeding is much worse than the national average. These findings are concerning, given that a dose-responsive association between breastfeeding and lower rates of common infant and childhood conditions (i.e.: otitis media, diarrhea, respiratory infections, obesity) (Ip et al., 2007) has been well recognized. Suboptimal breastfeeding practices have a profound impact on the health and wellbeing of children, as well as their healthcare costs (Bartick & Reinhold, 2010).

The untimely and inappropriate introduction of complementary foods has shown to be risk factors for both over and underweight, stunting and micronutrient deficiencies. Moreover, improper feeding during infancy, such as early or late introduction of complementary foods and overfeeding can lead to adverse effects on children's health including weight status (Forsyth, Ogston, Clark, Florey & Howie, 1993). Although research studies on complementary feeding practices among Latinas are relatively scarce, those that have been conducted reveal a consistent pattern of very early introduction of solids and frequently report overfeeding. This is very concerning given that Latinos have higher obesity rates than the general U.S. population.

While future public health interventions are necessary to improve breastfeeding rates and complementary feeding practices in all sectors of the U.S. population, they are particularly important among Latinas. Breastfeeding is associated with reductions in several chronic health conditions such as diabetes and obesity (Ip et al., 2007), and these conditions occur at disproportionately high rates among Latinos (Pérez-Escamilla & Putnik, 2007). There is very limited research on the area of complementary foods and feeding practices of Latina mothers and caregivers.

Future research should include: culturally sensitive breastfeeding and complementary feeding promotion efforts, identification of Latino subgroups within studies and further refinement of the peer counseling model, with a possible expansion of the role to address appropriate complementary feeding practices. Additionally, further research is necessary to better understand the aspects of life in the United States that are negatively associated with breastfeeding rates among immigrant Latinas. Research elucidating barriers and effective interventions for introducing complementary foods at the appropriate time, with high nutrient quality and with suitable parenting styles in Latino families is also urgently needed. Addressing this research need will likely have a profound impact on the long-term health consequences for Latinos.

References

Anderson, A., Damio, G., Himmelgreen, D., Peng, Y.-K., Segura-Pérez, S., & Pérez-Escamilla, R. (2004). Social capital, acculturation, and breastfeeding initiation among Puerto Rican women in the United States. *J Hum Lact, 20*(1), 39-45.

Anderson, A., Damio, G., Young, S., Chapman, D., & Pérez-Escamilla, R. (2005). A randomized trial assessing the efficacy of peer counseling on exclusive breastfeeding in a predominantly Latina low-income community. *Arch Pediatr Adolesc Med, 159*(9), 836-841.

Bartick, M., & Reinhold, A. (2010). The burden of suboptimal breastfeeding in the United States: a pediatric cost analysis. *Pediatrics, 125*(5), e1048-1056.

Bonuck, K. A., Freeman, K., & Trombley, M. (2006). Randomized controlled trial of a prenatal and postnatal lactation consultant intervention on infant health care use. *Arch Pediatr Adolesc Med, 160*(9), 953-960.

Bonuck, K. A., Trombley, M., Freeman, K., & Mckee, D. (2005). Randomized, controlled trial of a prenatal and postnatal lactation consultant intervention on duration and intensity of breastfeeding up to 12 months. *Pediatrics, 116*(6), 1413-1426.

Brophy-Herb, H. E., Silk, K., Horodynski, M. A., Mercer, L., & Olson, B. (2009). Key theoretical frameworks for intervention: understanding and promoting behavior change in parent-infant feeding choices in a low-income population. *J Prim Prev, 30*(2), 191-208.

Bunik, M., Clark, L., Marquez Zimmer, L., Jimenez, L., O'Connor, M., Crane, L., & et al. (2006). Early infant feeding decisions in low-income Latinas. *Breastfeed Med, 1*(4), 225-235.

Bunik, M., Shobe, P., O'Connor, M. E., Beaty, B., Langendoerfer, S., Crane, L., & et al. (2010). Are 2 weeks of daily breastfeeding support insufficient to overcome the influences of formula? *Acad Pediatr, 10*(1), 21-28.

Centers for Disease Control and Prevention. (2010a). Provisional exclusive breastfeeding rates by socio-demographic factors, among children born in 2006. Retrieved January 20, 2010, from http://www.cdc.gov/breastfeeding/ data/NIS_data/2006/socio-demographic.htm

Centers for Disease Control and Prevention. (2010b). Provisional formula supplementation of breast milk rates by socio-demographic factors, among children born in 2006. Retrieved January 20, 2010, from http://www.cdc. gov/breastfeeding/data/NIS_data/2006/socio-demographic_formula.htm

Chapman, D., Damio, G., Young, S., & Pérez-Escamilla, R. (2004). Effectiveness of breastfeeding peer counseling in a low-income, predominantly Latina population: A randomized, controlled trial. *Arch Pediatr Adolesc Med, 158*(9), 897-902.

Chapman, D., Merewood, A., Ackatia-Armah, R., & Pérez-Escamilla, R. (2008). Breastfeeding status on U.S. birth certificates: Where do we go from here? *Pediatrics, 122*(6), e1159-e1163.

Chapman, D., Morel, K., Anderson, A., Damio, G., & Pérez-Escamilla, R. (2010). Breastfeeding Peer Counseling: From efficacy through scale-up. *J Hum Lact, 26*(3), 314-326.

Chapman, D., & Pérez-Escamilla, R. (2009). U.S. National Breastfeeding Surveillance: Current Status and Recommendations. *J Hum Lact, 25*(2), 139-150.

Crocetti, M., Dudas, R., & Krugman, S. (2004). Parental beliefs and practices regarding early introduction of solid foods to their children. *Clin Pediatr (Phila), 43*(6), 541-547.

Dewey, K., Cohen, R., Brown, K., & Rivera, L. (2001). Effects of exclusive breastfeeding for four versus six months on maternal nutritional status and infant motor development: Results of two randomized trials in Honduras. *J Nutr, 131*(2), 262-267.

Forsyth, J. S., Ogston, S. A., Clark, A., Florey, C. D., & Howie, P. W. (1993). Relation between early introduction of solid food to infants and their weight and illnesses during the first two years of life. *BMJ, 306*(6892), 1572-1576.

Gartner, L. M., Morton, J., Lawrence, R. A., Naylor, A. J., O'Hare, D., Schanler, R. J., & et al. (2005). Breastfeeding and the use of human milk. *Pediatrics, 115*(2), 496-506.

Gerrish, C. J., & Mennella, J. A. (2001). Flavor variety enhances food acceptance in formula-fed infants. *Am J Clin Nutr, 73*(6), 1080-1085.

Gibson-Davis, C., & Brooks-Gunn, J. (2006). Couples' immigration status and ethnicity as determinants of breastfeeding. *Am J Public Health, 96*(4), 641-646.

Gill, S., Reifsnider, E., Mann, A., Villarreal, P., & Tinkle, M. (2004). Assessing infant breastfeeding beliefs among low-income Mexican Americans. *J Perinat Educ, 13*(3), 39-50.

Gonzalez-Reyes, G. (2003). *Determinants of infant feeding behaviors among a predominantly Latino population in Hartford, Connecticut.* University of Connecticut, Storrs.

Gorman, J. R., Madlensky, L., Jackson, D. J., Ganiats, T. G., & Boies, E. (2007). Early postpartum breastfeeding and acculturation among Hispanic women. *Birth, 34*(4), 308-315.

Gorman, T., Byrd, T., & VanDerslice, J. (1995). Breast-feeding practices, attitudes, and beliefs among Hispanic women and men in a border community. *Fam Community Health, 18*(2), 17-27.

Gross, R. S., Fierman, A. H., Mendelsohn, A. L., Chiasson, M. A., Rosenberg, T. J., Scheinmann, R., & et al. (2009). Maternal perceptions of infant hunger, satiety, and pressuring feeding styles in an urban Latina WIC population. *Acad Pediatr, 10*(1), 29-35.

Hannon, P. R., Willis, S. K., Bishop-Townsend, V., Martinez, I. M., & Scrimshaw, S. C. (2000). African-American and Latina adolescent mothers' infant feeding decisions and breastfeeding practices: a qualitative study. *J Adolesc Health, 26*(6), 399-407.

Harley, K., Stamm, N., & Eskenazi, B. (2007). The effect of time in the U.S. on the duration of breastfeeding in women of Mexican descent. *Matern Child Health, 11*(2), 119-125.

Heinig, M. J., Follett, J. R., Ishii, K. D., Kavanagh-Prochaska, K., Cohen, R., & Panchula, J. (2006). Barriers to compliance with infant-feeding recommendations among low-income women. *J Hum Lact, 22*(1), 27-38.

Higgins, B. (2000). Puerto Rican cultural beliefs: Influence on infant feeding practices in Western New York. *J Transcult Nurs, 11*(1), 19-30.

Hopkinson, J., & Konefal Gallagher, M. (2009). Assignment to a hospital based breastfeeding clinic and exclusive breastfeeding among immigrant Hispanic mothers: A randomized, controlled trial. *J Hum Lact, 25*(3), 287-296.

Ip, S., Chung, M., Raman, G., Chew, P., Magula, N., DeVine, D., et al. (2007). Breastfeeding and maternal and infant health outcomes in developed countries. *Evid Rep Technol Assess (Full Rep)*(153), 1-186.

Johnson, S. L., Clark, L., Goree, K., O'Connor, M., & Zimmer, L. M. (2008). Healthcare providers' perceptions of the factors contributing to infant obesity in a low-income Mexican-American community. *J Spec Pediatr Nurs, 13*(3), 180-190.

Kaufman, L., Deenadayalan, S., & Karpati, A. (2010). Breastfeeding Ambivalence Among Low-Income African American and Puerto Rican Women in North and Central Brooklyn. *Matern Child Health J, 14*(5), 696-704.

Kugyelka, J., Rasmussen, K., & Frongillo, E. (2004). Maternal obesity is negatively associated with breastfeeding success among Hispanic but not black women. *J Nutr, 134*(7), 1746-1753.

Lee, H., Elo, I., McCollum, K., & Culhane, J. (2009). Racial/ethnic differences in breastfeeding initiation and duration among low-income, inner-city mothers. *Soc Sci Q, 90*(5), 1251–1271.

Mennella, J. A., Ziegler, P., Briefel, R., & Novak, T. (2006). Feeding Infants and Toddlers Study: the types of foods fed to Hispanic infants and toddlers. *J Am Diet Assoc, 106*(1 Suppl 1), S96-106.

Newton, K., Chaudhuri, J., Grossman, X., & Merewood, A. (2009). Factors associated with exclusive brestfeeding among Latina women giving birth at an inner-city Baby-Friendly hospital. *J Hum Lact, 25*(1), 28-33.

Pachon, H., Olson, C. (1999). Retrospective analysis of exclusive breastfeeding practices among four Hispanic subgroups in New York's EFNEP. *JNE, 31*(1), 39-46.

Pérez-Escamilla, R., Himmelgreen, D., Segura-Millan, S., Gonzalez, A., Ferris, A., Damio, G., & et al. (1998). Prenatal and perinatal factors associated with breast-feeding initiation among inner-city Puerto Rican women. *J Am Diet Assoc, 98*(6), 657-663.

Pérez-Escamilla, R., & Putnik, P. (2007). The role of acculturation in nutrition, lifestyle, and incidence of type 2 diabetes among Latinos. *J Nutr, 137*(4), 860-870.

Petrova, A., Hegyi, T., & Mehta, R. (2007). Maternal race/ethnicity and one-month exclusive breastfeeding in association with the in-hospital feeding modality. *Breastfeed Med, 2*(2), 92-98.

Ramirez, R. (2004). We the people: Hispanics in the United States. Census 2000 Special Report. In U.S. Department of Commerce. Economics and Statistics Administration (Ed.): U.S. Census Bureau.

Rassin, D., Markides, K., Baranowski, T., Bee, D., Richardson, C., Mikrut, W., & et al. (1993). Acculturation and breastfeeding on the United States-Mexico border. *Am J Med Sci, 306*(1), 28-34.

Sandy, J. M., Anisfeld, E., & Ramirez, E. (2009). Effects of a prenatal intervention on breastfeeding initiation rates in a Latina immigrant sample. *J Hum Lact, 25*(4), 404-411; quiz 458-409.

Scanlon, K., Grummer-Strawn, L., Li, R., & Chen, J. (2010). Racial and ethnic differences in breastfeeding initiation and duration, by state—National Immunization Survey, United States, 2004-2008. *MMWR, 59*(11), 327-334.

Sussner, K. M., Lindsay, A. C., & Peterson, K. E. (2008). The influence of acculturation on breast-feeding initiation and duration in low-income women in the U.S. *J Biosoc Sci, 40*(5), 673-696.

Wood, S. P., Sasonoff, K. M., & Beal, J. A. (1998). Breast-feeding attitudes and practices of Latino women: a descriptive study. *J Am Acad Nurse Pract, 10*(6), 253-260.

World Health Organization. (2002a). *Guiding principles for complementary feeding of the breastfed child.* Geneva, Switzerland: World Health Organization.

World Health Organization. (2002b). *Infant and young child nutrition: Global strategy on infant and young child feeding* (Vol. A55). Geneva, Switzerland: World Health Organization.

World Health Organization. (2005). *Guiding principles for feeding non-breastfed children 6-24 months of age.* Geneva: World Health Organization.

Ziegler, P., Hanson, C., Ponza, M., Novak, T., & Hendricks, K. (2006). Feeding Infants and Toddlers Study: meal and snack intakes of Hispanic and non-Hispanic infants and toddlers. *J Am Diet Assoc, 106*(1 Suppl 1), S107-123.

CHAPTER FOUR

MY CHILD IS NOT FAT, HE'S JUST CHUBBY
A LATINO/A[1] PARENTING PERSPECTIVE

Norma Olvera,[2] Gretchen George[3] and Lucia L. Kaiser[3]

Introduction

"No come nada" (he doesn't eat anything) said a Latino mother of an obese toddler to her pediatrician (Garcia, 2004). Many Latino parents, especially those of younger children, may be unaware that their children are overweight[4] and eating too much unhealthy food. They may not realize how their own beliefs, attitudes and behaviors work against their intentions of raising a healthy child. To work more effectively with Latino parents, health practitioners and policy-makers need to know how and why certain parenting practices related to food and physical activity increase the chances of a child becoming overweight. This information is needed to increase awareness and to motivate and enable parents to adopt positive parenting practices and a lifestyle that supports optimal health for all members of their family. The purpose of this chapter is to discuss the role of Latino parents in promoting normal growth and health in their children. We

[1]The Latino or Hispanic terms will be used interchangeably across the entire chapter to maintain the original ethnic affiliation terminology used in cited articles.
[2]University of Houston.
[3]University of California-Davis.
[4]Overweight in children is defined as having a body mass index (BMI) for age and sex at or above the 85th percentile of the growth reference. Obesity is defined as having a BMI for age and sex at or above the 95th percentile.

begin with a brief overview of the prevalence of childhood obesity in the United States, followed by a discussion of dietary patterns, physical activity and sociocultural factors that contribute to the childhood obesity problem in Latinos. Next, the relationship of parenting and feeding styles and practices to child nutritional outcomes is examined. We conclude this chapter with recommendations for researchers, practitioners and policy-makers.

PREVALENCE OF OVERWEIGHT IN LATINO CHILDREN AND YOUTH

An estimated 31.7% of U.S. children ages 2-19 years are overweight or obese (Ogden, Carroll, Curtin, Lamb and Flegal, 2010). For non-Hispanic white children ages 6-19, 17% are obese. In Mexican-American children ages 6-19 years, 23.4% are obese. Even by 2-5 years of age, ethnic disparities in childhood obesity are apparent. Overweight and obesity in children raise health concerns of type 2 diabetes, hypertension, high cholesterol, stroke, heart disease, cancer and arthritis occurring in adulthood (Flegal, Ogden & Carroll, 2004).

CONTRIBUTORS TO OVERWEIGHT IN CHILDREN

Children need a balanced, healthy diet and regular physical activity to grow and develop normally. A healthy, balanced diet includes whole grains; a wide variety of vegetables and fruits; low-fat dairy products; lean fish, poultry and meat; and legumes, nuts and seeds (U.S. Department of Agriculture, 2005). Especially among children, foods and beverages that are high in fat or added sugar can easily replace healthier food and beverage choices, making their diets less nutritious overall (i.e., less nutrient dense). When children consume extra calories, above what is needed for normal growth, development and physical activity, they gain weight too rapidly and become overweight. It is crucial to understand that children can become overweight and still lack important nutrients needed for normal development and health. For example, iron-deficiency, along with obesity, is a concern in young Latino children (Brotanek, Halterman, Auinger, Flores & Weitzman, 2005). Some of the same child-feeding practices (for example prolonged bottle feeding with cow's milk) can influence both outcomes (Bonuck & Kahn, 2002). Deficiencies of iron and other nutrients can affect early brain development and behavior, resulting in lower cognitive performance that persists over time (Lozoff, Jimenez & Smith, 2006; Benton, 2008). Focus group research suggests that many Latino parents can identify foods that are healthy for the body and those that are not; however, the link between over-consumption of high fat/high sugar food, lack of physical activity and childhood obesity is not always clear (Kaiser, Martinez, Harwood & Garcia,1999; Gomel & Zamora, 2007; Guendelman, Fernald, Neufeld & Fuentes-Afflick, 2010).

SPECIFIC DIETARY AND PHYSICAL ACTIVITY PRACTICES

To promote normal growth and good health among children, health practitioners and policy-makers should be aware of specific behaviors that contribute to or interfere with healthy eating, active lifestyle and related attitudes and perceptions among Latino parents.

100% JUICE AND SWEETENED BEVERAGES

In Latino children, intake of sweetened beverages (carbonated sodas and fruit-flavored drinks) and even excessive 100% juice consumption is related to an increased risk of overweight (Tanasescu, Ferris, Himmelgreen, Rodriguez & Pérez-Escamilla, 2000; Ariza, Chen, Binns & Christoffel, 2004; Warner, Harley, Bradman, Vargas & Eskenazi, 2006). Although cross-sectional studies do not prove that excessive consumption of sweetened beverages actually causes Latino children to become overweight, there are several nutritional reasons to be concerned about excessive consumption of sweetened beverages and juice. Soft drinks, fruit-flavored beverages and juice do not provide the satiety that solid foods or whole fruit provide and may increase total energy consumption (O'Connor, Yang & Nicklas, 2006). The American Academy of Pediatrics (AAP) has noted that 100% fruit juice, while more nutritious than soda, is still not nutritionally superior to whole fruits (Committee on Nutrition, 2001). Whole fruits contain more fiber, vitamins and minerals and are consumed at a slower rate than juice, fruit drinks or sweetened beverages. Early introduction to 100% juice and fruit-flavored drinks may replace more nutritious beverages (like milk) in the child's diet (Skinner, Ziegler & Ponza, 2004). As children grow older, their preferences begin to shift from juice to less nutritious beverage choices, including carbonated drinks (Skinner & Carruth, 2001). According to a national study, infants and toddlers begin to increase intake of sweetened beverages by 9 to 24 months of age (Briefel, Reidy, Karwc, Jankowski & Hendricks, 2004). Intake of fruit-flavored beverages is higher among Hispanic than non-Hispanic infants and toddlers (Mennella, Ziegler, Briefel & Novak, 2006). Latino parents should be aware of the American Academy of Pediatrics guidelines (Table 1) regarding juice consumption and provide nutritious beverages, including milk and water, to their children.

Table 1. AAP Guidelines for Maximum Daily Fruit Juice Consumption

Child's Age	Amount of Fruit Juice
0—6 Months	Not Recommended
6 Months—6 Years	4—6 Fluid Ounces
7—18 Years	8—12 Fluid Ounces

Source: Committee on Nutrition, 2001.

Fried and high-fat foods

Fried and high-fat fast foods may be very high in calories and are linked to excess weight gain in U.S. children and youth (Taveras et al., 2005). By the age of 18 to 24 months, 25% of U.S. children consume chips or other salty, high-fat snacks (Briefel et al., 2004). Television advertising influences Latino families to spend more money on snack foods and provide more high-fat foods to their children (Ayala et al., 2007). To enable children to grow normally, Latino parents should be encouraged to use lower fat cooking methods (less fried foods and fatty cuts of meat) and good sources of fat (nuts, seeds, plant oils) in the home and to reduce consumption of fast food and high-fat snack foods away from home.

Overall diet quality

High quality diets include foods that are low in energy or calories and good sources of vitamins, minerals, fiber and other nutrients. Examples of nutrient-rich, also known as nutrient-dense, foods in the Latino diet are vegetables (tomato, squash, carrot, salsa); fruits (mango, orange, banana); legumes; corn tortillas; and low-fat animal products (without skin, not fried). In national studies of U.S. preschool children, higher quality diets, as measured by a healthy eating index, are associated with a lower prevalence of childhood obesity (Kranz, Findeis & Shrestha, 2008). Compared to other ethnic groups, young Mexican-American children have higher quality diets. Intake of fruit (including juice) is higher in Mexican-American children ages 2-18 years than in non-Hispanic white children (Lorson, Melgar-Quiñonez & Taylor, 2009) whereas, vegetable intake is similar. However, 66% of Mexican-American children do not meet MyPyramid recommendations for fruit and 82% do not meet the recommendations for vegetables. In the *Viva la Familia*[6] study of 1,030 low-income Hispanic children (mostly Mexican-origin), few differences in dietary intake were found between overweight and normal weight children (Wilson, Adolph & Butte, 2009). Diets of both overweight and normal weight children were low in fruit, vegetables, fiber and high in saturated fat, sodium and cholesterol. Compared to normal weight girls, those who were overweight consumed less fruit. Overweight children—boys and girls—did consume more total energy and fat than normal weight children. Overweight children also consumed more beverages (other than juice and milk), compared to normal weight children. Beverage intake in this population appears to be a key factor associated with lower intakes of most nutrients, except sodium and vitamin C. Making high quality foods and beverages available for meals and snacks, especially more fruit and vegetables, is an important responsibility of the parents, other caregivers, and schools to support normal child growth and to promote good health.

---

[6]Viva la Familia was a cross-sectional study, conducted in Houston Texas from 2000-2004, among 1,030 Hispanic children and adolescents, ages 4-19 years.

MEAL AND SNACK PATTERNS

Another important responsibility of parents is to provide a regular structure of meals and snacks. Common advice to parents of young children is to take responsibility for deciding what foods to serve and when to serve them, while allowing the child to decide how much to eat and even whether to eat (Satter, 1986). When parents provide limited structure or routines and respond too easily to requests, the children may fill up during the day on high-fat, high-sugar snack foods and sweetened beverages that they can easily access by themselves from the refrigerator or pantry. Young children tend to eat according to their appetite, but their parents can override their natural ability to stop eating when full. After snacking all day, they are not hungry at mealtime but can be coaxed into eating more food by parental use of threats and bribes. In many Latino households with young children, child-led snacking and the use of bribes and threats are both very common (Kaiser et al.,1999; Kaiser, Melgar-Quiñonez, Lamp, Johns & Harwood, 2001). Where there is less family support for healthy lifestyle patterns and larger families, more child-led snacking occurs (Ayala et al., 2007). In focus groups, Mexican-American parents of preschoolers have expressed ambivalence about the desirability of sticking to regular meal and snack schedules for young children but some also recognize a potential connection between constant snacking and overweight (Kaiser et al., 1999; Guendelman et al., 2010). Serving a large portion of food to a young child and insisting that he or she eat a certain amount can also lead to overfeeding and an unlearning of natural satiety signals (Fisher, Arreola, Birch & Rolls, 2007). Moreover, when the child is not hungry at mealtime, the opportunity to taste new foods or develop a preference for traditional Latino foods may be missed (Kaiser et al., 2001). Free access to foods has been associated with increased body weight in younger children (Ariza et al, 2004). Rather than a steady stream of chips, cookies, candy and sweetened beverages throughout the day, young children need three meals and at least two regular snacks that provide whole grains; a wide variety of vegetables and fruits; low-fat dairy products; lean fish, poultry and meat; and legumes, nuts and seeds (US Department of Agriculture, 2005). Latino parents may need reassurance that, in providing more structure and opportunities for physical activity, the goal of bringing children to the table with an appetite to enjoy family meals will be easier to attain.

PHYSICAL ACTIVITY

Obtaining enough calories from a balanced, healthy diet and regular physical activity (at least one hour on most days of the week) are key ingredients for normal child growth and development (U.S. Department of Agriculture, 2005). Physical activity levels significantly decrease in Mexican-American children as they grow older. In the *Viva la Familia* study conducted among 897 Latino children, the percentage of children engaging in at least one hour per day declined from 87% in four- to eight-year-olds to only 37% in twelve- to nineteen-year-olds (Butte, Puyau, Adolph, Vohra & Zakeri, 2007). Mexican-American boys stay more active than girls over time. Compared to normal weight children, overweight Latino children are less active, and their parents provide less support for them to engage in physical activity (Butte et al., 2007; Elder et al., 2010). Low physical activity may not only be due to a lack of parent encouragement but also to an unsafe environment. Depending on the socioeconomic status of the family, neighborhoods and access to safe outdoor play areas may vary. This can contribute to overall reduced activity for the child and family (Martinez, Arredondo, Perez & Baquero, 2009). Parents can support habits of physical activity in children to sustain these lifestyle patterns and prevent obesity later in life.

OTHER FACTORS

Besides these specific nutrition and physical activity behaviors, certain familial factors contribute to overweight in Latino children. These factors are described elsewhere in this book with more detail but are mentioned briefly here. In Puerto Rican and Mexican children, mother's weight status is associated with an increased risk of the child being overweight (Tanasescu et al, 2000; Melgar-Quiñonez & Kaiser ,2004). Maternal obesity before pregnancy and high birth weight are other risk factors in this population and suggest that the prenatal environment influences later development of obesity.

ROLE OF SOCIOCULTURAL FACTORS

Acculturation As immigrants adopt the attitudes, beliefs, practices and lifestyle of their new country, child-feeding practices may also change and thus influence childhood obesity (Kaiser et al., 2001; Hays, Power & Olvera, 2001). Does acculturation increase the risk of childhood obesity? The research findings on this question are conflicting. One study reported no relationship between maternal acculturation and risk of overweight among Latino preschoolers in Chicago (Ariza et al., 2004). A California study also found that greater maternal acculturation, based on the Marin scale, was not associated with risk of overweight among Mexican-American preschoolers, but was related to larger tricep skinfolds, a measure of body fatness (Kaiser et al., 2001). In contrast, an observational study reported that exclusive Spanish-language usage was associated with higher body mass index in a cohort of Latino children in Massachusetts (Sussner, Lindsay & Peterson, 2009). In other studies, longer residence in United States, maternal "Americanization score," or having a U.S.-born mother increased the risk of overweight in children (Ahn, Juon & Gittelsohn, 2008;

Fuentes-Afflick & Hessol, 2008; Reifsnider & Ritsema, 2008). Potential explanations for the discrepancies include failure to control for confounders; differences in the measures of acculturation and anthropometry used; and place of origin differences including not only country of birth, but also whether immigrants have come from rural or urban communities (Pérez-Escamilla, 2009).

FOOD INSECURITY

Parenting practices and attitudes of Latino parents have different effects on dietary intake and weight status of children, depending on the level of current food insecurity (Matheson, Robinson, Varady & Killen, 2006). Both past and current experience of food insecurity may influence child-feeding practices in Latino families. Focus group studies among Latino mothers describe how immigrants, who experienced food deprivation during childhood, may feel the need to compensate by giving their children "what they didn't have," going out to eat more often or serving large portions of food (Kuyper et al., 2006; Sussner, Greaney & Peterson, 2008). Latino mothers who report greater past food insecurity are less likely to monitor sweets and snack foods closely (Kuyper, Smith & Kaiser, 2009). Current periodic household shortages of foods due to food insecurity are associated with lower intake of fruit and vegetables among children (Dave, Evans, Saunders, Watkins & Pfeiffer, 2009). A bi-national study found that food insecurity affects dietary patterns differently among young children in rural Mexico and their immigrant counterparts in California (Rosas et al., 2009). In rural Mexico, greater food insecurity is associated with lower consumption of meat, dairy products and fruit and higher consumption of beans, resulting in lower energy intake overall. In contrast, greater food insecurity among the immigrant children living in California is associated with higher intake of sweets and fried snacks and higher energy, total fat and saturated fat intakes. One possible reason for this result is the relative affordability and availability of high-fat snack foods in low-income communities in the United States.

PERCEPTION OF OVERWEIGHT

A review of the literature from 2000-2007 suggest that parents, including Latino parents, do not perceive their children to be overweight (Olvera, Sharma, Suminski, Rodriguez & Power, 2007; Ward, 2008). From the perspective of an immigrant Latino parent who previously resided in a setting with high incidence of infections and parasites, the thin child, rather than the chubby one, is at risk of health problems. In the United States, a Latino parent's perception of health appears related to the absence of conditions that interfere with normal activities (Crawford et al., 2004). In a cohort study (n=184), a mother's perception that her child's health is poor or fair was associated with decreased risk of overweight (Fuentes-Afflick & Hessol, 2008). Thus, a "chubby child" who is happy, active, and "eating well" by the mother's standards would not necessarily be viewed as having a health risk.

With more exposure to public health messages about the extent and consequences of childhood obesity, parental attitudes about weight may be changing. A binational study examined maternal perceptions and attitudes in focus group discussions conducted among 84 Mexican-origin mothers in Mexico and California (Guendelman et al., 2010). In California, particularly in the urban groups, mothers expressed more concerns and fears and less acceptance of overweight than their Mexican counterparts. The California mothers also identified a smaller body size (on the Stunkard scale) as being ideal compared to Mexican mothers. In a Texas study of Mexican-American six- to twelve-year-old children, maternal acculturation level was associated positively with the girls', but not with boys', choice of thinner figures as an ideal body size (Olvera, Suminski & Power, 2005). Thus, health practitioners need to be aware that Latino attitudes regarding the relationships between child diet, weight status and health may be changing over time and need to pay attention to assess current attitudes and beliefs in their service populations.

GENERAL PARENTING AND FEEDING STYLES

Characterized by the levels of parental control and responsiveness, general parenting style is defined as a constellation of attitudes that are communicated to the child and create an emotional climate in which the parent's behaviors are expressed (Baumrind, 1966; Darling & Steinberg, 1993). Overall parenting style influences not only parental feeding style and practices but also the approach to other areas of child care, like potty training, bedtime routines, discipline, etc. Most researchers describe general parenting style in terms of the four types shown in Table 2 (Baumrind, 1966; Maccoby & Martin, 1983). *Authoritative* parenting is generally considered to be the most helpful for child socialization of healthy behaviors (Baumrind, 1966). *Authoritative* parenting seems to provide both the structure and support needed for children to internalize and sustain positive behaviors (Grolnick & Farkas, 2002). Similarly, in terms of health outcomes in children, authoritative parenting, compared to other parenting styles, is often associated with better nutrition outcomes, including higher levels of fruit consumption (Kremers, Brug, de Vries & Engels, 2003), more physical activity (Schmitz et al., 2002) and *lowest* risk for child obesity (Rhee, Lumeng, Appugliese, Kaciroti & Bradley, 2006; Wake, Nicholson, Hardy & Smith, 2007). Authoritative parenting may help children regulate food intake

Table 2: Four Parenting Styles

Responsiveness (Warmth)	Control (Demandingness)	
	Low	High
Low	Neglectful, uninvolved • Very few demands and non-supportive • No rules or structure • Little input from parent	Authoritarian • Use of directive strategies such as commands • Strict rules • Little input from child
High	Permissive, indulgent • Makes few demands, but when a demand is made, it is supportive and non-directive • Inconsistent rules or structure • Little input from parent	Authoritative • Use non-directive strategies such as questions, suggestions, offer choices • Age-appropriate rules •Considers input from child

Source: Baumrind, 1966; Maccoby & Martin, 1983.

through promoting the development of children's self-regulation (Kitzman, Dalton & Buscemi, 2008). Studies differ, however, on the parenting styles associated with the *highest* risk for obesity. In a longitudinal study, Rhee and colleagues (2006) reported that children of authoritarian parents were at the greatest risk. In contrast, Wake et al. (2007) found that children of indulgent and uninvolved fathers, but not mothers, showed the greatest risk. It is also noteworthy to point out that some studies have reported no association between parenting style and child weight status (Agras, Hammer, McNicholas & Kraemer, 2004; Gable & Lutz, 2000).

Few studies have examined parenting styles in Latino parents, particularly related to child weight. A cross-sectional study in Mexico found a positive relationship between permissive parenting style and body weight of middle-class school children (Brewis, 2003). In a longitudinal study in a sample of 69 low-income Mexican-American mothers and their four- to eight-year-old children, children of indulgent mothers were more likely to become overweight three years later than children of authoritative or authoritarian mothers (Olvera & Power, 2010).

Researchers have argued for the studying of parenting styles as they related to a specific context (Constanzo & Woody, 1985; Hoerr et al., 2009). Based on this paradigm, the concept of *feeding* styles has been introduced in this area of research. The focus of the feeding style is on the structure and responsiveness of the parent to the child's cues of hunger or satiety within a general parenting style framework. Thus, the difference between parenting style and parental feeding style is that the latter applies only to the domain of feeding children and not to other aspects of the parent-child relationship. A parent's feeding style can then be characterized according to the four types shown in Table 2 as the measures (e.g., Caregiver Feeding Style) were developed based on the general parenting paradigm.

Studies using this new conceptualization have shown positive associations between indulgent and uninvolved/neglectful parenting *feeding* styles and weight status in minority children (Hughes, Power, Fisher, Mueller & Nicklas, 2005; Hughes, Shewchuk, Baskin, Nicklas & Qu, 2008). These findings are inconsistent with studies showing a positive association between children's weight status and authoritarian feeding practices (Clark, Goyder, Bissell, Blank & Peters J., 2007). Studies conducted in Latino populations have found that an authoritative feeding style is associated with a healthier dietary pattern (more vegetables and dairy), compared to the permissive, uninvolved and authoritarian styles (Patrick & Nicklas, 2005; Hoerr et al., 2009).

Latino children of indulgent mothers may be at high risk for the development of obesity for a number of reasons. First, indulgent mothers may show low levels of control in the feeding context, allowing children too many choices in today's obesogenic food environment. Second, an indulgent approach to parenting may not provide children with the guidance they need for the development of self-regulation in both the eating and non-eating domains (Lengua, Honorado & Bush, 2007). Other possible mechanisms are that indulgent mothers may not only cater more to their children's unhealthy food preferences and serve them less healthy food but also allow their children to engage in more sedentary behaviors (e.g., screen time).

CHILD-FEEDING PRACTICES

Parenting styles remain consistent but parenting practices, specifically child-feeding practices, can differ across children even within the same family depending on the child's age, gender, eating behavior and weight status (Ventura & Birch, 2008). Since parents have goals for their children's growth and development, it makes sense that their feeding practices might vary depending on their perceptions of how well their children are doing.

Child-feeding practices include the level of control the parent exerts over the type and amount of food the child eats, role modeling of eating behaviors, feeding cues or prompts given to the child and the actual mealtime environment and routine. Often, in this context, "high control" refers to not only parental attempts to restrict the amount of all or specific foods (like sweets or salty snacks), but also pressuring a child to finish a meal.

Along with overall parenting style, specific child *feeding* practices are thought to influence a child's risk for becoming overweight. Infants and very young children can self-regulate energy intake. That is, they eat when they are hungry and then stop eating when they are full. Parents who are not responsive or misunderstand their infant's cues may attempt to follow-up with a bottle of formula even when the babies are not hungry. Calming an infant with a bottle, adding cereal to the bottle and prolonged bottle-feeding are feeding practices that have been associated with increased risk of overweight in Latino children (Sherman, Alexander, Dean & Kim, 1995; Bonuck & Kahn, 2002). Thus, beginning during infancy, specific child feeding practices may play a role in the development of overweight.

In a comprehensive literature review, 19 out of 22 studies determined at least one significant association between parent feeding practices, child eating and weight status (Faith, Scanlon, Birch, Francis & Sherry., 2004). Parental restriction is most commonly associated with increased energy intake and body weight. In a study of white middle-class families, parents with "anti-fat" attitudes are more likely to use restrictive feeding practices, independently of their child's actual body size (Musher-Eizenman, Holub, Hauser & Young, 2007). However, parental attempts to restrict intake of certain foods may be counterproductive and actually lead to a stronger child demand for that food (Fisher & Birch, 1999). In white middle-class girls, the mother's perception that her daughter is too heavy is associated with attempts to restrict the daughter's intake, which in turn predicts eating even more calories and higher body weight (Birch & Fisher, 2000). Child feeding practices may vary not only as a function of characteristics of the child, such as gender and weight status, but also of the mother. Latinas who show more restraint in the selection of their own diets also offer healthier food choices to their children, whereas overeating (also referred to as a disinhibition) among mothers is associated with more frequent high-fat, high-sugar food choices in their children (Contento, Zybert & Williams, 2005).

Most studies of general parenting practices in Latino parents have focused on individual parenting dimensions (control and responsiveness) and have usually characterized them as showing high levels of parental control (Cardona, Nicholson & Fox, 2000; Chao & Kanatsu, 2008; Hill, Bush & Roosa, 2003; Varela et al, 2004). Such findings are interpreted to reflect the importance of respect for authority in Latino cultures (Knight, Virdin & Roosa, 1994). In studies examining child feeding practices (see Table 3), Latino mothers' controlling feeding practices are inconsistently related to children's eating habits and BMI.

However, a major problem with the literature related to child feeding practices is that most studies have used cross-sectional designs. This is true of the general literature, as well as those studies that have included Latino families in the samples (Ventura & Birch, 2008). Since the impact of parenting practices on children's health is not unidirectional, cross-sectional studies cannot determine

Table 3: Summary of findings related to parenting styles, child feeding practices and nutrition outcomes in quantitative studies including Latino parents

Source (Author, Year)	Study Design	Sample Size and Characteristics	Independent Variables and Instruments	Outcome (Diet)	Outcome (Overweight)
(Ariza, 2004)	Cross-sectional, interview	250 Hispanic (mostly Mex.-Am.) 5th-6th-graders, Chicago		NA	Child has free access to food at home (+) wt-for-ht > 95th (p=0.06)
(Arredondo et al. 2006)	Cross-section-al, self- admin-istered parent survey	812, Latino parents with K-2-graders, San Diego	Parenting strategies for eating and activ-ity (PEAS) scale with 5 subscales related to monitor-ing, limit setting, reinforcement, dis-cipline, control Food frequency questionnaire	Monitoring and reinforcement (+) on intake of healthy foods Control (-) on intake of healthy foods Limit-setting (-) on intake of healthy foods in boys only	NA
(Bonuck and Kahn, 2002)	Cross-sectional, interview	95, Hispanic and African American mothers and chil-dren (18-56 mos.), WIC, NY	2 items related to bottle-feeding	NA	Prolonged bot-tle-feeding (+): BMI $\geq$ 95th
(Brewis, 2003)	Cross-sectional, interview	216 Mexican chil-dren, 6-12 yrs, affluent, school, Veracruz, MX	20-item parenting beliefs scale (0-10) where high=authori-tarian and low=per-missive	NA	Permissive (+) wt for age $\geq$ 95th perc
(Elder et al., 2010)	Cross-sectional	606 Hispanic chil-dren, K-2, San Diego, school	PEAS scale (see Arredondo above)	NA	Limit setting (on snacks and TV) (+)BMI for age z-score (BMZ) Less support for physical activity (+) BMZ Control (pressure to eat) (-) BMZ
(Faith et al. 2003)	Cross-sectional, National Longi-tudinal Survey of Youth, 1986	1790 youth (18% Hispanic, 30% Afr. Am. 52% white)	3 items related to mother-child feed-ing practices Measured wt and ht of child or self-reported by the mother	NA	Allowing greater food choice (+) (p=0.06) Child compli-ance with moth-er's request (+) (p=0.06)

Source (Author, Year)	Study Design	Sample Size and Characteristics	Independent Variables and Instruments	Outcome (Diet)	Outcome (Overweight)
(Hoerr et al., 2009)	Cross-sectional, interview	715 Head Start parents (29% Hispanic, 43% Afr. Am., 28% white), TX and AL	Hughes Caregivers Feeding Styles 24 hr diet recall	Permissive and uninvolved styles (-) on intake of fruit, vegetables and dairy at home	NA
(Kersey, Lipton, Quinn and Lantos, 2010)	Cross-sectional, interview	369 immigrant Mexican parents of 2-5 year olds		NA	Attitudes/beliefs about ideal body size (0) BMI >95th percentile
(Larios, Ayala, Arredondo, Baquero, and Elder, 2009)	Cross-sectional, Instrument development	714 Latino mothers, San Diego CA	Focus groups, interviews PEAS scale, 26 items	NA	Controlling parenting strategies (-) on BMI z-scores
(Matheson, Robinson, Varady, and Killen, 2006)	Cross-sectional, interview	108 Mex. Am parents and 5th-grade children, CA	Child Feeding Questionnaire 3- 24 hr diet recalls	Pressure to eat (+) on vegetable intake (in food-secure households only)	Pressure to eat (-) on BMI percentiles Restriction (0) Modeling (0)
(May et al., 2007)	Cross-sectional, Pediatric Nutrition Surveillance System	967 low-income mothers of preschoolers, WIC, Minnesota	4 Items from Child Feeding Questionnaire related to restriction and pressure to eat	NA	Mother's concern about child's becoming overweight positively related to restriction Restriction and BMI-for age z-scores (BMZ) (0) Pressure to eat all or enough (0) and BMZ
(Melgar-Quiñonez and Kaiser, 2004)	Cross-sectional, interview	206 Mex-Am, parents of preschoolers, CA	12 items based on child feeding strategies reported by Latino parents	NA	Child has free access to food at home (-) on BMI >95th percentile
(Olvera and Power, 2009)	Longitudinal, 4-year follow-up	69 Mex. Am 4-8 year olds	Parent Dimension Inventory, 58 items to define parenting style	NA	Indulgent style associated with greater wt gain (+), compared to authoritative or authoritarian

Source (Author, Year)	Study Design	Sample Size and Characteristics	Independent Variables and Instruments	Outcome (Diet)	Outcome (Overweight)
(Patrick et al., 2005)	Cross-sectional	231 Caregivers (53% Hispanic), Head Start, TX	Caregivers Feeding Style questionnaire Food frequency items to assess food patterns	Authoritative feeding (+) on dairy and veg-etable intake Authoritarian (-) vegetable intake	NA
(Robinson, Kiernan, Matheson and Haydel,2001)	Cross-sectional, population-based	792 third-graders, CA, 18.5 -20% Lati-no	6 items from Child Feeding Question-naire	NA	Parent control (-) to BMI and triceps skin-folds in girls only (p=0.05)
(Sherman, Alexander, Dean and Kim, 1995)	Cross-sectional, interview	189 Mex.-Am. and 188 Anglo mother-child pairs, WIC	Maternal Feeding Practices (21-item)	NA	Calming baby with a bottle to stop crying (+) and wt-for-ht $\geq$ 85th percentile Putting cereal in the bottle (+) & wt-for-ht: $\geq$ 85th percentile

BMI: body mass index (kg/ meters squared)
(+)Indicates a significant positive association or relationship
(-) Indicates a significant negative or inverse association or relationship
(0) Indicates no significant association or relationship
(+)Indicates a significant positive association or relationship
(-) Indicates a significant negative or inverse association or relationship
(0) Indicates no significant association or relationship

whether parenting practices actually cause children to be overweight. For exam-ple, does setting limits lead children to overeat *because* their favorite foods are withheld or do parents begin to set limits *because* the children are overweight? Due to lack of longitudinal and intervention studies, at best one can only con-clude that an association exists.

Recommendations for Researchers, Practitioners and Policy-Makers

Although there is a growing body of work related to parenting styles, feed-ing styles, feeding practices and child growth in Latinos, there are no published, controlled interventions to establish evidence-based recommendations for this population. At best, we can identify the gaps and several potential "best prac-tices" that might be implemented and evaluated in future studies.

RESEARCHERS

- Most of the research has used cross-sectional designs. More longitudinal and intervention studies are needed. Studies examining child feeding practices yield some conflicting findings. Reasons may in part be due to the cross-sectional design but also to the use of different instruments or methods to measure feeding practices. More research is needed to validate the accuracy of existing feeding questionnaire in Latino populations and to develop more culturally appropriate feeding measures if needed.
- More research is needed related to the influence of parenting styles and feeding practices in both late infancy and toddler phases also among children who are normal weight and overweight.
- Future work should examine how to intervene effectively among parents with different feeding styles. The role of food insecurity—both past and current may be an important factor influencing how parenting styles, feeding practices and attitudes affect nutrition outcomes and should be examined.

PRACTITIONERS

- Especially among parents of young children (preschoolers and younger), parental awareness of a weight issue is low, regardless of ethnic group (May et al., 2007). Thus, public health efforts should focus on educating Latino parents about weight guidelines for children. Implementation of better screening, counseling and referral protocols within the health care system are important to persuade Latino parents that childhood obesity is a serious problem that increases the risk of obesity, type 2 diabetes and other health problems later in life.
- Physicians and other health professionals should encourage breastfeeding in the first year of life, with appropriate introduction to solid foods.
- Physicians and other health professionals should advocate for healthy eating and regular physical activity to prevent obesity-related problems.
- Practitioners need to ask parents about their perceptions of the child's healthy weight and overall development, without assuming Latino parents automatically prefer a "chubby" or "thin" child body size.
- In recent years, the focus for intervention has been heavily on the preschool years, with the premise that earlier interventions is likely to be more effective. However, teaching Latino parents of infants and toddlers how to read and respond appropriately to the child's cues is very important.
- Although overall parenting style, especially a permissive style, appears to be most consistently related to poorer outcomes in Latinos, changing parenting style, which reflects in part personality, is not necessarily the target for intervention. Instead, emphasize providing advice or education on child feeding practices that is most appropriate to that parent's style. For example, parents

with a permissive or indulgent style might be encouraged to establish meal-time routines, shop for foods without bringing their children, become aware of how advertising influences their family's food choices and stock the refrigerator and pantry with more nutritious foods. Parents with an authoritarian style and those who expect children to finish their plate may need additional education about what is an appropriate portion size for a young child and how allowing frequent child-led snacking undermines appetite at meal times.

• Latino parents need parenting advice that enables them to strike a balance between offering too little and too much choice, not just in the realm of feeding but other areas as well.

POLICY-MAKERS

Health interventions that take into account Latino parenting styles can only become effective if the environment changes needed for providing the access necessary for better child food choices are implemented at the same time. Thus, policy-makers must consider the potential for complementing behaviorally focused interventions targeting parents with supportive environmental changes. For example, some policies to consider may include the following:

• Restrict soda and candy sales in schools

• Require fast food outlets and other restaurants to list the nutritional content of the foods they sell. Limit providing free toys with unhealthy foods. Consider options for adding a tax to soda and other sweetened beverages.

• Support physical education classes at schools and other opportunities for physical activity during recess and through participation in sports after school programs.

• Improve safety at parks and neighborhoods to increase minutes of recreational activity.

• Increase funding for behavior change theory-based education that takes into account parenting styles and feeding styles.

Summary and Conclusions on Parenting and Nutrition

Because parental attitudes toward child rearing are influenced by cultural norms and contextual factors, the effects of different parenting styles often vary and need to be studied carefully across ethnic groups. Thus, to intervene effectively in Latino populations, a culture-specific framework related to parenting and child nutrition is needed. A major limitation with the current literature related to parenting styles and child feeding practices is that most studies have used cross-sectional designs. Findings from these studies are often conflicting and difficult to interpret. More longitudinal and intervention studies are needed. Studies that have examined the overall parenting style or parent feeding style are yielding a more consistent picture than those focused on specific feeding practices, with permissive or indulgent styles being related to lower quality diets, higher body weight and greater weight gain. It may well be possible that both permissive feeding related to snacking and more controlling parental behaviors at mealtimes work in combination to influence excessive weight gain in Latino children. Especially for parents who say *"no come nada,"* greater awareness is needed of how much food is actually consumed by children who snack all day long and the long-term health consequences of childhood obesity.

References

Agras, W., Hammer, L., McNicholas, F., & Kraemer, H. (2004). Risk factors for childhood overweight: A prospective study from birth to 9.5 years. *Journal of Pediatrics, 145,* 20-25.

Ahn, M. K., Juon, H. S., & Gittelsohn, J. (2008). Association of race/ethnicity, socioeconomic status, acculturation, and environmental factors with risk of overweight among adolescents in California, 2003. *Prevention of Chronic Disease 5*(3), A75.

Ariza, A. J, Chen, E. H., Binns, H. J., & Christoffel, K. K. (2004). Risk factors for overweight in five- to six-year-old Hispanic-American children: A pilot study. *Journal Urban Health, 81*(1): 150-161.

Arredondo, E. M., Elder, J. P., Ayala, G. X., Campbell, N., Baquero, B., & Duerksen, S. (2006). Is parenting style related to children's healthy eating and physical activity in Latino families? *Health Education Reseach, 21*(6): 862-871.

Ayala, G. X., Baquero, B., Arredondo, E. M., Campbell, N., Larios, S., & Elder, J. P. (2007). Association between family variables and Mexican-American children's dietary behaviors. *Journal of Nutrition Education Behavior, 39*(2): 62-69.

Baumrind, D. (1966). Effects of authoritative control on child behavior. *Child Development, 37*: 887-907.

Benton, D. (2008). Micronutrient status, cognition and behavioral problems in childhood. *European Journal of Nutrition, 47*(3): 38-50.

Birch, L. L., & Fisher, J. O. (2000). Mothers' child-feeding practices influence daughters' eating and weight. *American Journal of Clinical Nutrition, 71*(5): 1054-1061.

Bonuck, K. A., & Kahn R. (2002). Prolonged bottle use and its association with iron deficiency anemia and overweight: A preliminary study. *Clinical Pediatrics (Phila), 41*(8): 603-607.

Brewis, A. (2003). Biocultural aspects of obesity in young Mexican schoolchildren. *American Journal of Human Biology, 15*(3): 446-460.

Briefel, R. R, Reidy, K., Karwe V., Jankowski, L., & Hendricks K. (2004). Toddlers' transition to table foods: Impact on nutrient intakes and food patterns. *Journal of American Diet Association, 104* (1): S38-44.

Brotanek, J. M., Halterman, J. S., Auinger, P., Flores, G., & Weitzman, M. (2005). Iron deficiency, prolonged bottle-feeding, and racial/ethnic disparities in young children. *Archives of Pediatric Adolescent Medicine, 159*(11): 1038-1042.

Butte, N. F., Puyau, M. R., Adolph, A. L.,Vohra, F. A., & Zakeri, I. (2007). Physical activity in non-overweight and overweight Hispanic children and adolescents. *Medicine & Science in Sports & Exercise, 39*: 1257-1266.

Cardona, P. G., B. Nicholson, C., & Fox, R. A. (2000). Parenting among Hispanic and Anglo-American mothers with young children. *Journal of Social Psychology, 140*: 357-365.

Chao, R., & Kanatsu A. (2008). Beyond socioeconomics: Explaining ethnic group differences in parenting through cultural and immigration processes. *Applied Developmental Science, 12*: 181-187.

Clark, H. R., Goyder, E., Bissell, P., Blank, L., & Peters J. (2007). How do parents' child-feeding behaviours influence child weight? Implications for childhood obesity policy. *Journal of Public Health, 29*, 132-141.

Committee on Nutrition, American Academy of Pediatrics. (2001). The use and misuse of fruit juice in pediatrics. *Pediatrics, 107*(5): 1210-1213.

Contento, I. R., Zybert, P., & Williams, S. S. (2005). Relationship of cognitive restraint of eating and disinhibition to the quality of food choices of Latina women and their young children. *Preventive Medicine, 40*(3): 326-336.

Costanzo, P. R., & Woody, E. Z. (1985). Domain-specific parenting styles and their impact on the child's development of particular deviance: the example of obesity proneness. *Journal of Social and Clinical Psychology, 4*: 425-445.

Crawford, P. B., Gosliner, W., Anderson, C., Strode, P., Becerra-Jones, Y., Samuels, S., Carroll, A. M., & Ritchie, L. D. (2004). Counseling Latina mothers of preschool children about weight issues: suggestions for a new framework. *Journal of American Diet Association, 104*(3): 387-94.

Darling, N., & Steinberg L. (1993). Parenting style as context: an integrative model. *Psychological Bulletin, 113*(3): 487-496.

Dave, J. M., Evans, A. E., Saunders, R. P., Watkins, K. W., & Pfeiffer, K. A. (2009). Associations among food insecurity, acculturation, demographic factors, and fruit and vegetable intake at home in Hispanic children. *Journal of American Diet Association, 109*(4), 697-701.

Elder, J. P., Arredondo, E. M., Campbell, N., Baquero, B., Duerksen, S., Ayala, G., Crespo N. C., Slymen, D., & McKenzie, T. (2010). Individual, family, and community environmental correlates of obesity in Latino elementary school children. *Journal of School Health, 80*(1): 20-30.

Faith, M. S., Heshka S., Keller, K. L., Sherry, K. L., B., Matz, P. E., Pietrobelli, A. & Allison, D. B. (2003). Maternal-child feeding patterns and child body weight: findings from a population-based sample. *Archive of Pediatric Adolescent Medicine, 157*(9): 926-932.

Faith, M. S., Scanlon, K. S., Birch, L. L., Francis, L. A., & Sherry, B. (2004). Parent-child feeding strategies and their relationships to child eating and weight status. *Obesity Research, 12*(11): 1711-1722.

Fisher, J. O., Arreola, A., Birch, L. L., & Rolls, B. J. (2007). Portion size effects on daily energy intake in low-income Hispanic and African American children and their mothers. *American Journal of Clinical Nutrition, 86*(6): 1709-1716.

Fisher, J. O., & Birch L. L. (1999). Restricting access to palatable foods affects children's behavioral response, food selection, and intake. *American Journal of Clinical Nutrition, 69*(6): 1264-1272.

Flegal, K. M., Ogden, C. L., & Carroll, M. D. (2004). Prevalence and trends in overweight in Mexican-American adults and children. *Nutrition Review, 62*(7): S144-148.

Fuentes-Afflick, E., & Hessol N. A. (2008). Overweight in young Latino children. *Archive of Medical Research, 39*(5): 511-518.

Gable, S., & Lutz, S. (2000). Household, parent, and child contributions to childhood obesity. *Family Relations, 49*, 293-300.

Garcia, R. S. (2004). No come nada. *Health Affairs, (Millwood) 23*(2): 215-219.

Gomel, J. N., & Zamora A. (2007). English- and Spanish-speaking Latina mothers' beliefs about food, health, and mothering. *Journal of Immigrant & Minority Health, 9*(4): 359-367.

Grolnick, W. S., & Farkas, M. Eds. (2002). Parenting and the development of children's self-regulation. In *Handbook of parenting:* Vol. 5. *Practical issues in parenting* Mahwah, NJ, Lawrence Erlbaum Associates.

Guendelman, S., Fernald, L. C, Neufeld, L. M., & Fuentes-Afflick, E. (2010). Maternal perceptions of early childhood ideal body weight differ among Mexican-origin mothers residing in Mexico compared to California. *Journal of the American Dietetic Association, 110*(2): 222-229.

Hays, J., Power, T. G., & Olvera, N. (2001). Effects of maternal socialization strategies on children's nutrition knowledge and behavior. *Applied Developmental Psychology, 22*, 421-437.

Hill, N. E., Bush, K. R., & Roosa, M. W. (2003). Parenting and family socialization strategies and children's mental health: Low-income Mexican-American and Euro-American mothers and children. *Child Development, 74*: 189-204.

Hoerr, S. L., Hughes, S. O., Fisher, J. O., Nicklas, T. A., Liu, Y., & Shewchuk, R. M. (2009). Associations among parental feeding styles and children's food intake in families with limited incomes. *International Journal of Behavioral Nutrition & Physical Activity, 6*: 55.

Hughes, S. O., Power, T. G., Fisher, J. O., Mueller, S., & Nicklas, T. A. (2005). Revisiting a neglected construct: Parenting styles in a child-feeding context. *Appetite, 44*(1): 83-92.

Hughes, S. O., Shewchuk, R. M., Baskin, M. L., Nicklas, T. A., & Qu, H. (2008). Indulgent feeding style and children's weight status in preschool. *Journal of Developmental Behavior and Pediatrics, 29*(5): 403-410

Kaiser, L. L., Martinez, N. A., Harwood, J. O., & Garcia, L. C. (1999). Child feeding strategies in low-income Latino households: focus group observations. *Journal of American Dietetic Association, 99*(5): 601-603.

Kaiser, L. L., Melgar-Quiñonez, H. R., Lamp, C. L., Johns, M. C., & Harwood, J. O. (2001). Acculturation of Mexican-American mothers influences child feeding strategies. *Journal of the American Dietetic Association, 101*(5): 542-547.

Kersey, M., R. Lipton, R., Quinn, M. T., & Lantos, J. D. (2010). Overweight in Latino preschoolers: do parental health beliefs matter? *American Journal of Health Behavior, 34*(3): 340-348.

Kranz, S., Findeis, J. L., & Shrestha, S. S. (2008). Use of the Revised Children's Diet Quality Index to assess preschooler's diet quality, its sociodemographic predictors, and its association with body weight status. *Journal of Pediatrics, 84*(1): 26-34.

Kitzmann, K. M., Dalton, W. T., & Buscemi, J. (2008). Beyond parenting practices: Family context and the treatment of pediatric obesity. *Family Relations, 57*, 13-23.

Kremers, S., Brug, J., de Vries, H., & Engels, R. C. (2003). Parenting style and adolescent fruit consumption. *Appetite, 41*: 43-50.

Kuyper, E. M., Espinosa-Hall, G., Lamp, C. L., Martin, A. C., Metz, D. L., Smith, D., Townsend, M.S., & Kaiser, L.L. (2006). Development of a tool to assess past food insecurity of immigrant Latino mothers. *Journal of Nutrition Education and Behavior, 38*(6): 378-382.

Kuyper, E. M., Smith, D., & Kaiser, L.L. (2009). Does food insecurity influence child feeding practices? *Journal of Hunger and Environmental Nutrition, 4*: 1-11.

Larios, S. E., Ayala, G. X., Arredondo, E. M., Baquero, B., & Elder, J. P. (2009). Development and validation of a scale to measure Latino parenting strategies related to children's obesigenic behaviors. The parenting strategies for eating and activity scale (PEAS). *Appetite, 52*(1): 166-172.

Lengua, L. J., Honorado, E., & Bush, N. R. (2007). Contextual risk and parenting as predictors of effortful control and social competence in preschool children. *Journal of Applied Developmental Psychology, 28*: 40-55.

Lorson, B. A., Melgar-Quiñonez, H. R., & Taylor, C. A., (2009). Correlates of fruit and vegetable intakes in U.S. children. *Journal of the American Dietetic Association, 109*(3): 474-478.

Lozoff, B., Jimenez E., & Smith J. B. (2006). Double burden of iron deficiency in infancy and low socioeconomic status: a longitudinal analysis of cognitive test scores to age 19 years. *Archives of Pediatric Adolescent Medicine, 160*(11): 1108-1113.

Maccoby, E. E., & Martin J.(1983). Socialization in the context of the family: Parent-child interaction. *Handbook of child psychology*: Vol. 4. *Socialization, personality, and social development.* New York, Wiley.

Martinez, S. M., Arredondo, E. M., Perez G., & Baquero B. (2009). Individual, social, and environmental barriers to and facilitators of physical activity among Latinas living in San Diego County: focus group results. *Family & Community Health*, 32(1): 22-33.

Matheson, D. M., Robinson, T. N., Varady, A., & Killen, J. D. (2006) Do Mexican-American mothers' food-related parenting practices influence their children's weight and dietary intake? *Journal of the American Diet Association, 106*(11): 1861-1865.

May, A. L., Donohue, M. Scanlon, K. S., Sherry, B., Dalenius, K., Faulkner, P., & Birch, L. L. (2007). Child-feeding strategies are associated with maternal concern about children becoming overweight, but not children's weight status. *Journal of the American Diet Association, 107*(7): 1167-1175.

Melgar-Quiñonez, H. R., & Kaiser L. L. (2004). Relationship of child-feeding practices to overweight in low-income Mexican-American preschool-aged children. *Journal of the American Dietetic Association, 104*(7): 1110-1119.

Mennella, J. A., Ziegler, P., Briefel, R., & Novak, T. (2006). Feeding Infants and Toddlers Study: The types of foods fed to Hispanic infants and toddlers. *Journal of the American Dietetic Association, 106*(1): S96-106.

Musher-Eizenman, D. R., Holub, S. C., Hauser, J. C., & Young, K. M. (2007). The relationship between parents' anti-fat attitudes and restrictive feeding. *Obesity, 15*(8): 2095-2102.

O'Connor, T. M., Yang, S. J., & Nicklas, T. A. (2006) Beverage intake among preschool children and its effect on weight status. *Pediatrics, 118*(4): e1010-1018.

Ogden, C. L., Carroll, M. D., Curtin, L. R., Lamb, M. M., & Flegal, K. M. (2010). Prevalence of high body mass index in U.S. children and adolescents, 2007-2008. *Journal of the American Medical Association, 303*(3): 242-249.

Olvera, N., & Power, T. (2010). Parenting styles and obesity in Mexican-American children: A longitudinal study. *Journal of Pediatric Psychology,* 35(3): 243-249.

Olvera, N., Sharma, S., Suminski, R., Rodriguez, A., & Power, T. (2007). BMI tracking in Mexican-American children in relation to maternal BMI. *Ethnicity and Disease, 17*(4) 707-713.

Olvera, N., Suminski, R., & Power, T. (2005). Intergenerational perceptions of body image in Hispanics: role of BMI, gender, and acculturation. *Obesity Research, 13*(11): 1970-1979.

Patrick, H., Nicklas, T. A, Hughes, S. O., & Morales, M. (2005). The benefits of authoritative feeding style: caregiver feeding styles and children's food consumption patterns. *Appetite, 44*(2): 243-249.

Pérez-Escamilla, R. (2009). Dietary quality among Latinos: Is acculturation making us sick? *Journal of the American Dietetic Association, 109*(6): 988-991.

Reifsnider, E., & Ritsema, M. (2008). Ecological differences in weight, length, and weight for length of Mexican-American children in the WIC program. *Journal of Specialists in Pediatric Nursing, 13*(3): 154-167.

Rhee, K. E., Lumeng, J. C., Appugliese, D. P., Kaciroti, N., & Bradley, R. H. (2006). Parenting styles and overweight status in first grade. *Pediatrics, 117*(6): 2047-2054.

Robinson, T. N., Kiernan, M., Matheson, D. M., & Haydel, K. F. (2001). Is parental control over children's eating associated with childhood obesity? Results from a population-based sample of third-graders. *Obesity Research, 9*(5): 306-312.

Rosas, L. G., Harley, K. G., Fernald, L. C., Guendelman, S., Mejia, F., Neufeld, L. M., & Eskenazi, B. (2009). Household food insecurity and dietary intake among children of Mexican descent: results of a binational study among Mexicans in California and Mexico. *Journal of the American Dietetic Association, 109*: 2001-2009

Satter, E. (1986). *Child of mine.* Palo Alto, Bull Publishing Co.

Schmitz, K.H., Lytle, L.A., Phillips, G.A., Murray, D.M., Birnbaum, A. S., & Kubik, M.Y. (2002). Psychological correlates of physical activity and sedentary leisure habits in young adolescents: The Teens Eating for Energy and Nutrition at School Study. *Preventive Medicine: An International Journal Devoted to Practice and Theory, 34*: 266-278.

Sherman, J. B., Alexander, M. A., Dean, A. H., & Kim, M. (1995). Obesity in Mexican-American and Anglo children. *Progressive Cardiovascular Nursing, 10*(1): 27-34.

Sherry, B., McDivitt, J., Birch, L. L., Cook, F. H., Sanders, S., Prish, J. L., Francis, L. A., & Scanlon, K. S. (2004). Attitudes, practices, and concerns about child feeding and child weight status among socioeconomically diverse white, Hispanic, and African-American mothers. *Journal of the American Dietetic Association, 104*(2): 215-221.

Skinner, J. D., & Carruth, B.R. (2001). A longitudinal study of children's juice intake and growth: the juice controversy revisited. *Journal of the American Dietetic Association, 101*(4): 432-437.

Skinner, J. D., Ziegler, P., & Ponza, M. (2004). Transitions in infants' and toddlers' beverage patterns. *Journal of the American Dietetic Association, 104*(1): s45-50.

Sussner, K. M., Lindsay, A.C., Greaney, M. L., & Peterson, K. E. (2008). The influence of immigrant status and acculturation on the development of overweight in Latino families: A qualitative study. *Journal of Immigrant & Minority Health, 10*(6): 497-505.

Sussner, K. M., Lindsay, A.C., & Peterson, K. E. (2009). The influence of maternal acculturation on child body mass index at age 24 months. *Journal of the American Dietetic Association, 109*(2): 218-225.

Tanasescu, M., Ferris, A. M., Himmelgreen, D. A., Rodriguez, N., & Pérez-Escamilla, R. (2000). Biobehavioral factors are associated with obesity in Puerto Rican children. *Journal of Nutrition, 130*(7): 1734-1742.

Taveras, E. M., Berkey, C. S., Rifas-Shiman, S. L., Ludwig, D. S., Rockett, H. R. Field, A. E., Colditz, G. A., & Gillman, M. W. (2005). Association of consumption of fried food away from home with body mass index and diet quality in older children and adolescents. *Pediatrics, 116*(4), e518-524.

U.S. Department of Agriculture. (2005). MyPyramid.gov: Steps to a healthier you. Retrieved April 30, 2010 from www.mypyramid.gov

Varela, R. E., E. M. Vernberg, Sanchez-Sosa, J. J., Riveros, A., Mitchell, M., & Mashunkashey, J. (2004). Parenting style of Mexican, Mexican-American, and Caucasian non-Hispanic families: Social context and cultural influences. *Journal of Family Psychology, 18*(4): 651-657.

Ventura, A. K., & Birch, L. L. (2008). Does parenting affect children's eating and weight status? *The International Journal of Behavioral Nutrition and Physical Activity, 5*, 15.

Wake, M., Nicholson, J. M., Hardy, P., & Smith, K. (2007). Preschooler obesity and parenting styles of mothers and fathers: Australian National Population Study. *Pediatrics, 120*, 1520-1527.

Ward, C. L. (2008). Parental perceptions of childhood overweight in the Mexican-American population: An integrative review. *The Journal of School Nursing, 24*(6): 407-416.

Warner, M. L., Harley, K., Bradman, A., Vargas, G., & Eskenazi, B. (2006). Soda consumption and overweight status of 2-year-old Mexican-American children in California. *Obesity, 14*(11): 1966-1974.

Wilson, T. A., Adolph, A. L., & Butte, N.F. (2009). Nutrient adequacy and diet quality in non-overweight and overweight Hispanic children of low socioeconomic status: The Viva la Familia Study. *Journal of the American Dietetic Association, 109*(6): 1012-1021.

CHAPTER FIVE

OBESITY AND SCHOOL NUTRITION PROGRAMS

Gail Woodward-Lopez[1] and Wendi Gosliner[1]

The Obesity Epidemic

The United States spends more per capita on health care than any other nation in the world, yet ranks 42nd in life expectancy (United Nations, 2007). Obesity[3]—an indicator of poor nutrition and inadequate physical activity —likely contributes to this unfortunate situation. In fact, the consequences of obesity are predicted to overturn historical gains in the health of Americans. If the current obesity trends are not reversed, experts predict one in three children—and nearly half of Latino[4] and African-American children—born in the year 2000 will develop type 2 diabetes in their lifetime (Narayan, 2003). This generation of children is predicted to be the first to have a life expectancy shorter than that of their parents (Olshakshy, 2005).

---

[1]Robert C. and Veronica Atkins, Center for Weight and Health, University of California, Berkeley.
[2]Overweight in adults is defined as having a body mass index (BMI) $\geq$ 25 and < 30; obesity in adults is defined as BMI of $\geq$ 30.
[3]Latino and Hispanic are used interchangeably to describe individuals of Central American, South American or Mexican ancestry. Mexican American refers specifically to those of Mexican descent residing in the United States.

Figure 1. Estimated Lifetime Risk of Developing Diabetes for Children Born in 2000.

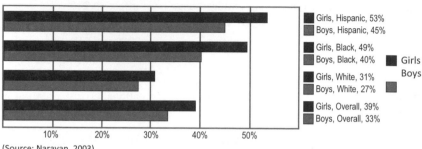

(Source: Narayan, 2003)

Obesity increases the risk for many chronic conditions such as hypertension, type 2 diabetes, metabolic syndrome, heart disease, gallbladder disease, certain types of cancer, arthritis, asthma and breathing problems (IOM, 2004; Joliffe, 2006; Must, 1999; Strong, 2005; Wolf, 1998). From 60 to over 80% of obese adults have type 2 diabetes, high blood cholesterol, high blood pressure or other related conditions (Must, 1999). Although most of the consequences of childhood obesity aren't experienced until adulthood, extremely obese children may experience medical problems associated with their weight, including high blood pressure, increased stress on weight bearing joints, type 2 diabetes, sleep apnea, asthma, hyperlipidemia and hypoxemia (Bray, 1985; Dietz, 1998; Falkner, 1999; Schonfeld-Warden, 1997). Alarmingly, up to 60% of obese children aged 5-10 years have early signs of heart disease (Freedman, 1999). Type 2 diabetes, previously only seen in adults, is now increasingly found in children. Even if an overweight child escapes major medical problems during youth, childhood overweight commonly persists into adulthood; approximately 26-41% of overweight preschoolers and 50-70% of 10-18 year olds will be obese as adults (Dietz, 1998; Freedman, 1999; Goran, 1998; Serdula 1993). Although the human costs are most concerning, the economic costs are also staggering; experts estimate that annual health-related costs in the United States due to obesity are approximately $147 billion (Finkelstein, 2009) and total economic losses cost the nation $1.3 trillion each year (DeVol, 2007).

Obesity Rates

The sharp rise in obesity which began in the 1970s has been especially rapid among children. Since the early 1970s, the prevalence of overweight children and youth has more than quadrupled among 6-11 year olds and tripled among 12-19 year olds (Ogden, 2002, 2006, 2008, 2010). Currently, more than one-third, or about 23 million children and youth in the United States, are overweight or obese[4] (36% of children aged 6-11 and 34% of children aged 12-19) (Ogden, 2010). Even very young children have been affected: 21% of 2-5 year olds are overweight or obese. After years of skyrocketing obesity rates, the Healthy People 2010 report to the nation in the year 2000 (DHHS, 2000) identified overweight and obesity as one of the ten leading health indicators on which the nation would focus during the decade. In 2003, then Surgeon General Richard Carmona dubbed the obesity epidemic a national crisis. Attention to the issue may be beginning to have a positive impact; recent data suggests obesity rates among children, although they remain high, are starting to reach a plateau (Ogden, 2010).

No ethnic or socioeconomic group in the United States has escaped the obesity epidemic; however, Latinos, African Americans and Native Americans are disproportionately affected (Crawford, 2001; Flegal, 1998, 2010; Hedley, 2004; Ogden 2006, 2010). Among male children, Mexican-American boys have the highest rates of obesity. Forty-six percent of Mexican-American adolescent boys (ages 12-19) and 44% of Mexican-American six- to eleven-year-old boys are overweight or obese. Rates are only slightly lower for Mexican-American girls: 42% of adolescent and 39% of six- to eleven-year-old Mexican-American girls are overweight or obese. Among Mexican Americans aged 2-5, more than one in four (28%) is overweight or obese compared to 17% of non-Hispanic whites and 26% of non-Hispanic blacks. Mexican-American boys in the 2-5 age range have especially high rates of overweight and obesity: almost one in three[5].

While all socioeconomic groups are affected by obesity, low-income Americans suffer disproportionately (Goodman, 1999). Regardless of ethnicity, rates of obesity among California preschoolers (aged 2-5) from low-income families are considerably higher (17%) than for their higher income peers (14%) (CMS, 2008). In an analysis of a nationally representative sample, children from families with lower income, lower parental education and lack of health insurance were more likely to be overweight or obese (Haas, 2003); Latinos are more likely to fit into these categories than other ethnic groups (Brown, 2003; Centrella-Nigro, 2009).

---

[4]According to the Centers for Disease Control and Prevention, overweight for children is defined as having a Body Mass Index (BMI) of $\geq$ 85th and < 95th percentiles for a given gender and age. Obesity in children is defined as a BMI of $\geq$ the 95th gender and age specific percentile.

[5]Starting with the 2007-2008 National Health and Nutrition Examination Survey, the United States began to report obesity rates for Hispanics (including Mexican Americans) in general in addition to reporting specifically on Mexican Americans; the rates of overweight and obesity for these two groups were similar in 2007-2008 and therefore are not both presented here.

Figure 2. Prevalence of Overweight in U.S. Children and Adolescents Aged 2 Through 19 Years by Sex, Age and Race/Ethnicity, 1976–2008. (Ogden, 2002, 2006, 2008, 2010)

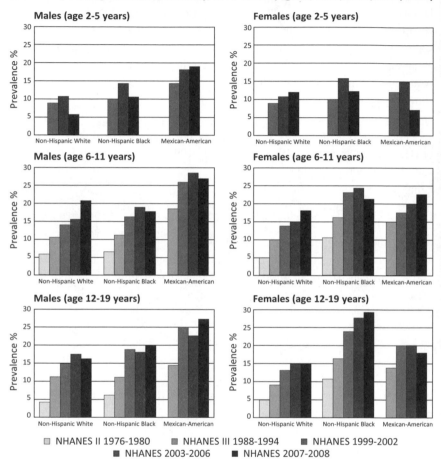

□ NHANES II 1976-1980   ■ NHANES III 1988-1994   ■ NHANES 1999-2002
■ NHANES 2003-2006   ■ NHANES 2007-2008

Causes of Obesity

Poor Dietary Intake. Obesity is associated with the consumption of high-calorie, nutrient-poor foods such as high-fat and high-sugar snack foods, fast foods, soda and other sweetened beverages. The consumption of fresh fruits and vegetables, whole-grain products and low-fat dairy and protein is associated with healthier weights (Woodward-Lopez, 2006). Although the diets of most children in the United States do not conform to U.S. dietary guidelines (Lorson, 2009; Muñoz, 1997), the diets of Latino children put them at a particularly high risk for obesity. In the past, studies have shown that compared to other ethnic groups, the diets of Latino children are higher in dietary fat and sweetened beverages, and lower in fruits and vegetables (Giammattei, 2003; Neumark-Sztainer, 1996; Troiano, 2000). Recent national survey data suggest that Latino adolescents drink less dairy and eat fewer fruits and vegetables than white students, but are more or equally likely to consume these items as black students (CDC, 2007). A survey of Californians supports this finding, with Latino and African-American children about equally likely to eat fast food, but more likely to do so than non-Hispanic white and Asian American children (CHIS, 2009). Recent national surveys have shown that Mexican-Americans' diets are higher in carbohydrates, dietary fiber and cholesterol than those of white or black Americans (CDC, 2001-2006).

Lack of Physical Activity. Lack of physical activity also contributes to obesity (Harsha; 1995; Moore, 1993; Obarzanek, 1994; Parsons, 1999; Sallis, 1998) and children who are physically active are more likely than others to continue being active as adults (Tammelin, 2003). The CDC recommends that children engage in 60 minutes of physical activity at least five days per week (CDC, 2008a). Although on average younger Mexican Americans (6-11 years old) are meeting these goals, national studies show that approximately 70% of Hispanic adolescents are not getting the recommended amount of physical activity (CDC, 2007). Mexican-American girls, ages 12-15 and 16-19, only get 22 and 26 minutes respectively of moderate to vigorous physical activity per day on average. Adolescent boys fare somewhat better at 51 and 41 minutes per day (Troiano, 2008). Interestingly, Mexican-American boys of all ages and adolescent girls get, on average, more physical activity than their non-Hispanic white peers, but younger girls, despite meeting minimal CDC standards, get less (Troiano, 2008).

TV Viewing. Adolescents are spending increasing amounts of their leisure time in sedentary activities. The National Youth Risk Behavior Survey found that 43% of Hispanic adolescents watch television for three or more hours daily, while one in four uses computers for three or more hours on an average school day (CDC, 2008b). In addition to decreasing physical activity time, TV viewing results in increased exposure to commercials that teach children to demand the high-sugar, high-fat snack and convenience foods that are most frequently advertised (Brody, 1981; Donkin, 1993; Galst, 1976; Isler, 1979; Linn, 2008; Stoneman, 1982; Taras, 1989, 2000). In 2004, the food and beverage industry spent over $260 million to advertise their products on Latino-oriented TV, magazines and radio (CPEHN, 2005). An analysis of Saturday morning children's television programming found that nine out of ten food and beverage advertisements were for products low in most essential nutrients and high in fat, sodium or added sugars (Batada, 2008).

Socioeconomic and Environmental Factors. Mounting evidence confirms that the nutrition and physical activity behaviors that lead to obesity are not merely the result of individual choice, traits and preferences, but are substantially affected by exposure to environments in which unhealthy foods are ubiquitous, less expensive and more heavily marketed than healthier options, and opportunities for physical activity are limited (California Nutrition Network, 2005; Galvez, 2010; Powell, 2007; Sallis, 2009). Although all communities are affected, low-income communities—where many Latinos live—tend to be less conducive to healthy eating and active living than higher-income communities (Baker, 2006). Even when healthy food choices are available within low-income Latino neighborhoods, limited purchasing power makes it more difficult to buy lower-calorie, nutrient-rich foods, which tend to be more expensive than high-calorie, nutrient-poor options (DPH, 2005; Drewnowski, 2005a, 2005b). Low-income Latino neighborhoods frequently lack well-equipped playgrounds, parks and recreational facilities, pedestrian- and bike-friendly streets, and other safe and affordable places to exercise, play and be active. (Babey, 2005; Evenson, 2002; Trust for Public Land, 2004; Weir 2006). Further, low-income parents often lack adequate transportation, time and money to support their children's participation in extramural sports, youth programs and other recreational activities.

Culture. Among immigrant Americans, subsequent generations tend to be heavier, suggesting that the U.S. lifestyle contributes to obesity (Bates, 2008). Traditional Latino culture appears protective against obesity, partially ameliorating the negative association between poverty and dietary intake among Latino youths. Although acculturation is unrelated to fat intake, traditional culture is associated with diets lower in sugar and sugar-sweetened beverages (Ayala, 2008) and higher in fruit, rice, beans and whole milk (Ayala, 2008; Centrella-Nigro, 2009). Latino immigrant families also are more likely to prepare meals at home and to eat meals together. Less acculturation is linked to reduced time watching TV (Gordon-Larsen, 2003), more physical activity and lower rates of obesity (Unger, 2004; Ravussin, 1994).

Genetics. The contribution of genetics to obesity is estimated to be between 40-70% (NHLBI, 2004). Genetics should not, however, be confused with destiny. Genetics determines one's susceptibility to obesity, but does not determine the actual weight that one will attain. Awareness of the genetic aspects of obesity helps us understand that differences in body fatness are not the result of differences in willpower, self-control or emotional stability, but rather have a physiologic basis. Latinos appear to be one of the ethnic groups with a greater genetic susceptibility to obesity. This genetic risk is amplified by the fact that Latinos, especially low-income Latinos, tend to live in communities where environmental risk is concentrated (Yancey, 2004); therefore, this genetic susceptibility is more likely to be expressed.

Obesity Prevention

Prevention of obesity is more efficient and cost-effective than treatment. Weight loss programs are seductive because dramatic results may be achieved over a relatively short period of time; however, studies have consistently shown that weight loss is only minimally successful and rarely sustainable (Curioni, 2005; Sarlio-Lähteenkorva, 2000). Rather than weight loss, the greatest challenge and greatest opportunity is prevention of excess weight gain. If adults maintain their current weights and if children gain weight at an appropriate rate, the obesity epidemic can be reversed in just a few generations (Woodward-Lopez, 2006).

Latinos may be particularly receptive to a preventive approach, given cultural values and perspectives that place family concerns and social cohesiveness above individual achievement (Centrella-Nigro, 2009; Hovell, 1991; Wilcox, 2000). It has been shown that Latinos emphasize broad concepts of social and physical health rather than relying on more narrowly defined concepts such as BMI or a focus on individual action or self-control (Crawford, 2004a). Therefore, a focus on the benefits of healthy eating and active living, as well as on family involvement, strengthening of social networks and development of social support (UCCE DANR, 2003) is likely to be more effective than a focus on individual weight loss or a sole reliance on BMI as the outcome of interest (Crawford, 2004b). Efforts to prevent obesity among Latino immigrants would also be well advised to protect and support healthy traditional dietary practices and physical activity patterns, while reinforcing cultural identification and pride. Increasing access to traditional foods and identifying appropriate and affordable replacements for traditional ingredients that are not readily available in the United States are important strategies for supporting healthy eating among recent immigrants as well as subsequent generations that could benefit from a return to traditional eating patterns (Brown, 2005).

To contain and reverse the obesity epidemic, prevention strategies must focus on children. Given the more rapid rise of obesity rates in children compared to adults, the tendency of weight problems to persist into adulthood and the fact that habits associated with eating and physical activity are formed early in life, children are an essential and logical target for obesity prevention. Many recent obesity prevention interventions have focused on the institution where children are most easily reached: schools.

Why Focus on Schools?

While multiple factors influence a child's dietary intake and risk for obesity, much attention of late has been directed at schools. As publicly funded and regulated environments, schools offer a natural setting for regulatory approaches. Since children are required to attend school and are a "captive audience," interventions in the school setting provide the unique opportunity to reach nearly all children and youth. Federal nutrition programs reach 60% of students that attend schools that participate in the federal meal program (Story, 2009a). In 2008, the National School Lunch program provided free or low-cost meals to more than 30.5 million children in the United States (NSLP, 2009) and about 10.6 million students participated in the School Breakfast Program (SBP, 2009). Furthermore, youth spend a large portion of their day in the school environment (IOM 2006), and consume, on average, 35% of their daily calories at school (Briefel, 2009b). Students who eat both breakfast and lunch at school consume nearly half (47%) of their daily energy intake there. It is therefore understandable that schools have been identified as a critical partner in the development of children's dietary behaviors (IOM, 2004; Murphy, 1998).

Schools not only provide food to students in various venues throughout the school day, but also define a food and nutrition culture through choices made regarding nutrition education and food promotion activities, provision of physical space for food service and other similar activities. The comprehensive policies and practices that shape a school's overall food environment likely affect not only what students consume at school but also what students and parents perceive to be normal and appropriate food choices for children and youth.

The military has long recognized the role schools play in supporting nutrition and health. The initial government effort to establish school meals in the 1940s was designed in large part to address a national health concern: undernourished young men who were not fit for military service. Currently, a group of veterans and military leaders have identified a different problem compromising the fitness of many youth for military service—obesity—and have argued that foods provided at school can help reverse this trend as well (Christeson, 2010).

Demographic changes also have contributed to the importance of school foods. As fewer families have a parent at home not participating in the paid labor force, reliance on obtaining food at school has increased. Many students spend longer hours at school each day than in earlier eras, beginning with early morning care and stretching through after-school programming.

The school food environment may have an especially important impact on Latino families. More than three-quarters of Hispanic children participate in the National School Lunch Program (NSLP), with the majority qualifying for free or reduced price meals; overall, Hispanics represent 24% of all NSLP participants (ERS, 2009). While until the early 1980s more children paid full price for school meals than received them for free or reduced price, in 2009 nearly 63%

of the meals were provided to low-income children (FNS, 2010). Research has found that food insecure Latino families are very likely to have their children participate in the school meal programs, but are unlikely to participate in the Food Stamp Program, (recently renamed Supplemental Nutrition Assistance Program "SNAP") (Chávez, 2007).

Schools also serve as role models, especially for immigrant families who look to public institutions to learn about cultural norms and practices (Gordon-Larsen, 2003). Immigrant parents may view the school menus and cafeteria environments as examples of what American children should consume. If the school serves pizza, burgers, french fries, chicken nuggets and other similar fare, it is possible that this teaches parents that these are the foods they should serve their children. However, if the school menu provides a healthier variety of foods, this, too, could educate parents.

Although, it is not known how the school environment contributes to acculturation and adoption of more typical American food practices among Latinos, it is known that foods served at school have the potential to positively impact childrens' health. Students who consume the school meal eat meals of higher dietary quality compared to non-participants (Story, 2009). Although the image of a wholesome lunch sent from home persists, studies have shown that school lunches are healthier than lunches sent from home, which often rely on processed packaged items rather than home-prepared fresh foods (Bergman, 2003; Woodward-Lopez, 2010a). Research also has found that students who participated in the National School Lunch Program consumed more energy at school than those who did not participate (Briefel, 2009b). Although these school lunch consumers ate more calories from some low-nutrient energy dense foods at school (like baked goods and French fries), they consumed fewer calories from sweetened beverages than students who did not participate (Briefel, 2009a). While there has been some degree of controversy over whether school meals contribute to obesity, a recent analysis controlling for selection bias, found no association overall between students who consume school lunch and rates of obesity, and actually found that students who eat school breakfast had a significantly lower BMI overall (Gleason, 2009), though this relationship was less clear among Hispanics. However, *what* is served in school meals matters: elementary school students attending schools that serve french fries or desserts more than once a week were found to be at increased risk for overweight (Fox, 2009a).

The potential impact of the school food environment goes well beyond physical health but also extends to academic performance. Well-nourished children are more able to learn and less likely to miss school for health reasons (Florence, 2008; Fu, 2007; Taras, 2005). There are also reports of improved classroom behavior and attentiveness (Hollar, 2010a; Kleinman, 1998; Nansel, 2010; Shilts, 2009). For example, studies have shown that low-income children participating in the School Breakfast Program score higher on standardized tests and have better school attendance than similar children not participating in the Program (Hoyland, 2009; Kleinman, 2002; Meyers, 1989; Rampersaud, 2005).

School food environments have become quite complex. In addition to breakfast and lunch, individual food items are sold to students throughout the school day in order to generate much needed funds. Because these foods often "compete" with the meal program they are commonly referred to as "competitive foods." Competitive foods are sold in vending machines, snack bars, carts and stores throughout campus and in school cafeterias during breaks, lunchtime, and before and after school. They are sold by student groups, athletic departments, school administration and other special programs as well as school food service operations which commonly sell individual foods and beverages, referred to as food service a la carte. Foods are also offered to children free of charge during classroom parties, at various school events and as rewards for good behavior or academic performance.

Food marketing has crept into schools and classrooms and may appear on score boards, other school equipment and facilities, vending machines, classroom television, posters, disposable cups and utensils, cafeteria offerings and even textbooks and other instructional materials. Promotional events may feature branded food and beverage products and incentives may be paid to the school for selling certain food and beverage items. "Pouring rights contracts" are common, whereby schools receive cash or material bonuses for exclusively carrying one brand of beverage (Ludwig, 2001; Nestle, 2000). Studies have shown that students are affected by the branding icons to which they are exposed at school (McDermott, 2006), and that food advertising and marketing affect children's preferences and behaviors toward particular products (IOM, 2006). Unfortunately, most of the products and brands marketed to students at school promote unhealthy items, like sweetened beverages, candy, snack and fast foods (Molnar, 2003). Although it is well known that the food industry targets the general Latino population (CPEHN, 2005), data are not available regarding school food marketing to Hispanic/Latino students in particular.

School Meals: Challenges and Opportunities

Within this complex school food environment, school meals provide the greatest opportunity to contribute to student health and children's readiness to learn. School meal foods are required by the U.S. Department of Agriculture (USDA) to meet particular nutritional guidelines, outlined in the USDA's

School Meals Initiative for Healthy Children (SMI). School lunches must provide ⅓ and school breakfast must provide ¼ of the recommended dietary allowances (RDA) for key nutrients including calories, protein, vitamin A, vitamin C, calcium and iron. Since the current meal standards were developed to address undernutrition and hunger, no maximum calorie levels or sugar content of meal foods have been set.[6] However, meals are required to limit the proportion of calories from fat to 30% (<10% from saturated fat), and must reduce cholesterol and sodium and increase dietary fiber. Despite these requirements, school meals frequently fall short of the healthy, wholesome offerings one might envision.

Across the nation, only a small minority of schools (6%) meet all of the USDA standards, with most failing to meet the fat and sodium limits (Crepinsek, 2009). Most of the fat in school meals comes from salad dressing and condiments, pizza, peanut butter and french fries (Crepinsek, 2009). Nearly ⅓ of schools provide whole milk as a choice to students (Condon, 2009), despite the fact that the Dietary Guidelines recommend low- or nonfat milk for children older than age 2.

In predominately Latino high schools in California in 2008, 45% of entrées offered were fast foods such as chicken burgers, pizza, hamburgers and chicken nuggets and 40% of schools offered french fries as a vegetable option on a given day. Of milks served in California schools (all grade levels), about half were sugar-sweetened flavored milks. Heat and serve items, such as packaged burritos, prepared by central processors off-site, have become the norm. Fewer than 25% of high schools reported that at least half of the entrées served were prepared on site from fresh basic ingredients (Woodward-Lopez, 2010a and 2010c).

As schools have increasingly relied upon heat-and-serve items, many have eliminated or downsized their kitchen facilities such that meal preparation from scratch is no longer possible (CWH, 2007a). Lack of computerized points of service (stations where students pay for the meals) and inadequate staffing lead to long meal lines that result in students buying less healthy a la carte items that can be served more rapidly. In California, where 49% of public school students are Latino, over 25% of schools had no indoor dining facilities for students; when it rains children must crowd into hallways and under awnings or eaves without seats and tables at which to eat (Woodward-Lopez, 2010b). Further, the

---

[6]In December of 2010 Congress passed the Healthy Hunger-Free Kids Act (HHKA). This act directs the USDA to develop nutrition standards for all foods sold and/or served to children during the school day. The HHKA requires that new standards be consistent with the Dietary Guidelines and therefore will likely address gaps in the current requirements such as the fat content of milk and upper calorie limits for meals.

facilities that do exist tend to be basic and plain, with an institutional ambience that is unlikely to attract students.

The good news is that nearly all schools in the United States meet the federal standards for protein, vitamins A and C, calcium and iron, (Crepinsek, 2009) and nearly all schools offer a fruit or vegetable with school meals. However 42% of schools do not offer a *fresh* fruit or *raw* vegetable daily (Crepinsek, 2009; Gordon, 2009), and fresh produce items are less common in schools with a higher percentage of low-income students (Finkelstein, 2008). Encouragingly, 18% of secondary schools and 13% of elementary schools offer salad bars on a daily basis. School lunch participants have also been shown to consume more of certain healthy foods such as vegetables and milk, fewer unhealthy foods such as pastries and sweetened beverages and have more meal pattern consistency (Woodward-Lopez, 2000).

Promising trends also have been observed in schools with high numbers of Latino students. In one study, 24 elementary, middle and high schools in California (47% Latino on average) offered an average of over four different fruit and vegetable options, half of which were fresh and one third of which were less common varieties (i.e. not apples, bananas or oranges) (Woodward-Lopez, 2010c). All milks were either low- or nonfat, 57% of schools offered a whole-grain option, and juice was only offered at one-third of schools. However, Latino students still complain about the quality and taste of the foods served. Studies have reported that Latino students want more variety, more fresh foods, more of their cultural favorites and foods that are more like what is served at home (Gosliner, 2011; Woodward-Lopez, 2008).

Although USDA currently only has minimum calorie requirements, recent proposals to reform school meal requirements include maximum calorie limits for meals (in addition to other recommendations); these may provide particular benefits for Latino students who consume school meals in large numbers and who are at increased risk of overweight and obesity.

Efforts to improve school meals generally focus on improving the nutritional quality of the meals and on improving their taste and appeal to students, so that students will actually eat the healthier options. Increasing the number of students served (meal participation) is also a common objective in order to ensure that more students benefit from a balanced school meal as opposed to less healthy sack lunches and competitive foods. Increasing meal participation has the added benefit of improving food service department revenues (CWH, 2007b; Woodward-Lopez, 2010b, 2010d). Therefore, more schools are adding salad bars, renovating dining areas and converting to food court style service in order to attract students. Schools are also starting to switch from facilities designed to heat and serve foods processed off-site to fully equipped kitchens that allow for more cooking from scratch (CWH, 2007a). Many school interventions serving large percentages of Latino students have included improvements to the meals and/or cafeteria facilities (Coleman, 2005; Heath 2002; Heath, 2003; Hoelscher, 2010; Hollar, 2010a, 2010b; Resnicow, 1992; Sallis, 2003; Treviño, 1998). A few efforts have focused primarily or exclusively on the meal program (Bartholomew, 2006; Folta, 2006). Many of the changes made were quite modest. Almost all the meal program improvement interventions reported in the literature include a switch to lower fat entrées and/or side dishes. Some made additional nutritional changes, including increases in dietary fiber/whole grain options, decreases in glycemic index, decreases in sodium and/or an increase in the fruits and vegetables offered. Many of the multicomponent programs and even those that focused primarily on the meal program and other school foods resulted in improvements in student dietary intakes (Bartholomew, 2006; Folta, 2006; Hoelscher, 2010; Treviño, 1998), increased breakfast consumption, increased meal participation (Bartholomew, 2006), reductions in adiposity (Coleman, 2005; Hoelscher, 2010; Hollar, 2010a, 2010b; Sallis, 2003) and improvements in other health measures (Hollar, 2010a, 2010b; Resnicow, 1992), suggesting that improvements to the school meal are an important component of any effort to improve student nutrition and health. Critical elements for success of these interventions include food service staff training, parent involvement and promotion and education activities with students.

Unfortunately, in many cases, schools lack the resources needed to make comprehensive changes to school meals and instead compromise by making modest adjustments to their programs. Often, processed heat-and-serve and fast foods continue to predominate even when schools undertake these modest reform efforts (Woodward-Lopez, 2010a, 2010b, 2010c). Findings suggest that in order to get more substantive improvements to the meals and therefore more significant impacts on student health, funds for facilities upgrades, staff training, reduced competition from snacks and beverages (competitive foods) sold on campus and more adequate meal reimbursements will be required.

Although inadequately studied, meal scheduling likely is also important. Meals offered too early or late in the day may lead to snacking on unneeded or less healthy foods. Inadequate time to eat may cause students to forgo the meal altogether. Many schools have found that when elementary students are sent outside to play before, rather than after lunch, they eat a more nutrient-dense lunch (Bergman, 2003; Gettlinger, 1996). Teachers say that these students return to the classroom more ready to learn, and schools report significantly less food waste at lunchtime.

A successful effort to improve school meals needs to go well beyond modest changes, such as merely substituting baked for regular fries, flavored low-fat milk for whole milk or simply reducing the fat content of entrées. Given that schools serve as powerful role models to students and parents and students are forming taste preferences and habits that may last a lifetime, it is critical that schools receive support that enables them to offer a wide array of not just nutrient-adequate meals, but also fresh, wholesome, minimally processed meals.

Competitive Foods

In contrast to the meal program, competitive foods in schools likely contribute to obesity and poor nutrition. Both obesity and the availability of competitive foods have increased in recent years. In 2005, competitive foods were available in all high schools, 97% of middle schools, and 73% of elementary schools (Fox, 2009b). Nearly all high schools and most middle schools have a la carte foods and vending machines available to students. The majority of elementary schools sell a la carte foods, but only 27% have vending machines (Fox, 2009a). It has been reported that 44% of middle school students and 55% of high school students consume competitive foods on a typical school day (Fox, 2009b).

Competitive foods are often of low nutritional quality. A survey conducted in California in 2000 revealed the plethora of fast foods, candies, soda and other junk foods available in schools (Craypo, 2002). More recent research found that most competitive food calories consumed by students come from items such as sweetened juice drinks, cookies, cakes, brownies, candy and soda (Fox, 2009a). At low-income primarily Latino schools in California in 2005, the most common competitive foods and beverages available were chips, candies, cookies/pastries and sugar-sweetened beverages such as soda, sports drinks and sweetened juice drinks (Woodward-Lopez, 2010d).

Further, because they are so prevalent and convenient, competitive foods tend to divert children from the more balanced school meals. The availability of competitive foods has been found to be associated with increased dietary fat intake and decreased consumption of fruits and vegetables (Cullen, 2004; Kubik, 2003). Students attending schools that sell foods a la carte, and/or have snack bars, stores or an exclusive beverage pouring rights contract, consume more calories from sweetened beverages than students attending schools without these venues (Briefel, 2009b). Among students consuming competitive foods, those foods contributed 216 calories to elementary school students' diets, 171 calories to middle school students' diets and 219 calories to high school students' diets. The most commonly consumed competitive foods include desserts and snacks, beverages other than milk and 100% juice, grain products, and entrée items. Children who ate a school lunch were less likely to consume competitive foods.

It is not surprising therefore that school nutrition efforts have focused heavily on improving, reducing or even eliminating competitive foods. After years of negotiation, in 2005 California became the first state to adopt comprehensive nutrition standards for competitive foods sold at K-12 schools (Table 1). This approach quickly spread across the county, with many other states adopting the same or similar standards. At the request of USDA, in 2007, the Institute of Medicine (IOM) released recommendations for national standards to govern competitive foods in schools (Table 1). The Healthy Hunger-Free Kids Act of 2010 directs the USDA to develop nutrition standards for all foods sold and served at schools during the school day. The development of these standards will likely be influenced substantially by the IOM standards.

To determine the effects of California's nutrition standards legislation on school food environments and students' consumption patterns, three studies were conducted by the Dr. Robert C. and Veronica Atkins Center for Weight and Health at the University of California, Berkeley (Samuels, 2009; Woodward-Lopez, 2010a, 2010b, 2010c, 2010d). Each of the studies included many schools with large Latino populations, ranging from 37-65% Latino on average for each study. Results showed that after the legislation went into effect, significant improvements were made in compliance of foods and beverages sold at the study schools; thus, the levels of fat, sugar and calories in the competitive foods and beverages available to students were reduced, and fewer of the most energy-dense, nutrient-poor items, such as candy, soda and regular chips, were offered. However, though there was a large degree of variability by school, most schools continued to offer some non-compliant items. Further, sports drinks and baked chips, which continued to be allowed by law, remained among the most common products offered.

School personnel reported challenges with implementing the California nutrition standards. Staff reported difficulty determining which foods were compliant, because of the challenge in determining a food's nutrient content and subsequently translating that into an assessment of compliance with the standards. Interpretation of beverage standards was easier, but not problem free. In general, schools struggled with monitoring adherence to the standards, especially when multiple school-based groups conducted food and beverage sales, a very common situation particularly in the high school setting.

The impact of the implementation of the competitive foods standards on student dietary intake in these California studies was favorable but modest, for

Table 1. Nutrition guidelines for competitive foods sold at school

	Institute of Medicine Standards	California Standards (SB 12 and 965)
Foods		
What can be sold	All grade levels: Food items must include at least one serving fruit, vegetable and/or whole grain, or non-/low-fat dairy product*	MS/HS: No restriction on type of food ES: Only individual portions of nuts, nut butters, seeds, eggs, cheese, legumes, dairy, whole grains and fruit and vegetables that are not deep-fried
Calorie restrictions	≤200 kcal	MS/HS: ≤250 kcal ES: ≤175 kcal for dairy and whole grain items (other items exempt)
Total fat	≤35% total calories	≤35% total calories (nuts, nut butters, seeds, eggs, cheese, fruit, vegetable, legumes exempt)
Saturated fat	<10% total calories	<10% total calories (eggs or cheese exempt)
Trans fat	Trans fat free (≤ 0.5 g/serving)	Not addressed
Total sugars	≤35% total calories, except: • Yogurt: ≤30g total sugars/8 oz • 100% fruits, vegetables and juices	≤35% total weight (fruit and vegetables, not deep-fried exempt)
Sodium	≤200 mg sodium	Not addressed
Entrées	Must meet fat and sugar limits above, and: • Must be NSLP menu items • Must not exceed calorie content of comparable NSLP items • ≤480 mg sodium	ES: no restrictions on "full meals" MS/HS: Must be categorized as School breakfast or NSLP items and: • ≤4 g fat/100 kcals • ≤400 kcals/entrée
Beverages		
Water	Water without flavoring, additives or carbonation	Drinking water with no added sweetener
Milk	1% and nonfat milk, including: • Lactose-free and soy beverages • Flavored milk w/ ≤22 g total sugars/8 oz serving	2%, 1%, nonfat milk, including: • Soy milk, rice milk, other non-dairy milk • Flavored milks
Juice	ES/MS: 100% fruit juice in 4-oz portions HS: 100% fruit juice in 8-oz portions	Fruit- or vegetable-based drinks composed of ≥50% fruit or vegetable juice with no added sweetener
Beverages		
Caffeine	Caffeine-free	The allowed beverages do not generally include caffeine
Sports drinks	Sports drinks are not allowed except for athletes participating >1 hr vigorous physical activity	MS/HS: electrolyte replacement beverage w/ ≤42 g added sweetener/20-oz serving
Non-nutritive sweeteners	Non-nutritive sweetened, non-caffeinated, non-fortified beverages with <5 kcals/portion are Tier 2**	The only compliant beverages allowed to have added sweeteners are sports drinks, which can only be sold in MS/HS

* The IOM separates foods and beverages into those that can be sold during school hours (Tier 1) and those that can only be sold on high school campuses after school hours (Tier 2). Tier 1 foods should also be available after school to elementary and middle schools.

** Tier 2 foods have the same calorie, fat, sugar and sodium restrictions, but are not restricted on the type of food (i.e. they don't need to include 1 serving of fruit, vegetable, whole grain or dairy).

[ES= Elementary School; MS = Middle School; HS = High School; NSLP=National School Lunch Program]

example from 4-8% fewer students consumed candy, chips and soda after the changes were made. These findings suggest that either stricter or improved standards are needed in order to more meaningfully impact students' dietary intake in the school setting. To address this concern, the 2007 Institute of Medicine report recommended that if competitive foods and beverages are made available to students, only fruits, vegetables, whole grains and low-fat dairy should be offered (IOM, 2007). Others have recommended that competitive food sales should be eliminated entirely, based on observations that students increase their participation in the meal program when access to competitive foods is reduced. The switch from snack foods and beverages to meals has a favorable impact on students' nutrient intake, and has been shown to benefit school food service operations financially. This favorable financial impact has been observed in several predominately Latino schools (CWH, 2007b; Woodward-Lopez, 2010a, 2010b, 2010c, 2010d). Further, Latino students have high rates of school meal program participation, and schools with high percentages of students participating find it easier to transition to fewer or even no competitive food sales.

Other studies of schools with relatively large Latino student populations have found that local or state school nutrition standards resulted in improvements in the types of snack foods and beverages sold (Cullen, 2009; Schwartz, 2009; Snelling, 2009) along with some improvements in student intake and food purchasing behaviors (Cullen, 2006; Schwartz, 2009; Snelling, 2009; Wojcicki, 2006). One study reported an overall reduction in snack foods sales which was accompanied by an increase in meal sales (Wojcicki, 2006).

The impact of switching to healthier competitive food options can be enhanced both by providing healthy alternatives that are priced lower than comparable less healthy options (French, 1997, 2001) and by incorporating effective promotion of the healthy options. Providing free, chilled water in cafeterias and other areas on school grounds has been an effective component of strategies to reduce sweetened beverage intake (Haerens, 2007; Loughridge, 2005; Taylor, 2007). Point of purchase prompts (signage or oral encouragement by staff) have also been to shown to be effective in influencing selection of healthier options (Andersoe, 2005; Bere, 2006; Conklin, 2005; Foerster, 1995).

One concern regarding recent competitive food policies is that they most commonly restrict fat, sugar and portion size; thus, the food industry responds by creating compliant fat- or sugar-modified versions of processed unhealthy foods that schools sell in order to maintain their business model. In this scenario, consumption of unhealthy items such as candy and soda were observed to decrease, but consumption of healthy items did not increase (Woodward-Lopez, 2010a, 2010b, 2010c, 2010d). Although no studies to date have been able to assess the independent impact of competitive food policies on adiposity, a recently published study suggests an association between California's statewide competitive food policy and a reduction in adiposity among California students as a whole as well as students from predominantly Latino schools (Sanchez, 2010). However, when a school only makes modest improvements to the competitive foods and does not change any other aspects of the school food environment improvement in students' adiposity will likely be limited. Therefore the elimination or large reductions in the availability of competitive foods may be needed in order to substantively improve student intake and reduce adiposity.

Nutrition Education and Promotion

Nutrition education appears to be a critical component of successful school-based strategies to improve student dietary intake and reduce obesity. In the majority of the studies identified (with large numbers of Latino students) where nutrition education and/or promotion was part of a multi-component intervention and adiposity outcomes were assessed, improvements in student adiposity were observed (Coleman, 2005; Foster, 2008; Hoeschler, 2010; Hollar, 2010a, 2010b; Rosenbaum, 2007). Many also reported improvements in various aspects of student dietary intake, blood pressure, cholesterol, nutrition knowledge and intent. However because nutrition education and promotion strategies are often part of a more comprehensive school-based intervention effort, it can be difficult to assess their independent effect. One study that measured the impact of an education-only program at schools found a favorable impact on adiposity (Casazza, 2007). Other education-only programs reported increases in fruit and vegetable intake and/or decreases in calorie and fat intake (Auld, 1999; Baranowski, 2003; Frenn, 2005). It appears therefore that when nutrition education is delivered effectively, it can positively impact students' health. These effects have been observed both when education is delivered alone and more commonly when it is part of a comprehensive effort.

Unfortunately, however, few schools offer the intensity and quality of nutrition education needed to foster healthy behaviors. While most states require nutrition to be taught in schools, health education teachers generally only devote about 5 hours a year to this topic, which is not enough to have a substantial impact on students' behaviors (Story, 2006).

The successful programs described above most commonly included the use of nutrition and health curricula taught by the regular classroom teacher, usually in conjunction with one or more other wellness related components involving physical activity and/or healthy food (Coleman, 2005; Foster, 2008; Hoeschler, 2010; Hollar, 2010a, 2010b; Rosenbaum, 2007; Sallis, 2003; Walter, 1985,

1988). The nutrition education offered in the classroom often consisted of several (i.e., 6-8) 30-60 minute lessons over part of the school year. Sometimes these lessons were integrated throughout the school year for as much as 2 hours per week. Much of the curricula were hands-on and interactive, including food games, taste testing, cooking, food demonstrations and information about portion sizes (Devault, 2009). The use of goal setting, rewards, prizes, parties and other types of recognition and acknowledgements were also common and deemed critical for success.

The use of technology for nutrition education has been well-received among student populations that include large proportions of Latinos. Multimedia games for elementary school students (Baranowski, 2003) and computer games (Casazza, 2007) for teens have been successful at not only improving intake but also lowering adiposity. Teens reportedly prefer computer-based curricula to more conventional classroom based nutrition education. A series of interactive internet-based sessions and short videos was successful at reducing students' dietary fat intake and increasing physical activity (Frenn, 2005).

School gardens have been an important element of some successful nutrition education programs (Hollar 2010a, 2010b; McAleese, 2007). In one case, compared to the same curriculum without a gardening component, the added gardening activities resulted in dramatic increases in fruit and vegetable consumption (McAleese, 2007).

Some of the most effective programs not only offer education to the students, but also include parent involvement in various forms including gatherings with parents to discourage use of unhealthy foods at fundraisers and parties; parent assistance in teaching nutrition education; family fun nights and similar promotional events that include parents; and various education activities for parents ranging from newsletters to workshops (Auld, 1999; Foster, 2008; Hoeschler, 2010; Resnicow, 1992; Treviño, 1998).

In many cases nutrition education does not occur exclusively in the classroom but also includes an array of social marketing/promotional activities, such as broadcasts to promote healthy food and beverage alternatives being offered at school that day, raffles, characters, slogans, newsletters, posters, taste-testing, rewards, prizes and school celebrations, and activities and events such as wellness fairs (Coleman, 2005; Folta, 2006; Foster, 2008; Hoeslscher, 2010; Hollar 2010a, 2010b; Resnicow, 1992). These promotional activities alone or in combination with other efforts to improve the school food and nutrition environment have been shown to impact student behavior. One of the strategies that has been most effective is point of purchase prompts or labeling. Point of purchase signage encouraging purchase of a healthy alternatives in the cafeteria and verbal prompts such as "Would you like fruit or juice?" by school foodservice staff (Conklin, 2005; Schwartz, 2007) have been shown to increase the number of students selecting these healthier options in studies that included schools that were predominately Latino. Promoting new healthy offerings using school broadcasts also has been effective (Folta, 2006).

Price is also a powerful marketing tool that schools can use. Several studies with substantial Latino populations have found that providing free fruits and vegetables in the classroom is effective at improving student preferences for and/or intake these foods (Cassady, 2006; Cullen, 2009; Davis, 2009). Studies conducted at schools serving predominately white students have shown that when the prices of low-fat items (fresh fruit and baby carrots) in a vending machine were lowered by 10-50% relative to the price of less healthy options, purchases of the healthy options increased dramatically—particularly among schools in urban settings (French, 1997, 2001, 2005).

These types of promotional efforts are a critical component of any effort to improve schools foods. In order for students to accept the new healthy offerings, they need to be marketed effectively and priced competitively. In order to provide a consistent message to students, schools should not only provide quality nutrition education and promotion but also curb the currently pervasive marketing of unhealthy foods.

Putting It Together: A Comprehensive Approach to Improving Student Nutrition

Given 1) the limited impact that a piecemeal approach, such as only addressing competitive foods, can have on student nutrition; 2) the inter-related nature of the various elements of the school food environment; and 3) the importance of providing a consistent message and role modeling to students, a comprehensive approach to improving school nutrition environments is warranted. Indeed research suggests that comprehensive programs including both nutrition education and changes to various aspects of the food and activity environments, are the most likely to favorably impact student health and wellness. Notable among these programs that have been evaluated in schools serving Latino students are: CATCH (Coleman, 2005), HOPS (Hollar, 2010a), the School Nutrition Policy Initiative (Foster, 2008), Bienestar (Treviño, 1998), Know Your Body (Resnicow, 1992) and M-SPAN (Sallis, 2003). Several were assessed in schools where half to all participating students were Latino (Coleman, 2005; Hollar, 2010a; Treviño, 1998). For example CATCH was implemented in elementary schools where 93% of students were Latino. These multi-component programs have demonstrated positive and sometimes sustained improvements in 1) students' dietary intake including reduced fat intake, switch to purchases of healthier options, increased fruit and vegetable intake, increased breakfast consumption and decreased consumption of unhealthy foods (Devault, 2009; Hoeschler, 2010; Treviño, 1998), 2) adiposity (Coleman, 2005; Foster, 2008; Hollar, 2010b; Sallis, 2009), 3) other health indicators such as blood pressure or cholesterol (Resnicow, 1992) and 4) test scores (Hollar, 2010b). Studies conducted with students of other ethnic groups have found similar results (Cunningham-Sabo, 2003; Economos, 2007; Katz, 2008; Taylor, 2007). These impacts are impressive and have been shown to be both replicable and sustainable (Coleman, 2005). In addition to improvements in school meals, meal facilities and competitive foods, these programs often had strong nutrition education and promotion components, addressed physical education and physical activity during the school day, included activities and education to get families involved, provided incentives, awards and recognition, conducted high-profile school wide and community events, engaged in community partnerships and established school gardens. Many also addressed foods available at classroom parties and school events. Some of these programs also extended beyond the school setting and included the promotion of healthy eating and active living in the surrounding community, after-school and health care settings. Training at all levels for food service staff, physical education teachers and classroom teachers was very common as were various types of social marketing strategies and the formation of school health and wellness committees and sometimes student committees and other forms of student involvement. Keys to success included: flexibility in adapting their program to local needs and priorities, community involvement and partnerships, and having the school personnel (as opposed to researchers or external staff) deliver the intervention. This suggests the importance of local ownership and institutionalization of efforts to ensure the program becomes an integrated part of how the school conducts business.

These successes at all grade levels (preschool through high school) were made possible by adaptation of program elements to reflect the ethnic heritage of the students (Flores, 1995; Gortmaker, 1999; Lytle, 1996a,1996b; Treviño, 2004) including:

- Incorporation of culturally meaningful activities, foods and materials
- Student involvement in selecting foods and physical activities
- Interactive education strategies that engage students
- Physical activities that are fun and appropriate for students of various sizes and physical capacities
- A focus on *specific* dietary changes, physical activities and reduction in sedentary activities (i.e., television viewing reduction) that can have an observable short term impact on weight and fitness.

In conclusion, the challenges presented by the obesity epidemic must be confronted, with the goal of prevention in childhood before unhealthy nutrition and activity patterns are ingrained. The school food environment presents a critical opportunity for improving the health and wellbeing of America's children in general and Latino children in particular. Numerous programs and policies have begun to be developed and tested, and understanding of best practices and most promising approaches continues to grow. Due to the magnitude of the obesity epidemic, particularly among Latinos, and the devastating consequences of poor nutrition and physical inactivity during childhood, devoting increased resources to schools to optimize the food and nutrition environments would be a wise investment in the future of our children and our nation.

Acknowledgements

The authors gratefully acknowledge that parts of this paper were based on previously conducted literature reviews funded by The California Endowment, the California Taskforce on Youth and Workplace Wellness, Kaiser Permanente and the American Dietetic Association. The authors wish to thank Aileen Baecker for locating articles and abstracting information included in this chapter, Juan Yang for conducting parts of the literature search and Sheila Stern, Jess Thacher and Peg Farrell for reviewing and editing the document.

The authors would also like to acknowledge the agencies that funded the research (conducted by the authors) that informed the development of, and provided data, for this chapter: The Robert Wood Johnson Foundation, the California Endowment, the Nutrition Services Division of the California of Education and the U.S. Department of Agriculture.

References

Agras, W. S., Hammer, L. D., McNicholas, F., & Kraemer, H. C. (2004). Risk factors for childhood overweight: A prospective study from birth to 9.5 years. *J Pediatr, 145*(1):20-5.

Andersen, L. F., Lillegaard, I. T. L., Øverby, N., Lytle, L., Klepp, K., & Johansson, L. (2005). Overweight and obesity among Norwegian schoolchildren: Changes form 1993-2000. *Scan J Public Health, 33*(2):99-106.

Auld, G. W., Romaniello, C., Heimendinger, J., Hambridge, C., & Hambridge, M. (1999). Outcomes from a school-based nutrition education program alternating special resource teachers and classroom teachers. *J Sch Health, 69*(10):403-8.

Ayala, G. X., Baquero, B., & Klinger, S. (2008). A systematic review of the relationship between acculturation and diet among Latinos in the United States: implications for future research. *J Am Diet Assoc, 108*:1330-44.

Babey, S., Diamant, A., Brown, R., & Hastert, T. (2005). California adolescents increasingly inactive. *Health Policy Research Brief,* 2005. Los Angeles, CA: UCLA Center for Health Policy Research. Available at: http://www.health policy.ucla.edu/pubs/files/TeensInactive_PB_040105_.pdf

Baker E., Schootman M., Barnidge, E., & Kelly, C. (2006). The role of race and poverty in access to foods that enable individuals to adhere to dietary guidelines. *Prev Chron Dis, 3*(3):1-11.

Baranowski, T., Baranowski, J., Cullen, K. W., Marsh, T., Islam, N., Zakeri, I., Honess-Morreale, L., & de Moor, C. (2003). Squire's Quest! Dietary outcome evaluation of a multimedia game. *Am J Prev Med, 24*(1):52–61.

Bartholomew, J. B., & Jowers, E. M. (2006). Increasing frequency of lower-fat entrées offered at school lunch: an environmental change strategy to increase healthful selections. *J Am Diet Assoc, 106*:248-52.

Batada, A., Seitz, M., Wootan, M., & Story, M. (2008). Nine out of 10 food advertisements shown during Saturday morning children's television programming are for foods high in fat, sodium, or added sugars, or low in nutrients. *J Am Diet Assoc, 108*:673-78.

Bates, L. M., Acevedo-Garcia, D., Alegria, M., & Krieger, N. (2008). Immigration and generational trends in body mass index and obesity in the United States: results of the National Latino and Asian American Survey, 2002-2003. *Am J Public Health, 98*(1):70-7.

Bere, E., Veierød, M. B., Bjelland, M., & Klepp, K. I. (2006). Outcome and process evaluation of a Norwegian school-randomized fruit and vegetable intervention: Fruits and Vegetables Make the Marks (FVMM). *Health Educ Res*, *21*(2):258-67.

Bergman, E. A., Buergel, N. S., Femrite, A., Englund, T. F., & Braunstein, M. R. (2003). Relationships of meal and recess schedules to plate waste in elementary schools. National Food Service Management Institute: The University of Mississippi. NFSMI Item Number R-71-03.

Björntorp, P. Heart and soul: Stress and the metabolic syndrome. (2001) *Scand Cardiovasc J*, *35*(3):172-7.

Bray, G. A. (1985). Complications of obesity. *Ann Int Med*; 103(6 Pt 2);1052-62.

Briefel, R. R., Crepinsek, M. K., Cabili, C., Wilson, A., & Gleason, P. M. (2009a). School food environments and practices affect dietary behaviors of U.S. public school children. *J Am Diet Assoc*, *109*:s91-s107.

Briefel, R. R., Wilson, A., & Gleason, P. M. (2009b). Consumption of low-nutrient, energy-dense foods and beverages at school, home, and other locations among school lunch participants and nonparticipants. *J Am Diet Assoc*, *109*:S79-S90.

Brody, G. H., Stoneman, Z., Lane, T. S., & Sanders, A. K. (1981). Television food commercials aimed at children, family grocery shopping, and mother-child interactions. *Family Relations*, *30*(3):435-9.

Brown, D. (2005). Dietary challenges of new Americans. *J Am Diet Assoc*, *105*(11):1704.

Brown, E., Ponce, N., Rice, T., & Lavarreda, S. (2003). The state of health insurance in California: long-term and intermittent lack of health insurance coverage. Los Angeles, CA: UCLA Center for Health Policy Research. Available at: http://www.healthpolicy.ucla.edu/pubs/files/SHIC_report_1114 2003.pdf

California Nutrition Network for Healthy, Active Families (2005). Nutrition and Health Barriers Facing California Latinos: Latino Community Leaders Recommend Practical Solutions. Sacramento, CA: California Department of Health Services. *Issue Brief*. Available at: http://www.dhs.ca.gov/ps/cdic/cpns/lat5aday/download/Issue_Brief-September05.pdf

Casazza, K., & Ciccazzo, M. (2007). The method of delivery of nutrition and physical activity information may play a role in eliciting behavior changes in adolescents. *Eating Behaviors*, *8*:73–82.

Cassady, D., Vogt, R., Oto-Kent, D., Mosley, R., & Lincoln, R. (2006). The power of policy: a case study of healthy eating among children. *Am J Public Health*, *96*:1570–1.

CDC (Centers for Disease Control and Prevention). (2007). *Health Risk Behaviors by Race/Ethnicity- National YRBS: 2007*. Retrieved May 25, 2010 from: http://www.cdc.gov/HealthyYouth/yrbs/pdf/yrbs07_us_disparity_race.pdf

CDC (Centers for Disease Control and Prevention) (2008a). *How much physical activity do you need?* Retrieved May 24, 2010 from: http://www.cdc. gov/physicalactivity/everyone/guidelines/index.html

CDC (Centers for Disease Control and Prevention) (2008b). *Behavioral Risk Factor Surveillance System.* Retrieved May 25, 2010 from: http://www.cdc. gov/nccdphp/dnpa/physical/stats/index.htm

CDC (Centers for Disease Control and Prevention) (2001-2006) National Center for Health Statistics (NCHS). National Health and Nutrition Examination Survey Data. Hyattsville, MD: U.S. Department of Health and Human Services, Centers for Disease Control and Prevention.

Centrella-Nigro, A. (2009). Hispanic children and overweight: Causes and interventions. *Ped Nursing, 35*(6):352-6.

Chávez, N., Tellcen, S., & Kim, Y. O. R. (2007). Food insufficiency in urban Latino families. *J Immigrant Minority Health, 9*:197–204.

CHIS (California Health Interview Survey) (2009). CHIS 2007 Child Public Use File. Los Angeles, CA: UCLA Center for Health Policy Research.

Christeson, W., Taggart, A. D., & Messner-Zidell, S. (2010). *Too fat to fight: Retired military leaders want junk food out of schools.* Mission: Readiness. Accessed June 24, 2010 at: http://cdn.missionreadiness.org/MR_Too_Fat_ to_Fight-1.pdf

CMS (Children's Medical Services) (2008). California Dept. of Public Health Pediatric Nutrition Surveillance System (PedNSS) in California Data tables. Accessed Feb 2008 at http://www.dhs.ca.gov/pcfh/cms/online archive/pdf/chdp/informationnotices/2004/chdpin04c/ contents.htm

Coleman, K. J., Tiller, C. L., Sanchez, J., Heath, E. M., Sy, O., Milliken, G., & Dzewaltowski, D. A. (2005). Prevention of the epidemic increase in child risk of overweight in low-income schools. The El Paso coordinated approach to child health. *Arch Pediatr Adolesc Med, 159*:217-24.

Condon, E. M., Crepinsek, M. K., & Fox, M. K. (2009). School meals: Types of foods offered to and consumed by children at lunch and breakfast. *J Am Diet Assoc, 109*:S67-S78.

Conklin, S., Parham, E., & Robison, J. (2005). Impact of a convincing guest lecturer. *J Nutr Educ Behav, 37*:S101-S102.)

Cottrell, L. A., Northrup, K., & Wittberg, R. (2007). The extended relationship between child cardiovascular risks and academic performance measures. *Obesity, 15*(12):3170-7.

CPEHN (California Pan Ethnic Health Network and the Consumers Union) (2005). *Out of Balance: Marketing of Soda, Candy, Snacks and Fast Foods*

Drowns Out Healthful Messages. San Francisco, CA. Available at: http://www.consumersunion.org/pdf/OutofBalance.pdf

Crawford, P. B., Story, M., Wang, M. C., Ritchie, L. D., & Sabry, Z. I. (2001). Ethnic issues in the epidemiology of childhood obesity. *Child Adolesc Obes*, *48*(4):855-78.

Crawford, P. B., Gosliner, W.; Anderson, C.; Strode, P, Becerra-Jones, Y.; Samuels, S. E.; Carroll, A. M., & Ritchie, L. D. (2004a). Counseling Latina mothers of preschool children about weight issues: suggestions for a new framework. *J Amer Dietetic Assoc*, *104*:387-94.

Crawford, P. B., Gosliner, W., Strode, P., Samuels, S. E., Burnett, C., Craypo, L., Antronette, K., & Yancey, A. K. (2004b). Walking the talk: Fit WIC Wellness Programs improve self-efficacy in pediatric obesity prevention counseling. *Am J Public Health*, *94*:1480–85.

Craypo, L., Purcell, A., Samuels, S. E., Agron, P., Bell, E., & Takada, E. (2002). Fast food sales on high school campuses: results from the 2000 California high school fast food survey. *J Sch Health*, *72*(2):78-82.

Crepinsek, M. K., Gordon, A. R., McKinney, P. M., Condon, E. M., & Wilson, A. (2009). Meals offered and served in U.S. public schools: Do they meet nutrient standards? *J Am Diet Assoc*, *109*:S31-S43.

Cullen, K. W., & Zakeri, I. (2004). Fruits, vegetables, milk and sweetened beverages consumption and access to à la carte/snack bar meals at school. *Am J Public Health*, *94*:463-7.

Cullen, K. W., Watson, K., Zakeri, I., & Ralston, K. (2006). Exploring changes in middle-school student lunch consumption after local school food service policy modifications. *Publ Health Nutr*, *9*(6):14–20.

Cullen, K. W., & Watson, K. B. (2009). The impact of the Texas public school nutrition policy on student food selection and sales in Texas. *Am J Public Health*, *99*:706-12.

Cunningham-Sabo, L., Snyder, M. P., Anliker, J., Thompson, J., Weber, J. L., Thomas, O., Ring, K., Stewart, D., Platero, H., & Nielsen L. (2003). Impact of the Pathways food service intervention on breakfast served in American-Indian schools. *Prev Med*, *37*:S46–S54.

Curioni, C., & Lourenco, P. (2005). Long-term weight loss after diet and exercise: a systematic review. *Int J Obesity*, *29*(10):1168-74.

CWH (Center for Weight & Health, UC Berkeley) (2007a). *School Cafeteria Facilities: Information Sheet*. Accessed on June 28, 2010; available at http://cwh.berkeley.edu/sites/default/files/primary_pdfs/Improved_School_Food%20Service_1.28.08_0.pdf

CWH (Center for Weight & Health, UC Berkeley) (2007b). *Dollars and Sense: The Financial Impact of Selling Healthier School Foods.* Information sheet. Accessed on June 28, 2010; available at http://cwh.berkeley.edu/sites/default/files/primary_pdfs/Dollars_and_Sense_FINAL_3.07.pdf

Davis, E. M., Cullen, K. W., Watson, K. B.; Konarik, M., & Radcliffe, J. (2009). A fresh fruit and vegetable program improves high school students' consumption of fresh produce. *J Am Diet Assoc, 109*:1227-31.

Devault, N., Kennedy, T., Hermann, J., Mwavita, M., Rask, P., & Jaworsky, A. (2009). It's all about kids: preventing overweight in elementary school children in Tulsa, OK. *J Am Diet Assoc, 109*:680-7.

DeVol, R., Bedroussian, A., Charuworn, A., Chatterjee, A., Kim, I. K., Kim, S., & Klowden, K. (2007). An unhealthy America: The economic burden of chronic disease—Charting a new course to save lives and increase productivity and economic growth. *Milken Institute Report.*

DHHS (U.S. Department of Health and Human Services). (2000). *Healthy People 2010—Understanding and Improving Health.* Retrieved June 2, 2010 from: http://www.healthypeople.gov/Document/tableofcontents.htm#under

Dietz, W. H. (1998). Health consequences of obesity in youth: childhood predictors of adult disease. *Pediatrics, 101*:518-25.

Donkin, A. J, Neale, R. J., & Tilston, C. (1993). Children's food purchase requests. *Appetite, 21*(3):291-4.

DPH (California Department of Public Health). (2005). California Dietary Practices Survey, Why Californians are not eating more fruits and vegetables, unpublished data tables.

Drewnowski, A., & Darmon, N. (2005a). The economics of obesity: dietary energy density and energy cost. *Am J Clin Nutr, 82*(suppl):265S-73S.

Drewnowski, A., & Darmon, N. (2005b). Food choices and diet costs: an economic analysis. *J Nutr, 135*(4):900-4.

Economos, C. D., Hyatt, R. R., Goldberg, J. P., Must, A., Naumova, E. N., Collins, J. J., & Nelson, M. E. (2007). A community intervention reduces BMI z-score in children: Shape Up Somerville first year results. *Obesity, 15*(5):1325-36.

ERS (U.S. Department of Agriculture Economic Research Service) (2009). *Food Security in the United States: Key Statistics and Graphics.* Retrieved May 27, 2010 from: http://www.ers.usda.gov/Briefing/FoodSecurity/stats_graphs.htm

Evenson, K. R., Sarmiento, O. L., Macon, M. L., Tawney, K. W., & Ammerman, A. S. (2002). Environmental, policy, and cultural factors related to physical activity among Latina immigrants. *Women and Health, 36*(2):43-57.

Falkner, B., & Michel, S. (1999). Obesity and other risk factors in children. *Eth Dis*, 9(2):284-9.

Finkelstein, D. M., Hill, E. L., & Whitaker, R. C., MD. (2008). School food environments and policies in U.S. public schools. *Pediatrics*, 122:e251–e259

Finkelstein, E. A., Trogdon, J. G., Cohen, J. W., & Dietz, W. (2009). Annual medical spending attributable to obesity: payer- and service-specific estimates. *Health Affairs*, 28(5):w822-w831.

Flegal, K. M., Carroll, M. D., Kuczmarski, R. J., & Johnson, C. L. (1998). Overweight and obesity in the United States: prevalence and trends, 1960-1994. *Int J Obes*, 22:9-47.

Flegal, K. M., Ogden, C. L., Yanovski, J. A., Freedman, D. S., Shepherd, J. A., Graubard, B. I., & Borrud, L. G. (2010). High adiposity and high body mass index-for-age in U.S. children and adolescents overall and by race-ethnic group. *Am J Clin Nutr*, 91(4):1020-26.

Florence, M. D., Asbridge, M., & Veugelers, P. J. (2008). Diet quality and academic performance. *J Sch Health*, 78(4):209-15; quiz 239-41.

Flores, R. (1995). Dance for Health: Improving fitness in African American and Hispanic adolescents. *Public Health Rep*, 110(2):189-93.

FNS (Food & Nutrition Services, U.S. Department of Agriculture (2010) *National School Lunch Program: Participation and Lunches Served, 1969-2009.* Accessed on June 24, 2010 from: http://www.fns.usda.gov/pd/slsummar.htm

Foerster, S. B., Kizer, K. W., Disogra, L. K., Bal, D. G., Krieg, B. F., & Bunch, K. L. (1995). California's "5 a day-for better health!" campaign: an innovative population-based effort to effect large-scale dietary change. *Am J Prev Med*, 11(2):124-31.

Folta, S. C., Goldberg, J. P., Economos, C., Bell, R., Landers, S., & Hyatt, R. (2006). Assessing the use of school public address systems to deliver nutrition messages to children: Shape Up Somerville—Audio Adventures. *J Sch Health*, 76(9):459-64.

Foster, G. D., Sherman, S., Borradaile, K. E., Grundy, K. M., Vander Veur, S. S., Nachmani, J., Karpyn, A., Kumanyika, S., & Shults, J. (2008). A policy-based school intervention to prevent overweight and obesity. *Pediatrics*, 121;e794-e802.

Fox, M. K., Dodd, A. H., Wilson, A., & Gleason, P. M., (2009a). Association between school food environment and practices and body mass index of U.S. public school children. *J Am Diet Assoc*, 109:S108-S117.

Fox, M. F., Gordon, A., Nogales, R., & Wilson, A. (2009b). Availability and consumption of competitive foods in U.S. public schools. *J Am Diet Assoc, 109*(2,Supp 1):S57-S66.

Freedman, D. S., Dietz, W. H., Srinivasan, S. R., & Berenson, G. S. (1999). The relation of overweight to cardiovascular risk factors among children and adolescents: the Bogalusa Heart Study. *Pediatrics, 103*(6 Pt I):1175-82.

French, S. A., Story, M., & Jeffery, R. W. (2001). Environmental influences on eating and physical activity. *Ann Rev. Public Health, 22*:309–35.

French, S. A., Story, M., Jeffery, R. W., Snyder, P., Eisenberg, M., Sidebottom, A., & Murray, D. (1997). A pricing strategy to promote fruit and vegetable purchase in high school cafeterias. *J Am Diet Assoc, 97*(9):1008-10.

French, S. A. (2005). Public Health strategies for dietary change: schools and workplaces. *J Nutr, 135*: 910-12.

Frenn, M., Malin, S., Brown, R. L., Greer, Y., Fox, J., Greer, J., & Smyczek, S. (2005). Changing the tide: an Internet/video exercise and low-fat diet intervention with middle-school students. *Appl Nursing Res, 18*:13-21.

Fu, M. L., Cheng, L., Tu, S. H., & Pan, W. H. (2007). Association between unhealthful eating patterns and unfavorable overall school performance in children. *J Am Diet Assoc, 107*(11):1935-43.

Galst, J. P., & White, M. A. (1976). The unhealthy persuader: the reinforcing value of television and children's purchase-influencing attempts at the supermarket. *Child Devel, 47*(4):1089-96.

Galvez, M. P., Pearl, M., & Yen, I. H. (2010). Childhood obesity and the built environment. *Curr Opin Pediatr, 22*(2):202-7.

Getlinger, M. J., Laughlin, C. V. T., Bell, E., Akre, C., & Arjmandi, B. H. (1996). Food waste is reduced when elementary-school children have recess before lunch. *J Am Diet Assoc, 96*(9):906-8.

Giammattei, J., Blix, G., Marshak, H. H., Wollitzer, A. O., & Pettitt, D. J. (2003). Television watching and soft drink consumption: associations with obesity in 11 to 13 year old schoolchildren. *Arch Ped Adolesc Med, 157*(9):882-6.

Gleason, P. M., & Dodd, A. H. (2009). School Breakfast Program but not School Lunch Program participation is associated with lower body mass index. *J Am Diet Assoc, 109*:S118-S128.

Goodman, E. (1999). The role of socioeconomic status gradients in explaining differences in U.S. adolescents' health. *Am J Public Health, 89*(10):1522-8.

Goran, M. I., & Sun, M. (1998). Total energy expenditure and physical activity in prepubertal children: recent advances based on the application of the doubly labeled water method. *Am J Clin Nutr, 68*(4):9445-95.

Gordon, A. R., Cohen, R., Crepinsek, M. K., Fox, M. K., Hall, J., & Zeidman, E. (2009). The third School Nutrition Dietary Assessment Study: background and study design. *J Am Diet Assoc, 109*(2 Suppl):S20-30.

Gordon, A., Crepinsek, M. K., Nogales, R., & Condon, E. (2007). *School Nutrition Dietary Assessment Study-III: Volume I: School Foodservice, School Food Environment, and Meals Offered and Served.* Alexandria, VA: U.S. Department of Agriculture, Food and Nutrition Service, Office of Research, Nutrition and Analysis. Accessed at: http://www.fns.usda.gov/oane/MENU/Published/CNP/cnp.htm

Gordon-Larsen, P., Harris, K. M., Ward, D. S., & Popkin, B. M. (2003). Acculturation and overweight-related behaviors among Hispanic immigrants to the U.S.: The National Longitudinal Study of Adolescent Health. *Soc Sci Med, 57*(11):2023-34.

Gortmaker, S. Cheung, L., Peterson, K., Chomitz, G., Cradle, J., Dart, H., & et al. (1999). Impact of a school-based interdisciplinary intervention on diet and physical activity among urban primary school children. *Arch Ped Adol Med, 153*(9):975-83.

Gosliner, W., Madsen, K. A., Woodward-Lopez, G., & Crawford, P. B. (2010). Would students prefer to eat healthier foods at school? *J Schl Health, 81*:146-151.

Haas, J., Lee, L., Kaplan, C., Sonneborn, D., Phillips, K., & Liang, S. (2003). The association of race, socioeconomic status, and health insurance status with the prevalence of overweight among children and adolescents. *Am J Public Health, 93*(12):2105-10.

Haerens, L., De Bourdeaudhuij, I., Maes, L., Vereecken, C., Brug, J., & Deforche, B. (2007). The effects of a middle-school healthy eating intervention on adolescents' fat and fruit intake and soft drinks consumption. *Public Health Nutrition, 10*(5):443-9

Harsha, D. W. (1995). The benefits of physical activity in childhood. *Am J Med Sci, 310S*(1):S109-S111.

Heath, E. M., & Coleman, K. J. (2002). Evaluation of the institutionalization of the Coordinated Approach to Child Health (CATCH) in a U.S./Mexico border community. *Health Educ Behav, 29*:440-60.

Heath, E. M., & Coleman, K. J. (2003). Adoption and institutionalization of the Child and Adolescent Trial for Cardiovascular Health (CATCH). *Health Promot Pract, 4*:157-64.

Hedley, A. A., Ogden, C. L., Johnson, C. L., Carroll, M. D., Curtin, L. R., & Flegal, K. M. (2004). Prevalence of overweight and obesity among U.S. children, adolescents, and adults, 1999-2002. *JAMA, 291*(23):2847-50.

Hoelscher, D. M., Springer, A. E., Ranjit, N., Perry, C. L., Evans, A. E., Stigler, M., & Kelder, S. H. (2010). Reductions in child obesity among disadvantaged school children with community involvement: The Travis County CATCH Trial. *Obesity, 18*(Suppl 1):S36-S44.

Hollar, D., Messiah, S. E., Lopez-Mitnik, G., Hollar, T. L., Almon, M., & Agatston, A. S. (2010a). Effect of a two-year obesity prevention intervention on percentile changes in body mass index and academic performance in low-income elementary school children. *Am J Public Health, 100*:646-53.

Hollar, D., Lombardo, M., Lopez-Mitnik, G., Hollar, T. L., Almon, M., Agatston, A. S., & Messiah, S. E. (2010b). Effective multilevel, multisector, school-based obesity prevention programming improves weight, blood pressure, and academic performance, especially among low-income, minority children. *J Health Care Poor Underserved, 21*(2 Suppl):93-108.

Hovell, M., Sallis, J., Hofstetter, R., Barrington, E., Hackley, M., Elder, J., Castro, F., & Kilbourne, K. (1991). Identification of correlates of physical activity among Latino adults. *J Community Health, 16*(1):23-6.

Hoyland, A., Dye, L., & Lawton, C. L. (2009). A systematic review of the effect of breakfast on the cognitive performance of children and adolescents. *Nutr Res Rev, 22*(2):220-43.

IOM (Institute of Medicine). (2004) *Preventing Childhood Obesity: Health in the Balance.* [Koplan JP, Liverman CT, Kraak VI, Editors] The National Academies Press: Washington, D.C.

IOM (Institute of Medicine). (2006). *Food Marketing to Children and Youth: Threat or Opportunity?* [McGinnis JM, Gootman JA, Kraak VI, Editors] The National Academies Press: Washington, D.C.

IOM (Institute of Medicine) (2007) *Nutrition Standards for Foods in Schools: Leading the Way toward Healthier Youth.* [Stallings VA, Yaktine AL, Editors] The National Academies Press: Washington, D.C.

Isler, L., Popper, E., & Ward, S. (1979). Children's purchase requests and parental responses: Results from a diary study. *J Advertising Res, 27*:28-39.

Jolliffe, C. J., & Janssen, I. (2006). Vascular risks and management of obesity in children and adolescents. *Vasc Health Risk Manag, 2*(2):171-87.

Katz, D. L., O'Connell, M., Njike, V. Y., Yeh, M.-C., & Nawaz, H. (2008). Strategies for the prevention and control of obesity in the school setting: systematic review and meta-analysis. *Inter J Obes, 32*:1780-9.

Kleinman, R. E., Hall, S., Green, H., Korzec-Ramirez, D., Patton, K., Pagano, M. E., & Murphy, J. M. (1996). Diet, breakfast, and academic performance in children. *Ann Nutr Metab, 46 Suppl 1*:24-30.

Kleinman, R. E., Murphy, J. M., Little, M., Pagano, M., Wehler, C. A., Regal, K., & Jellinek, M. S. (1998). Hunger in children in the United States: Potential behavioral and emotional correlates. *Pediatrics, 101*(1):e3.

Kleinman, R. E., Hall, S., Green, H., Korzec-Ramirez, D., Patton, K., Pagano, M. E., & Murphy J. M. (2002) Diet, breakfast, and academic performance in children. *Ann Nutr Metab, 46*(Suppl 1):24-30.

Kubik, M. Y., Lytle, L. A., Hannan, P. J., Perry, C. L., & Story, M. (2003). The association of the school food environment with dietary behaviors of young adolescents. *Am J Public Health, 93*:1168-73

Linn, S. (2008) Calories for sale: food marketing to children in the Twenty-First Century. *Annals Am Acad Political Soc Sci, 615*(1):133-55.

Lorson, B. A., Melgar-Quiñonez, H. R., & Taylor, C. A. (2009). Correlates of fruit and vegetable intakes in U.S. children. *J Am Diet Assoc, 109*(3):474-8.

Loughridge, J. L., & Barrat, J. (2005) Does the provision of cooled filtered water in secondary school cafeterias increase water drinking and decrease the purchase of soft drinks? *J Hum Nutr Diet, 18*:281-6.

Ludwig, D. S., Peterson, K. E., & Gortmaker, S. L. (2001). Relation between consumption of sugar-sweetened drinks and childhood obesity: a prospective, observational analysis. *The Lancet, 357*:505-8.

Lytle, L. A., Murray, D. M., Evenson, K. R., Moody, J., Pratt, C. A., Metcalfe, L., & Parra-Medina, D. (2009). Mediators affecting girls' levels of physical activity outside of school: findings from the trial of activity in adolescent girls. *Ann Behav Med, 38*(2):124-36.

Lytle, L. A., Eszery, M. K., Nicklas, T., Montgomery, D., Zive, M., Evans, M., Snyder, P., Nichaman, M., Kelder, S. H., Reed, D., Busch, E., & Mitchell, P. (1996a) Nutrient intakes of third graders: results from the Child and Adolescent Trial for Cardiovascular Health (CATCH) Baseline Survey. *J Nutr Educ, 28*(6):338-47.

Lytle, L. A., Stone, E. J., Nichaman, M. Z., Perry, C. L., Montgomery, D. H., Nicklas, T. A., Zive, M. M., Mitchell, P., Dwyer, J. T., Ebzery, M. K., Evans, M. A., & Galati, T. P. (1996b). Changes in nutrient intakes of elementary school children following a school-based intervention: results from the CATCH Study. *Prev Med, 25*(4):465-77.

McAleese, J. D., & Rankin, L. L. (2007). Garden-based nutrition education affects fruit and vegetable consumption in sixth-grade adolescents. *J Am Diet Assoc, 107*:662-5.

McDermott, L., Stead, M., & Hastings, G. (2006). Does food promotion influence children's diet? A review of the evidence. In: *Childhood Obesity: Con-*

temporary Issues. [Cameron N, Norgan NG, Ellison GTH, Editors]. CRC Press: Boca Raton, FL.

Meyers, A. F., Sampson, A. E., Weitzman, M., Rogers, B. L., & Kayne, H., PhD. (1989). School breakfast program and school performance. *Am J Dis Child,* *143*:1234-9

Molnar, A. (2003). *School commercialism, student health, and the pressure to do more with less.* Commercialism in Education Research Unit, Arizona State University. Accessed June 28, 2010; available at http://www.epicpolicy.org/files/EPSL-0307-105-CERU.doc

Moore, D. C. (1993). Body image and eating behaviour in adolescents. *J Am Coll Nutr, 92*(7), 851-3.

Muñoz, K. A., Krebs-Smith, S. M., & et al. (1997). Food intakes of U.S. children and adolescents compared with recommendations. *Pediatrics, 100*(3 Pt 1):323-9.

Murphy, J. M., Pagano, M. E., Nachmani, J., Sperling, P.; Kane, S., & Kleinman, R. E. (1998). The relationship of school breakfast to psychosocial and academic functioning: cross-sectional and longitudinal observations in an inner-city school sample. *Arch Pediatr Adolesc Med, 152*:899-907.

Must, A., Spandano, J., Coakley, E. H., Field, A. E., Colditz, G. A., & Dietz, W. H. (1999). The disease burden associated with overweight and obesity. *JAMA, 282*(16):1523-9.

Nansel, T. R., Huang, T. T., Rovner, A. J., & Sanders-Butler, Y. (2010). Association of school performance indicators with implementation of the healthy kids, smart kids programme: case study. *Health Nutr, 13*(1):116-22.

Narayan, K. M. V., Boyle, J. P., Thompson, T. J., Sorensen, S. W., & Williamson, D. F. (2003). Lifetime risk for diabetes mellitus in the United States. *JAMA, 290*(14):1884-90.

Nestle, M. (2000). Soft drink "Pouring Rights": marketing empty calories to children. *Public Health Reports, 115*(4):308-19.

Neumark-Sztainer, D., Story, M., Resnick, M. D., & Blum, R. W. (1996). Correlates of inadequate fruit and vegetable consumption among adolescents. *Prev Med,* (5):497-505.

NHLBI (National Heart Lung and Blood Institute) (2004). *Think Tank on Enhancing Obesity Research at the National Heart, Lung and Blood Institute.* Bethesda, Maryland: National Institutes of Health. Available at: http://www.nhlbi.nih.gov/health/prof/heart/obesity/ob_res_exsum/obesity_tt.pdf

NSLP (National School Lunch Program), U.S. Department of Agriculture, Food & Nutrition Service. (2009) *National School Lunch Program Fact Sheet.*

Accessed June 24, 2010, from http://www.fns.usda.gov/cnd/Lunch/About Lunch/NSLPFactSheet.pdf

Obarzanek, E., Schreiber, G., Crawford, P., Goldman, S., Barrier, P., & Frederick, M. (1994). Energy intake and physical activity in relation to indices of body fat. *Am J Clin Nutr, 60*:15-22.

Ogden, C. L., Flegal, K. M., Carroll, M. D., & Johnson, C. L. (2002). Prevalence and trends in overweight among U.S. children and adolescents, 1999-2000. *JAMA, 288*(14):1728-32.

Ogden, C. L., Carroll, M. D., Curtin, L. R., McDowell, M. A., Tabak, C. J., & Flegal, K. M. (2006). Prevalence of overweight and obesity in the United States, 1999-2004. *JAMA, 295*(13):1549-55.

Ogden, C. L., Carroll, M. D., & Flegal, K. M. (2008). High body mass index for age among U.S. children and adolescents, 2003-2006. *JAMA, 299*(20):2401-05.

Ogden, C. L., Carroll, M. D., Curtin, L. R., Lamb, M. M., & Flegal, K. M. (2010). Prevalence of high body mass index in U.S. children and adolescents, 2007-2008. *JAMA, 303*(3):242-9.

Olshanksky, S. J., Passaro, D. J., Hershow, R. C., Lavden, J., Carnes, B. A., Brody, J., Hayflick, L., Butler, R. N., Allison, D. B., & Ludwig, D. S. (2005). A potential decline in life expectancy in the United States in the 21st century. *N Engl J Med, 352*(11):1138-45.

Parsons, T. J., Power, C., Logan, S., & Summerbell, C. D. (1999). Childhood predictors of adult obesity: a systematic review. *Int J Obes, 12*:S1-S107.

Powell, L. M., Auld, M. C., Chaloupka, F. J., & et al. (2007). Associations between access to food stores and adolescent body mass index. *Am J Health Promo, 33*(4 suppl):S301-7.

Rampersaud, G. C., Pereira, M. A., Girard, B. L., Adams, J., & Metzl, J. D. (2005). Breakfast habits, nutritional status, body weight, and academic performance in children and adolescents. *J Am Diet Assoc, 105*(5):743-60.

Ravussin, E., Valencia, M. E., Esparza, J., Bennett, P. H., & Schulz, L. O. (1994). Effects of a traditional lifestyle on obesity in Pima Indians. *Diabetes Care, 17*(9):1067-74.

Resnicow, K., Cohn, L., Reinhardt, J., Cross, D., Futterman, R., Kirschner, E., Wynder, E. L., & Allegrante, J. P. (1992) A three-year evaluation of the Know Your Body Program in inner-city schoolchildren. *Health Educ Behav, 19*:463.

Rhoades, J. A., & Vistnes, J. P. (2006). *Health Insurance Status of Hispanic Subpopulations in 2004: Estimates for the U.S. Civilian Noninstitutionalized Population under Age 65.* Statistical Brief #143. Agency for Healthcare

Research and Quality, Rockville, MD. http://www.meps.ahrq.gov/mepsweb/data_files/publications/st143/stat143.pdf

Rosenbaum, M., Nonas, C., Weil, R., Horlick, M., Fennoy, I., Vargas, I., & Kringas, P., The El Camino Diabetes Prevention Group. (2007). School-based intervention acutely improves insulin sensitivity and decreases inflammatory markers and body fatness in junior high school students. *J Clin Endocrinol Metab*, *92*:504-8.

Sallis, J. F., & Glanz, K. (2009). Physical activity and food environments: solutions to the obesity epidemic. *Milbank Q*, *87*(1):123-54.

Sallis, J. F., McKenzie, T. L., Conway, T. L., Elder, J. P., Prochaska, J. J., Brown, M., Zive, M. M., Marshall, S. J., & Alcaraz, J. E. (2003). Environmental interventions for eating and physical activity: a randomized controlled trial in middle schools. *Am J Prev Med*, *24*(3):209–217.

Sallis, J. F., Patterson, T. L., Buono, M. J., & Nader, P. R. (1998). Relation of cardiovascular fitness and physical activity to cardiovascular disease risk factors in children and adults. *Am J Epidemiol*, *86*(3):352-6.

Samuels, S. E., Bullock, S. L., Woodward-Lopez, G., & et al. (2009). To what extent have high schools in California been able to implement state-mandated nutrition standards? *J Adol Health*, *45*:S38-S44.

Sanchez-Vaznaugh, E. V., Sanchez, B. N., Baek, J., & Crawford, P. B. (2010). Competitive food and beverage policies: Are they influencing the trends in childhood overweight? *Health Affairs*, *29*(3):436-446.

Sarlio-Lähteenkorva, S., Rissanen, A., & Kaprio, J. (2000). A descriptive study of weight loss maintenance: 6- and 15-year follow-up of initially overweight adults. *Int J Obesity*, *24*(1):116-25.

SBP (School Breakfast Program), U.S. Department of Agriculture, Food & Nutrition Service. (2009) *School Breakfast Program Fact Sheet*. Accessed June 24, 2010, from http://www.fns.usda.gov/cnd/breakfast/AboutBFast/SBPFactSheet.pdf

Schonfeld-Warden, N., & Warden, C. H. (1997). Pediatric obesity: an overview of etiology and treatment. *Ped Clin No Amer*, *44*(2):339-61.

Schwartz, M. B. (2007). The influence of a verbal prompt on school lunch fruit consumption: a pilot study. *Int J Beh Nutr Phys Act*, *4*:6-11.

Schwartz, M. B., Novak, S. A., & Fiore, S. S. (2009). The impact of removing snacks of low nutritional value from middle schools. *Health Educ Behav*, *36*;999-1011.

Serdula, M. K., Ivery, D., Coates, R. J., Freedman, D. S., Williamson, D. F., & Byers, T. (1993). Do obese children become obese adults? A review of the literature. *Prev Med*, *22*:163-77.

Shilts, M. K., Lamp, C., Horowitz, M., & Townsend, M. S. (2009). Pilot study: EatFit impacts sixth graders' academic performance on achievement of mathematics and English education standards. *J Nutr Educ Behav*, *41*(2):127-31.

Snelling, A. M., & Kennard, T. (2009). The impact of nutrition standards on competitive food offerings and purchasing behaviors of high school students. *J School Health*, *79*(11):541-6.

Stoneman, Z., & Brody, G. H. (1982). The indirect impact of child-oriented advertisements on mother-child interaction. *J App Devel Psych*, *2*:369-76.

Story, M., Kaphingst, K. M., & French, S. (2006). The role of schools in obesity prevention. *The Future of Children, Childhood Obesity*, *16*(1):109-42.

Story, M. (2009). The Third School Nutrition Dietary Assessment Study: Findings and policy implications for improving the health of U.S. Children. *Am J Diet Assoc*, *109*(2, Suppl 1):S8-S13.

Strong, W. B, Malina, R. M. M., Blimkie, C. J., Daniels, S. R., Dishman, R. K., Gutin, B., Hergenroeder, A. C., Must, A., Nixon, P. A., Pivarnik, J. M., Rowland, T., Trost, S., & Trudeau, F. (2005). Evidence based physical activity for school-age youth. *J Pediatrics*, *146*(6):732-7.

Tammelin, T., Näyhä, S., Laitinen, J., Rintamäki, H., & Järvelin, M. R. (2003). Physical activity and social status in adolescence as predictors of physical inactivity in adulthood. *Prev Med*, *37*:375-81.

Taras, H. (2005). Nutrition and student performance at school. *J Sch Health*, *75*(6):199-213.

Taras, H., Sallis, J. F., Patterson, T. L., Nader, P. R., & Nelson, J. A. (1989). Television's influence on children's diet and physical activity. *J Dev Behav Pediatr*, *10*(4):176-80.

Taras, H., Zive, M., Nader, P., Berry, C. C, Hoy, T., & Boyd, C. (2000). Television advertising and classes of food products consumed in a paediatric population. *Int J Ad*, *19*:487-93.

Taylor, R. W., McAuley, K. A., Barbezat, W., Strong, A., Williams, S. M., & Mann, J. I. (2007). APPLE Project: 2-y findings of a community-based obesity prevention program in primary school–age children. *Am J Clin Nutr*, *86*:735-42.

Treviño, R. P., Pugh, J. A., Hernandez, A. E., Menchaca, V. D., Ramirez, R. R., & Mendoza, M. (1998). Bienestar: a diabetes risk-factor prevention program. *J School Health*, *68*(2):62-7.

Treviño, R. P., Yin, Z., Hernandez, A., Hale, D. E., Garcia, O. A., & Mobley, C. (2004). Impact of the Bienestar school-based diabetes mellitus prevention program on fasting capillary glucose levels: a randomized controlled trial. *Arch Pediatr Adolesc Med*, *158*(9):911-7.

Troiano, R. P., Briefel, R. R., Carroll, M. D., & Bialostosky, K. (2000). Energy and fat intakes of children and adolescents in the United States: data from the National Health and Nutrition Examination Surveys. *Am J Clin Nutr,* 72(suppl):1343S-53S.

Troiano, R. P., Berrigan, D., Dodd, K. W., Mâsse, L. C., Tilert, T., & McDowel, L. M. (2008). Physical activity in the United States measured by accelerometer. *Med Sci Sports Exerc, 40*(1):181-8.

Trust for Public Land. (2004). *Parks for People: Los Angeles Case Statement.* San Francisco, CA: The Trust for Public Land. Available at: http://www.tpl.org/tier3_cd.cfm?content_item_id=17655&folder_id=2627

UCCE DANR (University of California Cooperative Extension Division of Agriculture and Natural Resources) (2003). *Learning from Latino Community Efforts. Youth, Families, and Communities Workgroup.* Retrieved November 11, 2005 from http://ucce.ucdavis.edu/files/filelibrary/5433/11197.pdf

Unger, J. B., Reynolds K., Shakib S., Spruijt-Metz D., Sun P., & Johnson C. A. (2004). Acculturation, physical activity, and fast-food consumption among Asian-American and Hispanic adolescents. *J Comm Health, 29*(6):467-81.

United Nations Department of Economic and Social Affairs. (2007). *World Population Prospects: The 2006 Revision.* Retrieved June 2, 2010 from: http://www.un.org/esa/population/publications/wpp2006/WPP2006_Highlights_rev.pdf

Walter, H. J., Hofman, A., Connelly, P. A., Barrett, L. T., & Kost, K. L. (1985). Primary prevention of chronic disease in childhood: changes in risk factors after one year of intervention. *Am J Epidemiol, 122*:772-81.

Walter, H. J., Hofman, A., Vaughan, R. D., & Wynder E. L. (1988). Modification of risk factors for coronary heart disease. Five-year results of a school-based intervention trial. *N Engl J Med, 318*(17):1093-100.

Weir, L. A., Etelson, D., & Brand, D. A. (2006). Parents' perceptions of neighborhood safety and children's physical activity. *Prev Med, 43* 212–7.

Wilcox, S., Castro, C., King, A. C., Housemann, R., & Brownson, R. C. (2000). Determinants of leisure time physical activity in rural compared with urban older and ethnically diverse women in the United States. *J Epidemiol Comm Health, 54*(9):667-72.

Wojcicki, J. M., & Heyman, M. B. (2006). Healthier choices and increased participation in a middle school lunch program: effects of nutrition policy changes in San Francisco. *Am J Public Health, 96*:1542-7.

Wolf, A. M., & Colditz, G. A. (1998). Current estimates of the economic costs of obesity in the United States. *Obes Res, 48*(1):5-12.

Woodward-Lopez, G., Flores, G., Garza A., Mendoza, F., Alonzo-Diaz, G., Jarra, E., Sunderland A., & Nguyen R. (2006). *Obesity in Latino Communities: Prevention, Principles and Action.* Latino Coalition for a Healthy California: Sacramento.

Woodward-Lopez, G., Ikeda, J., & Crawford, P. (2000). *Improving Children's Academic Performance, Health and Quality of Life:A Top Policy Commitment in Response to Children's Obesity and Health Crisis in California.* California Elected Women's Association for Education and Research (CEWAER).

Woodward-Lopez, G., Webb, K., Tujaque, J., Godbole, S., Gosliner, W., & Crawford, P. B. (2008). *Evaluation of the California Fresh Start Program: Report of Findings.* Center for Weight and Health, University of California, Berkeley.

Woodward-Lopez, G., Kao, J., & Crawford, P. B. (2010a). Unpublished findings from a survey of a random sample of 56 school food service directors in California as part of the study "Capturing the impact of new food and beverage standards in California high schools." Center for Weight and Health, University of California, Berkeley.

Woodward-Lopez, G., Kao, J., & Crawford, P. B. (2010b). Unpublished findings from observations of a random sample of 56 high schools in California as part of the study "Capturing the impact of new food and beverage standards in California high schools." Center for Weight and Health, University of California, Berkeley.

Woodward-Lopez G., Kao J., & Crawford P. B. (2010c). Unpublished findings from observations from 24 schools in California as part of the evaluation of the "School Wellness Policy Demonstration Project." Center for Weight and Health, University of California, Berkeley.

Woodward-Lopez, G., Gosliner, W., Samuels, S., Craypo, L., Kao, J., & Crawford, P. B. (2010d) Lessons learned from evaluations of California's statewide school nutrition standards. *Am J Public Health*, doi:10.2105/AJPH.2010.193490.

Yancey, A. K., Kumanyika, S. K., Ponce, N. A., McCarthy, W. J., Fielding, J. E., Leslie, J. P., & Akbar, J. (2004). Population-based interventions engaging communities of color in health eating and active living: a review. *Prev Cronic Dis, 1*(1):A09. Available at: www.cdc.gov/pcd/issues/2004/jan/03_0012.htm

CHAPTER SIX

TELEVISION VIEWING AND PHYSICAL ACTIVITY AMONG LATINO CHILDREN

Jason A. Mendoza[1] and Cristina S. Barroso[2]

Watching television and using other forms of media such as video games, computers, print, music and movies takes up a surprisingly large amount of our children's time. U.S. children spend more time watching television than any other activity except sleep (Dietz, 1991; Rideout, Foehr & Roberts, 2010). According to a recent nationwide report on children's media use in the United States conducted by the Kaiser Family Foundation, the average amount of time spent watching television by 8- to 18-year-olds was 4 hours and 29 minutes per day (4:29) (Rideout et al., 2010). If we add other forms of media including music, computer (non-homework related), video games, print and movies, their total media use was 7:38 hours per day, practically a full work day! Latino children eight to eighteen years old spent 5:21 hours daily watching television compared to their white peers who spent only 3:36 daily. Among Mexican-American preschool children, 27.5% watched television more than the recommended maximum of 1-2 hours per day (Mendoza, Zimmerman & Christakis, 2007).

[1]USDA/ARS Children's Nutrition Research Center and Academic General Pediatrics, Department of Pediatrics and the Dan L. Duncan Cancer Center, Baylor College of Medicine.
[2]Health Promotion and Behavioral Sciences, University of Texas Health Science Center at Houston, School of Public Health, Brownsville Regional Campus.

How were children watching all of this television programming? With so many television programs online, children can watch television programs on many devices. U.S. children now watch approximately 3½ hours of television per day on traditional television sets (whether live, recorded or on demand) and almost one additional hour of television viewing occurred using other devices, such as computers, iPod/MP3 players and cell phones (Rideout et al., 2010).

What influences children's television viewing and media use? Obviously, having access to televisions and other types of media devices allows children to use them. Children in the United States with a television in their bedrooms watched more television and were at greater risk for obesity (Dennison, Erb & Jenkins, 2002; Gorely, Marshall & Biddle, 2004). Despite this risk, 71% of eight- to eighteen-year-old U.S. children in 2008-2009 had a television in their bedroom and about half had a video game player or cable television in their bedroom as well (Rideout et al., 2010).

Parents' rules for their children's media use influence children's media and television use. Children in households with rules that limited their media and television time or content had almost 3 hours less exposure per day to media and television (Rideout et al., 2010). However, fewer Latino households imposed rules for their children on media content compared to white or black households (38% vs. 52% and 43%, respectively), which places them at greater risk for watching television. Children whose parents believed they lived in less safe neighborhoods had children who watched more television (Burdette & Whitaker, 2005). Neighborhoods with higher proportions of Latinos were perceived as less safe (Osypuk, Diez Roux, Hadley & Kandula, 2009), which places many Latino children at higher risk for greater television and media use.

Why are health professionals so interested in children's television viewing? Isn't it just entertainment? While television viewing can provide entertainment, it is also a powerful means to affect viewers' beliefs and behaviors (e.g. buy product A), and remains the dominant type of media today (Rideout et al., 2010). The American Academy of Pediatrics recognized the impact that media and television viewing has on children's behaviors and health and released recommendations to limit television viewing and media use for children 2 years and older to no more than 1-2 hours of quality programming per day (Barlow, 2007; Committee on Communications, 2006; Krebs et al., 2007). These recommendations recognized that television and media use are common to everyday life and can have both benefits and drawbacks, depending on the types of programs watched.

Child-oriented television channels and programs do exist, and some educational programming has been associated with better educational outcomes and racial attitudes (Thakkar, Garrison & Christakis, 2006). Diaz-Guerrero and Holtzman conducted a unique and well-designed experiment during the 1st telecast season of *Plaza Sésamo*, the Spanish-language version of *Sesame Street* (Diaz-Guerrero & Holtzman, 1974). The investigators randomly assigned 173 preschool children in Mexico City to watch either *Plaza Sésamo*, or cartoons and non-educational TV programs for 50 minutes per day over 6 months while attending daycare. Children who watched *Plaza Sésamo* scored higher on general knowledge, numbers, letters and words (all P<0.05), which were concepts directly taught by *Plaza Sésamo,* and had higher scores for cognitive and oral comprehension (all P<0.05), which were indirectly taught by the program. Among three- to five-year-old white children in Canada, Gorn and colleagues randomly assigned children to watch *Sesame Street* episodes either with or without inserts of non-white children playing together (Gorn, Goldberg & Kanungo, 1976). Children who saw *Sesame Street* with the inserts showed a preference (by selecting a photograph) for playing with non-white children compared to the control group (71.4% vs. 33.3%, respectively, P<0.01). Thus, some television programs, particularly educational ones like *Sesame Street* or *Plaza Sésamo*, have been shown to enhance educational achievement and to help shape racial attitudes.

However, in most homes, children are exposed to non-educational television programs and commercials designed for older audiences; viewing these may lead to undesired behaviors. For example, young children's television viewing was associated with greater risk of attention problems in later childhood and adolescence (Christakis, Zimmerman, DiGiuseppe & McCarty, 2004; Landhuis, Poulton, Welch & Hancox, 2007). School achievement may also be affected: 47% of children with heavy media use reported fair to poor grades versus 31% of moderate users and only 23% of light users (Rideout et al., 2010). Besides affecting children's attention and school achievement, watching excessive amounts of television may place children at high risk for developing childhood obesity, which remains at historically high levels in the United States (Ogden, Carroll, Curtin, Lamb & Flegal, 2010). Children who watched more television were at higher risk of obesity (Andersen, Crespo, Bartlett, Cheskin & Pratt, 1998), including preschool children (Mendoza et al., 2007). Moreover, decreasing children's television viewing resulted in lower body mass index in several randomized controlled trials (Epstein et al., 2008; Gortmaker et al., 1999; Robinson, 1999), although trials among Latino children are largely lacking.

How does television viewing put children at higher risk for obesity? Two main mechanisms have been proposed to explain the influence of TV viewing to obesity: (1) displacing physical activity, since watching television usually involves sitting down and not being very physically active, and (2) increasing caloric intake by children eating while watching television or being influenced by advertisements to later buy and eat high-calorie foods. While accurately measuring television viewing, physical activity and dietary intake is important to be able to detect these relationships, most measures commonly used in previous studies relied on children or parents recalling these items for the last 24 hours or even the last year. Recalls are problematic due to the difficulty in accurately remembering behaviors over these long periods of time. While objective measures of physical activity such as accelerometers or heart rate monitors have become more common (Trost, 2001; Trost, McIver & Pate, 2005), and should result in more accurate and consistent measurements, most previous studies used measures that relied on participant recall (Marshall, Biddle, Gorely, Cameron & Murdey, 2004). Despite these limitations, some evidence for the relationship between TV viewing and physical activity exists. A recent review that combined 24 previous studies reported that greater television viewing was associated with somewhat less physical activity (fully corrected sample-weighted mean effect size r=-0.129) (Marshall et al., 2004).

Watching television has also been associated with children eating more meals, snacks and calories in observational (Francis, Lee & Birch, 2003; Snoek, van Strien, Janssens & Engels, 2006) and small experimental studies (Blass et al., 2006; Stroebele & de Castro, 2004). Television advertisements influenced children's dietary intake toward increased consumption of snack foods and sweets, i.e. low-nutrient, high-energy foods. (Galst, 1980; Goldberg, Gorn & Gibson, 1978; Zajonc, 1968). Children as young as 2 to 5 years watched as many as 3 hours of food commercials each week (Cotugna, 1998). At least 56% of all commercials aired during children's hours in the United States were for food-related items, and the vast majority of these promoted foods high in sugar, fat or salt and low in nutritional value (Kotz & Story, 1994; Story & Faulkner, 1990). Bell and colleagues examined U.S. television commercial advertising among 12 broadcast and cable networks in 2005-2006, including the Spanish-language networks Telemundo and Univision. They reported that television commercials on the Spanish-language networks were more likely to be for fast-food restaurants compared to the full sample (46.7% vs. 28.4%) (Bell, Cassady, Culp & Alcalay, 2009). Similarly, Ramírez-Ley and colleagues reported that 50% of all food related advertising after school and on weekend mornings in Baja California, Mexico, were for fast foods and calorie-dense foods (Ramírez-Ley et al., 2009). For each hour increase in U.S. children's television viewing, Wiecha and colleagues estimated an additional 167 kcal eaten per day and an increase in the consumption of foods commonly advertised on TV (Wiecha et al., 2006).

Several studies helped explain the possible mechanism through which televised food advertisements influence children's behaviors and dietary intake. Borzekowski and Robinson conducted a series of experimental studies to examine the impact of advertisements on children. In the first experiment, they randomized thirty-nine preschool children (17 were Latino) to view videotapes of animated programs either with or without commercials for products commonly advertised on children's television programs. Brief exposure to commercials influenced children to select greater advertised versus non-advertised products (Borzekowski & Robinson, 2001). In a follow-up experiment, Robinson and colleagues randomized 63 preschool children (35 were Latino) to fast food/beverage items and carrots that the investigators branded as McDonald's or left unbranded. At the time of the experiment, carrots were not on the menu of McDonald's restaurants. Higher percentages of children indicated that they preferred the McDonald's-branded chicken nuggets, french fries, milk or apple juice and carrots versus the identical non-branded items (all P<0.05) (Robinson, Borzekowski, Matheson & Kraemer, 2007). This greater preference for branded items was stronger among children with more television sets in their homes.

In an observational study, Zimmerman and Bell used nationally representative data from the Panel Survey of Income Dynamics conducted by the National Science Foundation to examine the influence of television advertisements on children's weight status 5 years later (Zimmerman & Bell, 2010). Among children less than 7 years old (>1100 subjects), each hour per day of commercial viewing in 1997 was associated with higher BMI z-scores in 2002. No relationship was reported for non-commercial viewing and BMI z-scores. Nicklas and colleagues developed two 30-second commercials with one promoting fruit and another promoting vegetables and randomized 183 preschool children (61% were Latino) to watch a 15-minute television program either with or without the commercials. Children who watched the commercials showed a higher preference for the target vegetables (broccoli and carrots, P<0.02) after multiple exposures (Nicklas et al., 2011). Since advertisements for fruit and vegetables during children's typical television viewing times were rare (Bell et al., 2009), increasing children's exposure to "healthy" commercials appears to be a promising strategy to counter the impact of unhealthy advertised foods. The above studies suggest that television viewing influences children's dietary preferences, dietary intake and risk for obesity, likely through exposure to televised commercials.

According to a landmark report from the Institute of Medicine, the food, beverage and restaurant industry spent an estimated $11.26 billion dollars in food and beverage advertising in 2004, of which over half was spent on television advertising alone (not including cable networks, on which an additional

$1.8 billion was spent in advertising) (Committee on Food Marketing and the Diets of Children and Youth, 2006). Since children up to 11 years old lack the cognitive ability to differentiate between commercial and non-commercial content, they are developmentally vulnerable to the persuasive messages of advertising, i.e. they cannot distinguish the difference between a lesson from the television program and a commercial promoting a product (Committee on Food Marketing and the Diets of Children and Youth, 2006). In response, some countries in Europe have banned certain types of advertisements directed toward children or during children's programming. In the United States, the Children's Advertising Review Unit regulates child-directed advertising and promotional materials, but their effectiveness is controversial.

What about specifically targeting the reduction of television and media use to prevent obesity? Only a handful of published randomized controlled trials have successfully reduced children's television viewing in relation to child BMI and none specifically targeted Latino children. In one of the first experimental studies to examine this issue, Robinson enrolled 198 3rd- and 4th-grade students from two schools and randomized each school to either (1) a 6-month classroom curriculum designed to reduce their television, video and videogame use or (2) assessments only (Robinson, 1999). Most participants were white (>70%) with no further information on race/ethnicity reported. Compared to controls, intervention students watched 5.5 fewer hours of television and played 2.5 fewer hours of video games per week (P<0.01). They also had significant (all P<0.002) relative decreases in BMI (-0.45 kg/m^2), triceps skinfold thickness (-1.47 mm), waist circumference (-2.3 cm) and waist-to-hip ratio (-0.02). Neither changes to dietary intake nor moderate-to-vigorous physical activity were found to account for the changes in BMI and adiposity, although both dietary intake and physical activity were assessed by subjective recall methods, which generally limit the ability to test these relationships.

Epstein and colleagues enrolled seventy four- to seven-year-old children at or above the 75th BMI percentile for age and gender and randomized them into either a TV Allowance intervention or an Information Only control group (Epstein et al., 2008). Over 75% of the children were white with no information on percent of Latino children reported. The TV Allowance measured and controlled the use of household electronic equipment, including televisions, computers, video game consoles, etc. The Intervention children had their television and media use budgets reduced by 10% from baseline measurements each month until the budget was reduced by 50%. When the weekly budget was reached, the child's unique 4-digit code would not turn on the television or computer monitor for the remainder of the week. Intervention children received $0.25 for each ½ hour under budget but no greater than $2 per week. Control group children received unlimited access to television and computers and $2 per week for participating in the study; their families received a newsletter with parenting tips and activities for children. Results indicated that Intervention group children had greater decreases (-12 hours per week) in television viewing and computer game use at 24 months (P<0.001). BMI z-score on average decreased by -0.24 kg/m² compared to a decrease of -0.13 kg/m² by controls at 24 months (P<0.05). While the authors attributed changes to energy intake as mediating the affect between television viewing and BMI z-score, physical activity was assessed using accelerometers on a limited basis, which may have been inadequate to detect a relationship. Clearly, studies are necessary targeting Latino children and families, who may have culture-specific factors that influence their television and media use.

Qualitative Interviews on Limiting Children's Television Viewing

Prior to designing television reduction and obesity prevention interventions for Latino children, it is important to culturally adapt the intervention for the target population to improve the likelihood of adherence to the behavioral intervention (Resnicow, Baranowski, Ahluwalia & Braithwaite, 1999). Designing or adapting a culturally relevant intervention involves qualitative methods such as exploratory focus groups or qualitative interviews to obtain data on how cultural factors may influence the behaviors or responses to the intervention (Resnicow et al., 1999). Thus, focus groups or qualitative interviews provide target population members an opportunity to participate in the development of message content and format.

To inform future television reduction interventions for young Latino children, we conducted 25 semi-structured qualitative interviews with parents of Latino children enrolled in Head Start, i.e. a low income sample, in the Houston-metro area. The interviews were conducted September through November of 2007. The average age of parents participating in the interviews was 29.9 years, 24 of the parents were mothers, their children ranged in age from 2-5 years and 15 of the interviews were conducted in Spanish. The study protocol was approved by the institutional review board of Baylor College of Medicine.

Qualitative interviews explored parents' attitudes and beliefs about limiting their preschool children's television viewing. We used the Model of Goal Directed Behavior as a theoretical framework to design the interview questions and thereby explain how parents might influence limiting their children's television viewing. The Model of Goal Directed Behavior was proposed as an expansion and deepening of the Theory of Planned Behavior (Perugini & Bagozzi, 2001). The Theory of Planned Behavior posits that one's attitudes, subjective norms, and perceived behavioral control affect one's intentions which in turn predict behavior (Ajzen, 1991). Although one of the most popular theories applied to health behaviors, on average it accounted for only 30-40% of the variance in intentions and behaviors according to a recent review (Armitage & Conner, 2001). The Model of Goal Directed Behavior builds upon the Theory of Planned Behavior by adding 1) anticipated emotions (positive and negative) as predictors in the decision-making process, 2) desires as the motivational impetus for intentions and 3) recency and frequency of past behavior to the model. In direct comparisons of the two models using the same experiments, the Model of Goal Directed Behavior explained significantly more of the variance in intention for behavior. In a study of bodyweight regulation among university students, the Model of Goal Directed Behavior accounted for 34-88% more of the variance in intentions with regard to diet, exercising and behaviors (Perugini & Bagozzi, 2001). Similarly, in a study of the self-regulation of hypertension, the Model of Goal Directed Behavior accounted for 88% of the variance in intention among male hypertensive patients as compared to only 31% in studies using the Theory of Planned Behavior (Taylor, Bagozzi & Gaither, 2005).

A trained bilingual interviewer of Latino descent conducted one-on-one semi-structured interviews (n=25) using a standardized script in English or Spanish to guide the discussion. Participants were told in advance that the topic would be about their children's television viewing, the interviews would be audio-recorded, there were no right or wrong answers and they would be asked to explain their answers in detail. The semi-structured nature of the interview ensured each question was covered and allowed participants to raise important issues not foreseen by the researchers, which were explored in detail during the interview. Parents selected the language (English, Spanish) in which they preferred to converse.

A professional transcription/translation company (Chromolume, Inc. Santa Monica, CA) created verbatim transcripts; Spanish-language interviews underwent a Spanish to English translation process that included forward- and back-translations; and all interviews were transcribed. All final transcripts were in English. Transcriptions and translations were reviewed by bilingual research staff including the interviewer to ensure proper transcription/translation. The transcripts were preliminarily analyzed by a professional data company (DataSense, LLC, Tehachapi, CA) using the qualitative data analysis package QSR NVivo 8.0 (www.qsrinternational.com). A grounded-theory approach was used to identify categories and subcategories (Strauss & Corbin, 1998). The research questions defined main categories of interest and subcategories. However, given the semi-structured nature of the interviews, emerging topics were also elicited. Two trained researchers independently analyzed the categories and subcategories from the preliminary analysis to identify main themes and sub-themes. Results that were contradictory or inconsistent were resolved through discussion with the interviewer and the principal investigator (Dr. Mendoza). Themes that emerged from the analysis are discussed below.

Parent Attitude for Limiting Television

ATTITUDES: Most parents thought it was important to limit their child's television watching, with the most common reason being that the child should participate in healthier alternatives: "I only let them watch for an hour because then we go outside . . . do other activities together . . . " Eighty percent of parents chose either 0-1 or 1-2 hours as the daily limit for their child's television viewing, which were consistent with guidelines from the American Academy of Pediatrics. One of the main reasons cited for why parents may not want to limit their child's television viewing was babysitting: " . . . they use the TV as a babysitter . . . they're occupied, quiet in one place . . . " Also: "usually with TV, once you put something so interesting for these kids on TV, they're just quiet, they're watching TV. They're not gonna bother you or anything." Another reason was that television served as a learning resource, such as a method for learning English: "Like in our case, since we don't speak English, the children learn English from television. They are pronouncing words in English." Most parents did caution that only certain programs were educational: "In the morning there is a program that teach them about letters and numbers, things that can help the children, but in the afternoons there are no such educational programs." Toward the end of the interview, when asked about their agreement with the statement that watching too much television is related to children gaining weight, 72% agreed. For example: "Hmm, I have someone in my family, that I see watches too much television, and they're overweight. He's about I don't know, 9 years old, and he's 120 pounds. To me, that's too much for that age. He wastes too much time with television." Some parents connected television commercials with fast food and contributing to weight gain: "they see commercials, stuff like that, like McDonald's and that's all they want" while other parents associated eating unhealthy items during television viewing: "I think they are harming them if the children watch too much TV. Because they're eating during the time they're watching television. They are drinking sodas or eating candies. And they don't stop eating until the television program is over. And then they get up, but by then they've already eaten too many things."

SUBJECTIVE NORMS: While most participants seemed concerned about limiting their children's television viewing, the majority did not believe other family members and friends thought about limiting their own children's television viewing. This difference between parental attitudes and family or friends' subjective norms is illustrated by the following: "In reality, I can say that I have a family member that says, 'leave the children be. Let them enjoy. Let them watch television, let them do what they want to do'." Surprisingly, most participants also did not endorse wanting to be like other family members or friends regarding limiting their children's television viewing. Desire: Few participants were motivated to limit their children's television viewing. Intention: Additionally, few had plans to limit their children's television viewing. These low percentages for desire or intention to limit their children's television viewing likely reflects the finding that most parents interviewed had children who already watched only 1-2 hours of television per day, and thus they saw no need to further limit their children's television viewing.

PERCEIVED BEHAVIORAL CONTROL: The majority of participants agreed that the parents, usually the mother, decided how much television a child watches at home. Frequency: Some parents tried to limit their children's television viewing on a daily basis; fewer reported trying to do so on a weekly basis. Recency: Many parents limited their children's television viewing on the previous day. Anticipated emotions: When asked about the first emotion that comes to mind when limiting their children's television viewing, many endorsed good feelings: "I feel good 'cause I feel like if I would limit her time of television, I'll be doing something good for her." Alternatively, some endorsed feelings of guilt: "Well, at first, sometimes it bothers my conscience because I feel that I'm taking away something that they really want. I'll start to feel guilty."

Two emerging themes arose from the data analysis. The first involved concerns for television's affect on food-related behaviors: "so in reality, it is a motivator, to buy or eat something." Television commercials in particular were identified as influencing children's asking behaviors: "[TV] motivates the parents to spend on things that many times are not healthy. With regard to food, sometimes they show on there those commercials for [Restaurant X] . . . and so the kids get hungry . . . and then they say, 'mommy, let's go to [Restaurant X] or [Restaurant Y], or another place . . . ' So in reality, it is a motivator, to buy or eat something."

Another emerging theme raised by almost all of the participants was the topic of inappropriate television program content: "And sometimes there are programs that are not appropriate for them, being so young, and those are programs that they remember most and are most affected by." Some parents cited children's programs as influencing children's aggressive behaviors: "But I think it depends on the show because sometimes they'll watch like Power Rangers, Pokemon and other things with fighting and they think it's normal to fight and throw each other around. And no, I think it's hurting them more." Another participant explained: "And like I told you, there are many cases of a lot of violence, that they see on television, that young children see on the television, where they see violence, that they play with knives, or things like that, so I think too much is not a good thing."

Through the qualitative interviews with Latino parents of young children, we identified culturally specific concerns, using the Model of Goal Directed Behavior as a theoretical framework, to help explain how Latino parents influence their preschool children's television viewing. Applying these findings to the development of future interventions will be helpful to ensure cultural appropriateness and sensitivity. Specifically, television viewing appears to play several important and competing roles among Latino families. On the positive side, parents used television as a babysitter and educator or English teacher for their children. On the negative side most parents recognized that television viewing adversely affected their children's food-related behaviors, primarily through commercials, and exposed them to inappropriate content, including children's entertainment programs that encouraged aggressiveness or programs meant for older audiences.

Given these competing roles, simply telling Latino parents to reduce their children's television viewing to prevent obesity or other health problems ignores the complexity of this popular behavior. It may be more useful to recommend that Latino parents focus their children's television viewing to educational programs like *Sesame Street, Plaza Sésamo,* or similar programs, especially when parents cannot watch television with their children to ensure appropriate content. In this way, families may still benefit from the educational aspects of certain programs while being able to rely on the practical aspect of television as a "babysitter." Since parents raised concerns that television viewing, through commercial advertising and violent content, can adversely influence children's behaviors and health, television reduction interventions should be targeted to address those specific concerns. Besides helping parents identify programs that are age-appropriate and educational for their children, interventions should also identify channels and time periods when commercials for unhealthy foods tend to occur or when programming is geared toward older audiences with inappropriate content for children. For example, many channels had child-specific entertainment programs on Saturday mornings and weekdays after school and these time periods also contained a high number of advertisements for unhealthy foods (Bell et al., 2009); parents should be counseled to limit or supervise their children's television viewing during those times in order to decrease the influence of the commercials and the children's asking behaviors for

those items. Likewise, in order to avoid inappropriate content such as violent programs, parents may wish to limit their children's television viewing specifically
during evening or "primetime" hours on most major broadcast and cable channels and instead focus on child-specific entertainment or educational programs.
By taking these culture-specific factors into consideration, interventions to limit
Latino children's television viewing are more likely to be successful.

Physical Activity Among Latino Children

Physical activity (PA) is defined by the Surgeon General as "bodily movement that is produced by the contraction of skeletal muscle that substantially
increases energy expenditure" (USDHHS, 1996). It is generally agreed that
weight gain occurs when energy intake surpasses energy expenditure due to
excessive caloric consumption, low PA level or both. Habitual PA aids in weight
control and increased PA promotes weight reduction; utilization of energy and
development of lean muscle mass, which is metabolically active (USDHHS,
1996). Furthermore, regular PA reduces the risk of developing chronic diseases
such as obesity, cardiovascular disease, Type 2 Diabetes Mellitus and some
forms of cancer (IOM, 2005). Habitual PA also increases muscle and bone mass
(Branca, 1999) and promotes mental health by reducing symptoms of depression and anxiety (Fox, 1999). Because of the many positive health effects associated with PA the U.S. Department of Health and Human Services (2008) recommends the following for children and adolescents, ages 6-17:

1) 60 minutes or more of PA every day;
2) most of the 60 minutes should be moderate PA (increased heart rate, per-
   spiration and able to speak) or vigorous PA (increased heart rate, perspi-
   ration and breathing hard and fast—unable to hold a conversation);
3) vigorous intensity activity on at least three days per week; and
4) muscle-strengthening and bone-strengthening activity on at least three
   days per week

Establishment of PA behaviors in youth tracks into adulthood (Kelder et al.,
1994); however, Latino/Hispanic children, in particular Mexican-American
children, are more likely to be inactive (Dugas et al., 2008), placing them at
increased risk for unhealthy adult lives.

National self-reported data from the 2007 Youth Risk Behavior Survey
(YRBS) indicate that only about 35% of high school students engaged in a PA
that increased their heart rate and made them breathe hard for at least a total of
60 minutes/day on five or more days during the past week (CDC, 2008). The
2007 YRBS data also showed that male adolescents (44%) tended to be more
physically active than female adolescents (26%) and white (37%) high school

students had the highest prevalence of engaging in any kind of PA than black (31%) and Latino (30%) students (CDC, 2008). Additionally, PA levels rapidly declined throughout the adolescent years (CDC, 2008).

Texas is second only to California in Latino population size (U.S. Census Bureau, 2010). Assessment of states or geographic locations with a large Latino population may provide insight into the future needs of the United States given that the U.S. Census Bureau projects the Latino population will reach 47.8 million in mid-2010, 59.7 million in 2020 and 102.6 million in 2050 (U.S. Census Bureau, 2010). In a cross-sectional study conducted by Hoelscher et al. (2009) using a probability sample of Texas public school students to compare physical and sedentary activities by grade (fourth, eighth and eleventh) and ethnicity (African American, Latino and white/other), more than 70% of elementary and secondary school students reported engaging in vigorous PA on three or more days during the past week. However, 30-50% of students also reported three or more hours per day in a sedentary activity (Hoelscher et al., 2009). There was no difference in PA levels among fourth-grade boys (84%) and girls (83%), yet eighth- (77%) and eleventh- (66%) grade girls reported lower PA levels than their male counterparts (87% and 77%, respectively) (Hoelscher et al., 2009). Among Latinos, percentage of eighth- (74%) and eleventh- (66%) grade girls who engaged in vigorous PA on three or more days during the past week also differed from eighth- (83%) and eleventh- (79%) grade boys. Unlike national data, African-American secondary male students (92-93%) reported a higher prevalence of PA than Latino (79-83%) and white/other (75-90%) male students (Hoelscher et al., 2009). Additionally, PA levels decreased with increasing grade level (Hoelscher et al., 2009). Prevalence of PA in Latinos students declined from 84% in fourth- grade to 79% in eighth- grade to 72% in eleventh- grade (Hoelscher et al., 2009). Hence, low PA levels affect all children and adolescents but are more evident in underserved populations such as Latinos.

Factors Related to Physical Activity in Latino Children

Given that Latino children and adolescents tend to be more physically inactive than their counterparts from other ethnic/racial groups, research studies examining the reasons for this disparity and intervention methods to address the disparity are emerging. Although recommended by others since the late 1980s (McLeroy et al., 1988; Stokols, 1992), the use of multilevel interventions to attain aggregate level health behavior change has gained popularity in the last five to ten years. Public health researchers now emphasize the importance of ecological models as the basis for multilevel interventions (Sallis et al., 2006; Yancey, 2007). Ecological models encompass an individual's intrapersonal, interpersonal, social, physical and policy environments which work synergistically to influence a person's health decisions and behaviors (Sallis et al., 2006). In PA research use of ecological models has transformed the field into active living research (Sallis et al., 2006) where recreational or leisure-time activities, exercise, occupational activities including household tasks and transport are investigated to influence community practice and initiatives.

The first step in designing effective intervention strategies for health behavior change based on an ecological framework is to understand the factors related to the health behavior. Various PA researchers have identified correlates of PA of children and adolescents. Sallis et al. (2000) reported that the findings from 102 research studies on children, ages 4-12, primarily recognized male gender, intentions, enjoyment of PA, healthy food choices, previous experience with a PA, accessibility to programs and/or facilities as factors related to children's PA. Additionally, perceived barriers were inversely associated with children's PA (Sallis et al., 2000). For adolescents (ages 13-18), correlates of PA identified in 54 studies were male gender, white ethnicity, goal-oriented, perceived skill, intentions, thrill-seeking, previous experience with a PA and parental and "significant other" (siblings, peers, etc.) support (Sallis et al., 2000). Age, depression and sedentary behaviors were inversely related to adolescents' PA (Sallis et al., 2000). Data from this review demonstrate that many of the correlates of PA for young people include aspects of an individual's social (e.g., enjoyment), physical (e.g., accessibility) and policy (e.g., family policies) environments. Although the review by Sallis et al. (2000) was comprehensive, most of the articles examined did not include girls and underserved populations. Furthermore, most of the studies assessed only leisure-time activities and not active transport, "occupational" or other forms of active living (Sallis et al., 2000).

One recent study focused on the PA preferences of both girls and Latino children. Olvera et al. (2009) assessed the PA preferences of Latino and white pre-adolescent children, 10-13 years of age, and examined the relationship of PA preferences with ethnicity, gender, age and body mass index (BMI). A sample of 98 Latino children (49 girls) and 93 white children (52 girls) were matched for socioeconomic status and geographic location. Olvera et al. (2009) reported that of twenty activities, the preferred activity for both Latino and white children was water play (71% and 79%, respectively), followed by basketball (58% and 61%, respectively) and bicycling (57% and 61%, respectively). Neither ethnic group enjoyed household chores such as mopping, vacuuming or sweeping (Olvera et al., 2009). A few ethnic differences were noted. PA preferences for white children also included climbing trees and other outdoor activities as well as baseball/softball whereas soccer was a preferred PA for Latino children (Olvera et al., 2009). Based on factor loadings the authors grouped fifteen of the twenty activities into three categories; free play (water play, dance, tag, chase, outdoor activities, etc.), sports (soccer, basketball, baseball, etc. as well as weight lifting) and exercise (cardiovascular fitness activities). Linear regression analyses revealed that girls preferred free play activities whereas boys preferred sports (Olvera et al., 2009). White children preferred sports more so than Latino children. Younger children preferred exercise activities more than older children. Finally, children with lower BMI values preferred exercise activities more than children with higher BMI values (Olvera et al., 2009). More extensive studies on the PA preferences of Latino youth are needed given that the role of social and cultural factors such as socioeconomic status (income, educational attainment, etc.), acculturation and language preference, perceived general health, social support and self-efficacy is understudied in youth and debatable for Latino adults (Taverno et al., 2010; Arredondo et al., 2006; Marquez et al., 2006; Sanderson et al., 2006). Nonetheless these findings, PA preferences of Latino and white pre-adolescents, may aid in the design and implementation of culturally appropriate intervention strategies that address the intrapersonal, interpersonal and physical environmental needs of physically inactive Latino children.

SCHOOL- AND COMMUNITY-BASED APPROACHES TO INCREASE PHYSICAL ACTIVITY IN LATINO CHILDREN

The most common setting to implement active living programs for children and adolescents has been schools since school-aged children normally obtain 20% to 40% of their daily PA at schools, with a large proportion coming from structured physical education (PE) (Simons-Morton et al., 1999). School-based interventions also provide an important opportunity to concentrate on factors that influence children's social, physical and policy environments. One such coordinated school health program (CSHP) that has been successful nationally and in Texas is the Coordinated Approach to Child Health (CATCH). CATCH, a multisite randomized controlled field trial, 1991-1994, has proven effective at increasing PA levels among various ethnic groups (Luepker et al., 1996; Nader et al., 1999). The CATCH intervention consists of classroom curricula and school environmental changes concerning food services, PA and PE, and tobacco use, along with family and home-based assignments that reinforce the school-based activities. The heart of the CATCH PE component (presented elsewhere; McKenzie et al., 1994) is to engage students in moderate-to-vigorous PA for at least 40% of class time (30-40 minutes per class) during a minimum of three PE classes per week (McKenzie et al., 1996; McKenzie et al., 1995). Ultimately, CATCH PE introduces students to physical activities that can be easily incorporated into their daily routines and, most importantly, sustained into adolescence and adulthood.

The CATCH program has also been proven effective at limiting the percentage of risk of overweight or overweight among disadvantaged Latino elementary school students in the El Paso region of West Texas (Coleman et al., 2005).

Coleman et al. (2005) used a pre-test post-test (2-year), matched control group, quasi-experimental design to evaluate the El Paso CATCH program. Student participants were 93% Latino from four intervention (n=423) and four control (n=473) schools (Coleman et al., 2005). Child health outcomes were BMI, waist and hip circumference, and aerobic fitness while school health measures were PA during PE class (assessed using the System for Observing Fitness Instruction Time, SOFIT) and cafeteria meal quality (Coleman et al., 2005). Although control and intervention school students had similar increases in percentage of risk of overweight and overweight (as defined by CDC growth charts) at post-test, the rate of increase was lower for intervention students than control students (Coleman et al., 2005). All schools had similar percentages of students passing the 9-minute 1-mile run (aerobic fitness) at baseline, but more intervention school children passed the 9-minute 1-mile run at post-test than control school children (Coleman et al., 2005). Time spent in moderate-to-vigorous-PA during PE for intervention schools was greater during the spring semester of third grade and the fall semesters of fourth and fifth grades compared with control schools (Coleman et al., 2005). Whereas time spent in vigorous PA during PE class was greater in intervention schools during the fall semester of fourth grade and during both fall and spring semesters of fifth grade than in control schools (Coleman et al., 2005). Intervention schools met the recommended fat content of school lunches in year two of the program (Coleman et al., 2005). Although like other school-based interventions CATCH El Paso did not result in child weight reduction, CATCH El Paso slowed the risk of overweight or overweight. The authors speculated that the social and policy environments of the CATCH El Paso intervention schools were critical in the implementation and success of this CSHP. A non-profit foundation had implemented CATCH El Paso and obtained community support through community conferences, award banquets and school incentives which allowed the social and policy environment changes to be viewed by the target audience to be culturally relevant and beneficial (Coleman et al., 2005). Buy-in from community partners is a must for any health behavior change project.

Another successful CSHP in Texas is the Bienestar Health Program; which was specifically designed to reduce Type 2 Diabetes Mellitus (T2DM) risk factors and tailored for low-income Mexican-American children (Treviño et al., 2005). The construct of reciprocal determinism, where self-regulatory mechanisms are influenced by the interaction of personal, social and behavioral factors, from the Social Cognitive Theory (SCT) is the theoretical basis of the Bienestar Health Program. Four components (parent fun activities, health class, health club and school food service) comprise the Bienestar Health Program (Treviño et al., 2005). The parent fun activities consist of four events held throughout the school year: 1) a student dance recital to introduce and depict the health education aspects of the Bienestar Health Program; 2) a puppet craft project to describe the development of T2DM; 3) a lotería (Mexican bingo) game to teach healthy food choices; and 4) a salsa demonstration to teach simple movements and the benefits of PA (Treviño et al., 2005). The health class is a 16-lesson curriculum on nutrition, PA, self-image and T2DM. The health club consists of after-school meetings held once a week for 32 weeks to reinforce the concepts presented in the health class. The school food service component addressed both the food service staff and students. Food service staff and students are taught about the benefits of healthy food choices. Fourth-grade students from five intervention schools (n=200) and four control schools (n=187) from low-income neighborhoods in San Antonio, Texas participated in a pre-test post-test 8-month evaluation study (Treviño et al., 2005). Physical fitness measured using a modified Harvard step test was the main study outcome. Height, weight, age and gender were also collected. At baseline no difference in physical fitness score and BMI values were observed between the two study groups (intervention and control) (Treviño et al., 2005). At post-test, physical fitness scores increased significantly in the intervention group and slightly decreased in the control group. Treviño et al. (2005) posited that the improved physical fitness scores observed in the intervention group may have been attributable to the positive PA beliefs instilled by the various Bienestar Health Program components as well as the social support garnered from parents, teachers, after-school team members and peers. The use of culturally relevant parent fun activities (student dance recital, lotería, puppet show and salsa dance demonstrations) may have facilitated buy-in from study families which may have contributed to the differences observed in physical fitness scores. Overall, the Bienestar Health Program is a culturally relevant theory-based multilevel program that shows promise in encouraging active living in low-income Mexican-American families.

School-based programs have demonstrated success (Coleman et al., 2005; Treviño et al., 2005) but to reach other key components of a youth's social environment, community-based programs are needed. The Behavior Opportunities Using Nutrition, Counseling and Exercise (BOUNCE) intervention, a theory-based (SCT) 12-week program designed to improve physical fitness and activity, was delivered through both the community (community centers, grocery stores, park playgrounds) and school (gym, playground, cafeteria and classroom) settings for low-income Latino families (Olvera et al., 2010). Forty-six mother-daughter dyads, recruited via flyers mailed to the home, were enrolled. Mother-daughter dyads (daughters were 7-13 years old) in the intervention group received three weekly sessions of structured aerobic activity (salsa dance classes), sports training (basketball) or free play recreational activities, two weekly nutrition sessions, and one weekly behavioral counseling session (Olvera et al., 2010). All sessions last about 45 minutes. Daughter outcome measures included: acculturation level, BMI, aerobic fitness, measured PA and dietary intake. Mother outcome measures included: language preference, aerobic fitness and self-reported past PA. Daughters in both groups (intervention and control) were of similar age, but mothers in the intervention group were younger than mothers in the control group (Olvera et al., 2010). More than 80% of daughters were U.S.-born whereas all mothers were foreign-born (Mexico or Central America). Most of all dyads were overweight; 66% of daughters and 80% mothers. At post-test, intervention group daughters exhibited improved physical fitness than control group daughters whereas no statistically difference was observed in either mother group (Olvera et al., 2010). No difference was observed for PA levels or dietary intake at post-test for the dyads. The BOUNCE intervention study demonstrated that a community-based active living program can influence physical fitness of pre-adolescent girls. The authors noted that the mother-daughter interactions may have benefited the results of the BOUNCE program (Olvera et al., 2010); which adds credence to the importance of targeting the social, physical and policy environments when addressing families of underserved populations, in particular Latino families. Furthermore, because community-based active living research in Latino youth is in its infancy what works and what does not work is yet to be fully understood.

SCHOOL WELLNESS POLICY INITIATIVES TO INCREASE PHYSICAL ACTIVITY IN LATINO CHILDREN

Several U.S. states have enacted school wellness policy initiatives (Childhood Obesity Action Network, 2008) that focus on active living and healthy eating. In Texas, two such initiatives were passed, Texas Senate Bill 19 and Texas Senate Bill 42; which both now comprise Texas Senate Bill 530. (Texas Senate Bill 530 has similar requirements as Texas Senate Bills 19 and 42 but also mandated for all students in grades 3-12 fitness testing and public reporting of the results.) Texas Senate Bill 19 (SB19) passed in 2001, required elementary school children to participate in 30 minutes of daily PA or a total of 135 minutes per week. This initiative also required the Texas Education Agency (TEA) to identify CSHPs (classroom curriculum, PA, child food services and parental involvement) that schools could adopt and implement by 2007. Texas Senate

Bill 42 (SB42) had similar objectives as SB19. SB42, enacted in June 2005 and commenced in the 2006-2007 school year, required Texas middle school children to participate in 30 minutes of daily moderate-to-vigorous PA or a minimum of 135 minutes per week or 225 minutes per two week time period and to participate in physical education (PE) class for at least four of the six-semester middle school cycle. Additionally, SB42 obliged middle schools to implement an approved CSHP, school districts to follow nationally recognized guidelines for health and PE, restoration of the school health advisory council (SHAC) and TEA to annually summarize student health and PA data provided by school districts. Neither initiative, SB19 or SB42, mandated evaluation of implementation or funding for implementation.

Two evaluation studies were conducted by university researchers on the awareness and adherence to SB19 and SB42 (Kelder et al., 2009; Barroso et al., 2009). Kelder et al. (2009) reported on the implementation of SB19 at the state level as well as the impact on structured PA in PE and child self-reported PA and measured child obesity in two economically disadvantaged border regions (El Paso and Rio Grande Valley [RGV] of Texas). Barroso et al. (2009) evaluated the awareness of SB42 at the state level and the impact of SB42 in four border communities regarding structured PA in PE class, child self-reported PA and sedentary behaviors, and measured child obesity. Both evaluation studies used key informant interviews with school principals, PE instructors, nurses or designated school representatives to assess the awareness and adherence of the initiatives and both studies used the SOFIT to assess the impact of the initiatives on structured PA in PE, self-reported child data on PA and nutrition behaviors and measured child obesity (Kelder et al., 2009; Barroso et al., 2009). High awareness of the initiatives (SB19 and SB42) was reported in the two probability-based random study samples of statewide key informants (Kelder et al., 2009; Barroso et al., 2009). Key informants in the SB19 study were uninformed about the need to implement health education, child nutrition services and a parental involvement component in the CSHP (Kelder et al., 2009) whereas key informants in the SB42 study were unaware of the need to include a parental involvement component in the CSHP and to establish of a district SHAC (Barroso et al., 2009). SB19 key informants reported an average of 179 minutes of PE per week (Kelder et al., 2009) while SB42 key informants reported an average of 249 minutes of PE per week (Barroso et al., 2009). Kelder et al. (2009) reported greater PA minutes (231 minutes) and lower prevalence of obesity (21%) in fourth-grade students from the El Paso border schools compared with fourth-grade students from the RGV border schools (217 minutes of PA and 32% obesity). In the SB42 evaluation study, border schools reported an increase in the number of PE class days, however, child obesity and sedentary behavior did not differ (Barroso et al., 2009). The authors of both studies stated that although the school wellness initiatives examined are a good first step to promote child health and to address childhood obesity prevention by endorsing active living policy changes, differences in implementation of these school wellness initiatives by state regions may be due to both facilitators and barriers encountered by the regions (Kelder et al., 2009; Barroso et al., 2009). For example, the El Paso community, as mentioned previously, is committed to active living changes in order to address the obesity epidemic; hence, schools located within this community fared better than other schools in other communities in the implementation of SB19 and SB42 (Kelder et al., 2009; Barroso et al., 2009). The mixed findings from the evaluation of SB19 and SB42 call for continued monitoring of their implementation (now Texas Senate Bill 530) (Kelder et al., 2009; Barroso et al., 2009). Moreover, to truly achieve active living schools, school wellness initiatives are in need of funding, community support and modification to achieve the original health and academic outcomes proposed (Kelder et al., 2009; Barroso et al., 2009).

Habitual PA is a must for a healthy lifestyle (USDHHS, 1996; IOM, 2005; Branca, 1999; Fox, 1999). Physical inactivity in Latino youth is well documented (CDC, 2008; Hoelscher et al., 2009). The use of ecological models to better understand the gaps in knowledge regarding physical activity or inactivity in Latino youth allow for a more complete assessment of the various factors that influence active living in this underserved population (Olvera et al., 2009; Taverno et al., 2010; Arredondo et al., 2006; Coleman et al., 2005; Treviño et al., 2005; Olvera et al., 2010; Kelder et al., 2009; Barroso et al., 2009). Multilevel interventions including health policies based on an ecological framework (emphasizing social, physical and policy environments) are a must in creating active living communities (Stokols, 1992; Sallis et al., 2006; Yancey, 2007; Sallis et al., 2000). In addition, we hope that the findings summarized here will be used to develop and implement culturally and linguistically appropriate PA interventions for Latino children and adolescents.

Acknowledgements

For the section on television viewing, the author, JAM, would like to thank (1) Doris K. Uscanga for conducting the qualitative interviews; (2) Paul Aguilar and Melissa Alvarez for their help with the qualitative analysis; and (3) Deb Thompson, Tom Baranowski and Theresa A. Nicklas of Baylor College of Medicine for their guidance with the design and analysis of the qualitative study and for critically reviewing drafts of this work. The author, JAM, was supported in part, by a pilot award through the 2007 Bristol Myers-Squibb/Mead Johnson Unrestricted Nutrition Research Award of the Children's Nutrition Research Center, a career development award from the National Cancer Institute (1K07CA131178, PI: JAM) and with federal funds from the United States Department of Agriculture (USDA/ARS) under Cooperative Agreement No. 58-6250-6001. The funding agencies above had no role in the design, collection, analysis, interpretation of data, writing of the chapter or decision to submit the chapter for publication. The contents of this publication do not necessarily reflect the views or policies of the funding agencies or Baylor College of Medicine. For the section on physical activity, the author, CSB, would like to thank the Robert Wood Johnson Foundation and Active Living Research for their support in the creation of the data on Texas Senate Bill 19 and Texas Senate Bill 42 (#52467 and #56318, respectively). The author, CSB, was supported, in part, by a grant from the National Center on Minority Health and Health Disparities (NIH NCMHD 2P20MD000170-08). The funding agencies above had no role in the design, collection, analysis, interpretation of data, writing of the chapter or decision to submit the chapter for publication. The contents of this publication do not necessarily reflect the views or policies of the funding agencies or University of Texas Health Science Center at Houston, School of Public Health.

References

Ajzen, I. (1991). The theory of planned behavior. *Organizational Behavior and Human Decision Processes, 50*(2), 179-211.

Andersen, R. E., Crespo, C. J., Bartlett, S. J., Cheskin, L. J., & Pratt, M. (1998). Relationship of physical activity and television watching with body weight and level of fatness among children: results from the Third National Health and Nutrition Examination Survey. *JAMA, 279*(12), 938-942.

Armitage, C. J., & Conner, M. (2001). Efficacy of the Theory of Planned Behaviour: A meta-analytic review. *Br J Soc Psychol, 40*(Pt 4), 471-499.

Arredondo E. M., Elder J. P., Ayala, G. X., Campbell, N., Baquero, B., & Duerksen, S. (2006). Is parenting style related to children's healthy eating and physical activity in Latino families? *Health Educ Res, 21*(6), 862-871.

Barlow, S. E. (2007). Expert committee recommendations regarding the prevention, assessment, and treatment of child and adolescent overweight and obesity: Summary report. *Pediatrics, 120 Suppl 4*, S164-192.

Barroso, C. S., Kelder, S. H., Springer, A., Smith, C., Ranjit, N., Ledingham, C., & Hoelscher, D. M. (2009). Senate Bill 42: Implementation and impact on physical activity in middle schools. *Journal of Adolescent Health, 45*(3)Suppl, S82-S90.

Bell, R. A., Cassady, D., Culp, J., & Alcalay, R. (2009). Frequency and types of foods advertised on saturday morning and weekday afternoon English- and Spanish-language American television programs. [doi: DOI: 10.1016/j.jneb.2008.05.008]. *Journal of Nutrition Education and Behavior, 41*(6), 406-413.

Blass, E. M., Anderson, D. R., Kirkorian, H. L., Pempek, T. A., Price, I., & Koleini, M. F. (2006). On the road to obesity: television viewing increases intake of high-density foods. *Physiol Behav, 88*(4-5), 597-604.

Borzekowski, D. L., & Robinson, T. N. (2001). The 30-second effect: An experiment revealing the impact of television commercials on food preferences of preschoolers. *J Am Diet Assoc, 101*(1), 42-46.

Branca, F. (1999). Physical activity, diet and skeletal health. *Public Health Nutrition, 2*(3A), 391-396.

Burdette, H. L., & Whitaker, R. C. (2005). A national study of neighborhood safety, outdoor play, television viewing, and obesity in preschool children. *Pediatrics, 116*(3), 657-662.

Centers for Disease Control and Prevention. (2008) Youth Risk Behavior Surveillance—United States, (2007). Surveillance Summaries, *MMWR*, 57 (No. SS-4).

Childhood Obesity Action Network. (2008). *Childhood obesity: the role of health policy.* Miami, FL: Report to the Second National Childhood Obesity Congress.

Christakis, D. A., Zimmerman, F. J., DiGiuseppe, D. L., & McCarty, C. A. (2004). Early television exposure and subsequent attentional problems in children. *Pediatrics, 113*(4), 708-713.

Coleman, K. J., Tiller, C. L., Sanchez, J., Heath, E. M., Sy, O., Milliken, G., & Dzewaltowski, D. A. (2005). Prevention of the epidemic increase in child risk of overweight in low-income schools: The El Paso Coordinated Approach to Child Health. *Arch Pediatr Adolesc Med, 159*, 217-224.

Committee on Communications. (2006). Children, Adolescents, and Advertising. *Pediatrics, 118*(6), 2563-2569.

Committee on Food Marketing and the Diets of Children and Youth. (2006). *Food Marketing to Children and Youth: Threat or Opportunity?* Washington, DC: The National Academies Press.

Cotugna, N. (1998). TV ads on Saturday morning children's programming—what's new? *Journal of Nutrition Education 20*, 125-127.

Dennison, B. A., Erb, T. A., & Jenkins, P. L. (2002). Television viewing and television in bedroom associated with overweight risk among low-income preschool children. *Pediatrics, 109*(6), 1028-1035.

Diaz-Guerrero, R., & Holtzman, W. H. (1974). Learning by televised "Plaza Sésamo" in Mexico. [doi: DOI: 10.1037/h0037480]. *Journal of Educational Psychology, 66*(5), 632-643.

Dietz, W. (1991). Physical activity and childhood obesity. *Nutrition, 7*(4), 295-296.

Dugas, L. R., Ebersole, K., Schoeller, D., Yanovski, J. A., Barquera, S., Rivera, J., Durazo-Arzivu, R., & Luke, A. (2008). Very low levels of energy expenditure among pre-adolescent Mexican-American girls. *Int J Pediatr Obes, 3*, 123-126.

Epstein, L. H., Roemmich, J. N., Robinson, J. L., Paluch, R. A., Winiewicz, D. D., Fuerch, J. H., & et al. (2008). A randomized trial of the effects of reducing television viewing and computer use on body mass index in young children. *Arch Pediatr Adolesc Med, 162*(3), 239-245.

Fox, K. R. (1999). The influence of physical activity on mental wellbeing. *Public Health Nutrition, 2*(3A), 411-418.

Francis, L. A., Lee, Y., & Birch, L. L. (2003). Parental weight status and girls' television viewing, snacking, and body mass indexes. *Obes Res, 11*(1), 143-151.

Galst, J. P. (1980). Television food commercials and pro-nutritional public service announcements as determinants of young children's snack choices. *Child Dev, 51*, 935-938.

Goldberg, M. E., Gorn, G. J., & Gibson, W. (1978). TV messages for snack and breakfast foods: do they influence children's preferences? *Journal of Consumer Research, 5*, 73-81.

Gorely, T., Marshall, S. J., & Biddle, S. J. (2004). Couch kids: correlates of television viewing among youth. *Int J Behav Med, 11*(3), 152-163.

Gorn, G. J., Goldberg, M. E., & Kanungo, R. N. (1976). The role of educational television in changing the intergroup attitudes of children. [Article]. *Child Dev, 47*(1), 277-280.

Gortmaker, S. L., Peterson, K., Wiecha, J., Sobol, A. M., Dixit, S., Fox, M. K., & et al. (1999). Reducing obesity via a school-based interdisciplinary intervention among youth: Planet Health. *Arch Pediatr Adolesc Med, 153*(4), 409-418.

Hoelscher, D. M., Barroso, C., Springer, A., Castrucci, B., & Kelder, S. H. (2009). Prevalence of self-reported activity and sedentary behaviors among 4th-, 8th-, and 11th-grade Texas public school children: the school physical activity and nutrition study. *J Phys Act Health, 6*(5), 535-47.

Institute of Medicine (IOM). Committee on prevention of obesity in children and youth, food and nutrition board, board on health promotion and disease prevention committee on prevention of obesity in children and youth. (2005). *Preventing childhood obesity: Health in the balance.* Koplan JP, Liverman CT, Kraak VI, eds. Institute of Medicine (U.S.), Washington, DC.

Kelder, S. H., Perry, C. L., Klepp, K. I., & Lytle, L. L. (1994). Longitudinal tracking of adolescent smoking, physical activity, and food choice behaviors. *Am J Public Health, 84*, 1121-6.

Kelder, S. H., Springer, A., Barroso, C. S., Smith, C., Sanchez, E., Ranjit, N., & Hoelscher, D. M. (2009). Implementation of Texas Senate Bill 19 to increase physical activity in elementary schools. *Journal of Public Health Policy, 30(Suppl 1)*, S221-S247.

Kotz, K., & Story, M. (1994). Food advertisements during children's Saturday morning television programming: are they consistent with dietary recommendations? *J Am Diet Assoc, 94*(11), 1296-1300.

Krebs, N. F., Himes, J. H., Jacobson, D., Nicklas, T. A., Guilday, P., & Styne, D. (2007). Assessment of child and adolescent overweight and obesity. *Pediatrics, 120 Suppl 4*, S193-228.

Landhuis, C. E., Poulton, R., Welch, D., & Hancox, R. J. (2007). Does childhood television viewing lead to attention problems in adolescence? Results from a prospective longitudinal study. *Pediatrics, 120*(3), 532-537.

Luepker, R. V., Perry, C. L., McKinlay, S. M., Nader, P. R., Parcel, G. S., Stone, E. J., Webber, L. S., Elder, J. P., Feldman, H. A., Johnson, C. C., & et al. (1996). Outcomes of a field trial to improve children's dietary patterns and physical activity: the Child and Adolescent Trial for Cardiovascular Health (CATCH). *JAMA, 275*, 768-776.

Marquez, D. X., & McAuley, E. (2006). Social cognitive correlates of leisure time physical activity among Latinos. *J Behavioral Medicine, 29*(3), 281-289.

Marshall, S. J., Biddle, S. J., Gorely, T., Cameron, N., & Murdey, I. (2004). Relationships between media use, body fatness and physical activity in children and youth: a meta-analysis. *Int J Obes Relat Metab Disord, 28*(10), 1238-1246.

McKenzie, T. L., Feldman, H., Woods, S. E., Romero, K. A., Dahlstrom, V., Stone, E. J., Strikmiller, P. K., Williston, J. M., & Harsha, D. W. (1995). Children's activity levels and lesson context during third-grade physical education. *Res Q Exerc Sport, 66*(3), 184-193.

McKenzie, T. L, Nader, P. R., Strikmiller, P. K., Yang, M., Stone, E. J., Perry, C. L., Taylor, W. C., Epping, J. N., Feldman, H. A., Luepker, R. V., & Kelder, S. H. (1996). School physical education: effect of the Child and Adolescent Trial for Cardiovascular Health (CATCH). *Prev Med, 25*, 423-31.

McKenzie, T. L., Strikmiller, P. K., Stone, E. J., Woods, S. E., Ehlinger, S., Romero, K. A., & Budman, S. T. (1994). CATCH: Physical activity process evaluation in a multicenter trial. *Health Educ Q, Suppl 2*, S72–S89.

McLeroy, K. R., Bibeau, D., Steckler, A., & Glanz, K. (1988) An ecological perspective on health promotion programs. *Health & Educ Qtrly, 15*(4), 351-77.

Mendoza, J. A., Zimmerman, F. J., & Christakis, D. A. (2007). Television viewing, computer use, obesity, and adiposity in U.S. preschool children. *Int J Behav Nutr Phys Act, 4*(1), 44.

Nader, P., Stone, E. J., Lytle, L. A., Perry, C. L., Osganian, S. K., Kelder, S., Webber, L. S., Elder, J. P., Montgomery, D., Feldman, H. A., Wu, M., Johnson, C., Parcel, G. S., & Luepker, R. V. (1999). Three year maintenance of improved diet and physical activity: the CATCH study. *Arch Pediatr Adolesc Med, 153*(7), 695-704.

Nicklas, T. A., Goh, E. T., Goodel, L. S., Acuff, D. S., Reiher, R., Buday, R., & et al. (2011). Impact of commercials on food preferences of low-income,

176 *Jason A. Mendoza and Cristina S. Barroso*

minority preschoolers. *Journal of Nutrition Education and Behavior, 43* (1): 35-41.

Ogden, C. L., Carroll, M. D., Curtin, L. R., Lamb, M. M., & Flegal, K. M. (2010). Prevalence of high body mass index in U.S. children and adolescents, 2007-2008. *Jama, 303* (3): 242-249.

Olvera, N., Bush, A., Sharma, S., Knox, B. B., Scherer, R. L., & Butte, N. E. (2010). BOUNCE: A community-based mother-daughter healthy lifestyle intervention for low-income Latino families. *Obesity*, 18(Suppl), S102-S104.

Olvera, N., McCarley, K. E., Leung, P., McLeod, J., & Rodriguez, A. X. (2009). Assessing physical activity preferences in Latino and white preadolescents. *Pediatric Exerc Sci, 21*, 400-412.

Osypuk, T. L., Diez Roux, A. V., Hadley, C., & Kandula, N. R. (2009). Are immigrant enclaves healthy places to live? The multi-ethnic study of atherosclerosis. [doi: DOI: 10.1016/j.socscimed.2009.04.010]. *Social Science & Medicine, 69*(1), 110-120.

Perugini, M., & Bagozzi, R. P. (2001). The role of desires and anticipated emotions in goal-directed behaviours: broadening and deepening the theory of planned behaviour. *Br J Soc Psychol, 40*(Pt 1), 79-98.

Ramirez-Ley, K., De Lira-Garcia, C., Souto-Gallardo, M. d. l. C., Tejeda-Lopez, M. F., Castaneda-Gonzalez, L. M., Bacardi-Gascon, M., & et al. (2009). Food-related advertising geared toward Mexican children. *J Public Health, 31*(3), 383-388.

Resnicow, K., Baranowski, T., Ahluwalia, J. S., & Braithwaite, R. L. (1999). Cultural sensitivity in public health: defined and demystified. *Ethn Dis, 9*(1), 10-21.

Rideout, V. J., Foehr, U. G., & Roberts, D. F. (2010). *Generation M²: Media in the lives of 8-18 year olds.* Menlo Park, CA: Henry J. Kaiser Family Foundation.

Robinson, T. N. (1999). Reducing children's television viewing to prevent obesity: a randomized controlled trial. *Jama, 282*(16), 1561-1567.

Robinson, T. N., Borzekowski, D. L. G., Matheson, D. M., & Kraemer, H. C. (2007). Effects of fast food branding on young children's taste preferences. *Arch Pediatr Adolesc Med, 161*(8), 792-797.

Sallis, J. F., Cervero, R. B., Ascher, W., Henderson, K. A., Kraft, M. K., & Kerr, J. (2006). An ecological approach to creating active living communities. *Annu Rev Public Health*, 27, 297-322.

Sallis, J. F., Prochaska, J. J., & Taylor, W. C. (2000). A review of correlates of physical activity of children and adolescents. *Med Sci Sports, 32*(5), 963-75.

Sanderson, M., Fernandez, M. E., Dutton, R. J., Ponder, A., Sosa, D., & Peltz, G. (2006). Risk behaviors by ethnicity and Texas-Mexico border residence. *Ethnicity & Disease, 16*, 514-520.

Simons-Morton, B., Eitel, P., & Small, M. L.(1999). School physical education: secondary analyses of the School Health Policies and Programs Study. *J Health Educ, 30*(5), S21-S27.

Snoek, H. M., van Strien, T., Janssens, J. M., & Engels, R. C. (2006). The effect of television viewing on adolescents' snacking: individual differences explained by external, restrained and emotional eating. *J Adolesc Health, 39*(3), 448-451.

Stokols, D. (1992). Toward a social ecology of health promotion. *American Psychologist, 47*(1), 6-22.

Story, M., & Faulkner, P. (1990). The prime time diet: a content analysis of eating behavior and food messages in television program content and commercials. *Am J Public Health, 80*(6), 738-740.

Strauss, A., & Corbin, J. (1998). *Basics of qualitative research: Techniques and procedures for developing grounded theory* (2nd ed.). Thousand Oaks, California: Sage Publications, Inc.

Stroebele, N., & de Castro, J. M. (2004). Television viewing is associated with an increase in meal frequency in humans. *Appetite, 42*(1), 111-113.

Taverno, S. E., Rollins, B.Y., & Francis, L. A. (2010). Generation, language, body mass index, and activity patterns in Hispanic children. *Am J Prev Med, 38*(2), 145-153.

Taylor, S. D., Bagozzi, R. P., & Gaither, C. A. (2005). Decision-making and effort in the self-regulation of hypertension: Testing two competing theories. *Br J Health Psychol, 10*(Pt 4), 505-530.

Thakkar, R. R., Garrison, M. M., & Christakis, D. A. (2006). A systematic review for the effects of television viewing by infants and preschoolers. *Pediatrics, 118*(5), 2025-2031.

Treviño, R. P., Hernandez, A. E., Yin, Z., Garcia, O. A., & Hernandez, I. (2005). Effect of the Bienestar Health Program on physical fitness in low-income Mexican-American children. *Hispanic Journal of Behavioral Sciences, 27*(1), 120-132.

Trost, S. G. (2001). Objective measurement of physical activity in youth: current issues, future directions. *Exerc Sport Sci Rev, 29*(1), 32-36.

Trost, S. G., McIver, K. L., & Pate, R. R. (2005). Conducting accelerometer-based activity assessments in field-based research. *Med Sci Sports Exerc, 37*(11 Suppl), S531-543.

U.S. Census Bureau. Hispanics in the United States. Retrieved April 30, 2010 from http://www.census.gov/population/www/socdemo/hispanic/hispanic.html

U.S. Department of Health and Human Services. (1996) *Physical Activity and Health: A Report of the Surgeon General*. Atlanta, GA: U.S. Department of Health and Human Services. Center for Disease Control and Prevention, National Center for Chronic Disease and Prevention and Health Promotion,

U.S. Department of Health and Human Services. Physical Activity Guidelines Advisory Committee. (2008). *Physical Activity Guidelines Advisory Committee Report,* Washington, D.C.

Wiecha, J. L., Peterson, K. E., Ludwig, D. S., Kim, J., Sobol, A., & Gortmaker, S. L. (2006). When children eat what they watch: impact of television viewing on dietary intake in youth. *Arch Pediatr Adolesc Med, 160*(4), 436-442.

Yancey, A. (2007) Social ecological influences on obesity control: instigating problems and informing potential solutions. *Obesity Management, 3*(2), 74-79.

Zajonc, R. B. (1968). Attitudinal effects of mere exposure. *Journal of Personality and Social Psychology, 8*, 1-29.

Zimmerman, F. J., & Bell, J. F. (2010). Associations of television content type and obesity in children. *American Journal of Public Health, 100*(2), 334-340.

CHAPTER SEVEN

HOUSEHOLD FOOD INSECURITY AND CONSEQUENCES FOR LATINO CHILDREN

Hugo Melgar-Quiñonez[1] and Rafael Pérez-Escamilla[2]

Introduction

Compared to the national average, Latinos in the United States have a considerably higher rate of food insecurity (Nord et al., 2009). Household food insecurity is defined as the limited or uncertain ability to access through socially acceptable manners the nutritionally adequate and safe foods needed for a healthy and active life (Anderson, 1990). Food insecurity affects not only the quantity of the food available or accessed by the families; it is also reflected in the quality of the foods families consume. Thus, the impact of food insecurity on the health status of individuals might be multifold, ranging from undernourishment related outcomes (e.g., stunting and iron-deficiency anemia) to obesity and obesity-related illnesses (e.g. diabetes) (Hackett et al., 2009; Eicher-Miller et al., 2009; Townsend et al., 2001; Seligman et al., 2010). In addition, the constant uncertainty about not been able to meet their food needs generates anxiety in individuals, and might have also other psychosocial implications such as depression (Whitaker et al., 2006). Besides the negative impact food insecurity might have in the health and nutritional status of Latino children, an increased risk for food insecurity and hunger is also worrisome from a national perspec-

[1]Department of Human Nutrition, OSU Extension, The Ohio State University.
[2]School of Public Health, Yale University.

tive given the demographic and social characteristics that prevail in the Latino community (e.g. fastest growing, relatively young community with high fertility rates). In that regards, having an increasing proportion of the U.S. population under a high risk for food insecurity and its consequences might greatly affect the economical and social environment in the country. Increasing rates of food insecurity turn this phenomenon into a strategically important issue to address.

Demographic and Socioeconomical Characteristics of the Latino Community

As shown by recent U.S. Census Bureau statistics, the Latino community is considered the fastest growing population group in the United States (Pew Hispanic Center, 2010). From 2000 to 2008 Latinos contributed to over 50% of the population increase, both as U.S.-born individuals or as foreign-born immigrants. In this regards, of the total Latino population increase over two-thirds were born in the United States, whereas 32% reported been foreign-born. A consistent increase in its numbers turned Latinos to become the largest minority group in the country, or the second largest population group after non-Hispanic whites. By 2008, the Latino community represented 15.4% of the total U.S. population. As a community, Latinos in the United States are also a very diverse population group. Among the almost 47 million Latinos projected by the Census Bureau in 2008, 66% were of Mexican origin, 9% were of Puerto Rican origin, 8% were Central American (Guatemala, El Salvador, Honduras, Nicaragua and Costa Rica) and 3.5% were Cuban. Almost 3% were Dominican, and the rest 10% reported to be Colombian, Ecuadorian, Peruvian, Venezuelan, Argentinean, Panamanian, Chilean, Bolivian, Uruguayan, Paraguayan or of other Latino/Hispanic origin. Mexicans are in average 16 years younger than Cubans; 50% of all Peruvians are homeowners compared to 28% of all Dominicans; 66% of all Ecuadorians are foreign-born while the great majority of all Puerto Ricans are native-born; the poverty rate among Hondurans is almost twice the rate among Colombians (21.5% and 11%, respectively).

Besides its rapid growth, in average Latinos are younger than other population groups. When compared to non-Hispanic whites, Latinos are in average 15 years younger (median age in years: 42 and 27, respectively) and 7 years younger than non-Hispanic blacks (median age in years: 34). In terms of its distribution across the United States, the Latino community is located mainly in five states (over 70% of all Latinos): California (29%), Texas (19%), Florida (8%), New York (7%), Arizona and Illinois (4% in each). Around 10% of the Latinos in the United States live in four other states: New Jersey, Colorado, New Mexico, Georgia. Although only a small percentage of the total Latino population, Latinos in New Mexico represent over 45% of the state population (36%

of the population of California and Texas). Spanish constitutes the predominant language among Latinos. In that regard, 20% of adult Latinos in the United States report speaking English only at home, whereas about 44% report speaking English less than very well. One of the lowest levels in English proficiency can be found among Guatemalans (less than 40%).

As mentioned above, educational attainment differs among Latinos, but in general school education shows lower levels than any other population groups in the United States. Almost one out of four Latinos has completed ninth grade, and only 13% have a college degree. This statistics are even worst among foreign-born Latinos. Although showing a decreasing trend from 2000 to 2008, high school drop out rates among Latino youth are almost twice the national average (9.3% and 5.6%, respectively). The differences in country of origin within the Latino community determine also important disparities regarding education. Guatemalans show the lowest school attainment (over 53% have not obtained a high school diploma). Combining those with the highest and lowest educational level, over 25% of Colombians, Peruvians and Cubans in the United States have a college degree, while less than 10% of all Latinos of Mexican, Guatemalan and Salvadorian origin have such level of education. Subsequently, in average Latinos from these three last groups earn around 10,000 dollars less per year than those belonging to the first three groups.

HOUSEHOLD FOOD INSECURITY IN THE UNITED STATES

Despite the availability of food supplies in the United States, many homes do not have access to a diet that will allow them to cover their nutritional requirements. Since 1995, every year the Economic Research Service at the United States Department of Agriculture (ERS) releases a report on household food security in the United States, which is based on Current Population Survey (CPS) data (Nord et al., 2009). This report is derived from the results of a measurement instrument developed in the early 90s with the purpose of estimating the magnitude of food insecurity in the country and identifying the most affected population groups. During many years, one of the main obstacles to overseeing the state of household food security was the lack of valid tools for its measurement or assessment. Although in 1984 a Presidential Task Force report informed about signs of hunger in the United States, it was impossible to estimate its magnitude at that time (Olson, 1999). In 1992, the development of a food security scale began. This scale was previously called Central Food Security Module, and currently it is better known as Household Food Security Supplemental Module (HFSSM), which includes a total of 18 items (Hamilton et al., 1997). Most of the items in this tool derived from the Radimer/Cornell scale and the Community Childhood Hunger Identification Project (CCHIP), developed during the early stages of the measurement (Radimer et al., 1992; Wehler et al., 1992; Campbell, 1991). Ten of the HFSSM items refer to the situation faced by the household as a whole and by the adults in it. The rest refer to the situation of the children in the household. The assessment of food insecurity using such tool goes beyond the food sufficiency and includes: a) the quantitative component which refers to having enough food b) the qualitative aspect concerning the type and diversity of foods; c) the psychological element of uncertainty due to privation or restricted selection of foods. The measurement of food insecurity states that the underlying conditions to the items included in the HFSSM are due to restrained monetary resources (Campbell, 1991).

The conceptual framework of food insecurity states that this phenomenon is a "managed process" with a sequence of events (Radimer et al., 1992). Initially, anxiety and worry exist over food supplies (home level/mild). Then, adjustments are made in the household budget, which affect the quality of the diet. Later on, adults limit the quantity and quality of foods they consume (adult level/moderate). Finally, at the highest level of food insecurity, quantity and quality of food consumed by children are affected (child level/severe). Rigorous HFSSM tests have confirmed the underlying conceptual framework and its usefulness in overseeing the state of food security (Kendall et al., 1995; Frongillo, 1999). Different studies in the United States and in other countries have shown the association between food insecurity and adverse factors such as inadequate consumption of energy and nutrients (Rose & Oliviera, 1997); the decrease in household food supplies (Kendall et al., 1996); emotional problems in children (Kleinman et al., 1999); and obesity (Dietz, 1995; Townsend et al., 2001; Wilde & Peterman, 2006).

By 1999 the national rate of food insecurity in the United States showed its lowest point around 10%. Overall, during the first 7 years of the new century roughly 11% of U.S. households were affected, with the highest rate corresponding to 2004 (12%) (Nord et al., 2009). The last report available to date corresponding to 2008, showed the highest food insecurity rate ever since 1995. For the previous 2007, the ERS reported a national rate of 11.1% of U.S. households, meaning that 13 million U.S. households at some time during 2007 "had difficulty providing enough food for all their members due to a lack of resources." Roughly food insecurity affected about 36 million individuals. Around one third of all food insecure households were classified in the most severe food insecurity category, meaning that the food intake of one or more adults was reduced and their eating patterns were disrupted at times during the year because the household lacked money and other resources for food. In 2008 though, the food security status for the U.S. population suffered its lowest point with a 14.6% of food insecurity. This increase meant that the number of individuals affected by this phenomenon went up to almost 50 million individuals. Among the population categories with a higher prevalence of food insecurity the ERS reports households with children with a rate of 21% for 2008. This means that over 16.5 million children were affected by food insecurity during that year. The same report states that children in most food insecure households were protected from reductions in food intake. In some households it seems that only older children were impacted by the more severe effects of food insecurity, while their younger peers were protected from those effects. However, it was shown that in 2008 around 500,000 children were subject to reduced food intake and disrupted eating patterns.

In addition to the higher prevalence reported for households with children, family structure seems to have a big impact on food insecurity levels. In this regards, households with children headed by single females show a prevalence of over 37%, compared to a rate of 14.3% for married couples with children and 27.6% for households headed by a male without spouse.

Regarding the geographic distribution of food insecurity, the Southwest region shows higher rates than the Northeast. In average between 2006 and 2008 Texas and Arizona showed rates close to 16%, while New Hampshire and Massachusetts had a prevalence of around 8.5% for the same period of time. The food insecurity rate in 2008 was roughly the same for households located outside metropolitan areas, when compared to those located inside metropolitan areas (14.2% and 14.7%, respectively).

Obviously, food insecurity has its bigger impact in poor households (below 130% of the poverty line), and in those presenting some of the characteristics above the rates are much higher. For example, one out of two low-income households with children headed by a female without spouse experienced food insecurity in 2008. When examining food insecurity in Latino children in the United States, it is recommended to do it within a framework that takes into account its demographic, social and economical characteristics. Half of the Latino children have at least one parent born outside the United States (second-generation), while one in ten Latino children are first-generation immigrants themselves. The rest, are U.S.-born children whose parents were also born in this country, and are considered third-generation Latinos. A recent analysis by the Pew Hispanic Center found that first- and second-generation Latino children are less likely to be fluent in English and to have parents who completed high school than their third or higher generation peers. In consequence, they are more likely to live in poverty. The financial crisis of 2008 that might have determined the increase in the food insecurity rate reported by Nord et al., had a severe impact in the Latino community. The percentage of working-age Latinos (16 and older) who are employed fell to 64.7% by the end of 2008 (Pew Hispanic Center, 2010). A few more statistics might help to generate a more complete portrait of the underlying determinants to food insecurity among Latinos. By 2007, 27% of Latino households were headed by a single female, and/or were classified as being poor (Pew Hispanic Center, 2010). By 2009, 22% of all children under the age of 18 in the United States were Latinos, a number that will grow to around 33% by 2025 (Pew Hispanic Center, 2008).

HOUSEHOLD FOOD INSECURITY IN LATINO FAMILIES IN THE UNITED STATES

The ERS reported that Latino households in 2008 had a rate of food insecurity of 26.9%, higher than the prevalence among non-Hispanic white and black households (10.7% and 25.7%, respectively), as well as considerably above the national average of 14.6%. The increase in the prevalence of food insecurity observed from 2007 to 2008 affected especially Latino households, as well as those of single parents with children. Food insecurity among Latinos increased from 20.1% in 2007 to over 28% in 2008. Roughly, over 13 million Latinos in the United States experienced some level of food insecurity at some point during 2008; one third of them reported having experienced hunger. The situation among Latino households with children was even worst. In 2008, almost one in every three Latino household suffered food insecurity (32.1%), affecting around 5 million Latino children; an increase of almost 35% from 23.8% in 2007. In addition, 43% of the Latino households under the poverty line were considered to be food insecure.

At this point, a comment to better understand the ERS estimates on food insecurity is in place. The national measurement considers food insecure those households answering affirmatively to three or more of the items in the HFSSM (Bickel et al., 2000). As a consequence, households responding affirmatively to one or two of the items are categorized as food secure. In spite of that, the National Health and Nutrition Examination Survey, which includes the HFSSM, proposes that those households responding affirmatively to one or two items are to be categorized as "marginally food secure." In a recently published analysis of CPS data from 2003 to 2005, Coleman-Jensen suggests that because of the way food insecurity categories are determined the prevalence of this phenomenon might be underestimated, which also impacts the estimation of the needed food assistance in the United States. This author's analysis indicates that for the years assessed the actual prevalence of food insecurity might be about 70% higher than the official statistics. Thus, the corresponding rate for the U.S. Latino population would rise from an average of 20.9% to 34%. If the results of this analysis were applicable to 2008 data, the prevalence of food insecurity among Latinos in the United States would be over 40%, indicating the urgency for food assistance programs accessible to this population.

In addition to estimating an average national rate and the prevalence of food insecurity for different population categories, the ERS has been reporting estimates on food expenditure (Nord et al., 2009). In average for 2008 it was estimated that U.S. households spent weekly about 43.75 dollars in food per person. In contrast, Latino households spent weekly 35 dollars in food per person. Relative to the Thrifty Food Plan (TFP = 1.0), the median food expenditures for Latino households was 0.96, while among non-Hispanic white households it was 1.19. The TFP represents a minimal cost meal plan to achieve a nutritious diet with limited resources, assuming that all purchased foods are consumed at home. The TFP uses prices, assumed to be what low-income people pay for food. Taking into account the assumptions listed here, it is not difficult to see that Latinos on average not only spend less than what is needed to meet the TFP, but that 0.96 might be an overestimation of how close the most vulnerable Latino families are from meeting this minimal plan. As shown in some studies, food insecurity reaches very high levels among migrant farm working families, who given the locations and circumstances of their work are usually far from places where they can purchase foods at low prices, and might not have the facilities to prepare the foods suggested in the TFP. Also contributing to the problem of food insecurity is confusion about the selection of foods in U.S. supermarkets (i.e., how to select the most nutritious items for the best price), which might be due to language barriers confronted by Latinos disregarding their country of origin.

Given the differences in social and economical status within the Latino community in the United States, average statistics are only a rough reflection of the situation faced by the most vulnerable groups. In this regard, studies with Mexican immigrants have reported rates of food insecurity that are way above the national average estimates. Food insecurity among immigrants is often seasonal and exacerbated by limited transportation; especially in the winter (Melgar-Quiñonez et al., 2003). A series of studies in four different settings in North Carolina with Latino immigrant families showed that almost 50% of the families in each of the study samples were food insecure (Quandt et al., 2004, 2006). In one of the study settings food insecurity affected over 70% of the families interviewed. Researchers concluded that Latino families experience significant levels of food insecurity not been addressed by governmental assistance programs. More recently also in North Carolina, Borre et al., reported that in a sample of migrant seasonal farm workers food insecurity affected almost 64%

of the families interviewed. More than half of these families reported having experienced hunger.

In another study with migrants and seasonal farm workers in Texas, Weigel et al., reported a food insecurity prevalence of 82%, while hunger affected almost 50% of the study sample. Individuals in food insecure households were more likely to be affected by depression, learning disorders and probably by gastrointestinal infections. Besides the high levels of food insecurity, the study sample was characterized by adult obesity, central body adiposity and elevated blood pressure.

Urban Latino families are also highly vulnerable to food insecurity. In a study of low-income Latino communities in Chicago, researchers found a food insecurity prevalence of 30%. The sample includes a majority of Puerto Rican families (70% of the sample), who reported more severe food insecurity than Mexican families (22% of the sample). Interestingly, only 30% of the food insecure families were Food Stamp recipients. This is worrisome since their immigration status in the United States makes low-income Puerto Ricans eligible for food assistance programs.

In 1998, Himmelgreen et al., conducted a study among low-income Puerto Rican women from inner-city Hartford, Connecticut. The initial sample of women reporting no drug use was subsequently matched with a sample of drug users. The latter were more likely to be food insecure, and to confront increasingly severe food insufficiency. Drug users reported consuming fewer meals than non-drug users. Their consumption of vegetables and fish was lower, while their consumption of sweets/desserts and fried foods was significantly higher than among non-drug users.

In a study conducted in New York City with undocumented Mexican migrants Hadley et al., reported that hunger affected 28% of the survey respondents. Uncertainty about access to work seemed to be an important predictor for food insecurity; working as a day laborer was highly associated with hunger in this study. Researchers suggest that programs providing access to resources to undocumented migrants may help reducing food insecurity in this vulnerable population. Although lacking proper immigration documents in the United States might constitute a barrier for accessing governmental food assistance, food insecurity and hunger greatly impact Latinos who do comply with immigration regulations. A cross-sectional survey of documented Latino immigrants conducted in California, Texas and Illinois revealed that out of 630 respondents, 40% were food insecure without hunger, while 41% were suffering hunger (Kasper et al., 2000). Some of the independent predictors of hunger found by the researchers were income below federal poverty level and poor English proficiency. The authors state that "the prevalence of hunger among low-income legal immigrants is unacceptably high" and highlight the importance of improving access to food assistance programs for the health and wellbeing of the Latino population in the United States.

The limited ability to access enough food to meet the nutritional requirements represents a difficult burden to overcome for food insecure households. Even with increasing availability of healthful nutrition information in both English and Spanish, not having the needed resources to purchase what is being recommended by the dietary guidelines and nutrition education programs represents a concrete impediment for food insecure families to better feed their children. Several studies confirm the difficulties families face to supply and consume fruits and vegetables, which is particularly difficult for severely food insecure Latino households (Kendall et al., 1996; Kaiser et al., 2003). As previously mentioned, the paradox of food insecurity and obesity seems to greatly affect low-income Latinos in the United States. Especially in California, studies document that greater food insecurity might be associated with an increased risk of obesity (Adams et al., 2003; Kaiser et al., 2004).

THE IMPACT OF HOUSEHOLD FOOD INSECURITY IN LATINO CHILDREN IN THE UNITED STATES

The impact of food insecurity and hunger in children's health seems to be of diverse nature. As researchers have reported, children hunger seems to be associated with traumatic life, with low birth weight and with higher rates of chronic disease, as well as with behavioral problems, anxiety and depression (Weinreb et al., 2002).

Although young children seem to be spared the most severe effects of food insecurity, once food access becomes more restricted the possibility of providing children with the foods they need to meet their nutritional requirements turns more difficult. This might be especially true among groups at a very high risk of food insecurity. A study carried out in Minnesota comparing children of immigrant Latino parents with non-immigrant non-Latino children, both attending a low-income clinic population, found higher rates of child hunger among Latino children when compared to non-Latinos (Kersey et al., 2007). Other researchers have reported increasing risks for poor health among children of immigrants facing food insecurity (Chilton et al., 2009). In this regard, the risk of poor health was higher among children of recent immigrants when compared to children whose mothers were born in the United States. Other researchers have also found that children of immigrant non-citizens experience higher levels of food insecurity than the children of U.S. citizens (Kalil & Chen, 2008). This seems to be true especially among Latinos, and among households with low levels of maternal education. A study with Puerto Rican residents of Hartford, Connecticut, revealed high levels of food insecurity (Himmelgreen et al., 2000), especially among households running out of food stamps before the end of the month. A subsequent study in the same population group revealed the importance of food stamps in the dietary intake of micronutrients in Puerto Rican preschoolers in Hartford (Pérez-Escamilla et al., 2000).

Although hunger represents the most severe level of food insecurity, this phenomenon is not only associated with the lack of sufficient food. As researchers working with Latino families have shown, greater food insecurity is also associated with a lower variety of most foods. A study with Mexican-American children in California examining the relationship between food insecurity and food supplies (Kaiser et al., 2003) showed significantly inverse associations between increasing food insecurity and the availability in the homes of dairy products, fruits, grains, meats and vegetables. In this study the authors recommended that future research in Latino households should explore the effects of seasonal food insecurity on food intake of young children. Also in California, limited education, lack of English proficiency and low income were found to be negatively associated with food security (Kaiser et al., 2002).

With respect to the impact of food insecurity in the diet of Mexican-American children, few studies have been conducted. Nevertheless, in a consistent manner the available studies report a detrimental effect. In the late 90s researchers in California reported that children in severely food insecure households were less likely to meet Food Guide Pyramid guidelines than other children (Kaiser et al., 2002). Although not statistically significant, the rates of overweight tended to be higher among children in food insecure families when compared to children in food secure households. A recently published binational study with children living in the United States and Mexico found higher levels of food insecurity in both groups (39% and 75% in California and in Mexico, respectively (Rosas et al., 2009). In both cases though, the dietary intake showed patterns that might negatively affect the health status of the children. In the United States food insecure children consumed more fat, saturated fat, sweets and fried snacks than their food secure peers. In Mexico, food insecure children showed lower intakes of dairy and vitamin B-6. Another study with Latino children living in San Antonio, Texas, found significant associations between food insecurity and low fruit and vegetable consumption (Dave et al., 2009).

Although still controversial, the paradoxical relationship between food insecurity and overweight seems to affect Latino children. Buscemi et al., (2009) argue that as Latino children acculturate to the United States, they are at risk for excess weight gain. To examine this issue the authors recruited Latino children of both immigrant and non-immigrant parents. Their analysis revealed that acculturation was a moderating variable between food insecurity and weight status among the children of Latino immigrants. In addition, Ortiz-Hernandez et al., reported in 2007 that food insecurity and obesity are positively associated in school children living in Mexico City. In this study the highest rate of overweight was observed in children with severe food insecurity (15.8% compared to 6.9% among food secure children). This study reports also that food insecure children consumed more fatty cereals, salty foods and high-energy density sweets. In other Latin American countries, a higher risk for stunting and underweight has been found among children in food insecure households (Isanaka et al., 2007 & Hackett et al., 2009).

Other studies have shown increasing risks for iron deficiency anemia among children in food insecure households (Park et al., 2009). Although not specifically targeting Latino children, the prevalence of iron deficiency anemia in early childhood was significantly larger in low-income children, and Latinos showed elevated rates of this health problem.

MAIN PUBLIC HEALTH ISSUES IN LATINOS ASSOCIATED WITH FOOD INSECURITY

As reported by the Office of Minority Health and Health Disparities at the Centers for Disease Control (CDC, 2010), by 2006 the five leading causes of death among Latinos in the United States were: heart disease, cancer, unintentional injuries, stroke and diabetes. Although diabetes ranks sixth among the 10 main causes of death in the United States, it is usually found among the 5 main causes of death among Latinos. As reported by the CDC, the diabetes prevalence among Latinos is almost twice that the prevalence among Caucasians (9.8% vs. 5%). Furthermore, diabetes tends to affect young Latinos more than the non-Hispanic white youth. This is of great concern given that Latinos in the United States are younger than the non-Hispanic population. Increasing rates of overweight and obesity among Latino children might negatively affect diabetes rates in this population group. As shown in the Pediatric Nutrition Surveillance report of 2008, Latino preschoolers have higher rates of overweight and obesity when compared to their Caucasian and African-American peers (Polhamus et al., 2009). Finally, low educational attainment, as mentioned above, seems also to have detrimental effects in the diabetes status of Latinos. Latinos with less than a high school education showed a diabetes rate of 11.8% when compared to Latino college graduates, who had a rate of 7%.

Although the evidence on the association between food insecurity and diabetes is not consistent throughout the literature, which is not abundant, researchers have reported an increased risk of diabetes among severe food insecure individuals in the National Health and Nutrition Examination Survey (NHANES) of 1999—2002 (Seligman et al., 2007). Using a larger NHANES sample (NHANES 1999—2004), the same authors reported a non-significant association, although the trend was similar to the previous report (Seligman et al., 2010). In addition, they found significant associations of food insecurity with hypertension. Canadian investigators seem to ratify these findings when reporting that food insecurity rates are higher among individuals with diabetes when compared to those without diabetes (Gucciardi et al., 2009). A similar situation is found regarding an association between food insecurity and obesity. Among adults in the United States, most of the studies show significant associations between both phenomena in women and men. A study with low-income Latino women in California showed twice the risk for obesity among those classified as severely food insecure, when compared to their food secure peers. Among children though, the relationship is less clear and even controversial. While some authors report a positive association (Metallinos-Katsaras et al., 2009), others report no association (Gundersen et al., 2009). In any case, both phenomena seem to affect Latino children and their families at levels that urgently require effective interventions. The implications of the lack of action might greatly affect a large proportion of the U.S. population, and especially those integrating in increased numbers into the work force.

HOUSEHOLD FOOD INSECURITY AND CHILD PSYCHO-EMOTIONAL AND INTELLECTUAL DEVELOPMENT

Decades of research have conclusively shown that chronic and acute malnutrition have a negative impact on the physical and intellectual development of children. Furthermore these negative consequences can still be detected during adolescence and adulthood (Martorell & Scrimshaw 1995, Pollitt et al., 1993, Pollitt 1995). However, we are just starting to understand how household food insecurity (FI) affects the psycho-emotional and intellectual development of children in the United States.

Qualitative research has shown that FI in U.S. households can have a strong psycho-emotional impact on children and that these impacts are long lasting (Radimer 2002, Olson et al., 2007, Pérez-Escamilla et al., 2004, Sampaio et al., 2006, Wehler et al., 1992). These findings have been corroborated with epidemiological studies. Kleinman et al., (1998) examined the influence of FI on child behavior and school achievement among low-income primary school children from Pittsburgh. Almost two-thirds of children participating in this cross-sectional study lived in single-headed households. Based on the CCHIP scale, 16% of the children were classified as experiencing hunger and 36% as being at risk of hunger. FI was strongly associated with school behavioral problems, emotional problems and lower academic achievement. Specifically, 31 of the 35 items of the Pediatric Symptom Checklist (PSC) correlated significantly with hunger (r: 0.08-0.29). Correlation coefficients were stronger for "fighting with other children," "wanting to be in closer proximity to their mothers," "blaming others for their problems," "classroom behavioral problems," including not following teacher's rules and taking things from fellow classmates. Two of the eight factors derived from the PSC principal component analysis were associated with hunger and risk of hunger. These were the factors reflecting aggressiveness/disagreement and irritability/anxiety/worry. Findings suggest that adjusting for poverty, household FI can affect the behavioral, emotional and academic performance of children.

Whitaker et al. (2006) analyzed factors associated with FI using cross sectional data collected from low-income households located in 18 cities in the United States. About half of the women respondents were black (51%), 23% Hispanic, and the rest belonged to other ethnic/racial groups. Respondents' children were 3 years old on average. Based on the HFSSM scale (adult items), 71% of the households were food secure, 17% were marginally food insecure and 12% were food insecure. Multivariate analyses showed that the percentage of women with clinical depression and anxiety symptoms was 17% among food secure, 21% among the marginally food insecure and 30% among the food insecure (p<0.05). Among children there was also a dose-response relationship between FI and child behavioral/mental health problems, 23% vs. 31% vs. 37%, respectively (p<0.05). In this study behavioral/mental health problems were defined as aggressiveness, anxiety, depression, lack of concentration and/or hyperactivity.

Weinreb et al., (2002) conducted a cross-sectional study in Massachusetts where they interviewed women with preschool or school-aged children living under poverty conditions. Almost half of the women identified themselves as Puerto Rican (45%) and 30% as white. Based on the CCHIP scale, 33% of the school-aged children were classified as food secure, 51% as experiencing a moderate level of hunger and 16% as experiencing severe hunger. The corresponding percentages for the preschoolers were 41%, 51% and 8%, respectively. Women living in households experiencing severe hunger were significantly more likely to have experienced post-traumatic events during their lives. Multivariate analyses showed that among both school-aged children and preschoolers, severe hunger was associated with more likelihood of internalizing behavioral problems. Among school-aged children, severe hunger was also associated with more anxiety/depression. Among preschoolers severe hunger (vs. food security) was associated with extreme poverty (75% vs. 48%, respectively), higher likelihood of traumatic events (8.5% vs. 6%), and low birth weight (23% vs. 6%). Poor health was significantly associated with moderate hunger among preschoolers and with severe hunger among school-aged children. An interesting finding from this study is that maternal stress internalization was associated with more internalization of problems and worst health outcomes among their children.

Jyoti et al., (2005) found that 16% of households in a U.S. national cohort experienced FI as measured by the USDA scale. FI in kindergarten predicted delayed reading and mathematics, as well as less social skills in elementary school.

In conclusion, studies reviewed strongly suggest that FI represents not only a biological but also a psycho-emotional challenge to children exposed to it. This in turn is likely to translate into poor academic performance and intellectual achievement later on in life. All of these studies have been conducted in the United States and the great majority have included Hispanic children. Thus, improving food security in Hispanic households is likely to improve the overall wellbeing of their children, including their psycho-emotional and intellectual development. These conclusions need to be confirmed through additional longitudinal studies as most evidence to date is cross-sectional.

HOUSEHOLD FOOD INSECURITY IN LATIN AMERICA

In Latin America some countries have developed or adopted national measures of household food security, which is generating a wide range of research around causes and consequences of this phenomenon. In 2004, Brazil applied such a measure within a national households' survey showing the importance of such measure to understand the association of food insecurity and other factors closely associated with this phenomenon (Pérez-Escamilla et al., 2004). Researchers found significant correlations with daily consumption of fruits, vegetables, meat/fish and dairy. On the same line, Colombia applied a food security measure as part of a national survey, showing strong correlations with several social-demographic variables such as low food availability, begging and children's labor (Alvarez Uribe et al., 2006). A third Latin American country with national food security data is Mexico, where researchers found a national average food insecurity rate of 52%. The rates found in Brazil and Colombia were 35% and 40%, respectively (Parás and Pérez-Escamilla, 2004; Ministério do Desenvolvimento Social e Combate à Fome—Brazil, 2004; Instituto Colombiano de Bienestar Familiar, 2007). Studies in other Latin American and Caribbean countries have shown strong correlations with expenditures on food, household food availability, dietary diversity and illness (Melgar-Quiñonez et al., 2005 and 2006; Hackett et al., 2007; Pérez-Escamilla et al., 2009).

INTERVENTIONS AGAINST HOUSEHOLD FOOD INSECURITY

A wide range of programs in the United States support families in need of food assistance; in 2007, federally funded food and nutrition assistance programs provided benefits to 80% of low-income, food insecure households with children (Nord, 2009). Among others the following programs assist diverse population groups: the Supplemental Nutrition Assistance Program (SNAP), " . . . providing monthly benefits to eligible low-income families which can be used to purchase food" (http://www.fns.usda.gov/snap/); the Special Supplemental Nutrition Program for Women, Infants and Children (WIC), which " . . . serves to safeguard the health of low-income women, infants and children up to age 5 who are at nutritional risk by providing nutritious foods to supplement diets, information on healthy eating and referrals to health care" (http://www.fns. usda.gov/wic/); the School Meals Programs, which are federally funded child nutrition programs that include the National School Lunch Program, the School Breakfast Program and the Special Milk Program (http://www.fns.usda.gov/ cnd/); the Senior Farmers' Market Nutrition Program (SFMNP), which awards grants to provide low-income seniors with coupons for eligible foods at farmers' markets (http://www.fns.usda.gov/wic/SeniorFMNP/SFMNPmenu.htm); and the Food Distribution Program on Indian Reservations (FDPIR) providing assistance to low-income households in Indian reservations, and to Native American families (http://www.fns.usda.gov/fdd/programs/fdpir/).

Some, if not all of the programs in the United States have a strong nutrition education component such as SNAP-Education (SNAP-ED), with the goal of improving "the likelihood that persons eligible for SNAP will make healthy food choices within a limited budget and choose physically active lifestyles consistent with the current Dietary Guidelines for Americans and MyPyramid" (http://snap.nal.usda.gov/nal_display/index.php?info_center=15&tax_level=1& tax_subject=250); the Expanded Food and Nutrition Education Program (EFNEP), "designed to assist limited resource audiences in acquiring the knowledge, skills, attitudes and changed behavior necessary for nutritionally sound diets, and to contribute to their personal development and the improvement of the total family diet and nutritional wellbeing" (http://www.csrees.usda.gov/ nea/food/efnep/efnep.html). All these programs in combination with a wide network of food banks and food pantries play a major role in providing millions of American families with the means to access basic nutrition requirements, as well as valuable information on how to better utilize the available resources for a healthier diet and physical activity.

During the last 10 years, across Latin America several national or regional initiatives have been created to combat hunger and food insecurity such as: Fome Zero in Brazil (http://www.fomezero.org/), Oportunidades in Mexico (www.oportunidades.gob.mx), the Programa de Mejoramiento Alimentario y Nutricional de Antioquia (http://www.proyectofaomana.org.co/) or the Programa Regional de Seguridad Alimentaria y Nutricional para Centroamérica working in Guatemala, El Salvador, Honduras and Nicaragua (http://www.sica.int/san/).

Giving the high rates of food insecurity affecting millions of households in the United States and in Latin America it is imperative that the current efforts continue expanding their coverage and diversify the ways of approaching food insecurity. Programs to alleviate hunger should keep in mind that access to enough food goes hand in hand with accessing nutritionally adequate and safe food, and that nutrition education is a key component in supporting Latino families (in the United States and abroad) to maintain a balanced diet for a healthy and active life.

References

Adams, E. J., Grummer-Strawn, L., & Chavez, G. (2003). Food insecurity is associated with increased risk of obesity in California women. *J Nutr, 133*(4):1070-4.

Anderson, S. A. (1990). Core indicators of nutritional state for difficult-to-sample populations. *J Nutr, 121*:1559-1600.

Bickel, G., Nord, M., Price, C., Hamilton, W., & Cook J. (2000). Guide to measuring household food security, Revised 2000. U.S. Department of Agriculture, Food and Nutrition Service, Alexandria VA.

Borre, K., Ertle, L., & Graff, M. (2010). Working to eat: Vulnerability, food insecurity, and obesity among migrant and seasonal farm worker families. *Am J Ind Med, 53*(4):443-62.

Buscemi, J., Beech, B. M., & Relyea, G. (2009). Predictors of obesity in Latino Children: Acculturation as a moderator of the relationship between food insecurity and body mass index percentile. *J Immigr Minor Health* [Epub ahead of print]

Campbell, C. C. (1991). Food security: A nutritional outcome or a predictor variable? *J Nutr, 121*:408-415.

Centers for Disease Control (2010). 10 Leading Causes of Death Hispanic/Latino Population, U.S., 2006. Available at: http://www.cdc.gov/omhd/populations/HL/hl.htm#Ten (Accessed September 27, 2010)

Centers for Disease Control (2002). Prevalence of Diabetes among Hispanics in Six U.S. Geographic Locations Available at: http://www.cdc.gov/diabetes/pubs/pdf/hispanic.pdf (Accessed September 27, 2010)

Chilton M., Black M. M., Berkowitz C., Casey P. H., Cook J., Cutts D., Jacobs R. R., Heeren T., de Cuba S. E., Coleman S., Meyers A., & Frank D. A. (2009). Food insecurity and risk of poor health among U.S.-born children of immigrants. *Am J Public Health, 99*(3):556-62. Epub 2008 Dec 23.

Coleman-Jensen, A. J. (2010). U.S. food insecurity status: Toward a refined definition. *Soc Indic Res, 95*:215–230.

Dave, J. M., Evans, A. E., Saunders, R. P., Watkins, K. W., & Pfeiffer, K. A. (2009). Associations among food insecurity, acculturation, demographic factors, and fruit and vegetable intake at home in Hispanic children. *J Am Diet Assoc, 109*(4):697-701.

Dietz, W. H. (1995). Does hunger cause obesity? *Pediatrics, 95*:766-767.

Eicher-Miller, H. A., Mason, A. C., Weaver, C. M., McCabe, G. P., & Boushey, C. J. (2009). Food insecurity is associated with iron deficiency anemia in U.S. adolescents. *Am J Clin Nutr, 90*(5):1358-71. Epub 2009 Sep 23.

Frongillo, E. A. Jr. (1999). Validation of measures of food insecurity and hunger. *J Nutr, 129*:506S-509S.

Gucciardi, E., Vogt, J. A., DeMelo, M., & Stewart, D. E. (2009). Exploration of the relationship between household food insecurity and diabetes in Canada. *Diabetes Care, 32*(12):2218-24. Epub 2009 Aug 31.

Gundersen, C., Garasky, S., & Lohman, B. J. (2009). Food insecurity is not associated with childhood obesity as assessed using multiple measures of obesity. *J Nutr, 139*(6):1173-8. Epub 2009 Apr 29.

Hackett, M., Melgar-Quiñonez, H., & Alvarez, M. C. (2009). Household food insecurity associated with stunting and underweight among preschool children in Antioquia, Colombia. *Rev Panam Salud Pública, 25*(6):506-10

Hadley, C., Galea, S., Nandi, V., Nandi, A., Lopez, G., Strongarone, S., & Ompad, D. (2008). Hunger and health among undocumented Mexican migrants in a U.S. urban area. *Public Health Nutr, 11*(2):151-8. Epub 2007 Jul 5.

Hamilton, W. L., Cook, J. T., Thompson, W. W., Buron, L. F., Fronjillo, E. A., & Olson, C. M. (1997) Household food security in the United States in 1995: Executive Summary. Washington, DC: U.S. Department of Agriculture.

Himmelgreen, D. A., Pérez-Escamilla, R., Segura-Millán, S., Romero-Daza, N., Tanasescu, M., & Singer, M. (1998). A comparison of the nutritional status and food security of drug-using and non-drug-using Hispanic women in Hartford, Connecticut. *Am J Phys Anthropol, 107*(3):351-61.

Himmelgreen, D. A., Pérez-Escamilla R., Segura-Millán S., Peng Y. K., Gonzalez A., Singer M., & Ferris A. (2000) Food insecurity among low-income Hispanics in Hartford, Connecticut: Implications for public health policy. *Hum Org, 59*(3):334-42

Isanaka, S., Mora-Plazas, M., Lopez-Arana, S., Baylin, A., & Villamor, E. (2007). Food insecurity is highly prevalent and predicts underweight but not overweight in adults and school children from Bogotá, Colombia. *J Nutr, 137*(12):2747-55.

Instituto Colombiano de Bienestar Familiar. (2007). Presentación Encuesta Nacional de la Situación Nutricional en Colombia ENSIN 2005. Available at: http://nutrinet.org/servicios/biblioteca-digital/func-startdown/385/. (Accessed on September 27, 2010)

Jyoti, D. F., Frongillo, E. A., & Jones, S. J. (2005) Food insecurity affects school children's academic performance, weight gain, and social skills. *J Nutr, 135*:2831-9.

Kaiser L. L., Melgar-Quiñonez H., Townsend M. S., Nicholson Y., Fujii M. L., Martin A. C., & Lamp C. L. (2003). Food insecurity and food supplies in Latino households with young children. *J Nutr Educ Behav, 35*(3):148-53.

Kaiser, L. L., Melgar-Quiñonez, H. R., Lamp, C. L., Johns, M. C., Sutherlin, J. M., & Harwood, J. O. (2002). Food security and nutritional outcomes of preschool-age Mexican-American children. *J Am Diet Assoc, 102*(7):924-9.

Kaiser, L. L., Townsend, M. S., Melgar-Quiñonez, H. R., Fujii, M. L., & Crawford, P. B. (2004). Choice of instrument influences relations between food insecurity and obesity in Latino women. *Am J Clin Nutr, 80*(5):1372-8.

Kalil, A., & Chen, J. H. (2008) Mothers' citizenship status and household food insecurity among low-income children of immigrants. *New Dir Child Adolesc Dev,* (121):43-62.

Kasper, J., Gupta, S. K., Tran, P., Cook, J. T., & Meyers, A. F. (2000). Hunger in legal immigrants in California, Texas, and Illinois. *Am J Public Health, 90*(10):1629-33.

Kendall, A., Olson, C. M., & Frongillo, E. A., Jr. (1996). Relationship of hunger and food security to food availability and consumption. *J Am Diet Assoc, 6*:1019-1024.

Kendall, A., Olson, C. M., & Frongillo, E. A., Jr. (1995). Validation of the Radimer/Cornell measures of hunger and food security. *J Nutr, 125*:2793-2801.

Kersey, M., Geppert, J., & Cutts, D. B. (2007). Hunger in young children of Mexican immigrant families. *Public Health Nutr, 10*(4):390-5.

Kleinman, R. E., Murphy, J. M., Little, M., Pagano, M., Wehler, C. A., Regal, K., & Jellinek, M. S. (1998) Hunger in children in the United States: potential behavioral and emotional correlates. *Pediatrics, 101*:e3.

Martorell, R., & Scrimshaw, N. (1995) The effects of improved nutrition in early childhood: The Institute of Nutrition of Central America and Panama (INCAP) follow-up study. *J Nutr, 125*: 1027S-1138S.

Melgar-Quiñonez, H., Kaiser, L. L., Martin, A. C., Metz, D., & Olivares, A. (2003). Food insecurity among Californian Latinos: focus-group observations. *Salud Pública Mex., 45*(3):198-205.

Metallinos-Katsaras, E., Sherry, B., & Kallio, J. (2009). Food insecurity is associated with overweight in children younger than 5 years of age. *J Am Diet Assoc, 109*(10):1790-4.

Ministério do Desenvolvimento Social e Combate à Fome, Ministério do Planejamento, Orçamento e Gestão, Brazil (2006). Pesquisa Nacional por Amostra de Domicilios; Segurança Alimentar; 2004. Available at: http://www.ibge.gov.br/home/estatistica/ populacao/trabalhoerendimento/ pnad2004/ default.shtm. (Accessed on September 15 2010)

Nord, M., Andrews, M., & Carlson, S. (2009). Household Food Security in the United States, 2008. ERR-83, U.S. Dept. of Agriculture Econ. Res. Serv.

Nord, M. (2009). Food Insecurity in Households with Children: Prevalence, Severity, and Household Characteristics. EIB-56. U.S. Dept. of Agriculture, Econ. Res. Serv.

Olson, C. M., Bove, C. F., & Miller, E. O. (2007) Growing up poor: Long-term implications for eating patterns and body weight. *Appetite, 49*:198-207.

Olson, C. M. (1999). Nutrition and health outcomes associated with food insecurity and hunger. *J Nutr, 129*:521S-524S.

Olson, C. M. (1999). Symposium: Advances in measuring food insecurity and hunger in the U.S. (Introduction). *J Nutr, 129*:504S-505S.

Ortiz-Hernández, L., Acosta-Gutiérrez, M. N., Núñez-Pérez, A. E., Peralta-Fonseca, N., & Ruiz-Gómez, Y. (2007). Food insecurity and obesity are positively associated in Mexico City schoolchildren. *Rev Invest Clin, 59*(1):32-41.

Parás, P., & Pérez-Escamilla, R. (2004). El rostro de la pobreza: la inseguridad alimentaria en el Distrito Federal. *Rev Este País* 2004; 158(5):45-50.

Park, K., Kersey, M., Geppert, J., Story, M., Cutts, D., & Himes, J. H. (2009). Household food insecurity is a risk factor for iron-deficiency anaemia in a multi-ethnic, low-income sample of infants and toddlers. *Public Health Nutr, 12*(11):2120-8. Epub 2009 May 1.

Pérez-Escamilla, R., Ferris, A. M., Drake, L., Haldeman, L., Peranick, J., Campbell, M., Peng, Y. K., Burke, G., & Bernstein, B. (2000). Food stamps are associated with food security and dietary intake of inner-city preschoolers from Hartford, Connecticut. *J Nutr, 130*(11):2711-7.

Pérez-Escamilla, R., Segall-Correa, A. M., Kurdian Maranha, L., Sampaio, Md M de F., Marin-Leon, L., & Panigassi, G. (2004) An adapted version of the U.S. Department of Agriculture Food Insecurity module is a valid tool for assessing household food insecurity in Campinas, Brazil. *J Nutr, 134*:1923-8.

Pérez-Escamilla, R., Dessalines, M., Finnigan, M., Pachón, H., Hromi-Fiedler, A., & Gupta N. (2009). Household food insecurity is associated with childhood malaria in rural Haiti. *J Nutr, 139*(11):2132-8.

Pew Hispanic Center. (2008). U.S. Population Projections: 2005-2050 Available at: http://pewhispanic.org/reports/report.php?ReportID=85. (Accessed September 15, 2010)

Pew Hispanic Center. (2010). Statistical Portrait of Hispanics in the United States, 2008 Available at: http://pewhispanic.org/factsheets/factsheet.php?FactsheetID=58. (Accessed September 15, 2010)

Polhamus, B., Dalenius, K., Mackentosh, H., Smith, B., & Grummer-Strawn, L. (2009) Pediatric Nutrition Surveillance 2008 Report. Atlanta: U.S. Department of Health and Human Services, Centers for Disease Control and Prevention.

Pollitt, E. (editor). (1995) The relationship between undernutrition and behavioral development tin children. *J Nutr, 125*:2211S-2284S.

Pollitt, E., Gorman, K. S., Engle, P. L., Martorell, R., & Rivera, J. (1993) Early supplementary feeding and cognition. *Monographs of the Society for Research in Child Development, 58*:1-118.

Quandt, S. A., Arcury, T. A., Early, J., Tapia, J., & Davis, J. D. (2004). Household food security among migrant and seasonal latino farm workers in North Carolina. *Public Health Rep, 119*(6):568-76.

Quandt, S. A., Shoaf, J. I., Tapia, J., Hernández-Pelletier, M., Clark, H. M., & Arcury, T. A. (2006). Experiences of Latino immigrant families in North Carolina help explain elevated levels of food insecurity and hunger. *J Nutr, 136*(10):2638-44.

Radimer, K. L., Olson, C. M., Greene, J. C., Campbell, C. C., & Habicht, J. P. (1992) Understanding hunger and developing indicators to assess it in women and children. *J Nutr Educ, 24*: 36S-45S.

Radimer, K. (2002) Measurement of household food security in the USA and other industrialized countries. *Public Health Nutr, 5*:859-64.

Rosas, L. G., Guendelman, S., Harley, K., Fernald, L. C., Neufeld, L., Mejia, F., & Eskenazi, B. (2010). Factors Associated with Overweight and Obesity among Children of Mexican Descent: Results of a Binational Study. *J Immigr Minor Health* [Epub ahead of print].

Rose, D., & Oliviera, V. (1997) Validation of a self-reported measure of household food insufficiency with nutrient intake data. Washington, DC: U.S. Department of Agriculture; 1-13.

Sampaio, M. F. A., Kepple, A. W., Segall-Corrêa, A. M., de Oliveira, J. T. A., Panigassi, G., Kurdian Maranha, L., Marin-Leon, L., Bergamasco, S. M. P. P., & Pérez-Escamilla, R. (2006) (In) Segurança Alimentar: experiência de grupos focais com populações rurais do Estado de São Paulo. *Segur Alim Nutr* (Campinas, Brazil) *13*:64-77.

Seligman, H. K., Bindman, A. B., Vittinghoff, E., Kanaya, A. M., & Kushel, M. B. (2007). Food insecurity is associated with diabetes mellitus: Results from the National Health Examination and Nutrition Examination Survey (NHANES) 1999-2002. *J Gen Intern Med, 22*(7):1018-23.

Seligman, H. K., Laraia, B. A., & Kushel, M. B. (2010). Food insecurity is associated with chronic disease among low-income NHANES participants. *J Nutr, 140*(2):304-10.

Townsend, M. S., Love, B., Achteberg, C., & Murphy, S. (2001). Food insecurity is related to overweight in women. *J Nutr, 131*:1738-1745.

Wehler, C. A., Scott, R. I., & Anderson, J. J. (1992). The Community Childhood Hunger Identification Project: A Model of Domestic Hunger—Demonstration Project in Seattle, Washington." *J Nutr Educ, 24*: 29S-35S.

Weigel, M. M., Armijos, R. X., Hall, Y. P., Ramirez, Y., & Orozco, R. (2007). The household food insecurity and health outcomes of U.S.-Mexico border migrant and seasonal farm workers. *J Immigr Minor Health, 9*(3):157-69.

Weinreb, L., Wehler, C., Perloff, J., Scott, R., Hosmer, D., Sagor, L., & Gundersen, C. (2002) Hunger: its impact on children's health and mental health. *Pediatrics, 110*:e41.

Whitaker, R. C., Phillips, S. M., & Orzol, S. M. (2006) Food insecurity and the risks of depression and anxiety in mothers and behavior problems in their preschool-aged children. *Pediatrics, 118*:e859-68.

Wilde, P. E., & Peterman, J. N. (2006). Individual weight change is associated with household food security status. *J Nutr, 136*(5):1395-400.

CHAPTER EIGHT

THE BURDEN OF INJURY AMONG LATINO YOUTH

Federico E. Vaca[1] and Craig L. Anderson[2]

Introduction

Along with wellknown childhood racial and ethnic health disparities in disease entities such as diabetes, hypertension and obesity, there are substantial disparities in the burden of violence and injury. For those who work in the area of injury prevention and control, the lack of attention to these formidable public health threats have continued to be puzzling particularly because injury remains the leading cause of death for children and youth after the first year of life (Figure 1).

Regrettably, this is no different for Latino children in the United States where injury is the overwhelming leading cause of death (Figure 2).

Worse yet, it is injury that not only tops the list of diseases that take the lives of Latino children and youth but it also deprives local communities and American society of hundreds of thousands of years of potential productive life to be had by Latino children and youth (Figure 3).

This chapter will examine two important causes of injury among Latino youth—violence and motor vehicle crashes. We will discuss the overall burden of injury; the epidemiology, risk factors and proven intervention for each of

[1]Yale University School of Medicine, Department of Emergency Medicine.
[2]University of California, Irvine, Center for Trauma and Injury Prevention Research.

Figure 1. Leading Causes of Death Among All Races and Ethnicities. United States, 2007.

Rank	<1	1-4	5-9	10-14	15-24	25-34	35-44	44-54	55-64	65+	All Ages
1	Congenital Anomalies 5,785	Unintentional Injury 1,588	Unintentional Injury 965	Unintentional Injury 1,229	Unintentional Injury 15,897	Unintentional Injury 14,977	Unintentional Injury 16,931	Malignant Neoplasms 50,167	Malignant Neoplasms 103,171	Heart Diasease 496,095	Heart Diasease 616,067
2	Short Gestation 4,857	Congenital Anomalies 546	Malignant Neoplasms 480	Malignant Neoplasms 479	Homicide 5,551	Suicide 5,278	Malignant Neoplasms 13,288	Heart Diasease 37,434	Heart Diasease 65,527	Malignant Neoplasms 389,730	Malignant Neoplasms 562,875
3	SIDS 2,453	Homicide 398	Congenital Anomalies 196	Homicide 213	Suicide 4,140	Homicide 4,758	Heart Diasease 11,839	Unintentional Injury 20,315	Chronic Low. Respiratory Disease 12,777	Cerebro-vascular 115,961	Cerebro-vascular 135,952
4	Maternal Pregnancy Comp. 1,769	Malignant Neoplasms 364	Homicide 133	Suicide 180	Malignant Neoplasms 1,653	Malignant Neoplasms 3,463	Suicide 6,722	Liver Disease 8,212	Unintentional Injury 12,193	Chronic Low. Respiratory Disease 109,562	Chronic Low. Respiratory Disease 127,924
5	Unintentional Injury 1,285	Heart Diasease 173	Heart Diasease 110	Congenital Anomalies 178	Heart Diasease 1,084	Heart Diasease 3,223	HIV 3,572	Suicide 7,778	Diabetes Mellitus 11,304	Alzheimer's Disease 73,797	Unintentional Injury 123,706

Age Groups

(Centers for Disease Control and Prevention (CDC), 2010a).

Figure 2. Leading Causes of Death Among Latinos. United States, 2007.

Age Groups

Rank	<1	1-4	5-9	10-14	15-24	25-34	35-44	44-54	55-64	65+	All Ages
1	Congenital Anomalies 1,520	Unintentional Injury 348	Unintentional Injury 199	Unintentional Injury 188	Unintentional Injury 2,511	Unintentional Injury 2,321	Unintentional Injury 1,958	Malignant Neoplasms 3,554	Malignant Neoplasms 5,326	Heart Diasease 21,296	Heart Diasease 29,021
2	Short Gestation 917	Congenital Anomalies 132	Malignant Neoplasms 117	Malignant Neoplasms 111	Homicide 1,295	Homicide 1,028	Malignant Neoplasms 1,485	Heart Diasease 2,317	Heart Diasease 3,751	Malignant Neoplasms 16,026	Malignant Neoplasms 27,660
3	SIDS 2,453	Homicide 76	Congenital Anomalies 44	Homicide 53	Suicide 527	Suicide 649	Heart Diasease 962	Unintentional Injury 1,659	Diabetes Mellitus 1,131	Cerebro-vascular 5,020	Unintentional Injury 11,723
4	Maternal Pregnancy Comp. 307	Malignant Neoplasms 68	Heart Diasease 23	Congenital Anomalies 29	Malignant Neoplasms 345	Malignant Neoplasms 609	HIV 505	Liver Disease 1,167	Liver Disease 954	Diabetes Mellitus 4,343	Cerebro-vascular 7,078
5	Placenta Cord Membranes 240	Heart Diasease 39	Homicide 23	Suicide 19	Heart Diasease 145	Heart Diasease 378	Homicide 502	Cerebro-vascular 656	Cerebro-vascular 911	Chronic Low. Respiratory Disease 2,965	Diabetes Mellitus 6,417

(CDC, 2010a).

Figure 3. Leading Causes of Years of Potential Life Lost Before Age 65 due to Injury Deaths Among Latinos, United States, 2007.

		0%	5%	10%	15%	20%	25%	30%	35%	40%
Unintentional Motor Vehicle	189,753									
Homicide	126,948									
Suicide	67,805									
Unintentional Poisoning	63,402									
Unintentional Drowning	19,223									
Unintentional Suffocation	12,278									
Unintentional Fall	11,903									
Unintentional Fire/burn	7,429									
Unintentional All Others	48,133									

(CDC, 2010a).

these causes of injury; the developmental sources of crash injury risk, especially as it is related to driving; and present our conclusion.

To the surprise of many not familiar with the study of injury science, injury follows the conventional epidemiological model of disease causation in the same manner as diseases that garner considerably more attention in the popular media and medical literature such as cancer, cardiovascular and infectious disease. As a result, injury has epidemiological patterns of distribution that vary according to person, time, place and season. Injury is not a random or "accidental" event but a definable, predictable, correctable event with specific patterns of occurrence. Moreover, it is a disease that transcends all demographic, socioeconomic and sociocultural lines in society. It is also a disease with a persistently high societal burden that when not intervened upon regularly displays notable racial and ethnic disparities in its outcomes.

Paradox and Anomaly in Injury

Because of its historic rapid population growth coupled with attempts by researchers to better understand socioeconomic and cultural determinants of health in this vulnerable group, Latino populations in the United States have long been the focus of discussion and research in the public health and programmatic context regarding health disparities. A key example of this points to a landmark report by Markides and Coreil and their original description of the Latino Epidemiologic Paradox (LEP, also known as the Hispanic Paradox) (Markides & Coreil, 1986). This paradox describes favorable health profiles for Latinos compared to non-Latino whites despite poverty, low education and low access to health care. Close examination by Markides and Coreil of Latino key health indicators such as infant mortality, life-expectancy, mortality from cardiovascular diseases, mortality from major types of cancer and measures of functional health supported their claim. While this construct has been supported and refuted in later research (Cagney, Browning & Wallace, 2007; Hummer, Powers, Pullum, Gossman & Frisbie, 2007; Palloni & Arias, 2004; Eschbach, Kuo & Goodwin, 2006), it remains a focus of considerable interest in public health (Gallo, Penedo, de los Monteros & Arguelles, 2009; Arias, Eschbach, Schauman, Backlund & Sorlie, 2010) in hopes of arriving at clear delineation of protective factors that may account for health status resiliency that can be applied to other vulnerable populations.

Subsequent to the work by Markides & Coreil, Hayes-Bautista et al, identified an anomaly to the LEP that revealed increased mortality of Latino adolescent and young adult males in California mortality data (1989–1997) (Hayes-Bautista et al., 2002). They further note the identification of the Latino Adolescent Male Mortality Peak (LAMMP) that shows that it is homicide and motor vehicle crashes that overwhelmingly supersedes any other cause of death represented in the Latino youth mortality burden encompassed in this anomaly.

Homicide and Violence-Related Injury

Homicide is the third leading cause of death for Latino children age 10-14 years, and the second leading cause for ages 15-34 years (Figure 2). In the age group 15-24 years, the death rate due to homicide for Latino males is more than

Figure 4. Mortality Rates per 100,000 by Cause, Ethnic Group and Sex. Two Leading Causes of Death, Age 15-24 Years, United States, 2006 and 2007.

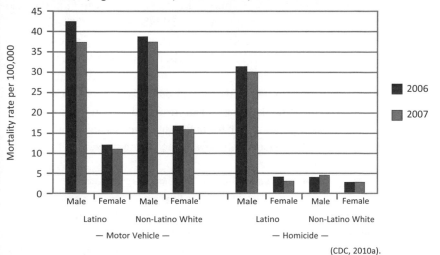

(CDC, 2010a).

6 times those of non-Latino white males, and the rate for Latinas is 1.6 times the rate for non-Latino whites females (Figure 4). From 1999 to 2007, the death rate due to homicide for Latino males increased 5% and the rate for Latinas decreased 20% (CDC, 2010a). However, since 1998, the death rate due to homicide among Latinos in this age group is lower than at any period since 1980 (Blumstein & Wallman, 2006).

A public health approach to the problems of interpersonal violence and homicide requires consideration of the host (the victim), vehicle (weapon), vector (perpetrator) and the environment. The Surgeon General's report on youth violence (U.S. Department of Health and Human Services, 2001) reviewed the extensive literature on risk factors for youth violence. Among the personal risk factors are male sex, poverty, other criminal offenses, aggressive behavior, substance use, weak social ties, antisocial peers and parents and gang membership. Environmental risk factors include neighborhood crime, drugs, disorganization and poverty. Warm, supportive relationships with parents or other adults and commitment to school are protective against violence. The use of weapons influences the severity of injuries resulting from violence and the risk of homicide.

In 2009, 17% of Latino high school students reported that they had carried a weapon in the past 30 days, and 5% reported that they had carried a gun (Eaton et al., 2010). Both weapon and gun carrying was similar for Latino and non-Latino white students and higher among Latino males than females. Weapon carrying among Latino students decreased from 1991 to 2001, but was stable from 2001 to 2009 (Centers for Disease Control and Prevention, 2010b). Thirty-six percent of Latino students said they had been in a physical fight in the previous 12 months. More Latino than non-Latino white students had been in a fight and more Latino males than females had been in a fight (Eaton et al., 2010).

Alcohol use is associated with fighting and weapon carrying among Latino high school students (Grunbaum, Basen-Engquist & Pandey, 1998), and alcohol availability in Latino neighborhoods is associated with violence (Alaniz, Cartmill & Parker, 1998; Lipton & Gruenewald, 2002; Zhu, Gorman & Horel, 2004). In 2009, 43% of Latino high school students had used alcohol in the last month, and this percentage is similar for males and females and to non-Latino whites (Eaton et al., 2010). Alcohol use by Latino students declined from 1991 to 2009 (CDC, 2010b).

Violence prevention interventions that have been systematically evaluated by the Task Force on Community Preventive Services, a group of independent public health and prevention experts convened by the CDC, are listed in Table 1. The guide is based on existing program evaluations, and notes that insufficient evidence of an intervention is not evidence of ineffectiveness. Early child-

Table 1. Interventions in the Community Guide to Violence Prevention.

Early Childhood Home Visitation	Recommended (Strong Evidence)
Firearms Laws	
"Shall issue" Concealed Weapons Carry Laws	Insufficient Evidence
Acquisition Restrictions	Insufficient Evidence
Bans on Specified Firearms or Ammunition	Insufficient Evidence
Child Access Prevention (CAP) Laws	Insufficient Evidence
Combinations of Firearms Laws	Insufficient Evidence
Firearm Registration and Licensing of Firearm Owners	Insufficient Evidence
Waiting Periods for Firearm Acquisition	Insufficient Evidence
Zero Tolerance of Firearms in Schools	Insufficient Evidence
Reducing Psychological Harm Among Children and Adolescents Following Traumatic Events	
Art Therapy	Insufficient Evidence
Group Cognitive-Behavioral Therapy	Recommended (Strong Evidence)
Individual Cognitive-Behavioral Therapy	Recommended (Strong Evidence)
Pharmacological Therapy	Insufficient Evidence
Play Therapy	Insufficient Evidence
Psychodynamic Therapy	Insufficient Evidence
Psychological Debriefing	Insufficient Evidence
School-Based Violence Prevention Programs	
School-Based Violence Prevention Programs	Recommended (Strong evidence)
Therapeutic Foster Care	
Therapeutic Foster Care for the Reduction of Violence by Children with Severe Emotional Disturbance	Insufficient Evidence
Therapeutic Foster Care for the Reduction of Violence by Chronically Delinquent Adolescents	Recommended (Sufficient Evidence)
Youth Transfer to Adult Criminal System	
Policies Facilitating the Transfer of Juveniles to Adult Justice Systems	Recommended Against (Strong Evidence)

(CDC, 2010).

hood home visitation is strongly recommended for its effect on decreasing child abuse but there was insufficient evidence to determine if home visitation decreased later violence by the visited child (Task Force on Community Preventive Services, 2005). According to the task force, none of the eight types of firearms laws have sufficient scientific evidence to support their implementation (Task Force on Community Preventive Services, 2005). Group and individual cognitive-behavioral therapy are recommended, but not other forms of therapy (Holly et al., 2008; Task Force on Community Preventive Services, 2008). The transfer of violent youth to the adult criminal justice system increases their violent behavior, and the task force has recommended against this policy (CDC, 2007). Many gaps remain because the scientific evidence base for injury programs in woefully inadequate.

School-based violence prevention programs are the only intervention recommended for the primary prevention of youth violence (Task Force on Community Preventive Services, 2007). Such programs have been implemented from the pre-kindergarten to the high school level. At the elementary school level, many programs seek to decrease antisocial and disruptive behavior. Many programs for older students seek to prevent violence or specific forms of violence. Programs have been effective at all grade levels (Hahn, Fuqua-Whitley, Wethington, Lowy, Crosby et al., 2007; Hahn, Fuqua-Whitley, Wethington, Lowy, Liberman et al., 2007; Wilson & Lipsey, 2007).

A number of school-based violence prevention programs have been implemented in communities with large numbers of Latino youth with cultural sensitivity and bilingual materials and staff. However, these programs have not specifically made use of Latino cultural values that could be expected to decrease violence. These values include *simpatía,* which discourages conflict, and *familismo,* which emphasizes the centrality of family life and thus should encourage protective relationships (Mirabal-Colón B. & Velez C. N., 2006).

Motor Vehicle Crash Injury

Motor vehicle crashes remain the leading cause of death for Latinos in the United States from age 1 to 44 (CDC, 2010a). These deaths include not only motor vehicle occupants, but pedestrians, bicyclists and motorcyclists. Latino children have been noted to be at a greater risk of dying or being admitted to the hospital as a result of injury (Agran, Winn, Anderson & Del Valle, 1998; Agran, Winn, Anderson & Del Valle, 1996). In 2007, motor vehicle crash fatalities contributed to an increasing proportion of all causes of deaths across the age spectrum of Latino children and youth (1–4 yrs. (16%), 5–9 yrs. (23%), 10–14 yrs. (22%), 15–20 yrs. (32%)) (CDC, 2010a). Population-based motor vehicle related death rates for Latino children have previously been noted to far exceed that of whites (Baker, Braver, Chen, Pantula & Massie, 1998; Harper, Marine, Garrett, Lezotte & Lowenstein, 2000; Hayes-Bautista et al., 2002; March, Evans, Ward & Brewer, 2003). Since the study by Hayes-Bautista et al. identifying the anomaly to the Latino Epidemiological Paradox in California mortality data (1989–1997), we have similarly studied this phenomena in more recent California mortality data (1999–2006) in order to show any progress in previously found injury mortality disparity (Vaca, Anderson & Hayes-Bautista, 2010). In our analysis of 1,866,743 deaths of California residents we found that both the Latino Epidemiological Paradox persisted along with the anomaly to the paradox. Moreover we identified a notable widening of injury mortality disparity for Latino adolescent males due

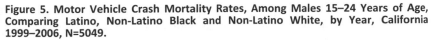

Figure 5. Motor Vehicle Crash Mortality Rates, Among Males 15–24 Years of Age, Comparing Latino, Non-Latino Black and Non-Latino White, by Year, California 1999–2006, N=5049.

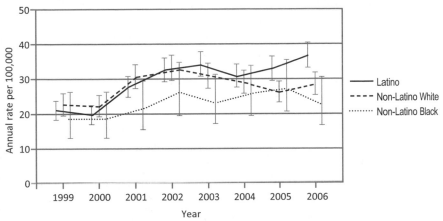

to motor vehicle crashes. Specifically, we found that crash mortality for Latino males 15-24 years increased from 2000-2006 (Figure 5).

Our study also showed that Latino crash mortality rates exceeded the rate for non-Latino whites overall and for each year from 2003-2006.

In order to further understand the national scope of crash fatality trends and changes in factors that influence crash fatality among young Latino males, we studied U.S. fatal crashes using data from the Center for Disease Control and Prevention's Web-based Injury Statistics Query and Reporting System (WISQARS) and the National Highway Traffic Safety Administration's Fatali-

Figure 6. Annual Motor Vehicle Death Rates per 100,000 for Latino, Non-Latino White and Non-Latino Black Males Age 15-24, by Year, U.S. 1999–2006, N=59,719.

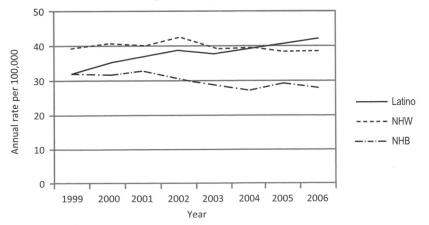

ty Analysis Reporting System (FARS) (Vaca & Anderson, 2009). The findings of our analysis showed that for the time period studied (1999–2006) Latino young males 15–24 years had the highest crash fatality rate compared to that of non-Latino white and non-Latino black males (Figure 6).

In the fatal crashes (Figure 7a), restraint use (including lap, shoulder and lap-shoulder belts) among Latino drivers was higher than that of non-Latino

Figure 7a. Percent Restraint Use for Latino, Non-Latino White and Non-Latino Black Males Age 15-24 Driver (dr) Fatalities in Passenger Vehicles, 40 States and District of Columbia, 2001-2006, N=18,487.

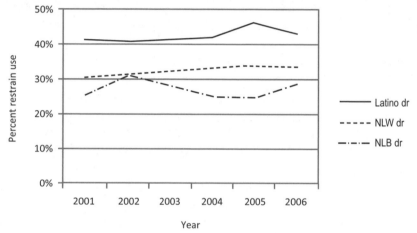

Figure 7b. Percent Restraint Use for Latino, Non-Latino White and Non-Latino Black Males Age 15-24 Passenger (ps) Fatalities in Passenger Vehicles, 40 States and District of Columbia, 2001–2006, N=9,053.

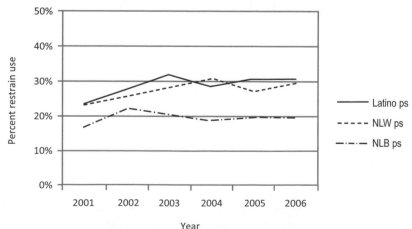

white drivers. Restraint use by passengers was similar for Latinos and non-Latino whites both in the fatal crashes (Figure 7b) and in a national survey of high school students (Eaton et al., 2010). Restraint use by Latino passengers increased in both data sources (CDC, 2010b; Vaca & Anderson, 2009).

The percent of driver fatalities with blood alcohol > 0.01 (BAC+) was greater for Latinos than non-Latino whites (Figure 8). Among high school students, the percent who drove after drinking was similar for Latinos and non-

Figure 8. Percent BAC+ for Latino, Non-Latino White and Non-Latino Black Males Age 15-24 Driver Fatalities, by Year, 40 States and District of Columbia, 2001–2006, N=23,778.

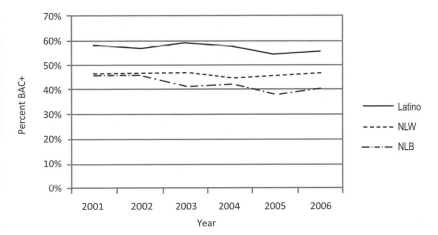

Latino whites but a greater percentages of Latino than non-Latino students reported that they rode with a driver who had been drinking (Eaton et al., 2010). The later proportion decreased from 1991 to 2009 (Centers for Disease Control and Prevention, 2010b).

Our study of FARS data further showed that the contribution of alcohol remains overrepresented among young Latino male pedestrians and bicyclists in fatal crashes. This is of considerable concern as Latino young males bear the largest proportion of blood alcohol concentration-positive crash fatalities in this setting. Alcohol use continues to contribute to the ongoing pervasive disparity in crash fatalities for Latino young males.

Acknowledging that there is a multitude of contributing factors linked to injury and fatal crashes in youth, such as driver training, seat belt use, alcohol and drug use, there are also important developmental factors to be taken into consideration in this context (Shope & Bingham, 2008). While adolescence has been described as a development period of strength and resilience, experts have

highlighted the dual paradox that exists during this time of life with regard to overall health statistics (Dahl, 2004). The dual paradox describes the adolescent period as a time of increased injury-related morbidity and mortality rates despite it also being a time of acquiring greater physical strength and capacity for decision making. Research on adolescent drivers indicates that brain development and mastery of driving tasks may lag behind the increased responsibility that teens experience with unsupervised driving.

The U.S. Census reported a national adolescent population of 42 million in 2008 with a decrease of 1% and an increase of 8% since the 2000 Census for ten to fourteen years old and fifteen to nineteen years old respectively (U.S. Census Bureau, 2009). In 2006, the injury death rates (per 100,000 population) for adolescents were found to widely range from 5.9 (10 yrs.)—79.9 (19 yrs) (CDC, 2010a). Adolescents face considerable health risk as they routinely operate motor vehicles to the extent that in 2008 2,739 fifteen- to twenty-year-old drivers were killed in U.S. motor vehicle crashes and 228,000 were injured (National Highway Traffic Safety Administration, 2009).

Developmental Sources of Crash Risk

More often than not, risky behavior or components thereof are associated with major causes of injury-related death. Several psychological adolescent developmental factors have been noted to play an important role in risk behavior (Kelley, Schochet & Landry, 2004; Steinberg, 2004). Specifically, when considering motor vehicle crashes in young male drivers, the developmental perspective points to adolescent impulsivity (emotionality), friend influence, optimistic bias and "maleness" as important developmental sources of crash risk (Arnett, 2002).

Adolescent impulsiveness remains as one of several important personality dimensions linked to developmental sources of crash risk (Arnett, Offer & Fine, 1997). While a multitude of constructs have been used to define impulsivity as a limited ability to control behavior (i.e. failure to consider consequences before acting, low-self control), it is closely associated with the adolescent's slow to mature self-regulatory competencies (Farrington, 2004). Delving further into the development of the adolescent brain, it is the continuum of maturation of the frontal cortical system that extends well into emerging adulthood (age 18-age 25) that has been implicated in governing executive function like impulse control (Giedd, 2004; Keating, 2004; Steinberg, 2004). While the brain maturation process during the peri-adolescent period is notably complex, the suggestions is, with variation, that adolescents are limited in their capacity to effectively regulate sensation or reward–seeking impulses well enough to limit their vulnerability to unintentional harm. Although, some have viewed risk behavior in adolescence as behavior with developmental worth, purpose and function; in the setting of traffic crashes the negative consequences that (Keating, 2004) routinely result always negate the worth (Jessor, 1991; Kelley et al., 2004). Friend influence or the power of friends is another noted developmental source of crash risk in young drivers. Adolescent drivers already hold some of the highest crash rates in relation to the national population of drivers. Further, at least one recent study shows that youth modeling of drinking behavior can predict impaired driving behavior in the emerging adult period (Gulliver & Begg, 2004). Coupling this with a lifestyle and environment largely oriented around friends, studies closely link the presence of additional passengers in the vehicle of young drivers with greater likelihood of at fault and fatal crashes (Doherty, Andrey & MacGregor, 1998; Preusser, Ferguson & Williams, 1998). In the larger context of risk behavior, friend influence has been correlated with adolescent drug and alcohol use and delinquent behavior (Andrews, Tildesley, Hops & Li, 2002; Prinstein, Boergers & Spirito, 2001; Sieving, Perry & Williams, 2000). The similarity of peer behavior may be the result of friend influence or of the selection of friends with similar behavior (Arnett, 2001). Further, it is well understood that while friend influence may generally have a connotation of adolescents encouraging fellow friend to engage in negative behavior, studies show that the influence can also be of a positive nature. Friends do influence each other against risk behavior (Keefe, 1994; Urberg, Degirmencioglu & Pilgrim, 1997). Herein lies considerable potential for opportunities to utilize this influence in order to modulate risk behavior in adolescent drivers.

Optimistic bias is commonly understood as the propensity to view the likelihood of negative events as something that happens to others far more often than to oneself. Generally, the adolescent period is a time when youth are optimistic about their future as well as their personal control over it (Weinstein, 1998). Moreover, those that engage in risk behavior are more apt to believe that negative consequences will not befall them (Arnett, 1992). This inflated positive outlook is similarly noted in the young driver's perception that risky driving behaviors pose a lesser risk to themselves than that perceived by older drivers (DeJoy, 1989; Finn & Bragg, 1986; Trankle, Gelau & Metker, 1990). Although not thoroughly studied in adolescents, optimistic bias in the setting of alcohol impaired driving remains prevalent in adults in their mid-to-late 20s (Ferguson, Burns, Fiorentino, Williams & Garcia, 2002). For the young driver, optimistic bias manifests itself in an overestimation of the degree of control that they believe they have over traffic-related events (National Highway Traffic Safety Administration, 1995).

While both male and female adolescent drivers are well noted to have high crash rates, it is the young male that is persistently overrepresented in traffic collisions and fatal crashes. Developmentally, this gender disparity has been suggested to be related to a greater propensity for the young males to pursue new and intense stimulation as well as possess higher levels of aggression. In this same context, sensation-seeking joined with aggressive driving behavior is likely to contribute to higher crash rates (Deery & Fildes, 1999; Ellisoin-Potter, Bell and Deffenbacher, 2001). However, involvement in alcohol-related crashes is growing faster among young females than among young males (Tsai, Anderson, Vaca, 2010).

It is reasonable to assume that culture, on some levels, plays an important role in "maleness" and driving behavior. As Arnett notes of Harre's observations that young males are "propped up with an entire social system of norms and media images that equate fast driving and skillful maneuvers with masculinity, adulthood and peer group approval" (Harre, 2000). When it comes to risky driving, young drivers have been portrayed of the mentality that *"it's not me, it's the other guy who is a problem"* (National Highway Traffic Safety Administration, 2003a). A report from the National Highway Traffic Safety Administration show that many young drivers commonly engage in risky and aggressive driving behavior including cutting in front of other drivers, making obscene or angry gestures toward other motorists and using the shoulder to pass in heavy traffic (National Highway Traffic Safety Administration, 2003b). It is also well noted in this report that drivers less than age 21 are more likely to engage in these types of driving behaviors.

Overall, notable strides have been made in decreasing the overall number of fatalities in young drivers, there remains considerable research and evidence-based applied prevention work to be done to reduce the burden of needless injury and loss of life of young people as a result of motor vehicle crashes. Moreover, significantly greater attention needs to focus on the injury disparities in Latino youth that already exist in this setting and have been noted to be growing.

Prevention and Best Practice Recommendations

Today's and future prevention work should be data driven and evidence-based. An important and current resource developed by the U.S. Department of Health and Human Services Task Force on Community Preventive Services (Briss et al., 2000; Truman et al., 2000) is the Guide to Community Preventive Services (Task Force on Community Preventive Service, 2010). Created through a scientific systematic review method, this guide can be accessed online at www.thecommunityguide.org. This credible guide was developed to give guidance to the public, public health workers and experts regarding community-based prevention and health promotion activities supported by the scientific literature. Furthermore, the guide can be used to develop evidence-based prevention and education programs as well as inform health promotion and disease-prevention policy development. It can also be used to further develop prevention and health promotion research in areas that lack robust scientific evidence for public health implementation and dissemination. While the guide covers eighteen core topic areas ranging from adolescent health to worksite health promotion, motor vehicle crash injury prevention is covered in the areas of seat belt use and alcohol-impaired driving (Table 2).

Conclusion

Table 2. Community Guide Prevention Recommendations for Motor Vehicle-Related Injury Prevention.

Alcohol-Impaired Driving	
0.08% Blood Alcohol Concentration (BAC) Laws	Recommended (Strong Evidence)
Designated Driver Promotion Programs: Incentive Programs	Insufficient Evidence
Designated Driver Promotion Programs: Population-Based Campaigns	Insufficient Evidence
Ignition Interlocks	Recommended (Strong Evidence)
Intervention Training Programs for Servers of Alcoholic Beverages	Recommended (Sufficient Evidence)
Lower BAC Laws for Young or Inexperienced Drivers	Recommended (Sufficient Evidence)
Maintaining Current Minimum Legal Drinking Age (MLDA) Laws	Recommended (Strong Evidence)
Mass Media Campaigns	Recommended (Sufficient Evidence)
Multi-component Interventions with Community Mobilization	Recommended (Strong Evidence)
Peer Organization Interventions	Insufficient Evidence
School-Based Instructional Programs	Recommended (Sufficient Evidence)
Sobriety Checkpoints	Recommended (Strong Evidence)
Social Norming Campaigns	Insufficient Evidence
Safety Belts	
Enhanced Enforcement Programs	Recommended (Strong Evidence)
Laws Mandating Use	Recommended (Strong Evidence)
Primary (vs. Secondary) Enforcement Laws	Recommended (Strong Evidence)

(CDC, 2010c).

Unintentional injuries, primarily from homicide and motor vehicle crashes, continue to be the leading causes of death for Latino youth, and to occur at higher rates in Latino males than non-Latino white males. For homicide the disparity is large, and for motor vehicle crashes it is increasing. A broader and more comprehensive understanding of these disparities must take into account adolescent development, including sensation-seeking and the resulting risk-taking and interpersonal aggression, as well as cultural definition of maleness. Effective interventions exist for both of these causes of injury. School violence prevention programs, and policies that limit the access of young people to alcohol and that increase safety belt use have demonstrated broad effectiveness in preventing deaths and injuries. Yet relatively few interventions are directed specifically to Latino youth or appeal to Latino cultural values. Such interventions may be necessary to eliminate injury disparities.

Acknowledgements

We would like to thank Dr. Corinne Peek-Asa, Professor of Occupational and Environmental Health and Director of the University of Iowa Injury Prevention Research Center, for her thoughtful and constructive review of this chapter. Dr. Vaca is supported, in part, by the Eunice Kennedy Shiver, National Institute for Child Health and Human Development (K23HD050630).

References

Agran, P. F., Winn, D. G., Anderson, C. L., & Del Valle, C. P. (1996). Pediatric injury hospitalization in Hispanic children and non-Hispanic white children in southern California. *Arch Pediatr Adolesc Med, 150*(4), 400-406.

Agran, P. F., Winn, D. G., Anderson, C. L., & Del Valle, C. (1998). Family, social, and cultural factors in pedestrian injuries among Hispanic children. *Inj Prev, 4*(3), 188-193.

Alaniz, M. L., Cartmill, R. S., & Parker, R. N. (1998). Immigrants and violence: The importance of neighborhood context. *Hispanic Journal of Behavioral Sciences, 20*(2), 155-174.

Andrews J. A., Tildesley E., Hops H., & Li F. (2002). The influence of peers on young adult substance use. *Health Psychol, 21*(4), 349-357.

Arias, E., Eschbach, K., Schauman, W. S., Backlund, E. L., & Sorlie, P. D. (2010). The Hispanic mortality advantage and ethnic misclassification on U.S. death certificates. *Am J Public Health, 100* Suppl 1, S171-177.

Arnett, J. (1992). Reckless behavior in adolescence: A developmental perspective. *Developmental Review* (12), 339-373.

Arnett, J. J., Offer, D., & Fine, M. A. (1997). Reckless driving in adolescence: "state" and "trait" factors. *Accid Anal Prev, 29*(1), 57-63.

Arnett, J. (2001). Friends and Peers *Adolescence and Emerging Adulthood: A Cultural Approach* (First ed., pp. 223—257). Upper Saddle River, New Jersey: Prentice Hall.

Arnett, J. J. (2002). Developmental sources of crash risk in young drivers. *Inj Prev, 8 Suppl 2*, ii17-21; discussion ii21-23.

Baker, S. P., Braver, E. R., Chen, L. H., Pantula, J. F., & Massie, D. (1998). Motor vehicle occupant deaths among Hispanic and black children and teenagers. *Arch Pediatr Adolesc Med, 152*(12), 1209-1212.

Blumstein, A., & Wallman, J. (2006). The Crime Drop and Beyond. *Annual Review of Law and Social Science, 2*(1), 125-146.

Briss, P. A., Zaza, S., Pappaioanou, M., Fielding, J., Wright-De Aguero, L., & Truman, B. I. et al. (2000). Developing an evidence-based guide to community preventive services—methods. The task force on community preventive services. *Am J Prev Med, 18*(1 Suppl), 35-43.

Cagney, K. A., Browning, C. R., & Wallace, D. M. (2007). The Latino paradox in neighborhood context: The case of asthma and other respiratory conditions. *American Journal of Public Health, 97*(5), 919-925.

Centers for Disease Control and Prevention (2007). Effects on violence of laws and policies facilitating the transfer of youth from the juvenile to the adult justice system. *MMWR* (56(RR-9)), 1-11.

Centers for Disease Control and Prevention (2010a). Injury Prevention & Control: data & statistics (WISQARS): Fatal injury data. Retrieved September 28, 2010, from http://www.cdc.gov/injury/wisqars/fatal.html

Centers for Disease Control and Prevention (2010b). Trends in the prevalence of selected risk behaviors and obesity for Hispanic students: national YRBS: 1991-2009. Retrieved September 28, 2010, from http://www.cdc. gov/HealthyYouth/yrbs/pdf/us_summary_hispanic_trend_yrbs.pdf

Centers for Disease Control and Prevention (2010c). Guide to community preventive services. Retrieved September 30, 2010 from http://www.the communityguide.org/index.html#topics

Dahl, R. E. (2004). Adolescent brain development: a period of vulnerabilities and opportunities. Keynote address. *Ann N Y Acad Sci, 1021*, 1-22.

Deery, H. A., & Fildes, B. N. (1999). Young novice driver subtypes: relationship to high-risk behavior, traffic accident record, and simulator driving performance. *Hum Factors, 41*(4), 628-643.

DeJoy, D. M. (1989). The optimism bias and traffic accident risk perception. *Accid Anal Prev, 21*(4), 333-340.

Doherty, S. T., Andrey, J. C., & MacGregor, C. (1998). The situational risks of young drivers: the influence of passengers, time of day and day of week on accident rates. *Accid Anal Prev, 30*(1), 45-52.

Eaton, D. K., Kann, L., Kinchen, S., Shanklin, S., Ross, J., Hawkins, J., Harris, W. A., Lowry, R., McManus, T., Chyen, D., Lim, C., Whittle, L., Brener, N. D., & Wechsler, H. (2010). Youth risk behavior surveillance—United States, 2009. *MMWR, 59*(SS-5), 1–142. Retrieved September 28, 2010, from http://www.cdc.gov/mmwr/pdf/ss/ss5905.pdf

Ellisoin-Potter, P., Bell, P., & Deffenbacher, J. L. (2001). The effect of trait driving anger, anonymity, and aggressive stimuli on aggressive driving behavior. *Journal of Applied Social Psychology, 31*, 431.

Eschbach, K., Kuo, Y. F., & Goodwin, J. S. (2006). Ascertainment of Hispanic ethnicity on California death certificates: implications for the explanation of the Hispanic mortality advantage. *Am J Public Health, 96*(12), 2209-2215.

Farrington, D. P. (2004). Conduct disorder, aggression, and delinquency. In Lerner RM & L. Steinberg (Eds.), *Handbook of Adolescent Psychology* (Second ed.). Hoboken, New York: Wiley.

Ferguson, S. A., Burns, M. M., Fiorentino, D., Williams, A. F., & Garcia, J. (2002). Drinking and driving among Mexican-American and non-Hispanic white males in Long Beach, California. *Accid Anal Prev, 34*(4), 429-437.

Finn, P., & Bragg, B. W. (1986). Perception of the risk of an accident by young and older drivers. *Accid Anal Prev, 18*(4), 289-298.

Gallo, L. C., Penedo, F. J., de los Monteros, K. E., & Arguelles, W. (2009). Resiliency in the face of disadvantage: do Hispanic cultural characteristics protect health outcomes? *Journal of Personality, 77*(6), 1707-1746.

Giedd, J. N. (2004). Structural magnetic resonance imaging of the adolescent brain. *Ann N Y Acad Sci, 1021*, 77-85.

Grunbaum, J. A., Basen-Engquist, K., & Pandey, D. (1998). Association between violent behaviors and substance use among Mexican-American and non-Hispanic white high school students. *J Adolesc Health, 23*(3), 153-159.

Gulliver, P., & Begg, D. (2004). Influences during adolescence on perceptions and behaviour related to alcohol use and unsafe driving as young adults. *Accid Anal Prev, 36*(5), 773-781.

Hahn, R., Fuqua-Whitley, D., Wethington, H., Lowy, J., Crosby, A., Fullilove, M., & et al. (2007). Effectiveness of universal school-based programs to prevent violent and aggressive behavior: a systematic review. *Am J Prev Med, 33*(2 Suppl), S114-129.

Hahn, R., Fuqua-Whitley, D., Wethington, H., Lowy, J., Liberman, A., Crosby, A., & et al. (2007). The effectiveness of universal school-based programs for the prevention of violent and aggressive behavior: a report on recommendations of the Task Force on Community Preventive Services. *MMWR Recomm Rep, 56*(RR-7), 1-12.

Harper, J. S., Marine, W. M., Garrett, C. J., Lezotte, D., & Lowenstein, S. R. (2000). Motor vehicle crash fatalities: A comparison of Hispanic and non-Hispanic motorists in Colorado. *Ann Emerg Med, 36*(6), 589-596.

Harre, N. (2000). Risk evaluation, driving, and adolescents: a typology. *Developmental Review, 20*, 206-226.

Hayes-Bautista, D. E, Hsu, P., Hayes-Bautista, M., Iniguez, D., Chamberlin, C. L., Rico, C., & et al. (2002). An anomaly within the Latino epidemiological paradox: the Latino adolescent male mortality peak. *Arch Pediatr Adolesc Med, 156*(5), 480-484.

Holly, R. W., Robert, A. H., Dawna, S. F.-W., Theresa Ann, S., Alex, E. C., Robert, L. J., & et al. (2008). The effectiveness of interventions to reduce psychological harm from traumatic events among children and adolescents: a systematic review. *Am J Prev Med, 35*(3), 287-313.

Hummer, R. A., Powers, D. A., Pullum, S. G., Gossman, G. L., & Frisbie, W. P. (2007). Paradox found (again): infant mortality among the Mexican-origin population in the United States. *Demography, 44*(3), 441-457.

Jessor, R. (1991). Risk behavior in adolescence: a psychosocial framework for understanding and action. *J Adolesc Health, 12*(8), 597-605.

Keating, D. (2004). Cognitive and brain development. In Lerner R. M., & L. Steinberg (Eds.), *Handbook of Adolescent Psychology* (Second ed.). Hoboken, NJ: Wiley.

Keefe, K. (1994). Perceptions of normative social pressure and attitudes toward alcohol use: changes during adolescence. *J Stud Alcohol, 55*(1), 46-54.

Kelley, A. E., Schochet, T., & Landry, C. F. (2004). Risk taking and novelty seeking in adolescence: introduction to part I. *Ann N Y Acad Sci, 1021*, 27-32.

Lipton, R., & Gruenewald, P. (2002). The spatial dynamics of violence and alcohol outlets. *J Stud Alcohol, 63*(2), 187-195.

March, J. A., Evans, M. A., Ward, B., & Brewer, K. L. (2003). Motor vehicle crash fatalities among Hispanics in rural North Carolina. *Acad Emerg Med, 10*(11), 1249-1252.

Markides, K. S., & Coreil, J. (1986). The health of Hispanics in the southwestern United States: an epidemiologic paradox. *Public Health Rep, 101*(3), 253-265.

Mirabal-Colón, B., & Velez, C. N. (2006). Youth violence prevention among Latino youth. In Guerra N. G., & Smith E. P. (Eds.), *Preventing youth violence in a multicultural society*. Washington, D.C: American Psychological Association.

National Highway Traffic Safety Administration (1995). *Understanding Youthful Risk Taking and Driving* (No. DOT HS 808-318). Washington, DC: U.S. Department of Transportation.

National Highway Traffic Safety Administration (2003a). National Survey of Speeding and Unsafe Driving Attitudes and Behavior 2002, Volume II Retrieved September 24, 2004, from http://www.nhtsa.dot.gov/people/injury/research/speed_volII_finding/SpeedVolumeIIFindingsFinal.pdf

National Highway Traffic Safety Administration (2003b). *Traffic Safety Facts: National Survey of Speeding and Unsafe Driving Attitudes and Behavior 2002* (No. 289). Washington, DC: U.S. Department of Transportation.

National Highway Traffic Safety Administration (2009). *Traffic Safety Facts: Data Young Drivers* (No. DOT HS 811 169). Washington, DC: U.S. Department of Transportation.

Palloni, A., & Arias E. (2004). Paradox lost: explaining the Hispanic adult mortality advantage. *Demography, 41*(3), 385-415.

Preusser, D. F., Ferguson, S. A., & Williams, A. F. (1998). The effect of teenage passengers on the fatal crash risk of teenage drivers. *Accid Anal Prev, 30*(2), 217-222.

Prinstein, M. J., Boergers, J., & Spirito, A. (2001). Adolescents' and their friends' health-risk behavior: factors that alter or add to peer influence. *J Pediatr Psychol, 26*(5), 287-298.

Shope, J. T., & Bingham, C. R. (2008). Teen driving: motor-vehicle crashes and factors that contribute. *Am J Prev Med, 35*(3 Suppl), S261-271.

Sieving, R. E., Perry, C. L., & Williams, C. L. (2000). Do friendships change behaviors, or do behaviors change friendships? Examining paths of influence in young adolescents' alcohol use. *J Adolesc Health, 26*(1), 27-35.

Steinberg, L. (2004). Risk taking in adolescence: what changes, and why? *Ann N Y Acad Sci, 1021*, 51-58.

Task Force on Community Preventive Service (2010). Task Force Findings: 1/1/1997 -5/5/2010. Retrieved from http://www.thecommunityguide.org/about/findings.html

Task Force on Community Preventive Services (2005). Recommendations to reduce violence through early childhood home visitation, therapeutic foster care, and firearms laws. *Am J Prev Med, 28*(2), 6-10.

Task Force on Community Preventive Services (2007). A Recommendation to Reduce Rates of Violence Among School-Aged Children and Youth by Means of Universal School-Based Violence Prevention Programs. *Am J Prev Med, 33*(2), S112-S113.

Task Force on Community Preventive Services (2008). Recommendations to Reduce Psychological Harm from Traumatic Events Among Children and Adolescents. *Am J Prev Med 35*(3), 314-316.

Trankle, U., Gelau, C., & Metker, T. (1990). Risk perception and age-specific accidents of young drivers. *Accid Anal Prev, 22*(2), 119-125.

Truman, B. I., Smith-Akin, C. K., Hinman, A. R., Gebbie, K. M., Brownson, R., Novick, L. F., & et al. (2000). Developing the guide to community preventive services—overview and rationale. The Task Force on Community Preventive Services. *Am J Prev Med, 18*(1 Suppl), 18-26.

Tsai, V. W., Anderson, C. L., & Vaca, F. E. (2010). Alcohol involvement among young female drivers in U.S. fatal crashes: unfavourable trends. *Inj Prev, 16*(1), 17-20.

U.S. Census Bureau. (2009). 2008 American Community Survey, from http://factfinder.census.gov

Urberg, K. A., Degirmencioglu, S. M., & Pilgrim, C. (1997). Close friend and group influence on adolescent cigarette smoking and alcohol use. *Dev Psychol, 33*(5), 834-844.

U.S. Department of Health and Human Services. (2001). *Youth Violence: A Report of the Surgeon General*. Washington, DC.

Vaca, F., & Anderson, C. L. (2009). U.S. motor vehicle fatality trends in young Latino males. *Annu Proc Assoc Adv Automot Med, 53*, 77-82.

Vaca, F. E., Anderson, C. L., & Hayes-Bautista D. E. (2010). The Latino adolescent male mortality peak revisited: attribution of homicide and motor vehicle crash fatality. *Inj Prev, (In Press, 2010)*.

Weinstein, N. D. (1998). Accuracy of smokers' risk perceptions. *Ann Behav Med, 20*(2), 135-140.

Wilson, S. J., & Lipsey, M. W. (2007). School-based interventions for aggressive and disruptive behavior: update of a meta-analysis. *Am J Prev Med, 33*(2 Suppl), S130-143.

Zhu, L., Gorman, D. M., & Horel, S. (2004). Alcohol outlet density and violence: a geospatial analysis. *Alcohol, 39*(4), 369-375.

CHAPTER NINE

LATINO YOUTHS' SUBSTANCE USE INTENTIONS: PARENTAL ACCULTURATION TRAJECTORIES AND PARENT-YOUTH RELATIONSHIP FACTORS

Felipe González Castro,[1] Stephen J. Boyd,[1]
Meghan M. Garvey[1] and Joshua G. Kellison[1]

Overview

This study examines a central question, "How may the lifetime acculturative trajectories of Latino parents from adolescence to adulthood influence their adolescent children's intentions to experiment with alcohol, tobacco and/or marijuana?" To address this question, this study employed a novel methodology involving a modeled approach to the study of acculturation as a temporal change process. An acculturation involves a change process that prompts adjustment and adaptation across time, location and context. Latino parents' acculturation experiences constitute developmental pathways that forge the formation of their own cultural identity, which in turn may influence the formation of cultural and familial norms which parents transmit to their children. In their roles as protectors and socializing agents for their children, parents will communicate various cultural messages that are derived from these cultural and familial norms.

From an analysis of parental *lifetime acculturative changes* we identified four distinct lifetime acculturative trajectories: (a) *major acculturative change*—a large magnitude of change toward the U.S. mainstream culture, (b) *minor acculturative change*—a small magnitude of change; (c) *no acculturative*

---

[1]Department of Psychology, Arizona State University.

change—no change in level of acculturation from adolescence to adulthood and (d) *enculturation,* that is, *enculturative change*—a change directed *away* from the mainstream American culture and toward the Mexican/Latino cultures. This study examined distal and proximal parent-child relationship factors as these would influence the adolescent's intentions to use alcohol, tobacco and/or marijuana. This study highlights the importance of parental and peer disapproval of youth substance use, as potent deterrents against youth experimentation with various substances.

Introduction

PARENT-YOUTH RELATIONSHIPS WITHIN LATINO FAMILIES

Parents as agents of culture. The construct of "culture" is a rich and complex entity (Chao & Moon, 2005), as indicated in part by the existence of over 150 definitions of culture. Generally culture refers to, "the distinctly human capacity for adapting to circumstances and transmitting this coping skill and knowledge to subsequent generations," (Harris & Morgan, 1987, p. 11, as cited in Baldwin & Lindsley, 1994). From this perspective, parents are the primary agents for transmitting cultural lifeways to their children. In part this occurs through the transmission of cultural or familial norms which contain the collective wisdom of elders (Triandis & Suh, 2002). These cultural norms convey rules or guidelines on correct or desirable behavior, as sanctioned by the cultural group's gatekeepers: community institutions including schools or churches and families, both nuclear and extended, in addition to parents themselves (McGoldrick & Giordano, 1996). Cultural norms consist of "common beliefs, expectations and practices," that confer to members of the group an "adaptive advantage," which promotes the group's survival and adjustment to changes in the environment (Lehman, Chiu & Schaller, 2004). These cultural norms also include expectations regarding the appropriate or acceptable use of alcohol, tobacco and other substances both legal and illegal.

Regarding the transmission of cultural norms from elders to children, one emerging question is, "Why are some normative beliefs and behaviors successfully transmitted to new cultural members whereas others fail to persist across time?" (Lehman et al., 2004, p. 691). Under this dynamic process of cultural transmission, *cultural traditions* are beliefs and practices that persist across time by conferring protective effects for families and communities (Cuadrado & Liberman, 1998). Cultural traditions may persist across generations by offering adaptive and functional guidelines that regulate a child's behavior in a manner that promotes adaptive integration into the local cultural milieu (Castro, Garfinkle,

Naranjo, Rollins, Brook & Brook, 2006; Castro & Gutierres, 1997). Ideally effective parenting practices promote a sound person-environment fit, that is, these culturally based practices offer guidelines that teach children how best to navigate the complex labyrinth of life challenges which they will face in adapting to their sociocultural environments. Ideally, best parenting practices foster youth *resilience* in the form of adaptive survival skills (Klohnen, 1996; Masten, 2001; Schwartz, Montgomery & Briones, 2006). For Latino and other ethnic minority youths, these skills would include capabilities for coping effectively in diverse sociocultural environments (Castro, Boyer & Balcazar, 2000; Ramirez, 1999).

Existing traditional parenting practices may be augmented by integrating new and potentially more adaptive methods of successful childrearing, in an effort to enhance parents' and children's ability to cope more effectively within their changing environment. At times, however, new or more permissive "modernistic" parenting practices will conflict with established and more conservative traditional lifeways (Ramirez, 1999). In other instances, for a new generation of parents, "old-fashioned" parenting traditions may re-emerge, as a new cohort of parents reject heretofore novel parenting practices which are no longer regarded as useful.

Moreover, within any cultural group or community, variations exist among parents regarding particular normative beliefs and behaviors which they endorse and choose to convey to their child. As one example, a Mexican father might teach his son "traditional" gender role expectation that boys and girls should be relegated different familial roles and household duties, whereby boys are conferred greater freedoms and family privileges. By contrast, another Mexican father from the same community may endorse "modernistic" gender role expectations, thus teaching his son that boys and girls should be assigned similar familial roles and household duties. In other words, boys when compared with girls should *not* be afforded greater freedoms or family privileges.

In addition to this within-group variation in parental endorsements of traditional gender norms, the process of acculturation change will introduce the challenge of reconciling competing, and at times conflicting norms that are drawn from two or more diverse cultural groups (e.g. American and Mexican). This situation often forces parents to reevaluate their native cultural norms, introducing complexity and at times conflict in situations that prompt a re-consideration of original or native cultural norms which may no longer be useful within the new environment.

Quality in the parent-youth relationship. Another emerging question within this complex cultural context is, "What constitutes a quality parent-child relationship?" In other words, which parent-child relationship patterns are associated with the most positive outcomes in childhood development into adolescence and beyond? As parents and their children develop affective bonds and mutual attachments, positive parent-child bonds enable parents to communicate effectively with their children and to exercise parental authority and control. Among traditional Latino families, parental expectations of youth respect and reverence toward parents and grandparents, coupled with parental affection and protectiveness of their children, constitute popular and perhaps idyllic Mexican cultural prescriptions. These beliefs also represent the traditional, and often conservative, Latino cultural norms that form the basis of strong traditional Latino parent-child relationships. Nonetheless, within-group variation exists among Mexican and other Latino families in parental endorsement and adoption of these traditional cultural expectations and norms, as contrasted with modernistic and more permissive cultural norms that include norms regarding the use of alcohol, tobacco and other drugs.

Several studies have identified parenting styles and behaviors that are indicative of "quality" in the parent-child relationship. The literature suggests that parenting styles which build strong parent-child relationships include: parental warmth and support for their child, clear and informative parent-child communications, parental monitoring that includes knowing their child's whereabouts and activities with friends (Velleman, Templeton & Copello, 2005), as well as parental disapproval of youth risk behaviors, including the use of alcohol, tobacco and other drugs. In the past, drug prevention programs have targeted parents by providing information about drug use to facilitate parent-youth discussions regarding drug-related issues with their children. However, the provision of information alone has *not* been an effective drug use prevention strategy (Hanson, 1992). A more complete parent education and training program would emphasize strengthening parental communications and developing parenting skills aimed at increasing parental self-efficacy or agency for communicating effectively with their child (Riggs, Elfenbaum & Pentz, 2006). Such parent education and training programs are designed to help parents set clear rules, provide explicit messages regarding their disapproval of drug use, and enforce these expectations. Effective parenting programs would also instruct parents on ways to protect their child from negative social influences, such as exposure to drug-using peers (Petrie, Bunn & Byrne, 2007). Effective parenting programs should also aim to increase parental self-confidence in their own parenting skills, reinforcing the message that they are experts on issues concerning their own families (Parsai, Castro, Marsiglia, Harthun & Valdez, 2011). In addition, *culturally sensitive parenting* for Latino parents may also include parent education regarding the issues and challenges of coping effectively with acculturation and acculturative stress, while including strategies on racial/ethnic socialization to help their child cope with discrimination (Carranza, 2007). From this analysis, a fundamental question is, "For which types of Latino parents may *authoritative* parenting serve as an effective and culturally congruent form of parenting?" And, by contrast, "For which Latino parents may a *permissive* or an *authoritarian* parenting style operate as an effective and culturally congruent form of parenting?"

Parental communication and monitoring. As parents develop skills for discussing difficult life issues with their adolescent child, they become more capable of protecting their children from harm (Barnes, Hoffman, Welte, Farrell & Dintcheff, 2006). Also, as parents monitor their child's activities with friends and ascertain their child's whereabouts, parents may be more capable of protecting their child from harm by discouraging their child's involvement with deviant peers and by disapproving of their child's experimentation with alcohol, tobacco and other drugs. By contrast, parenting styles and behaviors that are overly permissive, inconsistent and/or overly punitive have been associated with the onset of youth problem behaviors (Hoeve, Blokland, Dubas, Loeber, Gerris & van der Laan, 2008). However, differences exist between cultural groups and across families in how parents define the specific behaviors that constitute authoritative, permissive and punitive parenting practices.

Peer influences. As children progress through the stages of adolescence, they initiate and extend relationship bonds with their peers, which at times compete with parental authority and influence. Within this dynamic ecodevelopmental context (Pantin, Schwartz, Sullivan, Prado & Szapocznik, 2004), quality in the parent-child relationship may involve attaining a complex balance between several competing demands with a central aim of maintaining positive parent-child bonds. Whatever its configuration, this balance may be characterized by the presence of trust, effective communications and parental flexibility, yet also with a sustained parental authority that is instrumental in discouraging youth risk behaviors, including the disapproval of youth experimentation with alcohol, tobacco and other drugs.

Evidence from cross-ethnic studies has also identified ethnic group differences in forms of parental monitoring, whereby African-American and Mexican-American parents have differed in their parenting practices when compared with white non-Hispanic parents (Tragesser, Beauvais, Swaim, Edwards & Oetting, 2007). Similar within-group differences may also emerge among racial/ethnic groups, such as variation among Latino subcultural groups (Castro, Barrera & Holleran Steiker, 2010), in which Latino parents vary in levels or types of lifetime acculturation trajectories and the cultural norms which these parents endorse. Currently, little is known about such acculturation-related within-group differences that may exist among Latino parents, and ways in which such differences may influence the parent-child relationship and parental capabilities for discouraging youth risk behaviors.

Acculturative influences affecting the parent-child relationship. Among some Mexican and Mexican-American families, the stressors of acculturation will strain the quality of the parent-child relationship. Several studies have described acculturation-related stressors and the tensions that can and often occur among Latino and other ethnic minority parents and their children (Carranza, 2007; Farver, Narang & Bhadha, 2002). Among Cuban and other Latino families, the faster rates of acculturation that occur among immigrant children, as compared with their parents (known as *differential acculturation*), has been identified as a source of acculturation-related stress that often strains the parent-child relationship and places the child at greater risk for negative health outcomes (Elder, Broyles, Brennan, Zuniga de Nurcio & Nader, 2005; Tapia, Schwartz, Prado, Lopez & Pantin, 2006).

ACCULTURATION AND MENTAL WELLBEING

Acculturation and health-related outcomes. An early research contribution that examined levels of acculturation and health-related outcomes consisted of several articles on the Hispanic Health and Nutrition Examination Study (HHANES) published in 1990 in a special issue of the *American Journal of Public Health.* At that time, these studies used a one-factor measurement model, and the related unidimensional acculturation scale, or they used acculturation proxy measures, e.g., spoken language, as applied with Mexican-American, Cuban and/or Puerto Rican populations. These unidimensional acculturation scales and related proxy measures primarily assessed acculturation in terms of the influence of Spanish-English language usage, i.e., linguistic acculturation on health-related outcomes.

Although based on cross-sectional analyses, collectively these studies reported that *greater* levels of acculturation were associated with: (a) greater recency in health service utilization (Solis, Marks, Garcia & Shelton, 1990); (b) greater alcohol consumption, especially among Latinas (Marks, Garcia & Solis, 1990); (c) greater frequency of alcohol consumption among younger Mexican-American women, but *not* among Mexican-American men (Markides, Ray, Stroup-Benham & Treviño, 1990); (d) greater cigarette smoking among Mexican-American women, but not among Mexican-American men (Haynes, Harvey, Montes, Nickens & Cohen, 1990); and (e) higher prevalence rates of lifetime marijuana and cocaine use among Mexican-American and Puerto Rican men and women (Amaro, Whitaker, Coffman & Heeren, 1990). A recent review of studies that examined the influence of acculturation on health-related outcomes concluded that higher levels of acculturation have had a *negative* effect, that is, have been associated with *worse* health outcomes in the areas of: (a) substance use, (b) dietary practices and (c) birth outcomes. By contrast, higher levels of acculturation have had a *positive* effect, that is, *better* health-related outcomes in the areas of: (a) health care access and utilization and (b) self-perceptions of health (Lara, Gamboa, Kahramanian, Morales & Hayes-Bautista, 2005).

Issues in cross-sectional acculturation research. As a comparative context, in the past almost all acculturation research has examined levels of acculturation at a single-point-in-time, followed by cross-sectional analyses from which investigators have interred temporal effects. Unfortunately, in the past, this approach has yielded limited and at times conflicting information regarding the putative effects of acculturation on specific health-related outcomes (Rogler, Cortes & Malgady, 1991).

Within the natural environment, acculturation is a ubiquitous process of change that occurs worldwide and that often demands adaptive change to new environmental conditions. Given this complex and dynamic natural process, prior conventional cross-sectional assessments of "acculturation" have yielded shallow renditions of the actual process of acculturation change and its effects (Castro & Murray, 2010). Such limitations in the conceptualization and measurement of acculturation have prompted some health researchers to question the utility of the acculturation construct itself, particularly as applied to the study of health-related outcomes in Latino populations (Hunt, Schneider & Comer, 2004). Differences of opinion persist among social science investigators regarding the utility of the construct of acculturation with respect to Latino research (Schwartz, Ungar, Zamboanga & Szapocznik, 2010). A resolution of this controversy would appear to require improvements in the conceptualization and measurement of acculturation, in the form of re-framing of original and now archaic notions of acculturation, in favor of new, more relevant and more ecologically sound conceptions of acculturation that advance beyond the conventional use of language as an indicator of acculturation (Viruel-Fuentes, 2007).

MODELS OF ACCULTURATION AND ACCULTURATIVE CHANGE

Original anthropological A-B model of acculturation. To provide a context for possible new ways to re-frame the construct of acculturation, we will review the original conceptualizations of this construct. Figure 1 presents a simple A-B group-level model of acculturation as originally conceptualized by anthropologists (Redfield, Linton & Herskovits, 1936). At the individual and group levels, these acculturative changes were said to occur across several domains as these involve acculturative changes in attitudes, behaviors, values and sense of cultural identity (Ryder, Alden & Pauling, 2000). This simple A-B model conceptualizes acculturation as a process resulting from a cultural encounter between two distinct cultural groups, A and B. This perspective also implies that the smaller or "weaker" cultural group (Group A), will eventually be absorbed or "assimilated" into the larger and more influential group (Group B), i.e., *full assimilation*. The "weaker" cultural group is thus eradicated via its absorption into the "stronger" group, although under this process the dominant group will also change in its identity as it acquires and adopts some of the cultural lifeways of the weaker group.

Figure 1.

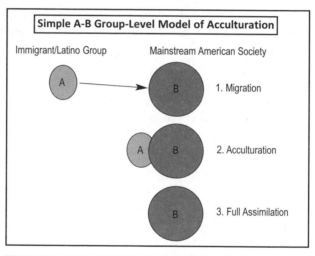

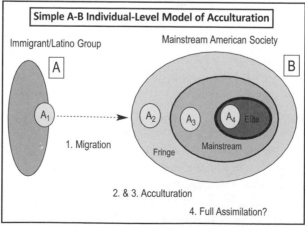

A variant of this group-level model is a simple *individual level* A-B model of acculturation. As shown in panel 2 of Figure 1, at the individual-level a person also undergoes a similar process of acculturation change and possible assimilation. Also at the individual level, this process of acculturation involves individual changes across several domains: changes in attitudes, behaviors, values and in cultural identity (Berry, 1997; Ryder, Alden & Pauling, 2000). Specifically an individual from cultural group A typically migrates into cultural group B, entering that cultural group or society at its outer sociocultural fringes. Many such immigrants enter into the new society with strong aspirations for upward sociocultural mobility. According to Segmented Assimilation Theory (Portes & Zhou, 1993; Zhou, 1997), the form and extent of this sociocultural mobility is determined by two principal factors: (a) the person's *human capital* (personal skills and resources), and (b) the extent of available *social capital* (the person's local network of social and environmental resources). Ostensibly, "ethnic enclaves" e.g., Mexican barrios, are communities rich in ethnic culture, thus serving as neighborhoods that are potentially rich in social capital. This process that produces differential acculturation trajectories and related variation in sociocultural mobility has been described as *segmented assimilation* (Portes, 1997; Portes & Rumbaut, 1996).

Thus, according to Segmented Assimilation Theory, the starting conditions under which an immigrant enters a new host society consist of specific governing factors that determine a person's life chances, that is, their likelihood of succeeding within the new host society based on opportunities provided them, conditions that launch their assimilation trajectory. The least advantaged immigrants face significant barriers to assimilation into the new cultural mainstream, and by implication they are almost assuredly excluded from assimilation into the *elite sector* of the new society (see Figure 1). By contrast, immigrants who are rich in social and/or human capital benefit from greater opportunities for upward sociocultural and economic mobility. For example, in the early 1960s when Fidel Castro took control of the Cuban government, a mass exodus occurred that first consisted of the middle- and upper-class residents. These sectors of Cuban society had the resources to establish and develop new social enclaves that were similar to those which they left behind, thus setting the stage for their future access to the *elite sector* of the new society (Pedraza, 2003). In response to the situational factors that influence acculturative motivations under this complex process of acculturation, immigrants can be motivated to: (a) retain most elements of their native ethnic identity, (b) completely abandon their ethnic identity in favor of a completely new identity—full assimilation or (c) develop a bicultural identity (Castro & Murray, 2010).

A one-factor model of acculturation. Within a one-factor model of acculturation, the process of migration and culture change has been depicted as a linear progression that occurs along a single-dimension of acculturation change. One end of this continuum consists of complete involvement in the original native or ethnic culture, a cultural state defined as a "low level of acculturation," given that this state is defined in terms of a low involvement in a reference group which is the mainstream dominant culture group or society. The opposite pole is described as consisting of a "high level of acculturation," as characterized by a complete involvement within this "mainstream" or "dominant culture" group or society, e.g., the white American culture. Here it is recognized that "white American culture" is an abstract and broad construct, within which there exists considerable within-group variability in what actually constitutes "white American culture," a factorially complex construct.

Several unidimensional acculturation scales have been developed to measure individual levels of acculturation as assessed along this single-acculturative dimension. These scales have generally focused on language proficiency, although other factors including food preferences, media usage, peer relations and cultural identification have also been assessed (Cabassa, 2003; Ryder, Alden & Paulhus, 2000). This one-factor model of acculturation has been criticized because it implies that acculturation is essentially a "zero-sum process," (Rogler, 1994; Rogler, Cortes & Malgady, 1991). Under this unidimensional model, "acculturative movement" toward the new cultural group, e.g., toward the white American (Anglo) mainstream culture (Locke, 1998), is depicted to induce a loss of native cultural values, beliefs and behaviors, thus producing full assimilation. In actuality, this "forced assimilation assumption" appears inaccurate as applied to many Latino and other ethnic minority or immigrant populations. Instead, immigrants tend to develop degrees of a bicultural identity in which they retain elements of their original cultural values, skills and behaviors, while also acquiring and adopting the linguistic skills and behaviors that are valued within the new host society.

A two-factor model of acculturation. The limitations of the one-factor model of acculturation have been partially addressed by emerging two-factor models of acculturation, such as the two-factor "orthogonal model" (Berry, 2005; Oetting & Beauvais, 1990). Proponents of this two-factor model have argued that the process of acculturation involves the acquisition of new mainstream cultural lifeways: language, skills, behaviors and identity formation, without necessarily introducing a loss or abandonment of native lifeways. An individual's level of acculturation can thus be determined based on his/her cultural affiliation on two dimensions: (a) an ethnic "heritage" dimension, and (b) a dominant-culture "mainstream" dimension. This dual-culture conceptualization also emphasizes that changes in these two acculturative processes occur independently, i.e., they are orthogonal. Berry is perhaps the best known proponent of this two-factor orthogonal model.

Berry (2005) proposed that specific types of acculturative states are definable based on variations (low to high) in a person's cultural position along each of these two dimensions of acculturation, thus producing four distinct acculturative states: *integration* (high on ethnic "heritage" dimension, high on "mainstream" dimension), *assimilation* (low on ethnic "heritage" dimension, high on "mainstream" dimension), *separation* (high on ethnic "heritage" dimension, low on "mainstream" dimension) *and marginalization* (low on ethnic "heritage" dimension, low on "mainstream" dimension).

This two-factor model, however, is not without criticisms. Rudmin (2003) has argued that these four types of acculturation are ill-defined and not necessarily evident within the natural environment. Moreover, while it has been argued in principle that the two dimensions of this two-factor model are uncorrelated, in practice these dimensions are often positively correlated (Castro & Murray, 2010). This suggests that these two acculturative dimensions, while conceptually distinct, are actually not as independent as was originally proposed.

Recent articles that have conducted multivariate latent class analyses to detect the presence of these acculturative subgroups have generated partial support for the existence of these subgroups (Castro, Marsiglia, Kulis & Kellison, 2010; Schwartz & Zamboanga, 2008). The study by Schwartz and Zamboanga (2008) examined these dual orientations to heritage and mainstream cultural practices as examined in terms of language use, foods and entertainment preferences, in a sample of 436 Hispanic college students who were enrolled in an introductory psychology class. Based on this two-factor orthogonal model, this latent class analysis yielded six distinct acculturation groups, thus providing partial support for Berry's orthogonal model. From these analyses, two new classes emerged and these were the subcultural groups of: (a) "Partial Bicultural," and (b) "Full Bicultural."

It is noteworthy that Berry's original conceptualization proposed the existence of a "Marginalized" acculturation group, although this group did not appear in the latent class outcomes that were reported by Schwartz and Zamboanga (2008). Notwithstanding that this latent class analysis, as conducted by Schwartz and Zamboanga, consisted of a sample of undergraduate college students, these investigators reported that the "Full Bicultural" subgroup exhibited the healthiest levels of psychosocial function (Schwartz & Zamboanga, 2008, p. 283). These results suggested and were interpreted as evidence that complete biculturality (La Frombois, Coleman & Gerton, 1993) may be the most adaptive of the acculturation states.

In summary, two-factor models of acculturation have been proposed and have been regarded as a broader and more valid framework for understanding acculturation. By contrast, the unidimensional model has been described as having the advantage of parsimony, although Ryder and colleagues (2000) also note that the one-factor model offers more limited and perhaps misleading descriptions of the acculturation process.

Psychological scales for the measurement of acculturation. Since the 1980s there has been a proliferation of scales and measures that purport to measure the construct of acculturation. This measurement approach has also popularized the "individual person" conception of acculturation thereby also narrowing the conceptualization of acculturation. The Acculturation Rating Scale for Mexican Americans (ARSMA) (Cuellar, Harris & Jasso, 1980) was one of the first and perhaps the most well known of these early scales that measured the individualized "trait" of acculturation in Mexican Americans and in other Latino populations. Since then, several revised two-factor scales have been developed, including the ARSMA II (Cuellar, Arnold & Maldonado, 1995) and the Bidimensional Acculturation Scale (BAS) (Marin & Gamboa, 1996), as well as second-generation scales that have utilized two or more dimensions for the measurement of acculturation.

Given this ability to succinctly measure and operationalize acculturation, the availability of these scales would suggest that changes in acculturation could now be examined. However, a fundamental problem has arisen involving the use of scale-based acculturation *change scores,* a procedure which introduces a fundamental measurement problem (Collins, 1991); which is that *change scores* alone do not take into account *start values,* i.e., the intercept, in the assessment of acculturative change. For example, under a simple change-score approach, one-unit of change in acculturation from adolescence to adulthood, i.e., acculturation change scores of +1.0, would have a different meaning for cases in which this change occurs from an intercept value of 1.0 to 2.0, as contrasted with a change from 3.0 to 4.0. In the first instance, the person initially exhibits a very low level of acculturation during adolescence, and then moves toward being bicultural. By contrast, in the second instance, a person initially exhibits a bicultural identity during their adolescence and then into adulthood moves toward developing a higher level of acculturation toward the dominant culture. As exemplified by these two cases, interpreting change scores in the absence of taking into account intercept values, the starting point, conflates two differing acculturation change trajectories, thus contributing to misleading interpretations regarding the meaning of these acculturation changes.

Latent growth models applied to acculturation change. A major methodological tool that is applicable to the study of acculturation and acculturation change is the statistical technique of latent growth modeling (Bollen & Curran, 2006). This approach examines the *initial state,* as well as the rate and direction of change, which are examined as distinct model parameters (McArdle & Hamagami, 1991). Within this methodology, as applied to the analysis of acculturation change, these two important culture change trajectory parameters are: (a) the acculturation *intercept*—the starting point in acculturation status which occurs at an early life stage, and (b) the acculturation *change slope*—the amount and direction of change, whether toward the mainstream American culture, *acculturation,* or away from it and toward the Mexican/Latino cultures, *enculturation.*

STUDY HYPOTHESES

The present study examines a central question. Among Latino parents, "How may parents' lifetime acculturation change trajectories operate as distal sources of acculturation that in turn may influence their child's intentions to use alcohol, tobacco and/or marijuana?" In other words, Latino parents' own lifetime acculturation experiences, their cultural life journey, may constitute distal but nonetheless influential sources in the formation of their own parental norms, which in turn may influence their child's orientations and intentions to experiment with alcohol, tobacco and other drugs.

Based on prior research on acculturation, health and parent-child relationships and youth drug use, we offer four specific hypotheses as applied to Latino families.

H$_1$—*Parent's Adolescent Acculturation Level and their Child's Substance Use Intentions.* Latino parents who exhibit a high acculturation intercept during their own adolescence (a bicultural and/or high acculturation status) will have children who report *higher* levels of substance use intentions.

H$_2$—*Parental Acculturation Trajectory and their Child's Substance Use Intentions.* Latino parents who exhibit an *increasing* acculturative trajectory (increasing lifetime acculturation toward the mainstream American society) will have adolescent children who exhibit *higher* levels of substance use intentions.

H$_3$—*Quality of Parent-Youth Relationship and Youth Substance Use Intentions.* A more positive (higher quality) parent-child relationship, as indicated by higher levels of parental monitoring, and greater effectiveness in parent-child communications, will be associated with *lower* levels of substance use intentions as reported by their adolescent child.

H$_4$—*Parental Conservative Norms and Youth Substance Use Intentions.* *Higher* levels of parental norms that communicate a disapproval of substance use will be associated with *lower* levels of youth substance use intentions.

Despite over 30 years of acculturation research with Latino/Hispanic populations, there still exists limited evidence on the effects of *acculturation change* on the lifeways and family norms of Latino parents, as aspects of this acculturation change are related to parental teachings toward their children. As an extension of prior research, we examined these four hypotheses, utilizing this novel methodology, to identify distinct acculturation subgroups that are defined by early life acculturation intercepts and by types of acculturative change, to attain new insights into Latino parenting practices and parent-youth relationships.

Procedures

SAMPLE AND CHARACTERISTICS

Participants were 203 Latino (primarily Mexican and Mexican-American) parents or guardians and their adolescent child; the children attended one of nine middle schools that are located in South Central Phoenix, Arizona. The sample for the present study is a subsample of a larger multi-ethnic sample of parents and adolescent children who participated in the *Familias: Preparando la Nueva Generación*, a five-year study funded by the National Center on Minority Health and Disparities of the National Institutes of Health, with the aim of developing a parent education intervention to aid in preventing problem behaviors in their middle school child. Parents' ages ranged from 23 to 75, with over 90% of these parents being between 32 and 54 years of age, with a mean age of 39.32 years (SD = 7.29). In this study the primary parent or guardian of the adolescent child was invited to participate; consequently, the sample includes some grandparents who were older than 54 years of age.

Table 1 presents demographic and acculturation characteristics for this sample of 203 participants. We eliminated a few cases of non-ethnic parents who, based on their cultural backgrounds, would not undergo the forms of acculturation change experienced by Latino and other immigrant populations. These "non-acculturative" cases were small in number, consisting of only six excluded cases: four white non-Hispanic parents and two African-American parents. Additionally, parents with missing data regarding their ethnicity or other personally identifying variables (n= 20) were also excluded. Accordingly, from this sample of 203 ethnic parents, a total of 183 parent-child dyads are included in the final data analyses.

As indicated in Table 1, for this sample of 183 parent-child dyads 124 parents were of "Mexican origin" (67.8%), and 51 were of another "Latino/Hispanic" origin (27.9%), for a total of 175 Latino parents (95.6% of the total sample). Thus, Mexican-heritage parents constituted the majority of this sample. Parents form other ethnic subgroups were three Native Americans/American Indians (1.6%), one parent from "other ethnic groups" (0.5%), and four parents who were of "mixed ethnic identities" (2.2%). The educational levels of parents in this sample varied considerably, ranging from those having only 3 years of education or

Table 1. Sample Characteristics

Variable	N	Percent	Min	Max	Mean	SD
Age	183	—	23	75	39.32	7.29
Education						
* 3 Years or Less	12	6.6				
* 4 to 6 Years	37	20.7				
* 6 to 11 Years	66	36.9				
* Completed High School or GED	25	14.0				
* Completed Trade or Vocational	11	6.1				
* Some College	19	10.6				
* Completed Undergrad—BA, BS	5	2.8				
* Some Grad School -	1	0.6				
* Completed Grad School—MD, PhD	3	1.6				
Nativity						
* Native Born	46	25.1				
* Immigrant	137	74.9				
Ethnic Identity						
* Mexican Origin	124	67.8				
* Other Latino/Hispanic	51	27.9				
* American Indian	3	1.6				
* Other Ethnicity	1	0.5				
* Multi-ethnic Identity	4	2.2				
Acculturation Level in Adolescence						
* High Acculturation (3.70 to 5.00)	13	7.1				
* Bicultural (2.40 to 3.69)	25	13.7				
* Low Acculturation (1.00 to 2.39)	145	79.2				
Acculturation Level in Adulthood						
* High Acculturation (3.70 to 5.00)	6	3.3				
* Bicultural (2.40 to 3.69)	57	31.1				
* Low Acculturation (1.00 to 2.39)	120	65.6				
Lifetime Acculturation Change						
* No Acculturative Change	49	26.8				
* Minor Acculturative Change	55	30.1				
* Major Acculturative Change	55	30.1				
* Enculturative Change	24	13.1				

less, to those who completed a graduate degree (see Table 1). The modal educational category for this group of parents was that of 6 to 11 years of education (n=73, 36.7%).

STUDY MEASURES

Table 2 presents the measures used in this study. This study included two parent-youth relationship scales, Parent-Child Communications and Parental Monitoring used with permission from the Miami research group (Pantin, Coasworth, Feaster, Newman, Briones, Prado, Schwartz & Szapocznik, 2003). The research instruments in our study also included scales to measure "Parental Investment" described as "Extent of Involvement and Positive Parenting" subscales from the Parenting Practices Scale (Gorman-Smith, Tolan, Zelli & Rowell, 1996), a 25-item measure that assesses various dimensions of parenting. Our project adopted two parenting practices scales based on the Pittsburgh Youth Survey (Wasserman, Miller, Pinner & Jaramillo, 1996). This scale was originally designed to measure: (a) positive parenting, (b) discipline effectiveness, (c) avoidance of discipline and (d) extent of monitoring and involvement in the child's life. These constructs have been used to measure parental monitoring and discipline practices in several studies (Dishion, Reid & Patterson, 1988). The parental measures also included the General Acculturation Index (Balcazar, Castro & Krull, 1995; Castro, Balcazar & Cota, 2007) as used to gather measurements of Acculturation in Adolescence, and Acculturation in Adulthood (Castro,

Table 2. Psychometric Properties of Study Measures

Scale	Items	Alpha
PARENTAL SCALES		
Parent-Child Relationships/ Communications	14	.77
Parental Monitoring	2	.63
Acculturation in Adolescence	5	.91
Acculturation in Adulthood	5	.86
YOUTH SCALES		
Youth Ethnic Pride	6	.80
Youth Perceived Parental Disapproval of Drug Use	3	.86
Friends' Disapproval of Youth Drug Use	3	.94
Youth Acculturation Stress	5	.77
Youth American Orientation	1	----
Youth Latino Orientation	1	----
OUTCOME MEASURE		
Youth Substance Use Intentions	3	.83

Marsiglia, Kulis & Kellison, 2010). Other youth scales were drawn from the baseline Phoenix Kids Survey, which was administered within the youth's classrooms. The youth variables for this study included the scales of: Ethnic Pride, Perceived Parental Disapproval of Drug Use, Friends' Disapproval of Youth Drug Use and youth Acculturative Stress. Also included as predictor variables were two single items: the youth's American Culture Orientation and Latino Culture Orientation (Castro, Garfinkle, Naranjo, Rollins, Brook & Brook, 2006).

The youth Substance Use Intentions variable consisted of the composite scale from three items. These items were assessed in response to the question, "If you had the chance *this weekend*, would you use . . . alcohol, cigarettes and/or marijuana?" Youth response choices were: (1) "Definitely yes," (2) "Yes," (3) "No" and (4) "Definitely no." These dimensional values were later reverse scored with higher scores indicating greater intentions to use one or more of these substances. For this sample of Latino adolescents, Cronbach's alpha coefficient for these three items measuring youth Substance Use Intentions was 83.

PARENTAL LEVELS OF ACCULTURATION DURING THEIR ADOLESCENCE AND ADULTHOOD

The present study examined the *acculturation change trajectories* of Latino parents as reported retrospectively and also concurrently for two life milestones: (a) adolescence and (b) currently in adulthood. This methodology utilized a "brief focused retrospective recall" procedure to examine early life and current-adult levels of acculturation. This methodology was developed to obtain reliable assessments of levels of acculturation for two or more specific life milestones. This "brief retrospective recall methodology" is a modified version of the timeline follow-back (TLFB) methodology which has been used often in substance abuse treatment research (Brown, Burgess, Sales, Whiteley, Evans & Miller, 1998; Sobell, Maisto, Sobell & Cooper, 1979; Sobell & Sobell, 1996). In this "brief retrospective recall," to enhance recall accuracy in a succinct manner, in place of using the conventional TLFB monthly calendar of events, we oriented participants and focused their attention via the identification of specific "anchoring events," personal events that occurred during the milestone period of interest, e.g., their life during their middle school years.

The timeline follow-back methodology. The timeline follow-back (TLFB) methodology is a well-established procedure that is used to obtain reliable retrospective estimates of specific behaviors that occurred during a specified period of time, such as episodes of alcohol use (Maisto, Sobell, Cooper & Sobell, 1979; Sobell & Sobell, 1978) and illegal drug use (Ehrman & Robbins, 1994). In research with clinical drug-using populations, such as injection drug users, this timeline follow-back procedure exhibited very similar data-gathering outcomes when this procedure was compared with a brief standardized quantity-frequency structured interview assessment instrument (Copersino, Meade, Bigelow & Brooner, 2010). A variant of this brief focused retrospective timeline follow back methodology has been tested and implemented in prior studies (Castro, Marsiglia, Kulis & Kellison, 2010).

Brief focused retrospective recall to facilitate recall of events at specific life milestones. Data gathering was conducted using parental and youth self-report surveys with project staff available to provide support to participants who requested clarifications in responding to this survey. The first section of this Parental Survey was section, "1. Your Background." This section consisted of two time-related subsections: (a) "When You Were an Adolescent" and (b) "Your Life Today as an Adult Parent." In parallel fashion, each section asked the participant to respond to features of their neighborhood, e.g., "I felt safe in my neighborhood," and also to respond to acculturation scale items that asked about specific acculturation-related aspects of their life.

This "brief focused retrospective recall" methodology consisted of a brief memory induction task that asked the parent to, "Please recall the time in your life when you were an adolescent, that is, when you were in middle school (grades 6 to 8), in other words, when you were 11 to 13 years old." This introduction focused the participant's attention on a specific period in their life, a "window of time" that was used to focus on and facilitate accurate recall of specific and salient life events that occurred during that time period. First, the participant was asked to identify the city, state and country where they lived during that period of time. They were then asked to recall specific features of the neighborhood where they lived during that period of their adolescence. They were then asked to respond to the acculturation items, as was true for them during the particular life milestone.

The General Acculturation Index. The participant was then asked to answer each of six items from a revised version of the General Acculturation Index (Balcazar, Castro & Krull, 1995; Castro & Gutierrez, 1997). As related to this adolescent milestone, these scale items asked about the person's Spanish-English-speaking and reading capabilities, mass media preferences, and also about the ethnic identity of their best friends and neighbors, using a dimension that ranged from (1) "almost all Latinos or other ethnic minorities" to (5) "almost all white Americans."

The first five items from the General Acculturation Index ask about concrete and specific aspects of acculturation, with the aim of eliciting easy-to-recall aspects of acculturation that were true for the participant during the specific life period, i.e., during the window from grades 6 to 8, and thus, between ages 11 to 13. Given that these scale items are concrete and specific, they have a low propensity for distortion in retrospective recall. We have found that study participants' memory have typically been accurate in response to such specific items that ask about the language spoken during a given period from their adolescence, i.e., they spoke (a) entirely or mostly English, (b) entirely or mostly Spanish or (c) both languages. By contrast, a sixth item from the General Acculturation Index asked about the participant's level of *ethnic pride* as it existed during that period from their adolescence, levels of ethnic pride ranging from: (1) Very Proud to (5) Ashamed. However, for this ethnic pride item which examines *affective* content, we believe that this scale item is subject to significant retrospective distortion and recall bias, and thus we *did not* include this sixth item in computing the participant's *adolescence* acculturation status score. Accordingly, this item was also *not* included in computing the parent's acculturation score in *adulthood*.

Acculturation scores for the adolescent and adult milestones. Thus, this milestone recall procedure generated an acculturation scale score that ranges from a high of 5.00 for *highest* level of cultural involvement in the mainstream white American dominant culture, to a *low* of 1.00 which refers to the lowest level of acculturation to this mainstream white American culture, and thus implicating greater cultural involvement within the Mexican/Latino core culture. While recognizing the advantages of a two-factor assessment of acculturation, to facilitate recall in the measurement of early-life levels of acculturation using this timeline follow-back approach, we utilized a single dimensional approach to the assessment of acculturation. And under this unidimensional approach, a value of 3.0 was indicative of having a bilingual/bicultural status. Based on prior research involving the development and use of this scale (Balcazar, Castro & Krull, 1995), we have established cut points to identify three levels of acculturation: Low Acculturation: 1.00 to 2.39; Bicultural: 2.40 to 3.69; and High Acculturation: 3.70 to 5.00.

In parallel fashion, and using this inductive procedure, acculturative status was also assessed for the present-day adult life milestone. As an additional methodological point, within the present study, some participants were in their 20s in age, and others in their 60s. Accordingly, for these parents, the time period from the participant's adolescence (ages 11 to 13) to their current adult age varied considerably. In related analyses using latent growth models, we have controlled for this between-subject variation across participants for the period of time from their adolescence to current adulthood (Castro, Marsiglia, Kulis & Kellison, 2010). However, in the present exploratory analyses we examined the two parameters: (a) the simple intercepts at the adolescence milestone, and (b) levels of acculturative change from adolescence to adulthood, as the method for defining distinct acculturation change groups, although without controlling for this between-subjects variation in time period in years from adolescence to adulthood.

Results

TYPES OF ACCULTURATION CHANGE AS CHANGE TRAJECTORIES

Figure 2 presents results from the identification of distinct acculturation-change trajectory groups as graphed along a two-dimensional field that is defined by the dimensions of: (a) acculturation level along the vertical axis, and by (b) time point along the horizontal axis, as indicated by the two life milestones: adolescence and current adulthood. Ideally the identification of acculturation groups would be conducted with a latent class analysis, although for the present sample, we did not conduct this more formal analysis. In a two-step process cases were identified in terms of: (1) low, bicultural or high levels in early-life acculturation intercepts, and then (2) lifetime acculturative change involving one of three types of acculturation change: (a) change toward greater acculturation (acculturation), (b) no acculturation change and (c) change toward lower acculturation (enculturation). In summary, the resulting acculturation change trajectory groups were thus identified on the basis of variations in: (a) the acculturation intercept during adolescence, and (b) the magnitude and direction of change in acculturation from adolescence to adulthood.

The basic aim of this exploratory identification of "latent classes" was to identify the smallest number of distinct and theoretically meaningful acculturation trajectory groups. For each of these emergent groups, the group's mean acculturation score for each of the two milestones (adolescence and adulthood) was also graphed along the dual acculturation axes (American cultural orientation, Latino cultural orientation) to aid in the interpretation of these emergent groups. Thus, for these 183 cases that were classified, the four distinct acculturation groups that were identified were: (a) (G1) *No Acculturative Change* (n = 49); (b) (G2) *Minor Acculturative Change* (n= 55); (c) (G3) *Major Acculturative Change* (n = 55); and (d) (G4) *Enculturative Change* (n = 24). The characteristics of these four groups are described below (see Figure 2).

These groups have the following characteristics:

No acculturative change. At the adolescence milestone, Group 1 exhibited an intercept with a level of acculturation of 1.54. For members of this group, the related acculturation scale score as assessed in adulthood was also 1.54, thus indicating *no lifetime acculturation change* as assessed for these two life mile-

Figure 2.

Lifetime Acculturation Trajectories in Latino and Other Minority Parents

Level of Acculturation

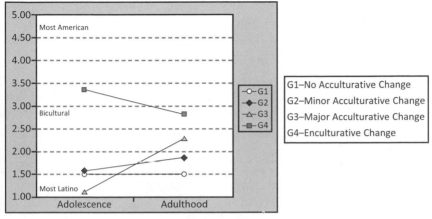

stones. Based on the values of these two parameters, the intercept in adolescence and the acculturation change slope of zero, this group's acculturation trajectory described lifelong stability in acculturation that centered at the low-acculturation range, as indicated by the acculturation score of 1.54. This score shows a level of acculturation consistent with the sociocultural features of: (a) being primarily Spanish-speaking with limited English-speaking skills, and (b) maintaining primarily Mexican/Latino sociocultural peers as friends and neighbors; and (c) the consumption of mass media primarily in Spanish.

Minor acculturative change. Group 2 exhibited a small magnitude of acculturative change that occurred in the direction of the dominant American mainstream culture. This group's lifetime acculturation trajectory was anchored at the adolescence milestone by an intercept acculturation score of 1.50. Then across their lifetime, these individuals exhibited a small positive acculturation slope that involved a modest increase in their level of acculturation into adulthood, rising to an acculturation value of 1.89. This small magnitude in acculturation change suggests a slight lifetime acculturation change toward "mainstream American society." This shift has the sociocultural features that involve linguistic and peer relations in the direction of: (a) learning some English, (b) the consumption of some English-learning media, while also (c) developing some relationships with white American persons and neighbors. This overall lower level of acculturation and its small magnitude of change into adulthood maintained these individuals within the low acculturation range (see Figure 2).

Major Acculturative Change. Members of Group 3 exhibited the largest amount of acculturation change, which was anchored in adolescence by an acculturation score of 1.07, and with a remarkable acculturation change that involved greatly increasing their level of acculturation into adulthood to an acculturation value of 2.27. This is a remarkable magnitude of lifetime acculturation change involving 1.20 units. This increase suggests the presence of a significant motivation and related success in integrating into the mainstream white American society and culture in terms of: (a) developing English-speaking and reading skills, (b) the consumption of English-language media and (c) developing friendships and social relations with white American friends and neighbors. This remarkable acculturative increase advanced this group of individuals culturally from the *lowest* levels of acculturation, consisting of complete cultural involvement within the Mexican/Latino culture(s) during their adolescence, followed by a remarkable acculturative shift toward developing a bilingual-bicultural identity and bicultural lifeways. This acculturative change involved the sociocultural features of: (a) bilingual/bicultural skills, (b) bilingual multimedia preferences, as well as (c) the acquisition of a more diverse set of friends and neighbors that included English-speaking white Americans, while still maintaining Spanish-speaking and Mexican/Latino cultural preferences.

Enculturative change. Group 4 was distinctly different from the three other groups. First, members of this enculturation change group exhibited an acculturation intercept during adolescence that was within the bicultural range, and was anchored at an acculturation score of 3.13. This acculturation score affirmed this group's bilingual-bicultural identity during adolescence. Accordingly, this group is described as consisting of "Mexican Americans" or "Chicanos/Chicanas," rather than as "Mexicans." Then, in their sociocultural development into adulthood, members of this group exhibited a "negative" acculturative change slope in the direction of developing a stronger Mexican/Latino sociocultural identification. Accordingly, they moved in their adulthood to an acculturation level of 2.54, which positioned members of this group near the low-acculturation cut point, although still within the bicultural range. This acculturative change from being a bicultural person during adolescence toward a lower level of acculturation in adulthood involved the sociocultural features of: (a) the acquisition of or an increase in Spanish-speaking skills, (b) Spanish-speaking mass media consumption, as well as (c) an increase in friends or neighbors who are of Mexican/Latino background. This shift suggests a desire and related actions to return to, or re-capture, their own Mexican/Latino cultural roots, and perhaps to expand or refine certain facets of their ethnic identity, which may not have been fully developed during their adolescence, a process that has been described as *enculturation*.

PREDICTORS OF YOUTH SUBSTANCE USE INTENTIONS

The youth substance use intentions variable. Due to the highly skewed form of the youth Substance Use Intentions index, we encoded this variable as: 1 "intentions to use alcohol, tobacco and/or marijuana" and 0 "no intentions to use alcohol, tobacco or marijuana." Then for this composite index of Substance Use Intentions, we conducted two planned logistic regression model analyses. The first model examined the *distal predictors* of parental lifetime acculturation change trajectories as predictors of Youth Substance Use Intentions. The second logistic regression model examined parent-youth relationship factors as *proximal predictors* of youth Substance Use Intentions. This dichotomous youth Substance Use Intentions variable for this sample of 142 Mexican or Mexican-American adolescent youth who were included in this logistic regression model, indicated that 50 (35.2%) intended to use one or more of these substances, whereas 92 (64.8%) *did not* intend to use these substances.

Model 1: Distal predictors. Model 1 consisted of a two-step hierarchical logistic regression analysis. It examined parental acculturative trajectory groups as early life sources of parental acculturative or enculturative change on these youth intentions to experiment with various substances. For Model 1, Step 1 controlled for potential non-equivalence across acculturation trajectory groups in their levels of education. Then Step 2 examined the predictive effects of these acculturation trajectory groups, when compared with the no-acculturation change trajectory group, which served as the reference group.

These analyses revealed that level of education was *not* a significant confounding variable in this model, OR= 1.0 (CI= .97, 103), p > .05 (see Table 3). Then in Step 2, we examined the effects of the parental acculturation trajectory groups as predictors of Youth Substance Use Intentions. This step revealed that the Enculturation Group contributed a significant elevated effect involving higher risks for Youth Substance Use Intentions, OR= 2.95, (CI= 1.31, 6.65), Wald= 6.76, p < .01. In other words, the bicultural Latino parental group, which exhibited an enculturative acquisition of Mexican-heritage lifeways, had adolescent children who expressed a greater willingness to try alcohol, tobacco and/or marijuana. For this subgroup of Latino parents it is unclear whether their child's greater intentions to experiment with substances were prompted by: (a) their parents' early life experiences within the United States, as indicated by their bicultural-level *intercept score* during adolescence; or (b) by their parent's

Table 3. Predictors of Youth Substance Use Intentions

Predictors	Model 1: Initial Model					Model 2: Final Model				
	Model	OR (95% CI)	b	Wald	p	Model	OR (95% CI)	b	Wald	p
Step 1—Control Variables										
* Education		1.00 (.97, 1.03)	.003	0.04	.847		1.09 (.86, 1.41)	.093	0.53	.465
Step 2—Parental Acculturation Group										
* No Acculturation Change Group		—	—	—	—		—	—	—	—
* Minor Acculturation Group		1.03 (.59, 1.82)	.032	0.01	.912		1.53 (.73, 3.17)	.423	1.30	.255
* Major Acculturation Group		0.68 (.39, 1.16)	-0.39	2.01	.156		1.01 (.50, 2.04)	.011	0.01	.976
* *Enculturation Group*		*2.95 (1.31, 6.65)*	*1.08*	*6.76*	*.009*		1.31 (.46, 3.76)	.268	0.25	.619
Step 3—Parental Factors										
* Parent-Child Communications							1.63 (.79, 3.38)	.489	1.73	.189
* *Parental Disapproval of Substance Use* [a]							*0.15 (.05, .44)*	*-1.906*	*12.04*	*.001*
* Parental Monitoring							2.09 (.86, 5.05)	.735	2.65	.103
Step 4—Youth Factors										
* Youth Ethnic Pride							0.90 (.38, 2.17)	-.102	0.05	.819
* Youth Acculturation Stress							2.21 (.97, 5.01)	.791	3.58	.059
* Youth American Cultural Orientation							1.71 (.92, 3.20)	.538	2.84	.092
* Youth Latino Cultural Orientation							1.17 (.56, 2.42)	.156	0.18	.675
Step 5—Peer Factors										
* *Friends Disapproval of Substance Use* [a]							*0.51 (.35, .74)*	*-.68*	*12.36*	*.000*
Block Chi-Square (df)	9.93 (3)					52.77 (8)				
p for Block	.040					.000				
Model Chi-Square (df)	9.96 (4)					62.73 (12)				
p for Model	.040					.000				
Nagelkerke R^2	.090					.476				
Hosmer & Lemeshow Fit Index (df)	13.14 (6)					5.60 (8)				
p for HLFI	.040					.692				

a. Refers to variable for this domain, but measured as youth-reported perceptions.

enculturative change as indicated by a negative acculturative *change trajectory* that indicates the acquisition of Mexican/Latino cultural lifeways.

Model 2: Proximal predictors. Model 2 examined the *proximal* influences of contemporary parent-youth relationship and peer factors, for their effects above and beyond the Model 1 influences of the parental acculturation trajectory groups. Accordingly, Model 2 consisted of three steps that in progressive hierarchical manner examined the effects of: (a) three Parental Factors—Parent-Child Communications, Parental Disapproval of Substance Use (as perceived by the adolescent) and Parental Monitoring; (b) four Youth Factors: Ethnic Pride, Acculturation Stress, American Cultural Orientation and Latino Cultural Orientation; and (c) one Peer Factor—Friends' Disapproval of Substance Use (as perceived by the adolescent).

As shown in Table 3, the results from Model 2 for these proximal variables as predictors of Youth Substance Use Intentions (the composite of model Steps 3, 4, and 5) accounted for a significant increase in predictive variance over and above Model 1, $\chi^2 = 52.77$, $p < .001$. Moreover, this block of proximal factors diminished the significant predictive effects of the distal Enculturation Group factor, as its influences were overshadowed by these more proximal parent-youth and peer-youth relationship factors. Model 2 revealed the presence of two significant protective predictors of Youth Substance Use Intentions: (a) a parental factor—Parental Disapproval of Substance Use, as perceived by the adolescent, OR= 0.15 (CI= .05, .44), $p < .001$; and (b) a peer factor—Friends' Disapproval of Substance Use also as perceived by the adolescent, OR= 0.51 (CI= .35, .74), p< .001. In both instances, the youth's *perceptions* of disapproval from parents and peers served as a potent protective factor against the youth's intentions to use alcohol, tobacco and/or marijuana.

For Model 2, the overall predictive variance was indicated by the Nagelkerke $R^2 = .476$. Also the Hosmer & Lemeshow Fit Index was 5.60 (df= 8) p= .692, which indicates that Model 2 fit the data well. In addition, Model 2 revealed two Youth Factors which were marginally significant at $p < .10$, although offering additional implications for potential predictors of Youth Substance Use Intentions. First, greater Youth Acculturation Stress was associated with higher Youth Substance Use Intentions, OR= 2.21, (CI= 0.97, 5.01; as was greater Youth American Cultural Orientation, OR= 1.71, (CI= 0.92, 3.20). While not significant at the conventional $p < .05$ level, these factors suggest that for Latino adolescents, higher acculturative stress along with a youth's greater orientation toward the mainstream American cultural lifeways are *potential* risk factors for youth intentions to experiment with the use of alcohol, tobacco and/or marijuana.

Effects related to study hypotheses. Study Hypothesis 1 asserted that a *higher* parental acculturative intercept during the parent's adolescence would be associated with *higher* youth intentions to experiment with substances. This hypothesis received partial support, as indicated by higher youth intentions for substance use among the children of parents from the Enculturation Group. However, as noted earlier, for this group it is not clear if the higher levels of youth substance use intentions were related to the parents' higher acculturation intercept (during the parents' adolescent years), or to the negative acculturation slope that depicts an enculturation effect for these parents. Hypothesis 2 that an increasing parental acculturation trajectory, toward the mainstream white American society would be associated with higher youth substance use intentions was *not* supported. Surprisingly, Hypothesis 3 that a positive youth relationship, as indicated by better parent-youth communications and more parental monitoring, was also *not* supported. By contrast, Hypothesis 4 that conservative parental norms that communicate disapproval of substance use would be associated with *lower* youth substance use intentions, did receive strong support.

Discussion

IMPLICATIONS OF STUDY RESULTS

This study examined Latino parents' lifetime acculturation trajectories as potential *distal* sources of influence on their adolescent child's willingness to experiment with the use of alcohol, tobacco and/or marijuana. This study also examined the effects of more *proximal* parent-youth relationship variables on the youth's intentions to experiment with substances. Results of this study provide new insights into the *process of acculturation change*, as it may exert direct and indirect influences on Latino parents' teachings and parenting behaviors, and these may subsequently influence the behaviors of their adolescent children. The present study may be one of the first to examine *lifetime acculturation change* as process-of-change factors, based on the identification of distinct parental acculturation trajectories, and to the relation of these trajectories with their adolescent's willingness to experiment with various "gateway" substances.

This line of research seeks to move beyond the contemporary stalemate in acculturation research that has been limited by the cross-sectional analysis of acculturation levels, which implicitly but inaccurately have been used to infer acculturative changes and their effects based on data from a single point in time. Even in their rudimentary form, the results of the present study offer a deeper level of analysis regarding cultural and other factors that may influence Latino youths' intentions to use various substances. Given the complexities and nuances involved in the study of *cultural factors* (Castro & Hernandez-Alarcon, 2002) as influences on the behaviors of Latino parents and their children, the present study results should be regarded as preliminary in nature and subject to further and more detailed analyses that examine other *contextual factors* that may modify the meaning of the present results (Schwartz, Ungar, Zamboanga & Szapocznik, 2010).

STUDY LIMITATIONS

In this study we utilized a one-factor scale, although with a consideration of the early-life acculturation intercept and of the adult acculturation level, to assess acculturation and enculturation trajectories. In the present study we conducted this data collection using a self-report survey approach for two life milestones (adolescence and current adulthood). This contrasts with other prior studies that utilized a more comprehensive in-depth face-to-face interview that assesses four life milestones (childhood, early adolescence, late adolescence and current adulthood), and in which participant responses could be clarified and confirmed by the interviewer. In summary, the present study presents preliminary acculturation trajectory outcomes that are based on this more abbreviated form of acculturation change assessment, involving only two life milestones, rather than for four life milestones as in a previous study utilizing this methodology (Castro, Marsiglia, Kulis & Kellison, 2010).

Nonetheless, the present approach offers preliminary yet informative and perhaps novel results which provide insights into distal and proximal parental influences on Latino youths' early substance use behaviors. This approach offers a new and more informative paradigm for the study of acculturation as a *process of change*, and how this process may influence the here-and-now behaviors of Latino parents and their children. As we advance beyond prior cross-sectional assessments of acculturation change, we seek to model such changes under a paradigm that depicts a more ecologically valid view of the dynamic process of acculturative change.

FUTURE DIRECTIONS

Improvements in future studies. As a direction for future research, future studies may expand on the use of this abbreviated retrospective assessment. Future studies may be improved by incorporating this retrospective assessment for more than two earlier life milestones, and also by the use of in-depth face-to-face interviews, as we have conducted in our prior research. The in-depth interview approach using a variation of the timeline follow-back allows for probing and clarification of participant self-reports in a manner that increases accuracy and validity of self-report (Brown et al., 1998). Future studies may also utilize a broader sampling frame to obtain a more diverse representation of acculturation levels, thus increasing the study's capacity to identify additional latent acculturation trajectories that were not represented by the lifetime acculturative change trajectories generated for this particular sample of parents. For example, the present study did not obtain a sample of *highly acculturated* Mexican-American and other Latino parents who would thus exhibit a high-acculturation intercept at their early adolescence (middle school) life milestone. Thus, other acculturation change trajectories could have emerged for these higher-acculturation cases, where these were not observed within the present study.

Remarkable observations. The present study conducted a disaggregation of differing acculturation trajectories for cases that would otherwise appear to have the same or similar levels of acculturation when examined solely under a single-point-in-time analysis that is conducted at the contemporary adult life milestone. This disaggregation thus identified important *subcultural groups* (Castro, Barrera & Holleran Steiker, 2010) based on their lifetime acculturation change trajectories. As noted, this methodology provides a modeled approach for understanding acculturation as a *temporal change process* that is congruent with the original conceptualization of acculturation as a naturally occurring process of change and adaptation occurring across time and location.

A notable observation from the present study is that for a large proportion of cases of Mexican-heritage adults, level of acculturation *does not change much*, even when examined across a life period of 10 to 50 years. Nonetheless, for a certain proportion of cases, acculturation change was significant and directional (acculturation to the mainstream dominant culture, or to the native minority Latino culture), thus identifying important subgroups of cases which changed remarkably in their acculturative status across time. In this regard, one important question is, "Why did some of these parents undergo remarkable levels of change in their acculturative status, whereas others exhibited no acculturative change?" Future studies may address this issue of individual differences in levels and types of acculturative change to identify factors, including those from Segmented Assimilation Theory, that influence the process of *acculturative change* and *enculturative change*. Furthermore, future research studies may examine the characteristics and predictive effects of each of the nine distinct acculturative change trajectories, based on systematic variations on two factors: (a) *Early Life Acculturation Intercept* (low acculturation level, bicultural level or high acculturation level), and (b) *Type of Acculturation Change* (increasing acculturation change, no change and decreasing acculturation change).

Improving Latino parenting practices. Regarding the promotion of protective parenting practices that can safeguard their adolescent children against various risk behaviors including experimentation with substance use, the present study highlights the importance of parental and peer disapproval of youth substance use as a potent deterrent against youth experimentation with various substances. This suggests that *conservative norms* that express disapproval of substance use operate as significant protective factors that should be incorporated into parent education for Latino and other parents of adolescent children, as a significant tool to discourage youth experimentation with various substances.

Given the importance of parental disapproval, it should be noted that the influence of parental disapproval exists *within the context* of a functional parent-youth relationship, i.e., a family having high levels of *family functioning*, as measured by (a) parental involvement, (b) parent-adolescent communications, (c) positive parenting and (d) family support (Prado et al., 2007). In this regard, youths will care about parental disapproval and respond to it if the youth lives within a functional family system in which the parent cares about and is involved with their child in a positive manner, and in which the adolescent child has a positive relationship with their parent. By contrast, in the extreme case in which the child lives in a dysfunctional family in which the parents lack care and involvement with their child, and the child has a poor or non-attached relationship with a parent, that adolescent child would disregard or dismiss a parent's disapprovals regarding substance use or experimentation. In this regard, the quality of the parent-child relationship matters as a *contextual basis* from which parental disapproval of youth substance use can be influential in protecting the child from engagement in risk behaviors, and in promoting positive youth development.

Finally, further study is indicated by the current finding with parents from this sample, that parents having an early life bicultural identity and who exhibit an enculturative trajectory had children who exhibited higher intentions to engage in substance use. Indeed, what is it about this acculturation profile, perhaps as mediated proximally by more permissive parental practices (including less disapproval of youth substance use), that may prompt greater youth intentions to engage in substance use? Based on preliminary findings from the present study of Latino parents, this is an interesting research question worthy of future study and greater depth of analysis.

Acknowledgements

We warmly thank Dr. Flavio F. Marsiglia and Dr. Monica Bermudez Parsai for their thoughtful comments in an earlier version of this chapter.

References

Amaro, H., Whittaker, R., & Heeren, T. (1990). Acculturation and marijuana and cocaine use: Findings from HHANES 1982-84. *American Journal of Public Health, Suppl. 80,* 54-60.

Balcazar, H., Castro, F. G., & Krull, J. L. (1995). Cancer risk reduction in Mexican-American women: The role of acculturation, education, and health risk factors. *Health Education Quarterly, 22(1),* 61-84.

Barnes, G. M., Hoffman, J. H., Welte, J. W., Farrell, M. P., & Dintcheff, B. A. (2006). Effects of parental monitoring and peer deviance on substance use and delinquency. *Journal of Marriage and the Family, 68,* 1084-1104.

Berry, J. W. (1997). Immigration, acculturation, and adaptation. *Applied Psychology: An International Review, 46,* 5-68.

Berry, J. W. (2005). Acculturation: Living successfully in two cultures. *International Journal of Intercultural Relations, 29,* 697-712.

Baldwin, J. R., & Lindsley, S. L. (1994). *Conceptualizations of culture.* Tempe, AZ: Arizona State University.

Bollen, K. A., & Curran, P. J. (2006). *Latent curve models: A structural equations perspective.* Hoboken, NJ: Wiley.

Brown, R. A., Burgess, E. S., Sales, S. D., Whiteley, J. A., Evans, D. M., & Miller, I. W. (1998). Reliability and validity of a smoking timeline follow-back interview. *Psychology of Addictive Behaviors, 12,* 101-112.

Cabassa, L. J. (2003). Measuring acculturation: Where we are and where we need to do. *Hispanic Journal of Behavioral Sciences, 25,* 127-146.

Carranza, M. E. (2007). Building resilience and resistance against racism and discrimination among Salvadoran female youth in Canada. *Child and Family Social Work, 12,* 390-398.

Castro, F. G., Barrera, M., & Holleran Steiker, L. K. (2010). Issues and challenges in the design of culturally-adapted evidence-based interventions. *Annual Review of Clinical Psychology, 6,* 213-239.

Castro, F. G., Balcazar, H., & Cota, M. (2007). Health promotion in Latino populations: Program planning, development, and evaluation. In M. V. Kline & R. M. Huff (Eds.), *Promoting health in multicultural populations* (2nd ed.) (pp. 222-253). Thousand Oaks, CA: Sage.

Castro, F. G., Boyer, G. R., & Balcazar, H. G. (2000). Healthy adjustment in Mexican-American and other Latino adolescents. In R. Montemayor, G. R. Adams & T. P. Gullotta (Eds.), *Adolescent diversity in ethnic, economic and cultural contexts* (pp. 141-178). Thousand Oaks, CA: Sage.

Castro, F. G., Garfinkle, J., Naranjo, D., Rollins, M, Brook, J. S., & Brook, D. (2006). Cultural traditions as protective factors among Latino children of illicit drug users. *Substance Use and Misuse, 42, 621-642.*

Castro, F. G., & Gutierres, S. (1997). Drug and alcohol use among rural Mexican Americans. In E. R. Robertson, Z. Sloboda, G. M. Boyd, L. Beatty, N. J. Kozel (Eds.), *Rural substance abuse: State of knowledge and issues.* NIDA Research Monograph No. 168 (pp. 499-533). Rockville, MD: National Institute on Drug Abuse.

Castro, F. G., & Hernández-Alarcón, E. (2002). Integrating cultural variables into drug abuse prevention and treatment with racial/ethnic minorities. *Journal of Drug Issues, 32,* 783-810.

Castro, F. G., Marsiglia, F. F., Kulis, S., & Kellison, J. G. (2010). Lifetime segmented assimilation trajectories and health outcomes in Latino and other community residents. *American Journal of Public Health, 100(4),* 669-676.

Castro, F. G., & Murray, K. E. (2010). Cultural adaptation and resilience: Controversies, issues, and emerging models. In J. W. Reich, A. J. Zautra & J. S. Hall (Eds.), *Handbook of adult resilience: Concepts, methods and applications* (pp. 375—403). New York: Guilford.

Chao, G. T., & Moon, H. (2005). The cultural mosaic: A metatheory for understanding the complexity of culture. *Journal of Applied Psychology, 90,* 1128-1140.

Collins, L. M. (1991). Measurement in longitudinal research. In L. M. Collins & J. L. Horn (Eds.), *Best methods for the analysis of change: Recent advances, unanswered questions, future directions* (pp. 137-148). Washington, DC: American Psychological Association.

Coersino, M. L., Meade, C. S., Bigelow, G. E., & Brooner, R. K. (2010). Measurement of self-reported HIV risk behaviors in injection drug users: Comparison of standard versus timeline follow-back administration procedures. *Journal of Substance Abuse Treatment, 38,* 60-65.

Cuadrado, M., & Lieberman, L. (1998). Traditionalism in the prevention of substance misuse among Puerto Ricans. *Substance Use and Misuse, 33,* 2737-2755.

Cuellar, I., Arnold, B., & Gonzalez, G. (1995). Cognitive referents of acculturation: Assessment of cultural constructs in Mexican Americans. *Journal of Community Psychology, 23,* 339-356.

Cuellar, I., Harris, L. C., & Jasso, R. (1980). An acculturation scale for Mexican-American normal and clinical populations. *Hispanic Journal of Behavioral Sciences, 2,* 199-217.

Cuellar, I., Arnold, B., & Maldonado, R. (1995). Acculturation rating scale for Mexican-Americans II: A revision of the original ARMSA scale. *Hispanic Journal of Behavioral Sciences, 17,* 275-304.

Dishion, T. J., Reid, J. B., & Patterson, G. R. (1988). Empirical guidelines for a family intervention for adolescent drug use. *Journal of Chemical Dependency Treatment, 1,* 189-224.

Ehrman, R. N., & Robbins, S. J. (1994). Reliability and validity of 6-month reports of cocaine and heroin use in a methadone population. *Journal of Consulting and Clinical Psychology, 62,* 843-850.

Elder, J. P., Broyles, S. L., Brennan, J. J., Zúñiga de Nuncio, M. L., & Nader, P. R. (2005). Acculturation, parent-child acculturation differential, and chronic disease risk factors in a Mexican-American population. *Journal of Immigrant Health, 7,* 1-9.

Farver, J. A., Narang, S. K., & Bhadha, B. R. (2002). East meets west: Ethnic identity, acculturation, and conflict in Asian Indian families. *Journal of Family Psychology, 16,* 338-350.

Gorman-Smith, D., Tolman, P. H., Zelli, A., & Rowell, H. L. (1996). The relation of family function to violence among inner-city minority youth. *Journal of Family Psychology, 10,* 115-129.

Hanson, W. (1992). School-based substance abuse prevention: A review of the state of the art in curriculum, 1980-1990. *Health Education and Research, 7,* 403-430.

Harris, P. R., & Morgan, R. T. (1987). *Managing cultural differences: Higher-performance strategies for today's global manager.* Houston: Gulf.

Haynes, S. G., Harvey, C., Montes, H., Nickens, H., & Cohen, B. H. (1990). Patterns of cigarette smoking among Hispanics in the United States: Results from HHANES 1982-84. *American Journal of Public Health, 80,* 47-53.

Hoeve, M., Blockland, A., Dubas, J. S., Loeber, R., Gerris, J. R., & van der Laan, P. H. (2008). Trajectories of delinquency and parenting styles. *Journal of Abnormal Child Psychology, 36,* 223-235.

Hunt, L. M., Schneider, S., & Comer, B. (2004). Should "acculturation" be a variable in health research? A critical review of research on U.S. Hispanics. *Social Science & Medicine, 59,* 973-986.

Klohnen, E. C. (1996). Conceptual analysis and measurement of the construct of ego-resiliency. *Journal of Personality and Social Psychology, 70,* 1067-1079.

LaFromboise, T., Coleman, H. L. K., & Gerton, J. (1993). Psychological impact of biculturalism: Evidence and theory. *Psychological Bulletin, 114,* 395-412.

Lara, M., Gamboa, C., Kahramanian, M. I., Morales, L. S., & Hayes-Bautista, D. E. (2005). Acculturation and Latino health in the United States: A review of the literature and its sociopolitical context. *Annual Review of Public Health, 26,* 367-397.

Lehman, D. R., Chiu, C., & Schaller, M. (2004). Psychology and culture. *Annual Review of Psychology, 55,* 689-714.

Locke, D. C. (1998). *Increasing multicultural understanding: A comprehensive model* (2nd ed.). Thousand Oaks, CA: Sage.

Maisto, S. A., Sobell, M. B., Cooper, A. M., & Sobell, L. C. (1979). Test-retest reliability of retrospective self-reports in three populations of alcohol abusers. *Journal of Behavioral Medicine, 1,* 315-326.

Marin, G., & Gamboa, R. J. (1996). A new measurement of acculturation for Latinos: The Bidimensional Acculturation Scale for Latinos (BAS). *Latino Journal of Behavioral Sciences, 18,* 297-316.

Markides, K. S., Ray, L. A., Stroup-Benham, C. A., & Treviño, F. (1990). Acculturation and alcohol consumption in the Mexican-American population of the Southwestern United States: Findings from HHANES 1982-84. *American Journal of Public Health, 80* (Supp.), 42-46.

Marks, G., Garcia, M., & Solis, J. M. (1990). Health risk behaviors of Hispanics in the United States: Findings from HHANES 1982-84. *American Journal of Public Health, 80,* 20-26.

Massey, D. S., Durand, J., & Malone, N. J. (2002). *Beyond smoke and mirrors: Mexican immigration in an era of economic integration.* New York: Russel Sage Foundation.

Masten, A. S. (2001). Ordinary people: Resilience process in development. *American Psychologist, 56,* 227-238.

McArdle, J. J., & Hamagami, F. (1991). Modeling incomplete longitudinal and cross-sectional data using latent growth structural models. In L. M. Collins & J. L. Horn (Eds.), *Best methods for the analysis of change: Recent advances, unanswered questions, future directions* (pp. 276-304). Washington, DC: American Psychological Association

McGoldrick, M., & Giordano, J. (1996). Overview: Ethnicity and family therapy. In M. McGoldrick, J. Giordano & J. K. Pearce (Eds.), *Ethnicity and family therapy* (2nd ed.) (pp. 1-27). New York: Guilford Press.

Oetting, E. R., & Beauvais, F. (1990). Orthogonal cultural identification theory: The cultural identification of minority adolescents. *International Journal of Addictions, 25*(5A-6A), 655-685.

Pantin, H., Coatsworth, J. D., & Feaster, D. J., Newman, F. L., Briones, E., Prado, G., Schwartz, S. J., Szapocznik, J. (2003). Familas Unidas: The efficacy of an intervention to promote parental investment in Hispanic immigrant families. *Prevention Science, 4,* 189-201.

Pantin, H., Schwartz, S. J., Sullivan, S., Prado, G., & Szapocznik, J. (2004). Ecodevelopmental HIV prevention program for Hispanic adolescents. *American Journal of Orthopsychiatry, 74,* 545-588.

Parsai, M. B., Castro, F. G., Marsiglia, F. F., Harthun, M., & Valdez, H. (2011). Using community based participatory research to create a culturally grounded intervention for parents and youth to prevent risky behaviors. *Prevention Science*, 12 (1): 34-47.

Pedraza, S. (2003). Cuba's refugees: Manifold migrations. In I. L. Horowitz & J. Suchlicki (Eds.), *Cuban communism: 1959-2003* (11th ed.) (pp. 308-328). New Brunswick, NJ: Transaction Publishers.

Petrie, J., Bunn, F., & Byrne, G. (2007). Parenting programmes for preventing tobacco, alcohol or drugs misuse in children < 18: A systematic review. *Health Education Research, 22,* 177-191.

Pilgrim, C. C., Schulenberg, J. E., O'Malley, P., Bachman, J. G., & Johnson, L. D. (2006). Mediators and moderators of parental involvement on substance use: A national study of adolescents. *Prevention Science, 7,* 75-89.

Portes, A. (1997). Immigration theory for a new century: some problems and opportunities. *International Migration Review, 31,* 799-825.

Portes, A., & Rumbaut, R. G. (1996). *Immigrant America: A portrait.* Berkeley: University of California Press.

Portes, A., & Zhou, M. (1993). The new second generation: Segmented assimilation and its variants. *Annals of the American Academy of Political and Social Science, 530,* 74-96.

Ramirez, M. (1999). *Multicultural psychotherapy: An approach to individual and cultural differences* (2nd ed.). Boston, MA: Allyn & Bacon.

Redfield, R., Linton, R., & Herskovits, M. J. (1936). Memorandum for the study of acculturation. *American Anthropologist, 38,* 149-152.

Riggs, N. R., Elfenbaum, P., & Pentz, M. A. (2006). Parent program component analysis in a Drug Abuse Prevention Trial. *Journal of Adolescent Health, 39,* 66-72.

Rogler, L. H. (1994). International migrations. A framework for directing research. *American Psychologist, 49,* 701-708.

Rogler, L. H., Cortes, D. E., & Malgady, R. G. (1991). Acculturation and mental health status among Hispanics. *American Psychologist, 46,* 585-597.

Rudmin, F. W. (2003). Critical history of the acculturation psychology of assimilation, separation, integration, and marginalization. *Review of General Psychology, 7,* 3-37.

Ryder, A. G. Alden, L. E., & Paulhus, D. L. (2000). Is acculturation unidirectional or bidirectional? A head-to-head comparison in the prediction of personality, self-identity and adjustment. *Journal of Personality and Social Psychology, 79,* 49-65.

Schwartz, S. J., Montgomery, M. J., & Briones, E. (2006). The role of identity in acculturation among immigrant people: Theoretical propositions, empirical questions, and applied recommendations. *Human Development, 49,* 1-30.

Schwartz, S. J., Ungar, J. B., Zamboanga, B. L., & Szapocznik, J. (2010). Rethinking the concept of acculturation: Implications for theory and research. *American Psychologist, 65,* 237-251.

Schwartz, S. J., & Zamboanga, B. L. (2008). Testing Berry's model of acculturation: A confirmatory latent class approach. *Cultural Diversity and Ethnic Minority Psychology, 14,* 275-285.

Sobell, L. C., Maisto, S. A., Sobell, M. B., & Cooper, A. M. (1979). Reliability of alcohol abusers' self-reports of drinking behavior. Behavior Research and Therapy, 17, 157-160.

Sobell, L. C., & Sobell, M. B. (1978). Validity of self-reports in three populations of alcoholics. *Journal of Consulting and Clinical Psychology, 46,* 901-907.

Sobell, L. C., & Sobell, M. B. (1996). *Alcohol timeline followback (TLFB) users manual.* Toronto: Addiction Research Foundation.

Solis, J. M., Marks, G., Garcia, M., & Shelton, D. (1990). Acculturation, access to care, and use of preventive services by Hispanics: Results from HHANES 1982-84. *American Journal of Public Health, 80,* 11-19.

Tapia, M. I., Schwartz, S. J., Prado, G., Lopez, B., & Pantin, H. (2006). Parent-centered intervention: A practical approach for preventing drug abuse in Hispanic adolescents. *Research in Social Work Practice, 16,* 146-165.

Tragesser, S. L., Beauvais, F., Swaim, R. C., Edwards, R. W., & Oetting, E. R. (2007). Parental monitoring, peer drug involvement, and marijuana use across three ethnicities. *Journal of Cross-Cultural Psychology, 38,* 670-694.

Triandis, H., & Suh, E. M. (2002). Cultural influences on personality. *Annual Review of Psychology, 53,* 133-160.

Velleman, R. D. B., Templeton, L. J., & Copello, A. G. (2005). The role of family in preventing and intervening with substance use and misuse: A comprehensive review of family interventions, with a focus on young people. *Drug and Alcohol Review, 24,* 93-109.

Viruell-Fuentes, E. A. (2007). Beyond acculturation: Immigration, discrimination, and health research among Mexicans in the United States. *Social Science and Medicine, 65,* 1524-1535.

Wasserman, G., Miller, L. S., Pinner, E., & Jaramillo, B. (1996). Parenting predictors of early conduct problems in urban high-risk boys. *Journal of the American Academy of Child & Adolescent Psychiatry, 35,* 1227-1236.

Zhou, M. (1997). Growing up American: The challenge confronting immigrant children and children of immigrants. *Annual Review of Sociology, 23,* 63-95.

CHAPTER 10

ECONOMIC ANALYSIS OF TREATING AND PREVENTING TYPE 2 DIABETES IMPLICATIONS FOR LATINO FAMILIES

Roberto P. Treviño[1]

Type 2 diabetes is prevalent among Latinos. Given that obesity is a major risk factor for type 2 diabetes, it is not surprising that obesity is also more prevalent among Latinos. Addressing childhood obesity prevention among Latino children is crucial to controlling type 2 diabetes among this population. Thus, the first objective of this chapter is to present the epidemiology of type 2 diabetes and obesity among Latino children. The second objective is to present evidence-based programs that have been shown to decrease blood glucose and obesity levels among this special children population. Because type 2 diabetes and obesity are costly diseases, the third objective is to present an economic analysis to determine if prevention is more cost-effective than treatment. The economic analysis, however, is in adults because no such studies have been conducted in children.

Type 2 Diabetes Rates and Economic Consequences

Type 2 diabetes is an old disease in a new host. Type 2 diabetes was unheard of in children before 1990 (Fajans, 1990). After 1990 more reports started coming out showing the increased number of new cases of type 2 diabetes and high levels of diabetes risk factors in children (Neufeld, Chen & Raffel, 1998; Treviño et al., 2009; Treviño et al., 1999). There is an estimated 2.8 million youth with either

---

[1]Director, Social and Health Research Center, San Antonio, Texas.

pre-diabetes or type 2 diabetes (Duncan, 2006). The percent of children with impaired fasting glucose, according to this study, was 15.3%, 11.3% and 7.4% for Latino, non-Hispanic white and non-Hispanic black children, respectively.

Diabetes complications are serious. People with diabetes are at increased risk for stroke, myocardial infarction, blindness, end-stage renal disease and lower extremity amputation (Ninomiya et al., 2004; Orchard et al., 1990). And diabetes is an exceedingly costly disease. In 2007, the cost of diabetes in medical expenditures and loss of worker productivity was estimated to be $174 billion in the United States (American Diabetes Association, 2008). Of these, $116 billion was attributed to medical cost and $58 billion to loss of productivity (absence from work, reduced productivity at work and at home, unemployment from chronic disability and premature mortality). The average annual cost to provide medical care to an individual with diabetes is estimated at $11,744. Annual health care expenditures are 2.3 times higher in people with diabetes than in people without diabetes ($11,744 vs. $5,095). Table 1 shows the expenses by health care system category. Hospitals and pharmaceutical drugs explain 74% of the annual medical expenditure. Because diabetes is a serious and costly disease, a prudent action would be to invest in primary prevention.

Table 1. Annual Medical Expenditures by Category and Percent to Treat One Patient with Diabetes

CATEGORY	COST	PERCENT
Hospital (in- and out-patient and E.R.)	6,459	55
Pharmaceutical (insulin, oral agents for diabetes and diabetes complication)	2,231	19
Physician	1,174	10
Nursing home	1,057	9
Home health care	587	5
Diabetes and non-diabetes medical supplies	235	2
Total	11,744	100

Source: ADA, Diabetes Care, 2008

Obesity Rates and Economic Consequences

Obesity is usually the precursor of diabetes. Studies have shown that the prevalence of diabetes increases by 9% for every kilogram gained in weight; and after a weight loss of 4.7% of total body weight, the incidence of diabetes decreases by 58% (Mokdad et al., 2001). Childhood obesity is an increasing problem. Obesity in children has been associated with higher rates of adult obesity, hypertension and diabetes (Lee, 2008; Mei et al., 1998). Figure 1 shows the prevalence of obesity of children over time by race/ethnicity (Malina, Zavaleta & Little, 1986; Ogden et al., 2006; Ogden, Carroll & Flegal, 2008; Troiano, Flegal, Kuczmarski, Campbell & Johnson, 1995; Zavaleta & Malina, 1980). Childhood obesity has increased in all ethnic/racial groups but the increase has been more pronounced in Latino children. Between 1965 and 2006 the prevalence of obesity increased 3-fold, 5-fold and 8-fold among non-Hispanic white, African-American and Latino children, respectively.

Figure 1. Obesity Prevalence Trends by Race/Ethnicity in Children Age 6 to 11 Years

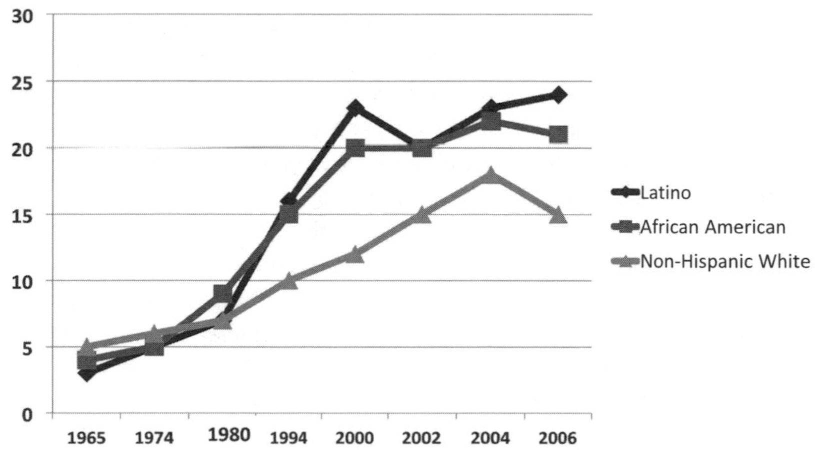

Source: Zavaleta, *Am J Clin Nutr*, 1980; Malina, *Int J Obes* 1986; Ogden, *JAMA*, 2006; Ogden, *JAMA*, 2008.

Obesity imposes a great financial burden in the form of medical expenditures (direct costs) and loss of worker productivity (indirect costs). Obese employees were 1.74 times more likely to experience high levels of absenteeism (7 or more absences per 6 mo) than were their leaner counterparts (Finkelstein, Ruhm & Kosa, 2005). Estimated obesity-attributable absenteeism cost employers $2.95 billion in 2003.

Not only do obese people and employers get affected financially. So does the general population. The average taxpayer spends approximately $175 more per year to finance obesity-related medical expenditures among Medicare and Medicaid recipients (Finkelstein, Trogdon, Cohen & Dietz, 2009). The reason is that annual health care expenditures are 1.4 times higher in people who are obese than in people who are not obese ($4,870 vs. $3,400).

Updated to 2003 dollars, the 2001 U.S. Surgeon General's report on obesity stated that annual indirect costs of obesity total $64 billion, which suggests that the total (direct and indirect) costs of obesity may now be $139 billion per year. This cost is about 5% to 7% of the total U.S. annual health care expenditure.

Dietary and Sedentary Lifestyle Trends Associated with Obesity

Obesity is usually the precursor to diabetes and to prevent diabetes, it is important to understand when and why obesity rates started to rise. Knowing the history of obesity gives society knowledge of how it got there, and provides a roadmap to get back on a healthy life track. Figure 1 shows a small increase in childhood obesity prevalence between 1965 and 1980 and a large increase between 1980 and 2004. The rapid rise of obesity that occurred in 1980 in the U.S. population, and particularly in Latinos, may be explained by the dietary and sedentary lifestyle patterns that occurred in this society at that time.

The U.S. Department of Agriculture has conducted two surveys biannually to measure what and how much food Americans consume. The Continuing Survey of Food Intakes by Individual records what respondents eat over a specific time period, and demographic information such as household size, income, race, age and sex. The U.S. Food Supply Series survey records what food producers produce annually and record their inventories at the beginning and end of a year. Following are results from the two surveys conducted by the USDA.

Figure 2 shows that in 1980 there was a sudden increase of flour and sweets consumption, and no increase in fresh fruits and vegetables consumption (Putnam, Allshouse & Kantor, 2002). Servings of flour per capita per day increased by 0.9% per year between 1970 and 1980, and by 1.7% per year between 1980

Figure 2. Servings Per Capita Per Day Over 30 Years

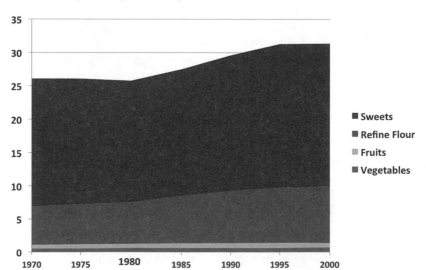

Source: Putnam, *Food Review*, 2002.

and 2000. Teaspoons of sweets per capita per day decreased by -0.05% per year between 1970 and 1980 and increased by 1.1% per year between 1980 and 2000.

Tablespoons of fats and oils per capita per day showed no difference in increase between 1970 and 1980 and between 1980 and 2000 (1.1% per year). Similarly, servings of meats per capita per day increased only by 0.2% per year between 1970 and 1980 and by 0.4% per year between 1980 and 2000.

The rapid rise of obesity seen in 1980 correlates more with increase consumption of processed carbohydrates than with proteins and lipids. Carbohydrates are converted to triglycerides, and triglycerides fill the adipose cell. It is triglycerides that "stuff" the adipose cell to increase their size. This is a problem because once an adipose cell increases to a certain size it triggers new adipose cell numbers to be formed. An adipose cell can be reduced in size but not reduced in numbers (terminal differentiation) (Rosenbaum & Leibel, 1998).

Another major national event that occurred around 1980 was the invention of personal computers. The first personal computers, Altair, Commodore, Radio Shack and Apple, came out in 1977; and the first IBM model in 1981 (Reimer, 2005). *Time* Magazine featured the personal computer in its front cover as the "Machine of the Year for 1982." This was the first time a non-human had won that award. Figure 3 shows the trend in personal computer sales. This graphs shows that starting in 1980 the personal computer may have transformed Amer-

Figure 3. Personal Computer Sales (thousands of units)

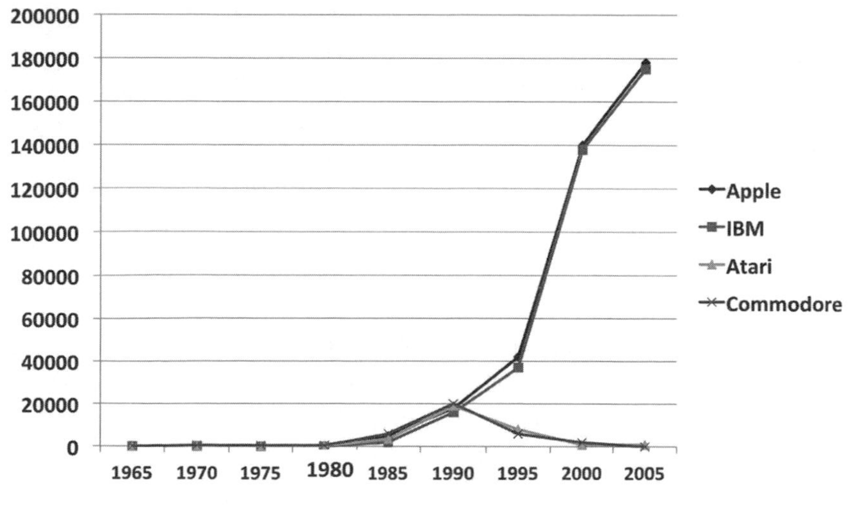

Source: Reimer, *Ars Technica*, 2005.

ican society lifestyle from active to sedentary. Thus, the major events that may have triggered the rise of obesity in the United States in 1980 were processed carbohydrates and sedentary lifestyles. For Latinos in particular, these new behaviors were counter-culture because of their ancestors historically consuming higher levels of complex carbohydrates (produce) and living more active lifestyles (labor).

Children's Diabetes Prevention Programs

BIENESTAR/NEEMA COORDINATED SCHOOL HEALTH PROGRAM

The increase of new cases of youth-onset type 2 diabetes and high levels of diabetes risk factors in children has led to the design of diabetes prevention programs for children. It is clear that school settings are ideal for influencing and regulating dietary intake and physical activity (PA) in children. Schools typically provide 1-2 meals per day, often provide opportunities for structured exercise and are a natural setting for instruction about healthy food choices and PA.

The *Bienestar*/NEEMA health program is a coordinated school health program designed to decrease blood glucose levels in high-risk children. *Bienestar* means wellbeing in Spanish and NEEMA means wellbeing in Swahili. Culturally appropriate interventions were developed for the four environments that are likely to influence children's health behaviors. The four environments include home, school classroom, school physical education (PE) and school cafeteria. All activities reinforce the four *Bienestar* healthy behavior aims—decrease dietary saturated fats and sugars; increase fruits, vegetables and grains; decrease TV viewing; and increase PA. The *Bienestar*/NEEMA health curricula is designed for pre-kindergarten to eight grades, and all the instructional material is bilingual (English and Spanish). Each grade level includes a Health Curriculum Teacher's Guide and Student Workbook; Cafeteria Program Teacher's Guide and Food Service Staff Workbook; Physical Education Curriculum Teacher's Guide; and Family Times Take Home Program. Following are the four components of the *Bienestar*/NEEMA health program (see Figure 4).

Physical Education Curriculum consists of 100 age-adjusted moderate to vigorous physical activity (MVPA). Lessons plans include skills and drills for basketball, football, soccer, softball, team handball, track and field, volleyball, badminton and tennis. Lessons were created to target the heart rate at or above 140 heartbeats per minute for half of the class period. PE lessons are taught four days a week and PE teachers teach the curriculum.

Health Curriculum consists of 12 to 24 lesson plans depending on the grade level. The lesson plans are taught once a week consecutively and are taught by the class-

Figure 4. Bienestar/NEEMA health program components

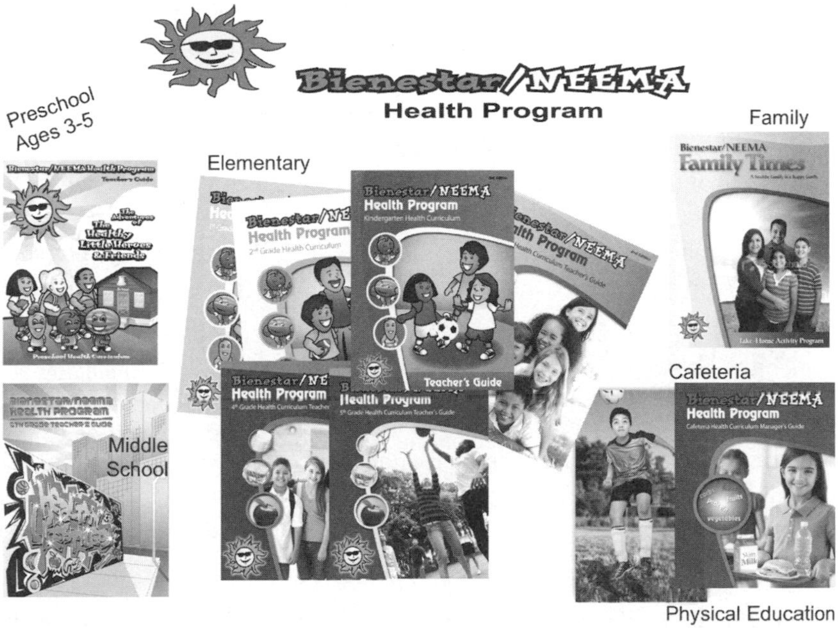

room teacher. Lesson plan topics include themes on nutrition, body awareness, physical fitness, obesity prevention, diabetes prevention and personal health. It also includes a pre-post knowledge test for each grade level.

Cafeteria Program consists of 9 lessons that are taught to food service staff once a week at the beginning of each school year. Lessons are taught by a trained food service manager or supervisor and takes approximately 20 minutes during morning breaks. Lessons include topics on basic nutrition, dietary guidelines, MyPyramid, preparing healthy meals and trays, food safety, portion control, reducing waste, diabetes prevention and healthy living.

Family Times Newsletters consists of 9 take-home issues that are distributed to families on a monthly basis. The issues encourage families to practice healthy behaviors at home. Some of the behaviors encouraged are to walk at least 150 minutes a week preferably after dinner, eat a combination of 5 fruits and vegetables a day, limit TV viewing to 2 hours a day and read food labels. The issue is reviewed with the child before it is sent home so the child can reinforce the health behaviors.

An efficacy trial was conducted to evaluate the impact of the *Bienestar*/NEEMA health program on fasting capillary glucose (FCG) levels in fourth-grade students (Treviño et al., 2004). Near 80% of the participating children were Mexican American. This study was undertaken during the 2001-2002 school year, and it involved a cluster randomized trial with 13 intervention (n=713) and 14 control (n=706) elementary schools located in socially deprived neighborhoods in San Antonio, Texas. Dietary intake was assessed using 24-hour dietary recalls. Three 24-hour dietary recalls, including 2 weekdays and a Sunday or holiday, were collected and recorded by trained staff. Physical fitness was measured using a modified Harvard step test. FCG was measured by collecting a blood drop from a student's finger-stick. The blood drop was placed in a reagent strip and inserted into an Ascencia Elite XL (Bayer Corp., Mishawaka, IN 46544). A FCG test result > 100 mg/dl was considered a positive screen.

Mean FCG levels decreased in intervention schools relative to control schools [mean difference (intervention minus control) =-2.24 mg/dl, p=0.03] at the end of the intervention. Intervention children experienced a significant increase in mean fitness score and mean dietary fiber intake. Intervention children did not differ significantly from control children with regard to the mean percentage of body fat (p=0.56) and mean dietary saturated fat intake (p=0.34).

NEEMA COORDINATED SCHOOL HEALTH PROGRAM

NEEMA, like *Bienestar*, is a coordinated school health program but aimed at decreasing blood glucose levels in high-risk African-American children. The four components of the *Bienestar* health program were translated into instructional materials more compatible with the African-American family life and culture. The translation team was composed of an African-American researcher and three African-American staff members from the Social and Health Research Center with combined six years' experience developing and implementing the *Bienestar* health program. The team modified pictures, names of people, activities, some language and foods in the curriculum to be more representative of the African-American culture and experience.

Five elementary schools were selected to participate because of their high African-American enrollment (Shaw-Perry et al., 2007). Of 162 African-American fourth-grade students enrolled in the five participating elementary schools, 68 (42%) gave assent and parent consent. Fasting capillary glucose, height and weight were obtained. Fitness was measured by the 20-meter shuttle run test (20-MST).

At baseline, 22% of students were obese (BMI ≥ 95th percentile) and 19% had high blood glucose levels (≥ 100 mg/dl). The laps completed in the 20-MST increased from 16.40 at baseline to 23.72 at follow-up (p=0.000). Fasting capillary glucose decreased from 89.17 mg/dl to 83.50 mg/dl, respectively (p=0.000). Although mean BMI increased from 20.30 to 20.81 (p=0.003), body fat decreased from 27.26 to 26.68 (p=0.537). BMI may have increased, despite decreased body fat, because of children's increased fitness levels increasing lean body mass.

HEALTHY Coordinated School Health Program

The HEALTHY study group developed and evaluated a multi-component middle school curricula aimed at reducing diabetes risk factors. The HEALTHY intervention is a middle school coordinated health program aimed at modifying school and home environments that may have an influence on youth's health behaviors. The four intervention components aimed at modifying the environments were behavior, nutrition, PE and social marketing. Following is a description of the four HEALTHY components.

Behavior Components consisted of the FLASH classroom lesson plans and Family Newsletters. The FLASH are sixth to eight grade health curriculums that include a teacher's guide and student's workbook. There were 10 lessons for each grade level, and the topics included healthy beverages, PA, nutrition, food labels, balanced meals, portion size, eating low-fat snacks and making healthy choices. The book contents were in color and the lessons were written in English and Spanish. The lessons were taught once a week by science or social study teachers over a 40-minute period class. The Family Newsletters were seven bilingual issues that included healthy tips, recipes, program updates and testimonials. Before distributing to the parents, the FLASH teachers reviewed the newsletters with the students, and encouraged them to practice the healthy activities learned in class with their family.

Physical Education Curriculum consisted of 100 PA lessons per grade level, and the aim of the activities was to increase heart rates to a MVPA level. Lessons, similar to the *Bienestar*/NEEMA health program, included skills and drills in fitness, basketball, flag football, Frisbee, dance, cooperative games, soccer, softball, team handball, track and field, volleyball, badminton and tennis. The curriculum was taught by PE teachers over a 40-minute PE period, five days a week.

Food Service Component consisted of working with food service staff to meet five nutrition goals, conduct taste tests and conduct cafeteria learning labs. The five goals were: 1) lower fat content food; 2) serve at least two servings at lunch and one serving at breakfast of fruits and vegetables; 3) serve deserts and snacks with ≤ 200 calories; 4) eliminate milk >1% and sugar sweetened beverages; and 5) serve at least two servings of whole grain foods with ≥ 2 grams of dietary fiber per serving. Taste test consisted of working with food service staff to introduce students to new healthy food options. Cafeteria learning labs were presentations during school lunch to educate students about healthy snacks, portion size, amount of fat in fatty food and amount of sugar in sweetened beverages. The goals were implemented by food service staff, and the taste test and cafeteria learning labs were conducted by study staff.

Social Marketing consisted of a schoolwide campaign that involved posting signs in the school hallways and cafeteria, handing out flyers to students and teachers and making schoolwide announcements through the intercom to promote healthful nutrition and behaviors, and encourage MVPA. Most marketing material and announcements were designed and delivered by students.

This study employed a cluster randomized design in 42 schools across 7 sites. Schools were the unit of randomization, intervention and analysis (Foster et al., 2010). Major inclusion criteria for schools were at least 50% of children eligible for federally subsidized, free or reduced-priced meals and/or at least 50% of its students whose ethnicity was black or Latino. Black (18.0%) and Latino (54.2%) children of lower socioeconomic status were oversampled given their higher risk for both obesity and type 2 diabetes. A total of 6,358 out of approximately 11,100 students (58%) had written parent/guardian consent and student assent prior to baseline measurement.

Fasting measures of weight, height, waist circumference, glucose and insulin were obtained. The primary outcome was the combined prevalence of overweight and obesity. Secondary outcomes included BMI $\geq$ 95th percentile (obesity), BMI z-score, waist circumference, fasting glucose and fasting insulin. All measures were conducted in the schools in fall of 6th grade (2006) and spring of 8th grade (2009).

Both intervention and control schools experienced reductions in the primary outcome measure (BMI percentile $\geq$ 85th), with no difference between the groups. The prevalence of obesity, however, was significantly lower in the intervention schools, with children in intervention schools having 19% (CI:0.66-1.00,p=.05) lower odds of being obese at the end of the study than those in control schools. Intervention schools also had significantly lower BMI z-score (p=0.05), percentage with waist circumference $\geq$ 90th percentile (p=0.05) and fasting insulin (p=0.04), at the end of study than did control schools.

The *Bienestar*/NEEMA and HEALTHY coordinated school health programs were well designed, and showed encouraging results decreasing blood glucose and obesity levels in mostly high-risk black and Latino children. Both of these studies, however, were efficacy trials and further research must be conducted to study how these programs perform in real world settings where school staff, rather than research staff, implement and evaluate the health curriculums (effectiveness trial). In addition, cost-effectiveness analysis must be conducted to determine the cost benefits of early age interventions. Unfortunately the only cost-effectiveness analyses that have been conducted are in adults. These, nonetheless, will be presented to determine if diabetes primary prevention is more cost-effective than treating the disease.

Adult Diabetes Prevention

The Diabetes Prevention Program (DPP) was the largest U.S. trial conducted between 1996 and 2001 to determine whether lifestyle modification or pharmacological therapy would prevent or delay the onset of diabetes (Diabetes Prevention Program Research Group, 1999). The study recruited 3234 individuals with impaired glucose tolerance (IGT; fasting glucose between 95 to 125 mg/dl). The participants were randomized to either placebo (n=1082), metformin therapy (n=1073) or lifestyle intervention (n=1079). Thirty-three percent of the participants were male; 55% were non-Hispanic white, 20% were African American, 16% were Latino, 5% were American Indian and 4% were Asian American. The mean age of the participants was 51 years.

Metformin was started at a dose of 850 mg once daily and increased to 850 mg twice daily. In addition, the metformin and placebo groups were offered a 30-minute lifestyle session once a year. Participants were encouraged to follow the Food Guide Pyramid to increase PA and reduce their weight.

The lifestyle intervention was designed to reduce weight by 7% of initial body weight and have participants walk at a brisk pace at least 150 minutes/week. The lifestyle intervention was intensive and individualized (Diabetes Prevention Program Research Group, 2002a). Each participant had their own personal trainer or lifestyle coach, and the sessions were scheduled around the participant's time. The lifestyle coaches were trained in nutrition, exercise or behavior modification. The intervention was divided into core and maintenance curriculums. The core curriculum consisted of 16 individual face-to-face sessions. The first eight sessions focused on nutrition, exercise and self-management, and the latter sessions focused on psychological, social and motivational courses. The 16-session core curriculum was taught during the first 24 weeks of the study, and the duration of each session was about an hour.

After completing the 16-session core curriculum in the first 24 weeks of the study, the maintenance curriculum consisted of face-to-face encounters with the participants every two months for the remainder of the trial. The maintenance curriculum combined both individual and group sessions. The health topics were similar to those in the core curriculum. If the participants had not reached their 7% weight loss goal, lifestyle coaches were encouraged to meet with them more frequently. Some of these participants were seen weekly or biweekly.

DPP RESULTS

The average follow-up of study participants was 2.8 years (Diabetes Prevention Program Research Group, 2002b). Over the course of the 2.8 years, the placebo and metformin groups attended on average one lifestyle session per year, and the lifestyle intervention group attended on average 11 sessions per year. Thirty-eight percent of participants in the lifestyle intervention group achieved their goal of weight loss of 7% or more, and 68% of the metformin group adhered to the medication dosage. The average weight loss was 5.6, 2.1 and 0.1 kilograms in the lifestyle intervention, metformin and placebo groups, respectively (p<0.001).

The incidence of diabetes was 4.8, 7.8 and 11.0 cases per 100 person-years for the lifestyle intervention, metformin and placebo groups, respectively. The incidence of diabetes was 58% lower in the lifestyle intervention group and 31% lower in the metformin group than in the placebo group. When lifestyle modification was compared to drug therapy, the incidence of diabetes was 39% lower in the lifestyle intervention group than in the metformin group.

The lifestyle intervention group was highly effective in every group regardless of physical, age, sex, race or ethnic characteristics. The metformin group, on the other hand, was less effective in groups with lower body mass index (BMI) and fasting glucose, and in older persons (≥60 years).

DPP OUTCOMES STUDY

The Diabetes Prevention Program Outcomes Study (DPPOS) was conducted between 2002 and 2008, and it was a long-term follow-up to the DPP (Diabetes Prevention Program Research Group, 2009). The purpose was to determine the long-term effects of the interventions on health, and if the delay in development of diabetes found in DPP can be sustained. For this study, 2766 (88%) of the DDP participants had enrolled.

Participants from the three treatment groups were informed of the DPP results. All participants were offered the 16-session core lifestyle curriculum as administered in the DPP but in group sessions. All participants were also offered the Healthy Lifestyle Program (HELP) maintenance sessions every 3 months. In addition to the HELP, participants in the lifestyle intervention were offered Boost Lifestyle sessions (BLS) in a group format, two times a year. Over the 6.8 year period of the DPPOS the placebo and metformin groups were offered 6 sessions per year of HELP programming, and the lifestyle intervention group was offered 9 sessions per year of HELP and BLS programming.

DPPOS RESULTS

The median follow-up from the beginning of the DPP to the most recent assessment in the DPPOS was 10 years (Diabetes Prevention Program Research Group, 2009). Fifty-seven percent of the metformin group adhered to the medication dosage. The average attendance rate for the 16-session core lifestyle curriculum was 40% for the lifestyle intervention group, 58% for the metformin group and 57% for the placebo group. The average attendance for the HELP sessions was 18% for the lifestyle intervention, 15% for the metformin group and 14% for the placebo groups. Attendance was nearly twice as high in participants aged 60-85 years than in those aged 25-44 years.

During the DPPOS, the lifestyle intervention group regained some of the weight they had lost in DPP and the placebo and metformin groups initially lost weight and then regained some. The lifestyle intervention group still weighed 2 kg less than they did at randomization and the metformin and placebo groups weighted 2.5 and 1 kg less, respectively. Diabetes incidence rates were stable in the lifestyle intervention group and decreased in placebo and metformin groups. Over the 10 years of both studies (DPP and DPPOS) the diabetes incidence of the lifestyle intervention and metformin groups were reduced by 34% and 18%, respectively, compared with placebo. The onset of diabetes was delayed by 4 years with lifestyle intervention and 2 years with metformin therapy. Although the use of anti-hypertensive and lipid-lowering medications was less frequent in the lifestyle intervention group, these participants still had lower systolic and diastolic blood pressure and lower triglyceride levels than the participants in the other two groups.

DOSE-RESPONSE OF LIFESTYLE SESSIONS

The amount of weight loss and diabetes incidence reduction was dose-related to the amount of lifestyle session attendance. Over the 10 years of the DPP and DPPOS, the average number of lifestyle sessions in the lifestyle group decreased from 11 sessions per year in the DPP to 9 sessions per year in the DPPOS (Diabetes Prevention Program Research Group, 2002b, 2009). The average weight loss of the lifestyle group decreased from 5.6 kg in the DPP to 2 kg in the DPPOS. The average lifestyle sessions in the placebo and metformin groups, on the other hand, increased from 1 session per year in the DPP to 6 sessions per year in the DPPOS. The average weight loss of the placebo and metformin groups increased from 0.1 and 2.1 kg, respectively, in the DPP to 1 kg and 2.5 kg, respectively, in the DPPOS. These findings show that as the number of lifestyle sessions decreased in the lifestyle intervention group, the weight of the participants increased. On the other hand, as the number of lifestyle sessions increased in the placebo and metformin groups, the weight of the participants decreased. In addition, participants who had the highest attendance rate to lifestyle sessions in the DPPOS, or those aged 60-85 years, also had the greatest reduction in diabetes incidence.

Economic Analysis

COST-BENEFIT ANALYSIS

Cost-benefit analysis is a term that refers to an appraisal where both the cost and benefits are expressed in monetary terms. An example is doing an analysis to determine the cost of building and maintaining a medical office building, and estimating revenues from rents to determine the profit or loss. Both cost (mortgage and operating expenses) and benefit (profit or loss) are expressed in monetary values.

COST-EFFECTIVENESS ANALYSES

In health services it is difficult to place a monetary value on the effects of a particular intervention. Economists, therefore, use cost-effectiveness analysis to determine how much health a certain investment purchases. One method is to measure the cost of two interventions to treat patients with diabetes and the health return for that cost. If interventions A and B cost the same but intervention A lowers hemoglobin A1c by three units and intervention B lowers it by one, then intervention A is more cost-effective than intervention B.

A second method is to measure the number of persons needed to be treated with a specific intervention over a given period of time to prevent one case of diabetes. If interventions A and B cost the same but with intervention A, 5 persons need to be treated and with intervention B, 10 persons need to be treated to prevent one case of diabetes, then intervention A is more cost-effective than intervention B.

A third method is to use quality-adjusted life year (QALY) questionnaires to measure health effects. QALY consist of health questions to determine global health (physical, emotional and cognitive function). A score of 1.0 is perfect health and a score of 0.0 is death. For example a woman with menopausal symptoms might score 0.99, a patient on hemodialysis might score 0.54 and a patient that needs mechanical aid to get out of bed and to walk might score 0.31 (Torrance & Feeny, 1989). There are patients that can score <0.00. For example a bedridden patient with chronic excruciating pain would rather be dead than alive. The scores take into consideration the quantity and quality of life. That is if the patient on hemodialysis lived one year, it is only worth 54% of a year with perfect health.

The incremental cost-effectiveness ratio (ICER) is the ratio between the difference in cost and difference in effect of two interventions. An example would be the comparison of two interventions (A and B) against doing nothing (control). If the cost of intervention A was $10,000 and it increased QALY from .80 to .90 (.10 QALY gained) and the cost of the control was $5,000 and it increased QALY from .80 to .82 (.02 QALY gained) then intervention A results in a cost of $62,500 per QALY gained [difference in cost between intervention A ($10,000) and control ($5,000) is $5,000 ÷ difference in QALY gained between intervention A (.10) and control (.02) is .08 = $62,500 per QALY gained]. If the cost of intervention B was $12,000 and it increased QALY from .80 to .98 (.18 QALY gained) and the cost and QALY gained for the control was unchanged, then intervention B results in a cost of $43,750 per QALY gained (difference in cost $7,000 ÷ difference in QALY 0.16 = $43,750 per QALY gained). In this case, intervention B is more cost-effective than intervention A even though intervention B was more expensive.

QALY also determine effects across different health outcomes or disease states. For example, if childhood immunizations cost $5,000 per QALY and angioplasty cost $100,000 per QALY then children immunizations is more cost effective than angioplasty.

There are two perspectives that should be considered when estimating cost of a health intervention or therapy: the health system and societal perspectives. From the health system perspective, only costs incurred by the health system are included (direct medical cost inside and outside of the prevention program). From the societal perspective, costs incurred by the health system plus cost incurred by the participants, their families and employers are included (direct medical, direct non-medical and indirect costs). Table 2 presents a case to show the difference between health system and societal cost. A system to rate interventions based on the societal perspective, however, has been proposed (Laupacis, Feeny, Detsky & Tugwell, 1992). Interventions that cost <$20,000 per QALY gained is highly recommended, interventions that cost between $20,000 and $100,000 are somewhat recommended and interventions that cost >$100,000 are not cost-effective.

The QALY instruments have shortcomings. The economist developing the QALY instruments incorporate their own viewpoints. Depending on how economists pose the questions, respondents will come up with different scores for the same medical condition. And the respondent's personal preferences and prejudices may also produce different scores for the same medical condition. Despite its limitations, there are no alternatives to measure health effectiveness, and the continued use of QALY questionnaires will allow the instruments to evolve and improve.

COST-EFFECTIVENESS OF THE DPP

Over the ten-year-period of the DPP and DPPOS studies, the effects of the lifestyle intervention group were more favorable than the metformin and placebo groups. But were the health effects procured with the lifestyle intervention cost less than those with metformin and placebo? To estimate cost it is important to capture direct medical cost, direct non-medical cost and indirect cost of the treatment groups. Table 2 summarizes the three categories of cost by treatment group (Diabetes Prevention Program Research Group, 2003a, 2003b).

Table 2. Per Capita Direct Medical, Direct Non-medical and Indirect Cost of the DPP Study over the Three Years

COSTS	PLACEBO	METFORMIN	LIFESTYLE
Direct Medical Costs (inside DPP)—laboratory test to identify individuals with IGT	$139	$139	$139
Direct Medical Costs (inside DPP)—medications; toolbox to promote treatment adherence; and implementing and maintaining DPP interventions (material, phone calls and personnel salaries).	$79	$2,542	$2,780
Direct Medical Costs (outside DPP)—medical treatment for serious adverse events that resulted from study interventions.	$5,011	$4,739	$4,579
Health System Perspective Costs	$5,229	$7,420	$7,498
Direct Non-medical Costs—time spend traveling to and from DPP appointments; time spent at DPP appointments; time spent outside the DPP appointments exercising; time spent shopping and cooking for healthy food; out-of-pocket purchases of health club memberships, and exercise and cooking equipment.	$15,692	$15,683	$17,137
Indirect Costs—time that participants lost from school or work as a result of DPP visits, illness, injury or death (lost productivity).	$2,604	$2,834	$2,430
Societal Perspective Costs	$23,525	$25,937	$27,065

Source: DPP, Diabetes Care, 2003.

According to the health system perspective, lifestyle and metformin were $2,269 and $2,191, respectively, more expensive than placebo. According to the societal perspective, lifestyle and metformin were $3,540 and $2,412, respectively, more expensive than placebo. These are the costs. Let's look at the effectiveness.

COST PER CASE OF DIABETES PREVENTED

From the health system perspective, the lifestyle intervention costs $2,269 more than placebo and 6.9 participants with IGT would need to be treated with the lifestyle intervention to prevent one case of diabetes (Diabetes Prevention Program Research Group, 2003b). The cost and number of people that would need to be treated multiplied equals $15,656 per case of diabetes prevented during the three years of the trial. Because metformin cost $2,191 more than placebo and 14.3 persons would need to be treated to prevent one case of diabetes, this pharmacological intervention would cost $31,300 per case of diabetes prevented.

From the societal perspective, lifestyle and metformin interventions cost $3,540 and $2,412, respectively, more than placebo and need to treat 6.9 and 14.3 participants, respectively, to prevent one case of diabetes. The total cost to prevent one case of diabetes, thus, would be $24,400 and $34,500 for lifestyle and metformin interventions, respectively.

From the health system perspective, the lifestyle intervention costs $15,700 per case of diabetes prevented over the three-year period of the study (Ratner, 2006). The alternative is to let the individual develop diabetes at a cost of $11,744 for annual medical expenditures (American Diabetes Association, 2008). If $11,744 is multiplied by 3 years to compare with the DPP, then the total cost to treat a patient with diabetes would be $35,232 over the three-year period. The cost to treat one patient with diabetes, therefore, is 2.2 times higher than to prevent one case with lifestyle intervention.

COST PER QALY GAINED

The difference between lifestyle and placebo in health system cost and QALY gained was $2,269 and 0.072, respectively (Diabetes Prevention Program Research Group, 2003b). The difference between metformin and placebo groups in health system cost and QALY gained was $2,191 and 0.022, respectively. Based on the ICER, the lifestyle and metformin therapy cost $31,514 ($2,269 ÷ 0.072) and $99,591 ($2,191 ÷ 0.022), respectively, per QALY gained.

From the perspective of society, the lifestyle intervention and metformin therapy cost $3,714 and $2,182, respectively, more than placebo, and improved QALY by 0.072 and 0.022, respectively, more than placebo. Based on the ICER, lifestyle and metformin cost $51,583 and $99,182 per QALY gained, respectively. According to the Laupacis cost-effective rating system, the lifestyle intervention would be somewhat recommended, and the metformin therapy would not be cost-effective.

The DPP was an outstanding study that showed the potential for diabetes prevention at a lower cost than treating it. But unfortunately the lifestyle intervention and drug therapy were still expensive preventative efforts. A more cost-effective alternative to preventing diabetes in adults with impaired glucose tolerance may be to intervene at an early age with children most at-risk for diabetes.

Future Research

Obesity and type 2 diabetes might be programmed developmentally between in-uterus and 9 years of age. The increase in adipose tissue, which occurs in obesity, is due to an enlargement in adipose cell size and an increase in adipose cell numbers. There are four known time intervals of physiologic adipose cell size enlargements: in the fetus between 15 and 30 weeks of gestation (Dauncey & Gairdner, 1975; Enzi et al., 1980; Enzi, Zanardo, Caretta, Inelmen & Rubaltelli, 1981); between newborn and 2 year of age (Hager, Sjostrom, Arvidsson, Bjorntorp & Smith, 1977; Knittle, Timmers, Ginsberg-Fellner, Brown & Katz, 1979); between 5 and 7 years of age (Rolland-Cachera et al., 1984; Whitaker, Pepe, Wright, Seidel & Dietz, 1998); and between 9 and 13 years of age (Knittle et al., 1979; Salans, Cushman & Weismann, 1973). Adipose cell numbers, increase only twice: between 15 weeks in uterus and 2 years of age and between 9 and 13 years of age (Enzi et al., 1981; Knittle et al., 1979).

Figures 5 and 6 show adipose cell size and number, respectively, between obese and non-obese children (Knittle et al., 1979). Non-obese children had a wave-like pattern and lesser increase in adipose cell size enlargement. Obese children, on the other hand, had a linear pattern and a greater increase in adipose cell size (Figure 5). Also, non-obese children had a later-onset and gradual increase in adipose cell number and obese children had an earlier-onset and rapid increase of adipose cell number (Figure 6). The increase in cell size in obese children may have triggered an early and rapid increase in cell number. Whereas cell size is increased and decreased by diet and physical activity, cell number cannot be influenced by external factors. So once a cell number is established, it cannot be changed (terminal differentiation).

Alteration in adipose cell size during any of these time intervals can result in abnormal adipose cell number proliferation and thus, obesity. Studies show, however, that of the four time intervals of physiologic adipose cell size enlargement, the period between in-uterus and 2 years of age is the most sensitive for adipose cell number multiplication (Brook, 1972; Enzi et al., 1981) and also, for

Figure 5. Fat Cell Size Changes Between Obese and Non-Obese Children

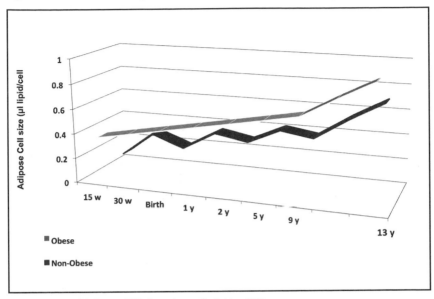

Source: Knittle, J Clin Invest, 1979; Rosenbaum, Pediatrics, 1998.

Figure 6. Fat Cell Number Changes Between Obese and Non-Obese Children

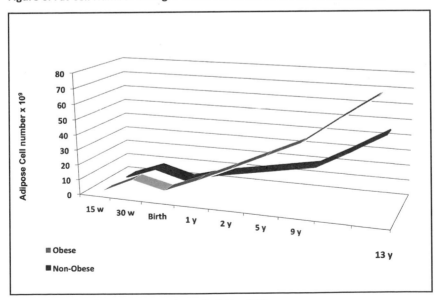

Source: Knittle, J Clin Invest, 1979; Rosenbaum, Pediatrics, 1998.

the development of adult obesity and insulin resistance (Bjorntorp, 1974; Hirsch & Han, 1969; Leunissen, Kerkhof, Stijnen & Hokken-Koelega, 2010).

The nutrient that increases adipose cell size is glucose, not fat (Knittle & Hirsch, 1968). Glucose is converted into triglycerides, and triglycerides fill the adipose cell content to increase its size. This may explain the relationship between increase in sweets and refined flour and increase in obesity in the United States in the 1980s. Future research, therefore, should assess the effect of home and family nutritional and physical activity interventions when the child is between in-uterus and 2 years of age. Earlier age interventions may be more cost-effective than interventions later in life. A Centers for Disease Control and Prevention study showed that society could save $15,887 in medical care cost and $25,104 in loss of productivity costs for each case of obesity that is prevented at an early age in life (Wang, Yang, Lowry & Wechsler, 2003).

Implications for Latino Families

- The excessive availability of processed carbohydrates (flour tortilla, chips, sugar-added beverages and the white breads in pizza, sandwiches, hamburgers and hot dogs), marketed by the U.S. food industry, may have contributed to the higher obesity rates in Latino children.
- The acculturation of the Latino family to western technology (TV, computers, and electronic games) changed their lifestyles from active to sedentary.
- Latino families need to do their part in reducing health care cost by practicing the healthier dietary and physical activity behaviors of their ancestors.
- Because obesity and type 2 diabetes may be programmed developmentally between in-uterus and age 2 years, Latino families need to inculcate by example healthy lifestyles in their children starting very early on in life.

Acknowledgements

I would like to acknowledge the National Institutes of Health's National Institute of Diabetes and Digestive and Kidney Disease (R01DK59213-01 and U01 DK0730994-01) and the WellMed Foundation for their support.

Reference

American Diabetes Association. (2008). Economic cost of diabetes in the U.S. in 2007. *Diabetes Care, 31*, 596-615.

Bjorntorp, P. (1974). Effects of age, sex, and clinical conditions on adipose tissue cellularity in man. *Metabolism, 23*(11), 1091-1102.

Brook, C. G. D. (1972). Evidence for a sensitive period in adipose cell replication in man. *Lancet, 2*, 624-627.

Dauncey, M. J., & Gairdner, D. (1975). Size of adipose cells in infancy. *Archives of Disease in Childhood, 50*, 286-290.

Diabetes Prevention Program Research Group. (1999). The Diabetes Prevention Program: Design and methods for a clinical trial in the prevention of type 2 diabetes. *Diabetes Care, 22*, 623-634.

Diabetes Prevention Program Research Group. (2002a). The Diabetes Prevention Program: Description of lifestyle intervention. *Diabetes Care, 25*(12), 2165-2171.

Diabetes Prevention Program Research Group. (2002b). Reduction in the incidence of type 2 diabetes with lifestyle intervention or metformin. *N Engl J Med, 346*(6), 393-403.

Diabetes Prevention Program Research Group. (2003a). Costs Associated with the primary prevention of type 2 diabetes mellitus in the Diabetes Prevention Program. *Diabetes Care, 26*(1), 36-47.

Diabetes Prevention Program Research Group. (2003b). Within-trial cost-effectiveness of lifestyle intervention or metformin for the primary prevention of type 2 diabetes. *Diabetes Care, 26*(9), 2518-2523.

Diabetes Prevention Program Research Group. (2009). 10-year follow-up of diabetes incidence and weight loss in the Diabetes Prevention Program Outcomes Study. *Lancet, 374*, 1677-1686.

Duncan, G. E. (2006). Prevalence of diabetes and impaired fasting glucose among U.S. adolescents. *Arch Pediatr Adolesc Med, 160*, 523-528.

Enzi, G., Inelmen, E. M., Caretta, F., Rubaltelli, F., Grella, P., & Baritussio, A. (1980). Adipose tissue development "in utero." *Diabetologia, 18*, 135-140.

Enzi, G., Zanardo, V., Caretta, F., Inelmen, E. M., & Rubaltelli, F. (1981). Intrauterine growth and adipose tissue development. *Am J Clin Nutr, 34*, 1785-1790.

Fajans, S. (1990). Scope and heterogeneous nature of MODY. *Diabetes Care, 13*, 49-64.

Finkelstein, E. A., Ruhm, C. J., & Kosa, K. M. (2005). Economic causes and consequences of obesity. *Annu Rev Public Health, 26*, 239-257.

Finkelstein, E. A., Trogdon, J., Cohen, J., & Dietz, W. H. (2009). Annual medical spending attributable to obesity: payer- and service-specific estimates. *Health Affairs, 28*(5), 822-831.

Foster, G. D., Linder, B., Baranowski, T., Cooper, D. M., Goldberg, L., Harrell, J. S., Kaufman, F., Marcus, M.D., Treviño, R. P., & Hirst, K. (2010). A school-based intervention for diabetes risk factors. *New England Journal of Medicine, 363*, 443-553.

Hager, A., Sjostrom, L., Arvidsson, B., Bjorntorp, P., & Smith, U. (1977). Body fat and adipose tissue cellularity in infants: A longitudinal study. *Metabolism, 26*(6), 607-614.

Hirsch, J., & Han, P. W. (1969). Cellularity of rat adipose tissue: effects of growth, starvation, and obesity. *Journal of Lipid Research, 10*, 77-82.

Knittle, J. L., & Hirsch, J. (1968). Effect of early nutrition on the development of rat epididymal fat pads: Cellularity and metabolism. *J Clin Invest, 47*, 2091-2098.

Knittle, J. L., Timmers, K., Ginsberg-Fellner, F., Brown, R. E., & Katz, D. P. (1979). The growth of adipose tissue in children and adolescents. Cross-sectional and longitudinal studies of adipose cell number and size. *Journal of Clinical Investigation, 63*(2), 239-246.

Laupacis, A., Feeny, D., Detsky, A. S., & Tugwell, P. X. (1992). How attractive does a new technology have to be to warrant adoption and utilization? Tentative guidelines for using clinical and economic evaluations. *Can Med Assoc J, 146*(4), 473-481.

Lee, J. M. (2008). Why young adults hold the key to assessing the obesity epidemic in children. *Arch Pediatr Adolesc Med, 162*(7), 682-687.

Leunissen, R. W. J., Kerkhof, G. F., Stijnen, T., & Hokken-Koelega, A. (2010). Timing and tempo of first-year rapid growth in relation to cardiovascular and metabolic risk profile in early adulthood. *JAMA, 301*(21), 2234-2242.

Malina, R. M., Zavaleta, A. N., & Little, B. B. (1986). Estimated overweight and obesity in Mexican-American school children. *International Journal of Obesity, 10*, 483-491.

Mei, Z., Scanlon, K. S., Grummer-Strawn, L. M., Freedman, D. S., Yip, R., & Trowbridge, F. L. (1998). Increasing prevalence of overweight among U.S. low-income preschool children: the Centers for Disease Control and Prevention pediatric nutrition surveillance, 1983 to 1995. *Pediatrics, 101*(1), E12.

Mokdad, A. H., Bowman, B. A., Ford, E. S., Vinicor, F., Marks, J. S., & Koplan, J. P. (2001). The continuing epidemics of obesity and diabetes in the United States. *JAMA, 286*(10), 1195-1200.

Neufeld, N. D., Chen, Y. I., & Raffel, L. J. (1998). Early presentation of type 2 diabetes in Mexican-American youth. *Diabetes Care, 21*, 80-86.

Ninomiya, J. K., L'Italien, G., Driqui, M. H., Whyte, J. L., Gamst, A., & Chen, R. S. (2004). Association of the metabolic syndrome with history of mycoardial infarction and stroike in the Third National Health and Examination Survey. *Circulation, 109*, 42-46.

Ogden, C. L., Carroll, M. D., Curtin, L. R., McDowell, M. A., Tabak, C. J., & Flegal, K. M. (2006). Prevalence of overweight and obesity in the United States, 1999-2004. *JAMA, 295*(13), 1549-1555.

Ogden, C. L., Carroll, M. D., & Flegal, K. M. (2008). High body mass index for age among U.S. children and adolescents, 2003-2006. *JAMA, 299*(20), 2401-2405.

Orchard, T. J., Dorman, J. S., Maser, R. E., Becker, D. J., Drash, A. L., Ellis, D., & et al. (1990). Prevalence of complications in IDDM by sex and duration: Pittsburgh Epidemiology of Diabetes Complications Study II. *Diabetes, 39*(9), 1116-1119.

Putnam, J., Allshouse, J., & Kantor, L. S. (2002). U.S. per capita food supply trends: More calories, refined carbohydrates, and fats. *Food Review, 25*(3), 2-15.

Ratner, R. E. (2006). An update on the Diabetes Prevention Program. *Endocrine Practice, 12*(1), 20-24.

Reimer, J. (2005). Total share: 30 years of personal computer market share figures. *Retrieved July 2010, from http://arstechnica.com/old/content/2005/12/total-share.ars*

Rolland-Cachera, M. F., Deheeger, M., Bellisle, F., Sempe, M., Guilloud-Bataille, M., & Patois, E. (1984). Adiposity rebound in children: a simple indicator for predicting obesity. *Am J Clin Nutr, 39*, 129-135.

Rosenbaum, M., & Leibel, R. L. (1998). The physiology of body weight regulation: Relevance to the etiology of obesity in children. *Pediatrics, 101*(3), 525-535.

Salans, L. B., Cushman, S. W., & Weismann, R. E. (1973). Studies of human adipose tissue. *J Clin Invest, 52*(929-941).

Shaw-Perry, M., Horner, C., Treviño, R. P., Sosa, E. T., Hernandez, I., & Bhardwaj, A. (2007). NEEMA: A school-based diabetes risk prevention program designed for African-American children. *Journal of the National Medical Association, 99*(4), 368-375.

Torrance, G. W., & Feeny, D. (1989). Utilities and quality-adjusted life years. *Intl J of Technology Assessment in Health Care, 5*, 559-575.

Treviño, R. P., Fogt, D., Wyatt, T. J., Leal-Vasquez, L., Sosa, E. T., & Woods, C. (2009). Diabetes risk, low fitness, and energy insufficiency levels among children from poor families. *J Am Diet Assoc, 108*, 1846-1853.

Treviño, R. P., Marshall, R. M., Hale, D. E., Rodriguez, R., Baker, G., & Gomez, J. E. (1999). Diabetes risk factors in low-income Mexican-American children. *Diabetes Care, 22*(2), 202-207.

Treviño, R. P., Yin, Z., Hernandez, A., Hale, D. E., Garcia, O. A., & Mobley, C. (2004). Impact of the *Bienestar* school-based diabetes mellitus prevention program on fasting capillary glucose levels: A randomized controlled trial. *Arch Pedriatr Adolesc Med., 158*, 911-917.

Troiano, R. P., Flegal, K. M., Kuczmarski, R. J., Campbell, S. M., & Johnson, C. 1. (1995). Overweight prevalence and trends for children and adolescents: the National Health and Nutrition Examination Surveys 1963 to 1991. *Arch Pediatr Adolesc Med, 149*, 1085-1091.

Wang, L. Y., Yang, Q., Lowry, R., & Wechsler, H. (2003). Economic analysis of a school-based obesity prevention program. *Obesity Research, 11*(11), 1313-1324.

Whitaker, R. C., Pepe, M. S., Wright, J. A., Seidel, K. D., & Dietz, W. H. (1998). Early adiposity rebound and the risk of adult obesity. *Pediatrics, 101*(3), http://www.pediatrics.org/cgi/content/full/101/103/e105.

Zavaleta, A. N., & Malina, R. M. (1980). Growth, fatness, and leanness in Mexican-American children. *Am J Clin Nutr, 33*, 2008-2020.

EDITOR AND CONTRIBUTOR BIOGRAPHIES

RAFAEL PÉREZ-ESCAMILLA, PhD is Professor of Epidemiology and Public Health and Director, Office of Community Health, Yale School of Public Health. He is also Director and PI of the Connecticut NIH EXPORT Center of Excellence for Eliminating Health Disparities among Latinos (CEHDL). His global public health nutrition and food security research has led to improvements in breastfeeding promotion, iron deficiency anemia among infants (by delaying the clamping of the umbilical cord after birth), household food security measurement and outcomes and community nutrition education programs worldwide. His current health disparities research involves assessing the impact of community health workers at improving behavioral and metabolic outcomes among Latinos with type 2 diabetes. He has published over 100 research articles and over 350 conference abstracts, book chapters and technical reports. He is currently chair-elect of the American Society for Nutrition International Nutrition Council and has served in the editorial boards of the *Journal of Nutrition*, the *Journal of Human Lactation* and the *Journal of Hunger and Environmental Nutrition*. Dr. Pérez-Escamilla served as a member of the 2009 IOM Gestational Weight Gain Guidelines Committee and of the 2010 Dietary Guidelines Advisory Committee. He is a trustee of the Pan American Health and Education Foundation (PAHEF) and an advisory board member of the Kellogg Foundation-supported "Salud Familia" initiative based at the University of Houston. Dr. Pérez-Escamilla obtained his BS in chemical engineering from the Universidad Iberoamericana in Mexico City. He earned an MS in food science and a PhD in nutrition from the University of California, Davis.

HUGO MELGAR-QUIÑONEZ, MD, Dr.Sc. is an Associate Professor and an Extension State Specialist in the Department of Human Nutrition at the Ohio State University with previous experience in nutrition and food security research at the Mexican Public Health Institute (1996-1997) and the Nutrition Department at the University of California, Davis (1998-2003). After graduating as a physician in 1992 at the University Friedrich Schiller in Germany, Dr. Melgar-Quiñonez received his doctoral degree in 1996 on a dissertation on the main causes of mortality in Mozambique. Once in the United States, where he arrived in 1998, Dr. Melgar-Quiñonez worked on food insecurity research with Latino immigrants, setting up the basis for subsequent studies in rural communities in several Latin American countries. His studies lead to further validation studies on adapted household food security instruments in a wide range of countries (Bolivia, Brazil, Burkina Faso, Colombia, Ecuador, Ghana, Guatemala, Mexico and The Philippines, among others). In the United States, Dr. Melgar-Quiñonez' research focuses on food insecurity and health-related outcomes in high-risk and minority populations, especially in Latino immigrants and food insecure groups. His work includes research with secondary survey data, which he uses to assess the association between food insecurity and nutrition and health outcomes. As an Extension Specialist, Dr. Melgar-Quiñonez conducts research to assess the impact of on nutrition education interventions such as the Rainbow of Healthy Choices program to promote healthy eating habits among food pantry users. In addition, he conducts validation studies on national food security scales applied within Demographic and Health Surveys in Latin American countries.

MANAL J. ABOELATA, MPH is Program Director at Prevention Institute, a national non-profit center focused on primary prevention of illness and injury. Ms. Aboelata coordinates the Strategic Alliance for Healthy Food and Activity Environments, an advocacy network which improves healthy food and physical activity opportunities for children and families throughout California. As chairperson of the Joint Use Statewide Taskforce (JUST), Ms Aboelata works to advance policies for equitable access to safe places to play for all children. In partnership with the Trust for Public Land, she developed and implemented the Healthy Parks, Healthy Communities program which linked park equity and health equity in low-income, Latino communities. Ms Aboelata has provided health and equity training to three cohorts of the National Association of Latino Elected Official's Health Leadership Program. She is principal author of *The Built Environment and Health: 11 Profiles of Neighborhood Transformation, Mapping the Movement for Healthy Food and Activity Environments: Organizational Snapshots*, and a forthcoming chapter on Community Engagement and the Built Environment. Previously, Ms Aboelata coordinated a statewide evaluation of in-school tobacco use prevention programs and managed Proyecto

Cuna, a research project focused on intimate partner violence. Ms Aboelata holds a bachelor's degree from UC Berkeley and received her MPH in Epidemiology from UCLA, where she was inducted into the Iota Chapter of the Delta Omega Honorary Society in 2001 and into the UCLA School of Public Health Alumni Hall of Fame in 2009.

HECTOR BALCAZAR is the Regional Dean of Public Health at the University of Texas Health Science Center at Houston, School of Public Health, El Paso Regional Campus. He is also a professor of health promotion and behavioral sciences. Prior to joining UT, he was a professor and Chair of the Department of Social and Behavioral Sciences, School of Public Health at the University of North Texas Health Science Center at Fort Worth, TX. He holds a PhD and MS degree in International Nutrition from Cornell University, Ithaca, NY, and a BS degree in Nutrition and Food Science from Iberoamericana University, Mexico City. Dr. Balcazar serves as the Co-Director of the Hispanic Health Disparities Research Center, an NIH-funded initiative in collaboration with the College of Health Sciences of the University of Texas at El Paso. Dr. Balcazar specializes in the study of public health problems of Latinos/Mexican Americans. Dr. Balcazar is a bilingual, bicultural family and public health scientist who has conducted numerous studies of Latino birth outcomes, acculturation and health-related behaviors, cardiovascular disease prevention programs in Latinos, and border health issues. His most recent funded work includes: an NIH-initiative to explore health disparity domains in the U.S.-Mexico border area of El Paso Texas; an NIH-initiative to test the effects of *promotoras de salud* in changing clinical outcomes for chronic diseases in El Paso, Texas; a CDC/ASPH project on promotoras de salud and hypertension control; an NHLBI/NIH project on the North Texas Salud Para Su Corazón (Health For Your Heart) Community Health Initiative. As a Latino health specialist Dr. Balcazar provides consultation and leadership to local and national health organizations. Dr. Balcazar has over 140 publications including peer-reviewed journal articles, book chapters, monographs and abstracts. Dr. Balcazar currently serves as Chair of the Editorial Board of *American Journal of Public Health*.

CRISTINA S. BARROSO, DrPH is Assistant Professor of Health Promotion and Behavioral Sciences at the University of Texas Health Science Center at Houston, School of Public Health, Brownsville Regional Campus. Her research on child and adolescent health focuses on health disparities in Latinos and African Americans; cancer control, obesity control research and the use of mass media to promote health promotion interventions. Her current work is on the design, development and evaluation of community-based participatory research interventions tailored for Mexican-American youth and families; with an emphasis on the reception of active living, healthy eating and other obesity-related messages by these priority groups. Additionally, she is the principal investigator of a study, sponsored by the Robert Wood Johnson Foundation through Salud America!, examining body image perceptions across generations in a Mexican-American population.

STEPHEN J. BOYD, MA is an advanced doctoral student in clinical psychology at Arizona State University. His research interests focus primarily on the prevention and treatment of alcohol and substance use disorders, and the potentially protective influences of ethnic and cultural variables against the development of these disorders. Mr. Boyd is currently using multi-group models to assess the effectiveness of substance abuse treatment programs across ethnic groups. Prior to entering graduate school, Mr. Boyd was involved in the development and implementation of several health-related behavioral interventions, including a nationwide tobacco cessation program and a risk reduction intervention for individuals at high-risk for acquiring HIV. Mr. Boyd is a graduate of the University of Oregon.

DONNA J. CHAPMAN an Associate Research Scientist at the Yale School of Public Health and is the Assistant Director of the Connecticut Center for Eliminating Health Disparities Among Latinos. Her research has focused on evaluating the effectiveness of breastfeeding peer counseling programs serving a low-income, predominantly Latina population in Hartford, CT. She is currently evaluating the impact of a breastfeeding peer counseling intervention targeting obese women. Her work is unique in that it addresses breastfeeding as a health disparities issue. Dr. Chapman has published 19 peer-reviewed articles and 15 reviews in scientific journals. She has presented at numerous scientific meetings. She serves as the Associate Editor for the *Journal of Human Lactation* and as an ad-hoc reviewer for several journals. Dr. Chapman received her BS degree in Nutritional Sciences from the University of Connecticut, a MS in Clinical Dietetics from Boston University and a PhD in Nutritional Sciences from the University of Connecticut. She is a Registered Dietitian, and completed her dietetic internship at New England Deaconess Hospital in Boston, Massachusetts.

GEORGE R. FLORES is a Program Manager for The California Endowment, one of the country's largest health foundations. His work focuses on grant-making at the intersection of health, equity and sustainable environments, through policy and systems change to create healthy and equitable community environments. Dr. Flores work builds on lessons from the Endowment's groundbreaking programs to prevent childhood obesity. Previously, Dr Flores served as Public Health Officer in San Diego County and in Sonoma County; Clinical Assistant Professor for the UCSF Family Practice Residency Program; Director, Project HOPE in Guatemala; and Deputy Health Officer in Santa Barbara County. Dr. Flores received his MD from the University of Utah, and MPH from Harvard. He is a member of the Institute of Medicine committees that published *Preventing Childhood Obesity: Health in the Balance*, and *The Future of the Public's Health in the 21st Century*.

ROBERT GARCIA is an attorney who engages, educates and empowers communities to achieve equal access to public resources. He is the Executive Director, Counsel and Founder of The City Project, a non-profit legal and policy advocacy organization based in Los Angeles, California. Mr. Garcia's work in the past decade has focused on the most influential Latinos in the United States in 2008, "men and women who are changing access to park, school and health resources throughout Los Angeles and California. The City Project is helping children move more, eat well, stay healthy and do their best in school and in life." He received the President's Award from the American Public Health Association in 2010. *Hispanic Business* Magazine recognized him as one of the 100 the nation." He has extensive experience in public policy and legal advocacy, mediation and litigation involving complex social justice, civil rights, human health, environmental, education and criminal justice matters. He graduated from Stanford University and Stanford Law School, where he served on the Board of Editors of the *Stanford Law Review*. As reported in *The New York Times*, "The City Project [is] working to broaden access to parks and open space for inner-city children, and . . . to fight childhood obesity by guaranteeing that . . . students get enough physical education."

MEGHAN M. GARVEY, BS is a doctoral student in clinical psychology in the Department of Psychology, Arizona State University, and a graduate research assistant at the Southwest Interdisciplinary Research Center. Her primary research interests include the assessment and development of culturally grounded drug prevention interventions and treatment programs for Hispanic adolescents. She has been the recipient of an APA Student Travel Award and has presented her research that examines the predictors of parenting self-agency in Latino families at the 2010 APA Convention. Ms. Garvey is interested in extending this research in an effort to improve parent-centered interventions aimed at reducing adolescent drug use and improving family functioning. Her current research focuses on the relationship between traditional family values, parenting practices and drug use intentions among Hispanic adolescents.

GRETCHEN GEORGE, MA, RD, is a doctoral student in Nutritional Biology with a Designated Emphasis in the Program of International and Community Nutrition at the University of California, Davis. Ms. George's research focuses on nutrition behavior modification and the slowing or prevention of chronic disease in overweight and/or obese children of minority populations and underserved communities. She is currently researching youth summer nutrition and physical activity intervention programs with parent involvement that are aimed at reducing risk factors of chronic disease. Ms. George received her BS in Nutritional Science from California Polytechnic University, San Luis Obispo, California. She completed her MA in Family and Consumer Studies with a focus on public health nutrition at Appalachian State University in North Carolina. Ms. George also completed her dietetic internship at Appalachian State University. Prior to returning to graduate school she worked as a Research Dietitian at Stanford Prevention Research Center in Palo Alto, California, and also was a lecturer at San Francisco State University.

LISA G.-ROSAS received her PhD in Epidemiology from the University of California, Berkeley, where she also completed her MPH in Maternal and Child Health. Previously, she worked as a social worker with migrant farm workers and their families and completed a research fellowship in Mexico City with the Population Council. Currently, Dr. Rosas is the Research Director for the Program on Prevention Outcomes and Practices at the Stanford Prevention Research Center. Her research focuses on prevention and treatment of obesity among Latino children and adults.

FELIPE GONZÁLEZ CASTRO, PhD, MSW is professor of clinical psychology in the Department of Psychology, Arizona State University, and a research affiliate at the Southwest Interdisciplinary Research Center (SIRC). His research focuses on multivariate model analyses of cultural factors as integral components in the design and evaluation of prevention interventions to reduce disease risks, including risk factors for substance abuse, type 2 diabetes and other addictive or health-compromising behaviors. In this regard, his research emphasizes the elimination of the health disparities that adversely affect Hispanic/Latino(a) populations. From a strength-based perspective, his research examines the cognitive, affective and behavioral determinants of effective coping with major life stressors, as factors in understanding the structure and expression of resilience and in the development of psychological wellbeing. Dr. Castro is a Fellow of APA Division 45, the Society for the Psychological Study of Ethnic Minority Issues. In 2005 Dr. Castro was awarded the National Award of Excellence in Mentorship by the National Hispanic Science Network. Also in 2005, he was awarded the Community, Culture and Prevention Science Award from the Society for Prevention Research. Dr. Castro serves as an Associate Editor for the journals: *Prevention Science* and the *American Journal of Public Health.*

WENDI GOSLINER has been a researcher and lecturer in community nutrition and nutrition policy at the Center for Weight and Health at UC Berkeley. The focus of her work is on improving the health of children and youth through interventions and policy changes designed to expand opportunities for healthy eating and physical activity. She has conducted research on community environmental and policy change, and has studied ways to help schools, child care centers, and the WIC program support children and youth to eat better and be more physically active. Wendi has also worked in the Peace Corps, Head Start, the California Children and Families Commission, and her former community of El Sobrante, CA. She received a Bachelor's degree in Nutritional Sciences from Cornell University and a Master's degree in Public Health from the University of California, Berkeley.

LUCIA L. KAISER is currently a Cooperative Extension Nutrition Specialist at the University of California, Davis in the Department of Nutrition. Dr Kaiser's responsibilities include developing nutrition education materials and evaluating programs offered through the University of California Cooperative Extension and presenting nutrition topics at workshops and conferences throughout the state. Her research interests include: examining the impact of acculturation and food insecurity on the child-parent feeding relationship among Latinos, developing tools to evaluate nutrition education and preventing diabetes. Dr. Kaiser received her BS in Biology from the College of William and Mary. She completed her MS and PhD in the Department of Nutrition at the University of California, Davis. She is also a Registered Dietitian, completing a dietetic internship at the Clinical Research Center at Stanford University Hospital.

JOSHUA G. KELLISON is an advanced doctoral student in clinical psychology in the Department of Psychology, Arizona State University, and he is a graduate research assistant at the Southwest Interdisciplinary Research Center. His research interests involve minority (both sexual and ethnic minority) health disparities, family dynamics, gender studies and the development of culturally sensitive preventive interventions. Currently his dissertation work will examine anti-gay discrimination coping and parenting strategies used by lesbian and gay parents when an act of discrimination has occurred where their children were present. Mr. Kellison also serves as the Co-Chair for the Health Initiative Task Force for Division 44, the Society of the Psychological Study of LGBT Issues of the American Psychological Association and is a Member of the American Psychological Association of Graduate Students' Committee on LGBT Concerns. In 2010 he was a Fellow of the University of Michigan's International LGBT Psychology Summer Institute, and in 2008 he was elected as a graduate student Fellow of the National Hispanic Science Network.

As a Program Associate at Samuels & Associates, MARIAH S. LAFLEUR works on proposal development, study design, data collection, qualitative research and development of briefs and reports for a variety of projects including grants from The Robert Wood Johnson Foundation's Active Living Research, Healthy Eating Research and Salud America! initiatives that promote healthy eating and physical activity in schools and communities. She is also involved in evaluating of the Statewide Health Improvement Program in Olmsted County, Minnesota, and the Consortium to Lower Obesity in Chicago's Children in Illinois. Her expertise encompasses chronic disease prevention in Latino populations, improving physical education and physical activity for children and working with diverse and low-income populations. Previously, Ms. Lafleur worked at Children's Hospital Oakland Research Institute to reduce obesity in low-income East Bay children and with La Clinica de La Raza to improve the nutritional status of Latinos living with HIV/AIDS. As a Peace Corps volunteer in Haiti and the Dominican Republic, she implemented projects to alleviate malnutrition and improve food security and sanitation in resource-poor rural communities. She holds an MPH from the UC Berkeley School of Public Health with an emphasis on Nutrition and is fluent in Spanish and Haitian Creole.

JASON A. MENDOZA, MD, MPH, is a board-certified pediatrician and an Assistant Professor of Pediatrics in the USDA/ARS Children's Nutrition Research Center and Academic General Pediatrics at Baylor College of Medicine. His research portfolio includes obesity and cancer prevention in children with a focus on minority and socioeconomically disadvantaged populations. He leads the design, implementation and evaluation of community and school-based behavioral programs aimed at (1) reducing sedentary activities and nutrition or (2) improving physical activity and injury prevention in children. He is leading a school-based intervention to reduce sedentary activities, such as watching television and videos, among Latino preschool children in Head Start. He is conducting series of studies examining the "walking school bus" and other Safe Routes to School programs to improve ethnic minority children's active commuting to school and physical activity. Finally, he is examining the role of food security in the health of HIV-positive children in Houston, Texas, and Gaborone, Botswana.

KATHERINE MOREL graduated with a Master of Science in Nutrition from the University of Connecticut in 2008. She has remained active in the field of community nutrition working in the areas of human lactation and type 2 diabetes. Katherine is currently working as a Senior Nutritionist in the Supplemental Nutrition Assistance Program-Education program at The Hispanic Health Council. She is passionate about working with low-income Latinos and other underserved populations. She has co-authored a paper in the *Journal of Human Lactation* and presented poster and oral presentations at the Experimental Biology and the International Lactation Consultant Association's annual conferences in 2009 and 2010.

AMANDA M. NAVARRO is an Associate Director at PolicyLink in New York, NY. Dr. Navarro oversees efforts of the national Convergence Partnership—a collaboration of funders aimed at achieving healthy people living in health places through environmental and policy change. She provides research, technical assistance and training on collaborative, multi-field strategies to improve community environments particularly in low-income communities and communities of color. Prior to joining PolicyLink, she worked at the Centers for Disease Control and Prevention in Atlanta, GA, coordinating several programmatic and research activities related to health disparities, social determinants of health, community health promotion and the impact of acculturation and mental health on chronic disease. She holds a Master in Public Health (MPH) from Boston University and a Doctor of Public Health (DrPH) from the University of Texas School of Public Health-Houston. Dr. Navarro has published on various health issues impacting poor communities and communities of color, including HIV/AIDS prevention, substance abuse treatment, access to health services among Medicaid and SCHIP families, the impact of policies on racial and ethnic health disparities and social determinants of health.

NORMA OLVERA, Associate Professor, Health Program, Educational Psychology, University of Houston, obtained her PhD, in Developmental Psychology from the University Houston in 1992 with an emphasis on minority health. Dr. Olvera's research interests have focused on assessing demographic, cultural, familial and environmental factors associated with eating and physical activity behaviors in low-income Hispanic Families. In addition, Dr. Olvera developed, implemented and evaluated community- and family-based lifestyle programs (after school and summer) for low-income Hispanic and African-American populations. One of her projects BOUNCE, a healthy lifestyle summer program, was recognized as one of the best nutrition and physical activity practices in Texas by the Texas Association of Public Health in 2006. Dr. Olvera has received numerous awards for her efforts to promote a healthy lifestyle in minority families. Dr. Olvera has received funding from the National Health Institutes, the Robert Wood Johnson Foundation, the Active Living Research and Salud Programs, the American Cancer Society, the Saint Luke Episcopal Health Charities and the University of Houston. Dr. Olvera has published numerous articles on child development, obesity, health education and behavior in the *Journal of Adolescent Health*.

EMMA V. SANCHEZ-VAZNAUGH is an assistant professor in the Department of Health Education at San Francisco State University. She received her doctorate degree from Harvard University's School of Public Health, and was a Kellogg Health Scholar within the Center on Social Disparities in Health, University of California San Francisco/Berkeley, where she completed a postdoctoral program in 2010. Dr. Sanchez-Vaznaugh's research aims to improve population health and reduce health disparities, devoting attention to the influence of policies and school environments on children's obesity risk. Currently, she is investigating whether compliance with State physical education policies is associated with fitness among children attending public schools in California, a project funded by the Robert Wood Johnson Foundation's Salud America! Research Network to Prevent Obesity among Latino Children.

As Senior Associate at Samuels & Associates, LIZ U. SCHWARTE, MPH, is engaged in evaluation and research design, implementation and reporting for a variety of community-based initiatives focused on increasing access to healthy eating and physical activity opportunities for children and families. She oversees the Mercado La Paloma/La Salud Tiene Sabor menu labeling program evaluation funded by the Robert Wood Johnson Foundation's Salud America! program, and leads the joint use evaluation components of the State and local Communities Putting Prevention to Work (CPPW)-funded obesity prevention efforts in California. Recent evaluation projects include The California Endowment's Healthy Eating Active Communities (HEAC) program and the Central California Regional Obesity Prevention Program (CCROPP). Ms. Schwarte advises The Rosalinde and Arthur Gilbert Foundation on its health grantmaking and serves as a strategic planning and evaluation consultant to the Oklahoma Tobacco Settlement Endowment Trust Nutrition and Fitness Initiative.

SOFIA SEGURA-PÉREZ received her BS in Nutritional Sciences from the Universidad Autónoma Metropolitana in Mexico City and her MS in Food and Nutrition from the Centro de Investigación en Alimentación y Desarrollo (CIAD) in Hermosillo, Sonora, Mexico. She also completed the Dietetic Program at the University of Connecticut, Department of Allied Health, which led her to become a Registered Dietitian. Her main areas of interest are food policy, nutrition education, diabetes prevention and community-based nutrition and health research. She is the Associate Center Director of the Center of Community Nutrition at the Hispanic Health Council (HHC), a non-profit organization located in Hartford, Connecticut. She has extensive experience in the management and evaluation of community nutrition programs targeting low-income Latinos and other underserved diverse population funded by the Supplemental Nutrition Assistance Program (SNAP). She has led the implementation of statewide social marketing campaigns in Connecticut and has also led the development of culturally appropriate nutrition and food access educational products including puppet shows, *fotonovelas* and *videonovelas*.

She has provided central coordination to diverse research studies including an NIH-funded trial seeking to improve diabetes self-management among Latinos through community health workers. She has worked at the WIC program as a nutrition consultant. She has been a presenter at national conferences such as the American Dietetic Association, the American Public Health Association and the American Society for Nutrition meetings. She has been an author and co-author of numerous peer-reviewed scientific articles published in high-impact journals. She is a member of the Hartford Food Policy Commission and the Hartford Childhood Obesity Task Force.

SETH H. STRONGIN is Policy and Research Manager at The City Project. His responsibilities include policy analysis, social science research and data analysis related to physical activity, public health, the natural environment and civil rights, including physical education, access to parks and the built environment. Mr. Strongin holds a Master's Degree in Environmental Science and Management from the Bren School at University of California, Santa Barbara and a BA in Biology from American University in Washington, D.C.

ROBERTO P. TREVIÑO, MD founded the South Alamo Medical Group in 1986 for the practice of primary care medicine in poor and underserved areas. The medical practice has grown to five clinics and 20 physicians. Dissatisfied with medical outcomes, however, he founded the Social and Health Research Center (SHRC) in 1995 to design and evaluate early-age obesity and type 2 diabetes school health prevention programs. He is the principal investigator of an efficacy trial (1 R01 DK 59213-01) an effectiveness trial (1 R18 DK073094-01), and a multi-center trial (5 U01 DK0730994-01). His research has been published in peer-reviewed journals and presented at national meetings.

FEDERICO E. VACA, MD, MPH, FACEP is a Professor of Emergency Medicine at the Yale University-School of Medicine. He was a previous Medical Fellow at the U.S. Department of Transportation's National Highway Traffic Safety Administration (NHTSA) in Washington D.C. The focus of his research has been to investigate and better understand the racial and ethnic disparities in traffic-related morbidity and mortality. He has continued to study traffic safety in a cultural context with a sociological and public health perspective in order to identify protective behavioral determinant as well as risk factors that would inform the development of effective clinical contact and community-based intervention strategies. Dr. Vaca has served on several national expert panels directed by the National Academies of Science and the Transportation Research Board, Centers for Disease Control and Prevention, Safe States Alliance (formerly State Territorial Injury Prevention Directors Association) and the National Highway Traffic Safety Administration

SANDRA VIERA, Program Coordinator at Prevention Institute (PI), works to promote safe and healthy communities for children, youth and families through projects focused on improving the built environment, preventing unintentional injuries and increasing equitable opportunities for physical activity and play. Among other responsibilities, Ms. Viera coordinates the Joint Use Statewide Task Force (JUST) whose mission is to increase community access to playgrounds through the policy of joint use agreements between school districts and local governments. Prior to joining PI in 2010, Ms. Viera was the Associate Director of Policy at Latino Health Access, a non-profit based in Santa Ana, California, where she led multi-sector healthy eating and active living initiatives focused on improving children's health environments.

GAIL WOODWARD-LOPEZ, MPH, RD is Associate Director of the Atkins Center for Weight & Health at the University of California, Berkeley. She has nearly 20 years experience developing, implementing and evaluating public health programs. The focus of her current work is the evaluation of school and community based programs to prevent overweight among children. She has evaluated multi-sector, place-based obesity prevention initiatives and has served as lead evaluator on various statewide and multi-state projects to evaluate school nutrition legislation and wellness policies. She is bilingual, has worked extensively with the Latino community in California and Latin America, and has served as a consultant for several international agencies including UNICEF in Nicaragua, the Arizona-Mexico Border Health Foundation in Tucson and PATH in Mexico. She has served on numerous obesity-related advisory groups, frequently speaks on the topic, and recently published a book on the dietary and developmental determinants of obesity.

ANA CLAUDIA ZUBIETA, PhD is currently the state director of the education component of the Supplemental Nutrition Assistance Program (SNAP-Ed) at The Ohio State University. She is in the Departments of Human Nutrition and Extension, College of Education and Human Ecology. Zubieta earned her PhD from the University of California, Davis. Her research focuses on infant nutrition, community nutrition and nutrition education in low-income populations including Latinos. She serves on the Association of SNAP-Ed Nutrition Networks and other Implementing Agencies (ASNNA) and has previously served on the Society for Nutrition Education. She is originally from Uruguay and has worked in several Latin American countries including Bolivia, Ecuador, Guatemala and Mexico.